THE CURRENT GLOBAL RECESSION

A Theoretical and Empirical Investigation into Developed and BRICS Economies

Emerald Group Publishing Limited
Howard House, Wagon Lane, Bingley BD16 1WA, UK

First edition 2017

British Library Cataloguing in Publication Data
A catalogue record for this book is available from the British Library

ISBN: 978-1-78635-158-6

Printed and bound by CPI Group (UK) Ltd, Croydon, CR0 4YY

ISOQAR REGISTERED

ISOQAR certified Management System, awarded to Emerald for adherence to Environmental standard ISO 14001:2004.

Certificate Number 1985
ISO 14001

INVESTOR IN PEOPLE

THE CURRENT GLOBAL RECESSION

A Theoretical and Empirical Investigation into Developed and BRICS Economies

BY

AKHILESH CHANDRA PRABHAKAR

Universiti Utara Malaysia (UUM), India

Emerald

United Kingdom – North America – Japan
India – Malaysia – China

Dedicated to the memory of my father Ram Singh with reverence and affection.

Contents

PART 2
EMPIRICAL INVESTIGATION

List of Tables

Chapter 8

Chapter 9

List of Figures

Chapter 7

Chapter 9

List of Abbreviations

DCIT	Developing Countries in International Trade
E7	Seven Emerging Economies
EU	European Union
EU15	EU Member States before 2004
EU10	EU Member States that Acceded in 2004
EVI	Economic Vulnerability Index
GDP	Gross Domestic Product
GNI	Gross National Income
GNTB	Group of Eminent Persons on Non-tariff Barriers
ICT	Information and Communication Technology
Input MI	Input Measure Index
LDC	Least Developed Country
MID	Middle-income Developing Country
NBER	National Bureau of Economic Research
NTBs	Non-tariff Barriers
Outcome MI	Outcome Measure Index
PCA	Principal Component Analysis
PPP	Purchasing Power Parity

SIC	Structural and Institutional Context
TDI	Trade and Development Index
TDP	Trade and Development Performance
TPP	Trade Policies and Processes
TRAINS	Trade Analyses and Information System
UNDP	United Nations Development Programme
QE	Quantitative Easing

Foreword

We are very lucky today. Our generations have an opportunity to see the implosion of socialism in the last decade of the twentieth century, and the great depression of capitalism in the first decade of twenty-first century. This study provides an overview of recent global economic performance and short-term prospects for the world economy and of some key global economic policy and development issues. One of its purposes is to serve as a point of reference for discussions on economic, social and related issues. The study discusses several policy directions to stimulate more direct job creation and investment in infrastructure, energy efficiency and sustainable energy supply, and food security; stronger financial safety nets; better coordination between fiscal and monetary policies; and the provision of sufficient support to developing countries in addressing the fallout from the crisis and the coordination of policy measures at the international level.

This book is designed for use in courses that focus on the effected countries from global economic depression (especially) in the United States and the EU, and Chinese responses to the global crisis. The study is based on theoretical and empirical investigation. It has designed to meet the requirements of the economic researchers as well university students who study the courses of economics, finance, banking and management at graduate and postgraduate levels, and various educational and research institutions and libraries, NGOs, Government Offices, etc. This study resulted from 10 years of teaching of development economics at various universities like Universiti Utara Malaysia (UUM), Addis Ababa University, Gondar University and Debre Birhan University in Ethiopia as well as travel Kenya as a researcher. These experiences have helped shape and refine a book that is unique in approach, organization and pedagogy in the context of a major set of problems, such as capitalist crisis, development problems, poverty, inequality, unemployment, environmental decay and rural stagnation. It proceeds to evaluate the economic growth in historical context, and focuses on major economic trends and current international trade trends as well as cooperation among the developing countries.

Acknowledgements

I am grateful to *Prof. Dato' Wira Dr. Mohamed Mustafa bin Ishak*, Vice-Chancellor of UUM, who have given me an opportunity to serve UUM. I am immensely indebted to Prof. Dr. Yusnidah Bt Ibrahim, the Dean of SEFB, COB for inspiring me to write this book. My gratitude to Dr. Siti Aznor Ahmad, the Deputy Dean of SEFB, Dr. Noor Azam, Head of the Department of Economics, and all colleagues and non-academic staffs including Assistant Registrar of SEFB, UUM. I am also very thankful to Prof. Prabhat Patnaik (Member of Planning Commission of India and the Dean of SSI, JNU, New Delhi), Prof Jayati Ghosh (JNU), Prof. Samir Amin (France) and many reviewers, both in Malaysia and abroad, who provided detailed and insightful comments for this book. I thank my current and former colleagues and friends who have provided a lot of suggestions and information, Dr. Mohammad Azam (Pakistaan), Dr. Rabiul Islam (Bangladesh), Prof.Asish Saha (India), Dr. Ahmad Sahidah (Indonesia), Dr. B. Bakhtiyar (Iran) and Dr. Abdullah Sumrahadi (Indonesia). I thank the several thousand students whom I have been privileged to teach. The instant response that comes from the look of puzzlement or enlightenment has taught me how to teach economics. Finally, I thank my mother Laxmi Devi, my life partner Julie Rani and lovely kids Raj and Neel, without whose generous cooperation and help this book would not have been possible.

Suggestions for improvements in the book from fellow teachers and readers are most welcome.

Part 1
Theoretical Investigation

1 Introduction

The world economy is in recession. The International Monetary Fund (IMF) chief predicts that the current global economic and financial crisis is a decade-long crisis as started in 2008, with slight recovery but fluctuating trends; there is no hope for recovery even before 2007 to maintain 3% growth rate until 2018. Some economists predict that it has been as large as in the 'Great Depression' of the 1930s. In the earlier episode (1929–1933), the collapse of the banking system led to the Great Depression. This financial crisis quickly transformed from the bursting of the housing bubble in the United States and the European Union (EU) to the worst full-fledged world economic crisis.

In the current crisis, economic policy reacted expeditiously, prudently, and to a surprising extent coordinated at an international level. The policymakers ignored the structural facts which served to mitigate the depth of the recent crisis such as the lower share of manufacturing and the higher share of services. The increasing financialisation of economy with marketisation at global levels fails to create the demand for ... and the supply of production, ultimately international trade and financial markets lead to a cumulative downward direction through weakening of the role of the state. The decline of trade occurred quickly and simultaneously across countries.

Economic science is an ideological construct which serves to camouflage and justify the world economic order. Unfortunately a set of dogmatic postulates serves to uphold free market capitalism by denying the existence of social inequality and the profit-driven nature of the system is denied. The role of powerful economic actors and how these actors are able to influence the workings of financial and commodity markets is not a matter of concern for the discipline's theoreticians. The powers of market manipulation which serve to appropriate vast amounts of wealth are rarely addressed. And when they are acknowledged, they are considered to belong to the realm of sociology or political science. This means that the policy and institutional framework behind this global economic system, which has been shaped over the course of the last 30 years, is rarely analysed by mainstream economists. It follows that economics as a discipline, with some exceptions, has not provided the analysis required to comprehend the economic crisis. In fact, its main free market postulates and denies the existence of a crisis. The focus of neoclassical economics is on equilibrium, disequilibrium and 'market correction' or 'adjustment' through the market mechanism, as a means to putting the economy back 'onto the path of self-sustained growth'.

Main issues have dominated headlines in recent times: sovereign debt problems in the two biggest economic groupings, the United States and the EU. To a dispassionate observer, it can be a source of wonder that what began as a crisis generated by the irresponsible excesses of financial markets has ended up as a problem of debt sustainability for the very governments that were forced to step in and clear up the mess. But this is an old story, for in history almost every financial crisis has been followed by a crisis of public debt because the crisis itself causes governments to spend more in bailouts as well as in reviving the economy during the subsequent recession.

It is surprising that global capitalism is in recession on the one hand, and world's wealth has reached a record US$263 trillion in mid-2014 (which is US$20.1 trillion more wealth, as increased with 8.3% ratio when compared to mid-2013) which has almost doubled from 2000 on other hand. The top richest 1% accumulated more wealth than the 3.5 billion people who survive on 1% of the world's wealth. The 500 richest people currently own US$1.54 trillion, which is more than the entire GDP of Africa.

The OXFAM International predicted that the wealth of 1% of the richest people in the world amounts to US$110 trillion, and if this trend continues then they can control more wealth than 99% of people in 2016. The world's 85 richest people have more assets with the same value as those owned by the poorer half of the world's population, or 3.5 billion people.

In other words, it is 65 times the total wealth of the bottom half of the world's population, 3.5 billion people who just survive with 1% wealth, resulting over 75% of the world's population, living in underdevelopment, and extreme poverty has already reached 1.2 billion people in the third world, as shown in international organisations' reports including UN, World Bank, Forbes, Oxfam, etc. Unemployment continues at a high level of 8.4% in the developed capitalist countries, according to the World Economic Studies and Prospects of the United Nations (Prabhakar, 2015).

For the purpose of capital formation and capital accumulation, mostly developing countries followed a 'market-oriented growth model' under the urban business leaders, neglecting the vast rural areas with huge populations in the last five to six decades, followed an urban-centred development model, and encouraged migration of surplus agricultural workforce from rural to urban areas to supply urban-based private corporate industries. In other words, the private corporate-led 'metropolitan-centred development model' of progress, the current 'capitalist mode of production systems', promotes free competition-based marketisation worldwide. Service sector dominated 'neo-liberal policies' through attracting foreign direct investment (FDI) with hi-tech (a jobless growth), and through public loans (as an extra burden placed on the country), which focus only on 'how to increase GDP', where vast populated agricultural-based rural areas have been neglected since the era of independence. As a result, it creates environmental degradation (through deforestation and creating all types of pollution), corruption, unemployment, regional imbalances and income inequality among people and between nations. This condition creates widespread poverty and malnutrition, as it is the output of a modern world historical product, the outcome of five centuries of global capitalist expansion under relations of imperialism. International finance capital led to imperialist dominated globalisation, technological change, corporate restructuring and strong support from a neo-liberal state to provide them with the knowledge and skills to cope with new technologies, where work practices are the responsible factors for all types of economic disorder (Prabhakar, 2015).

Any debate on how best to promote sustainable and inclusive development is incomplete without a full consideration of issues of science, technology and innovation (STI). Access to new and appropriate technologies promotes steady improvements in living conditions, which can be lifesaving for the most vulnerable populations, and drive productivity gains which ensure rising incomes. The digital revolution is opening up a great divide between a skilled and wealthy few and the rest of society. In the past, new technologies have usually raised wages by boosting productivity, with the gains being split between skilled and less-skilled workers, and between owners of capital, workers and consumers. Of course, technology is empowering talented individuals as never before and opening up yawning gaps between the earnings of the skilled and the unskilled, capital-owners and labour. At the same time, it is creating a large pool of underemployed labour that is depressing investment. The effect of technological change on trade is also changing the basis of tried-and-true methods of economic development in poorer economies. More manufacturing work can be automated, and skilled design work accounts for a larger share of the value of trade, leading to what economists call 'premature deindustrialisation' in developing countries. No longer can governments count on a growing industrial sector to absorb unskilled labour from rural areas. In both the rich and the emerging world, technology is creating opportunities for those previously held back by financial or geographical constraints; yet new work for those with modest skill levels is scarce compared with the bonanza created by earlier technological revolutions. All this is sorely testing governments, beset by new demands for intervention, regulation and support. If they get their response right, they will be able to channel technological change in ways that broadly benefit society. If they get it wrong, they could be under attack from both angry underemployed workers and resentful rich taxpayers (Prabhakar, 2015).

The Global Economic Scenario

The EU's recent economic experience is a double-dip recession — a prolonged recession that continues to this day. Like that of the U.S. economy, developments in the European economy have an influence on world trade, investments and economic growth.

The world's second-largest economic power house China's rapid growth over the last decade reshaped the world economy, creating a powerful driver of corporate strategies, financial markets and geopolitical decisions. But recently, China's dollar-denominated exports declined by 5.5% year-on-year in August 2015, while imports slid 13.8%, producing a trade surplus of $60.24 billion. China's foreign trade activity has weakened dramatically in recent months. Exports have been hit by sluggish global demand, while imports have been constrained by a slowing domestic economy and depressed commodity prices. Gross domestic product (GDP) growth is expected by some economists to slip below 7% in the third quarter — down from 7% in both the first and second quarters in 2015. Over the weekend, China's Finance Minister Lou Jiwei said that the world's second-largest economy had entered a 'new normal' of slower growth, adding that a growth rate of around 7% was to be expected in the coming four to five years. As the world's workshop, China is now facing its most protracted decline since the global financial crisis. Overseas shipments fell 5.5% last month compared with a year earlier. That has dragged total exports 1.4% lower in dollar terms in the first eight months of the year. It is a sign that the country's sprawling manufacturing sector is losing competitiveness: labour costs are rising relentlessly and the currency, the renminbi, remains relatively strong despite its devaluation last month.

Despite the currency move, Chinese goods are notably more expensive for foreign buyers than they were a year ago. At the same time, China's imports are falling even more sharply, declining last month for the 10th month in a row, with a drop of 14% by value. Sharp drops in global prices for commodities like oil and industrial metals have propelled the decline in import value. But the sheer volume of imports of crucial industrial raw materials like coal, iron ore, copper, aluminium and steel has also fallen this year. The declines are a clear sign of weakening domestic demand in China as a slump in manufacturing and new housing construction drag on economic growth (Gough, 2015).

China's economic downturn has sent shockwaves across the region, as evident in the deteriorating trade data of neighbouring Taiwan and South Korea, which reported plummeting exports in August 2015. Taiwan's exports plunged 14.8% the same year (August 2015), while Korea's exports contracted 14.7%, largely attributable to retreating mainland demand. Industrial and commodity multinationals face the most pressing concerns, as they scramble to stem the profit slide from weaker consumption. Caterpillar cut back factory production, with industry sales of construction equipment in China dropping by half in the first six months of the year. Smartphone makers, automobile manufacturers and retailers wonder about the staying power of Chinese buyers, even if it is not shaking their bottom line at this point. General Motors and Ford factories have been shipping fewer cars to Chinese dealerships this summer.

It is not just companies reassessing their assumptions. Russia had been turning to China to fill the financial gap left by low oil prices and western sanctions. Venezuela, Nigeria and Ukraine have been heavily dependent on investments and low-cost loans from China. The pain has been particularly acute for Brazil. The country is already faltering, as weaker Chinese imports of minerals and soybeans have jolted all of Latin America. The uncertainty over China could limit the manoeuvring room for officials to address the sluggish Brazilian economy at a time when resentment is festering over proposed austerity measures. The weakness in China is even compelling officials at the United States Federal Reserve to think more globally, as they consider raising interest rates.

India's trade deficit widened to US$12.5 billion in August 2015 from US$10.7 billion a year previously. This was the first instance of the trade deficit expanding in the past four months. Although export/import numbers have been weak in the last few months, in

August 2015, exports contracted at the steepest pace in five months while imports fell at the slowest pace in four months. This led to the widening of the trade deficit. Exports fell for the ninth consecutive month in August 2015, registering a decline of 20.7%. Low international commodity prices and tepid global demand continued to hurt India's exports. The fall in international crude oil prices has led to a decline in the value of India's exports. The price of the Indian basket of crude oil averaged 53.3% lower in August 2015 on a year-on-year basis. Prices have fallen over the last year on account of a global supply glut and weak international demand.

According to provisional data released by the Commerce Ministry, exports of 23 out of 30 items fell. Exports of a group of agriculture commodities (accounting for over 75% of total agri-exports) plunged by 18.9%. In addition, exports of items like engineering goods, electronic goods, readymade garments and leather products also fell during the month. India's imports fell by 10% in August 2015. Non-oil, non-gold and silver imports fell by 5.7% in August 2015. This was the steepest fall in these.

The world's third-largest economy Japan is back in recession. GDP fell at an annualised 1.6% from July to September 2014, compared with forecasts of a 2.1% rise due to consumption and exports remained weak, saddling companies with huge inventories to work off. The tax was increased to curb Japan's huge public debt, which is the highest among developed nations.

The data also showed that growth in private consumption, which accounts for about 60% of the economy, was much weaker than expected.

Billions of dollars were pumped into the economy through stimulus spending. The Bank of Japan went on an even bigger spree, printing hundreds of billions of dollars of new money and using it to buy government bonds. This had two effects:

- First, it pushed down the value of the yen, which made Japanese exports cheaper.
- Second, it pushed investors out of bonds and in to stocks.

The huge stock market rise only benefited a minority of rich people. About 80% of Japanese people do not own any shares. Instead, their incomes are stagnant or falling, and the tax rise has made them feel even poorer. Hence they have stopped spending.

China and the International Monetary Fund (IMF) want a yuan reserve currency — and are doing everything they can to make it happen. Their plan is already underway so that the U.S. dollar could be on its way out as the world's primary reserve currency.

A yuan reserve currency will trigger a transfer of $1 trillion into Chinese assets just in the first few years. It matters because much of the money pouring into the yuan will result in sales of U.S. Treasuries — how most governments hold dollars. When foreign governments start to dump the $6 trillion they hold, U.S. dollars will flood the market and trigger massive inflation. In fact, the race to dump the U.S. dollar has already started — even before we get a yuan reserve currency.

The IMF is so focused on taking out the U.S. dollar. It has to do with something called 'Special Drawing Rights', or SDRs. SDRs are just a softer term for 'world money'. That is why they came up with the name Special Drawing Rights — because if they called it 'world money' that would sound a little spooky and scary. The IMF's plan to dethrone the U.S. dollar is in fact part of a grand scheme to put the IMF in charge of the world's monetary system. In short, the IMF wants to be 'the central bank of the world'.

Structural Causes of the Global Financial Crisis

In the aftermath of the financial collapse in the United States that began in 1929, it was almost universally believed that unregulated financial markets are inherently unstable, subject to fraud and manipulation by insiders, and capable of triggering deep economic crises and political and social unrest. To protect the country from these dangers, in the mid-1930s the U.S. government created a strict financial regulatory system that worked effectively through the 1960s. These economic and political events found reflection in the financial market theories of endogenous financial instability created by John Maynard Keynes and Hyman Minsky. Their theories generated a policy perspective supportive of the sharp shift from light to tight financial market regulation that took place after the Great Crash. Economic and financial turbulence in the 1970s and early 1980s led to both a paradigm and a policy regime shift. Efficient financial market theory and new classical macro-theory replaced the theoretical visions of Keynes and Minsky, and the existing system of tight financial regulation was deconstructed through radical deregulation pushed by financial institutions and justified by efficient financial market theory. These developments facilitated the transition to a new globally integrated deregulated neo-liberal capitalism (Crotty, 2014).

The world has witnessed that some of the world's largest financial institutions (more than hundreds of banking and financial institutions, especially in the United States and the EU) have gone bankrupt, finally transmitted into the 'Great Depression' for a decades-long crisis. Key markets stopped functioning. Credit dried up, even for healthy borrowers. The IMF estimates that global recession seems to occur over a cycle lasting between 8 and 10 years. Its causes are still uncertain and controversial, the net effect was a sudden and general loss of confidence in the economic future, and there is no hope to recover until late 2018. The IMF Chief economist Olivier Blanchard warned that the Eurozone crisis, debt problems in Japan and the United States, and a slowdown in China meant that the world economy would not be in good shape until at least 2018. Blanchard said 'it will surely take at least a decade from the beginning of the crisis for the world economy to get back to decent shape'.[1] Plagued by uncertainty and fresh setbacks, the world economy has weakened further and will grow more slowly over the next coming year. This prolonged crisis indicates the unsustainability of international finance capital-led, 'oil Texas' and 'military-industrial complex' capital-intensive 'mode of production' in the United States, and heavily dependent

1. The IMF Forecasts (2014).

on 'financial sectors' led by euro money lending agency in the EU, neo-liberal regime has failed.

From 2008 to 2012, global output growth averaged just 1.7%. This is much slower than during any of the five-year periods that followed recessions in the global economy since the 1970s. The rate of world output was 2.2% in 2012 and at a similar rate in 2013. As in previous years, developed countries are expected to show the poorest performance, with around 1% increase in GDP). Developing and transition economies are likely to grow by almost 5% and 3%, respectively. Economic activity in many developed countries and a number of emerging market economies are still suffering from the impacts of the financial and economic crisis that started in 2008, and from the unsustainable financial processes and domestic and international imbalances that led to it. However, continuing weak growth in several countries may also be partly due to their current macroeconomic policy stance (Trade and Development Report, 2013).

In the EU, GDP is expected to shrink for the second consecutive year. Economic contraction is likely to be more severe in the euro area than in other EU countries. Private demand remains subdued, especially in the periphery economies, due to high unemployment, wage compression, low consumer confidence and the still incomplete process of balance sheet consolidation. Given the ongoing process of deleveraging, expansionary monetary policies have failed to induce banks to provide much-needed new credit to the private sector that could reinvigorate demand. In this context, the increased tendency towards fiscal tightening makes a quick return to a higher growth trajectory highly unlikely.

Indeed, attempts to resolve the crisis in the euro area through fiscal austerity may backfire badly, as it adds a deflationary impulse to already weak private demand. The countries in the eurozone that have been suffering the most from the crisis continue to operate under extremely adverse conditions, while growth in the surplus countries has largely relied on strong exports. Since governments in the latter countries have been reluctant to stimulate domestic demand by other means than monetary policy, disequilibrium within the zone persists (Trade and Development Report, 2013).

Countries in the eurozone system became enmeshed in the recession more deeply, especially as a consequence of the Greek debt crisis that broke open by 2010. By mid-2014, unemployment climbed: for Greece, 27.2%; Spain, 24.5%; Portugal, 14.3%; Italy, 12.6%; and France, 10.3%, among the big countries. The euro area unemployment rate (weighted) was 11.5%.

These unemployment rates reflected the recessionary changes in output in the region. Some countries have shown positive growth (for instance, United Kingdom and Germany). Weak growth of output however had been dragged down by the negative growth rates of bigger economies (Italy, Spain) between 2011 and 2013. Eurozone economies had real growth contractions close to half of 1% in these years.

Magnitude of the Problem

Europe was slow to adopt measures to counter the recessionary conditions. The policymakers in the region were dominated by believers that the cure to the problem was to tighten fiscal discipline — to reduce the fiscal deficit rather than raise expenditure and introduce direct economic stimulus. At a time when aggregate demand had fallen while unemployment rates were rising — sure indications that demand management in the macroeconomy was needed — governments in the region tightened fiscal policies. They could not effectively reform labour market policies. Many European governments did little to strengthen the position of the banks early enough. Then the Greek debt problem shook up the euro currency system. European banks were highly exposed to heavily indebted countries, not only to Greece, but also to the bigger countries, like Italy, Spain and others in the zone. The European Central Bank (ECB) followed the track to introduce non-conventional measures to ease monetary policy.

In the United States, an aggressive approach was undertaken to reform their capital structure which restored strength to the banks as a result of the financial debacle. In the United States, there was a way out — monetary policy to expand credit and liquidity in the economy. In the United States, the Federal Bank bought a wide range of secured private debts, including mortgage-backed debts, in order to introduce a sizable monetary and credit stimulus, and sold bonds to China to repay public debt. This led to a programme of raising capital of banks that were found after 'stress tests' were instituted.

Within the near zero-interest rates policy that the Federal bank of the United States has sustained, and credited at large scale to the private business centres which is facilitated for creating new job opportunities, induce greater demand for output and spur a rise in production. In turn, these measures also sustained a weaker dollar that made U.S. firms more internationally competitive. The ECB also followed the same road but limited its purchases of private debt only to lower risk, asset-backed securities. ECB's programme, though bold in its target quantity of private bond buying, was much more restricted in what it could buy from the region's banks.

ECB's programme was held back by German opposition to a bolder private debt-buying approach. German opposition was consistent with its more conservative stance regarding the measures designed to deal with the recession, which was more aligned with tighter fiscal and monetary policy. It could even be said that it is not succeeding in its goal of stimulating the restoration of growth. ECB's target has not been achieved. Apparently, banks took advantage of the scheme mainly to lend back to their governments or to boost their own balance sheets. Thus, there is still missing sufficient economic stimulus to restore the economy back to growth. ECB's quantitative easing (QE) did help, however, to restore calm to the European debt crisis arising from Greek, Italian, Spanish and other regional country debts. These countries have found relief in the fall of the cost of refinancing their debts.

At the global level, it is notable that Japan is bucking the current austerity trend by providing strong fiscal stimulus and monetary expansion that are aimed at reviving economic growth and curbing deflationary trends. These measures could help maintain its

GDP growth at close to 2% in 2013. The United States is expected to grow at a similar rate, but based on a different set of factors. Partly owing to significant progress made in the consolidation of its banking sector, private domestic demand has begun to recover. On the other hand, cuts in public spending, including for needed investment in infrastructure, are having a contractionary effect. Since the net outcome of these opposing tendencies is unclear, there is also considerable uncertainty about whether the expansionary monetary policy stance will be maintained (Trade and Development Report, 2013).

Growth in Emerging Developing Countries Driven by Domestic Demand

Developing countries are expected to grow by between 4.5% and 5% in 2013, similar to 2012. In many of them, growth has been driven more by domestic demand than by exports, as external demand from developed economies has remained weak. In addition, short-term capital inflows, attracted by higher interest rates than in the major developed countries, have been exerting appreciation pressure on the currencies of several emerging market economies, thus weakening their export sectors. As before, in 2012 output growth was strong in East, South and South-East Asia, at 5.3%, but recently there has been a slowdown, reflecting weak demand from some of the major export markets. In China, the contribution of net exports to GDP growth declined further, while fixed investment and private consumption, as a result of faster wage growth, continued to drive output expansion. Domestic demand, encouraged by various incomes policy measures in a number of other countries in the region, such as India, Indonesia, the Philippines and Thailand, is also supporting output growth, which may therefore accelerate moderately in the region as a whole in 2013 (Trade and Development Report, 2013).

The rapid expansion of developing economies as a group has further increased their weight in the world economy; a new pattern of global growth seems to be emerging. While developed countries remain the main export markets for developing countries, the share of the latter's contribution to growth in the world economy has increased, from 28% in the 1990s to about 40% in the period 2003–2007, and to close to 75% since 2008. However, more recently, growth in these economies has decelerated. If developing countries can increase the role of domestic demand and South-South trade in their development strategies, they may continue to grow at a relatively fast pace, with increasing potential to rely on each other for the expansion of aggregate demand. However, they cannot be expected to lift developed countries out of their sluggish growth pattern through higher imports from them.

The rate of world output, which was 2.2% in 2012, is forecast to grow at a similar rate in 2013. As in previous years, developed countries are expected to show the poorest performance, with around 1% increase in GDP. Developing and transition economies are likely to grow by almost 5% and 3%, respectively.

Economic activity in many developed countries and a number of emerging market economies is still suffering from the impacts of the financial and economic crisis that started in 2008, and from the unsustainable financial processes and domestic and international imbalances that led to it. However, continuing weak growth in several countries may also be partly due to their current macroeconomic policy stance (Trade and Development Report, 2013).

The 2012 Greek debt exchange was a watershed event in the euro area debt crisis. It generated fears of contagion and was viewed as a threat to the euro itself. There is a heated debate as to whether the debt restructuring should have taken place sooner. This chapter argues that a deep haircut up front, under threat of legislative action, would have been seen as unnecessary and deeply coercive. But delaying the restructuring beyond mid-2011, when it became clear that Greece's debt was unsustainable, was unjustified. The delay reduced the stock of privately held debt subject to a haircut, possibly making an official debt restructuring inevitable down the road. Initial fears that the Greek debt restructuring would pose a serious threat to the euro area's financial stability proved to be exaggerated. On the contrary, it demonstrated that an orderly default involving a pre-emptive debt restructuring is possible in a monetary union, provided appropriate firewalls are in place to limit contagion risks. With crisis management institutions and procedures now in place in the euro area, and with much stricter fiscal surveillance, the Greek experience is likely to remain unique in the history of debt restructurings; however, some lessons can be learned from its specific features (Xafa, 2012).

Greater Inequality

The world's most rich 1% control 50% of the world's the resources, and 50% world's population just survive with 1% of the world's resources (says Credit Suisse Bank). However, between 2000 and 2014 the world's wealth has increased almost doubly with maximum private corporate profits but no development in productive sectors. Some people argued that American capitalism is only responsible for both the world economic crisis and the social counter-revolution organised by the ruling class. World wealth has reached a record $263 trillion but is concentrated in fewer hands. The richest 1% has accumulated more wealth, and own almost 50% of it, which could trigger recession, according to a new report by Credit Suisse. The Credit Suisse Global Wealth Report, warns that the 'abnormally high wealth income ratios' may spark a recession, as high disparity leads to economic friction. Global wealth has grown to a record $263 trillion in mid-2014, $20.1 trillion more, and an 8.3% increase, over mid-2013. Household wealth has more than doubled since 2000, when the same report calculated it at $117 trillion. Leading the money trail is the United States, dubbed 'Land of Fortunes' by the report, which again boasts the highest average wealth. It is home to 34.7% ($91 trillion) of global wealth. Europe's portion comes in a close second with 32.4%, followed by India and China's 23.7% share, and then the 18.9% concentrated in the Asia-Pacific region.

North America has the highest average wealth and is also the world's leader in GDP, which the report estimates grew by $12.9 billion in 2013. Wealth in the United States and Europe was driven by a rather spectacular year on the stock exchanges. Since the financial crisis of 2008, the United States has added $31.5 trillion in household wealth. In the last year alone the stock market increased in value by 22.6%.

Germany, Canada and France all experienced huge spurts in capital markets, gaining more than 30%. Much of the world's 'new money' is coming from China and developing nations. Between 2000 and 2014, emerging markets accounted for 11.4% of wealth. 'As we noted last year, Asia and particularly China will account for the largest portion of newly created wealth among the emerging markets', the report says. Other emerging players on the international scene, according to Credit Suisse, are Russia, Brazil, India, Indonesia, South Africa and Turkey. The conclusion of the report offers predictions for 2019, where the authors suggest global wealth will grow by 40% and reach $369 trillion, but emerging markets will account for 26%, more than double of what they do now. The number of millionaires worldwide is projected to blossom from 35 million today to 53 million in 2019.

The wealth of the world's billionaires now stands at $7.3 trillion, an increase of 12% from last year, according to a report released by Wealth-X and Union Bank of Switzerland (UBS). There are a record 2325 billionaires in the world, up from 2170 in 2013 and 1360 in 2009, the first year following the financial collapse. Billionaires make up .000033% of the world's population, or to put in another way, there are about 3 million people for every one billionaire. Yet this exceedingly small social layer possesses about 4.5 times the total wealth of the bottom half of the population, or 3.5 billion people. All the money of bankers, shareholders, land owners and manufacturers is nothing else than accumulated unpaid for labour of the working class.

The stock market and finance capital are the driving forces behind the wealth of the world's billionaires. The top industry for billionaires, according to Wealth-X, is 'finance, banking and investment', which accounts for close to 20% of the total billionaire population, followed by industrial conglomerates at 12% and real estate at 7%. More than one in six billionaires resides in the financial capitals of New York, Hong Kong, London, Mumbai, Singapore and Moscow.

Behind these figures lies a social relationship essential to the functioning of the capitalist system. The corporate and financial aristocracy has benefited from a massive redistribution of wealth, aided and abetted by the major capitalist states and central banks. It is not just that enormous wealth stands side by side with enormous poverty, but the one is the direct product of the other.

American capitalism is at the centre of both the world economic crisis and the social counter-revolution organised by the ruling class. Since 2008, under the direction of the Obama administration, the resources of both the U.S. Treasury and the Federal Reserve have been opened up to Wall Street, which has engaged in an unprecedented orgy of speculation. Bank bailouts and 'quantitative easing' in the United States have been paralleled by similar measures internationally, particularly in Europe.

Six years later, stock markets continue to post record highs. Both benchmark U.S. indices — the Standard & Poor's 500 and the Dow Jones Industrial Average (DJIA) — closed above previous highs. The latest surge came after the Federal Chairman Janet Yellen said the central bank would keep interest rates at nearly zero (i.e., provide banks with essentially free cash) for a 'considerable time'. As a result, American billionaires have seen their number grow by 57 over the past year. The country is home to the largest number of billionaires in the world (571), nearly 25% of the total global billionaire population and three times more than any other country.

At the same time, as the World Socialist Web Site (WSWS) has previously documented, incomes for the majority of the population have continued to decline. Between 2010 and 2013, the period of Obama's 'recovery', average income for the bottom fifth of the population fell 8%, while the income of the top tenth of the population has increased 10%, with the extremely wealthy reaping the bulk of these gains. The cash paid out to the banks is to be covered by the destruction of social programmes and an historic reversal in the living conditions of the working class.

The response of the ruling class to the crisis has not only led to an explosive growth of social inequality, but has also created the conditions for an even more devastating economic catastrophe.

More perceptive media commentators have noted with concern the extraordinary disconnect between the surge in global stock markets and the state of the 'real economy'. Writing in the *Financial Times*, Jay Pelosky warned that, 'the state of the global economy resembles nothing so much as a soufflé on the brink of implosion'. He cited a number of warning signs: 'The US consumer remains quiescent, dramatic increases in Asian debt levels preclude a robust economic recovery there, while Europe stagnates. Global demand remains inadequate.'

As stock markets continue to rise, economic forecasts are being downgraded. The Organisation for Economic Cooperation and Development (OECD) this week cut its projection for economic growth in all major economies in 2014 and 2015. Among the billionaires themselves, there is growing concern. Sam Zell, the chairman of Equity Group Investments (net worth $4.8 billion), noted earlier this month that 'the stock market is at an all-time, but economic activity is not at an all-time'. Zell said that investors have 'no place else to put their money and the stock market is getting more than its share. It's very likely that something has to give here.'

Not only are Wall Street investors simply buying up stocks, but corporations themselves are also funnelling record cash hoards back into the market, rather than increasing production. In the first half of this year, U.S. companies bought back $338 billion in their own shares, more than any six-month period since 2007. This is the real state of world capitalism: sustained by an unending stream of cash, run by a financial aristocracy addicted to speculation and a sustained assault on the working class, and headed towards another and even greater collapse.

The extremely precarious state of the economic situation, and the parasitism of the ruling class that presides over it, is the central factor in explaining both the drive to war and dictatorship. With no way out of the crisis of the profit system, the ruling class, led by the American financial aristocracy, turns increasingly to militarism abroad and domestic repression at home. Such are the measures employed by a ruling class that has reached an historic impasse (Table 1.1).

Table 1.1: World GDP.

	Country	2013 (US$ Million)	2013 Growth (%)	2013 GDP per Capita (US$ Million)	2014 Estimate (US$ Million)	2015 Estimate (US$ Million)	2016 Estimate (US$ Million)	2017 Estimate (US$ Million)	2018 Estimate (US$ Million)
1.	USA	16,720,000	N/A	52,800	16,799,700	17,528,382	18,365,803	19,282,539	20,239,777
2.	China	9,330,000	7.4	6,900	9,181,377	10,027,558	10,940,377	11,878,659	12,908,392
3.	Japan	5,007,000	2.0	38,500	4,901,532	4,846,327	5,020,905	5,165,025	5,371,623
4.	Germany	3,593,000	0.5	44,300	3,635,959	3,875,755		4,263,547	4,464,412
5.	France	2,739,000	0.3	41,700	2,737,361	2,885,692	3,021,356	3,153,868	3,308,116
6.	UK	2,490,000	1.8	39,600	2,535,761	2,827,514	2,992,148	3,156,405	3,340,396
7.	Brazil	2,190,000	2.5	11,100	2,242,854	2,215,953	2,340,754	2,470,474	2,610,967
8.	Russia	2,113,000	1.3	14,600	2,118,006	2,092,205	2,108,837	2,201,726	2,270,810
9.	Italy	2,068,000	−1.8	33,600	2,071,955	2,171,482	2,263,472	2,352,507	2,451,564
10.	Canada	1,825,000	1.6	52,100	1,825,096	1,768,968	1,849,880	1,936,127	2,030,832
11.	India	1,670,000	4.3	1,500	1,870,651	1,995,776	2,172,320	2,369,907	2,592,258

Table 1.1: (*Continued*)

Country	2013 (US$ Million)	2013 Growth (%)	2013 GDP per Capita (US$ Million)	2014 Estimate (US$ Million)	2015 Estimate (US$ Million)	2016 Estimate (US$ Million)	2017 Estimate (US$ Million)	2018 Estimate (US$ Million)
12. Australia	1,488,000	2.5	65,100	1,505,277	1,435,830	1,481,592	1,537,920	1,597,522
13. Spain	1,356,000	−1.3	28,600	1,358,687	1,415,304	1,466,357	1,515,777	1,574,878
14. Netherlands	722,300	−1.3	47,600	800,007	838,036	876,171	911,957	954,660
15. Switzerland	646,200	2.0	80,800	650,814	693,532	718,758	740,809	765,693
16. Sweden	552,000	0.9	57,200	557,938	580,195	614,091	652,842	695,719
17. South Africa	353,900	2.0	6,600	350,779	354,150	373,254	394,274	417,327
18. Denmark	324,300	0.1	58,300	330,958	347,221	360,426	374,294	390,243
19. South Korea	1,198,000	2.8	24,400	1,221,801	1,307,887	1,395,703	1,493,681	1,609,528
20. Indonesia	867,500	5.3	3,500	870,275	859,339	900,270	991,286	1,068,507
21. Thailand	400,900	2.9	5,600	387,156	373,627	392,817	416,684	439,241

22. Malaysia	312,400	4.7	11,513	312,433	343,009	380,457	417,043	452,833
23. Singapore	295,700	4.1	54,700	295,744	304,105	317,749	330,766	345,301
24. Philippines	272,200	6.8	2,600	272,018	291,799	332,588	372,601	416,813
25. Hong Kong	272,100	2.9	38,100	273,658	293,709	315,396	336,967	360,390
26. Taiwan	484,700	2.2	20,900	489,213	502,284	534,217	568,827	608,571

Source: CIA 'The World Factbook'.

Governments of 158 countries have considered four main reforms:

I. Cutting or capping wage bills, which can impact the salaries of public sector workers that provide essential services to the population (under consideration in 73 countries).

II. Reducing or removing subsidies, including on food and fuel products at a time when food prices are at unprecedented high in many places (in 73 countries).

III. Targeting and rationalising social protection programmes, this is, reducing social protection coverage at a time when governments should be considering scaling up a social protection floor for all persons rather than scaling down benefits (in 55 countries).

IV. Governments are also pursuing other budget-slashing strategies that could lead to heightened vulnerabilities and cause further contraction of economic activities, such as tax increases on basic goods and services that are principally consumed by the poor (in 71 countries).

Those of us who investigate the great depression (2008–2018), and seek to intervene in policy debate, in favour of economic development with social justice and environmental sustainability, are regularly assured by the world's power brokers that they are fully committed to these goals so long as economic growth and expansion of free trade are not compromised by governmental restraints on the market. So sacred have growth and free trade become in our modern culture and habits that only rarely do we find the courage to ask why they should be given precedence over the needs of people and nature? Indeed, why should we consider accelerating growth and trade to be of any importance at all except to the extent that they serve people and nature? When the proponents of growth, market deregulation and free trade tout their benefits, it is well to bear in mind what some of the most outspoken of these proponents really have in mind.

The world's most powerful instrument of governance is not a government. Nor is it a global corporation. Rather it is a global financial system that is running dangerously out of control. Each day half a million to a million people — primarily Western Europeans, North Americans and Japanese — arise as dawn reaches their part of the world, turn on their computers, and leave the real world of people, things and nature of immerse themselves in playing the world's most lucrative computer game: the financial game. As their computers come online, they enter a world of cyberspace constructed of numbers that represent money and complex rules by which those numbers can be converted into a seemingly infinite variety of financial instruments, each with its own distinctive risks and reproductive qualities. Through their interactions, the players engage in competitive transactions aimed at acquiring for their own accounts the money that other players hold.

Players can also pyramid the amount of money in play by borrowing from one another and bidding up prices. Indeed, the money game players have been successful in creating play money that for every US$1 now circulating in the productive world economy of real goods and services, it is estimated that there is US$20 to US$50 circulating in the world of pure finance — 'investment' funds completely delinked from the creation of real value. In the international currency market alone, some US$800 billion to US$1 trillion changes hands each day unrelated to productive investment or trade in actual goods and services. Not only is the money game challenging, the play money it generates can be exchanged for real money to buy things from people who work in the real world — lots of things. Unfortunately for the rest of us, though it is played like a game and the transactions involve nothing more than moving numbers from one electronic account to another, through a global web of computers.

It is not only the advanced capitalist countries but almost all the capitalist nations who have been integrated or depending on the U.S. and the EU's markets face more serious economic and political challenges than the 1930s great depression. In other words, the global economy is in a very fragile situation — with mounting budget deficits and sovereign debt in advanced economies, asset and credit bubbles and growing current account deficits in several major emerging economies. It is increasingly recognised that the world economy is unlikely to make a smooth transition to stable, sustained and broad-based growth — hence the repeated talk of the 'next crisis'. As a result of the recent crisis more than 50 million new people were added below the poverty line and over 200 million became unemployed in Europe and the United States.

This prolonged crisis indicates the unsustainability of finance capital-driven globalisation. After spending billions of dollars to bail out the banks and financial institutions which were responsible for perpetuating the crisis, the governments in the United States and Europe have pursued austerity measures and cutbacks in public spending to shift the burden on to the people. The Eurozone countries are in the throes of a debt crisis with Greece at the epicentre. The people in all the advanced capitalist countries have been protesting and conducting struggles against the austerity measures and the cuts in social welfare. The Occupy Wall Street movement in the United States and the big strike struggle by workers, students and youth in Europe are noteworthy which is clear evidence that the classical Adam Smith's free market, free economy, laissez faire economic philosophy which was implemented by the first world since (the US former president Mr. Ronald Reagan and the British prime minister Ms. Margret Thatcher) what is called 'Reagan-Thatcher' imperialist-driven globalisation model has collapsed.

Unequal Exchange Rate Systems and Unequal Trading Patterns

The current world economic order is based on unequal exchange rate systems and unequal trading patterns. It has created the phenomenon of job-loss growth, where profits increase while unemployment also rises; a sharp widening of inequalities both within and between countries; and a sustained military-political drive to impose imperialist hegemony over the world's resources. The major international agencies such as the UN, the WTO, the

World Bank and the IMF which are dominated by the United States and the EU imposed neo-liberalism worldwide. A trend of global investment flows shifted away from the real, productive sector, more and more towards purely artificial, speculative profits in real estate, stock markets, futures markets and an exaggerated growth of service employment. This process, accompanied by a monstrous ballooning of debt, has finally led to a situation, in which the present global floating exchange rate financial system is hopelessly bankrupt, and accompanied by an accelerating decline in the performance of the real physical economies of nearly all nations of the world.

Production is not essentially determined by demand but owing to unrestricted competition where main motive of production is how to maximise profits. This unrestricted competition is the root cause of inequality, poverty, unemployment and all economic ills of society including economic depression. The terms of trade seem always to be working against the developing countries. International free trade theory suggest, if rich and poor nations concentrate on the production in which they enjoyed comparative advantage, for example, 'colonies' in raw materials and 'metro-poles' in manufactures and adequately supplied each other's demand through vigorous external trade, both would grow simultaneously.

However, what happened was that trading under these arrangements resulted in terms of trade invariably moving against the developing countries, for the prices of manufactured products that they imported rose faster than the prices of the primary commodities that they exported. As a consequence the motor force of growth engine, under such trade practices, was shifted to the metro-poles, and the development of the colonies was rendered utterly dependent on the mother countries.

This unequal relationship continued uninterrupted even after the Second World War, when most of the colonies had emerged as independent nations. The same relationship existed within the nations where the development model followed by the independent government under the leadership of domestic bourgeoisies through conflict and co-operation for sharing profits with international bourgeoisies. In the mercantilist environment of the eighteenth and nineteenth centuries the prevailing free trade notion was that what was good for Britain was good for the world. Free trade established inequality between nations and competition was agreeable only after Britain had established it was pre-eminent as the most advanced industrial nation. The artificial division of labour was broken when other countries adopted protectionism policies to counter the effects of Britain's pre-eminence. However, by the first half of the twentieth century protectionism was the norm in the developed world.

This prevented specialised exporters from using their export income to diversify into the various types of processing and manufacturing industries since these were protected by the developed world. However, after the Second World War, developed countries began once again to discuss the need for trade liberalisation, and as the beginning of the twenty-first century draws nearer, the rhetoric is towards free trade within trade blocs and regional groupings.

Financiarisation of the Global System

Service sectors and hi-tech manufacture (capital-intensive) dominated by a handful of oligopolies (around 5000 oligopolist; the top 2000 oligopolist are the most powerful) control the basic decision-making of the world economy. These oligopolies are not solely financial, such as the banks or the insurance companies, but also include enterprises involved in industrial production, services, transports and the like. The way they are financiarised is their chief characteristic. This financial capital sector was extremely profitable. Thus, the current financial system could not compete or qualify in the free market unless state sponsored highly subsidised and tax-relaxed crony capitalism of financiarised oligopolies. This system needs the expansion of financial investments worldwide.

In that respect the major market, the one which dominates all other markets, is precisely the monetary and financial market. This is my definition of the 'financiarisation' of the global system. Such a strategy is not the result of independent 'decisions' of banks, it is rather that the choice of the 'financiarised' groups. These oligopolies hence do not produce profits; they just swipe the monopolies' rent through financial investments. Oxfam International, a poverty fighting organisation, says at the World Economic Forum in Davos earlier this year with its report that the world's 85 richest people own assets with the same value as those owned by the poorer half of the world's population, or 3.5 billion people. The biggest group: almost 42% oligopolists are from the United States. Germany and Russia have the second-highest number. The rest are sprinkled among 13 countries in Western Europe, Asia-Pacific Economic Cooperation (APAC), China and India. The biggest group of the super-rich comes from the United States as the country holds almost a third of the world's wealth (30%), significantly more than any other country, according to the Global Wealth Data book, from Credit Suisse Research Institute. Europe, with a slightly bigger chunk of the world's wealth (32%), produced substantially fewer of the richest. That is due to less dynamic economies, which do not equal the United States in how they foster innovation, on which many of the newest U.S. fortunes are based.

However, financial investment could not continue indefinitely, while the productive basis was growing at a low rate. Consequently, we have the logic of a 'financial bubble', the sheer translation of the financial investments system. The gross amount of financial transactions reaches two thousand trillion alone, while the world GDP is 44 trillion only. Ultimately, the current economic regime has failed to provide full employment, equal distribution of wealth and income, and control inflation. It creates debt (both public and private) where everyday debt repayments are more than one hundred million dollars to the bank by the developing countries.

The oligopolist, through currency domination (dollar and euro), technology domination and trade domination (especially war equipment), maintained their own hegemony across the world since the Second World War. With the currency (dollar, pound and euro), oil and military-industrial complex related financial institutions, service sectors and hi-tech manufacture (capital-intensive), free market economic models established by Margret Thatcher (former British prime minister) and Ronald Reagan (former president of the United States) during the 1980s now dominate not only in the western rich or advanced countries but all over the world. This market economic system failed to provide full employment and equal distribution of wealth and income, or control inflation. Under the current global financial regime, developing countries, per day, pay debt repayments of more than one hundred million dollars to the World Bank.

Dirty Game Players

Second, the World Bank and the IMF always support the authoritarian regimes (see how Indonesia was redesigned by the United States, Britain and the western empire backed General Suharto in 1965 the Saudi Arabian monarch regime is still backed by the United States and the United Kingdom, and aggressively imposed economic sanctions and imposed war against Yugoslavia, Iraq, Afghanistan, Libya, Syria), to capture the vast mineral wealth and other natural resources, vast markets and cheap labour, and recently supported $1.7 billion to pro-EU and pro-western Ukrainian government.

The two biggest conflagrations ever, the First and Second World Wars — claiming total deaths of around 80 million — were both presaged by economic collapses in the capitalist system. The only way out for dead-end capitalism is the explosive force of war. That is what makes the U.S.-led western aggression towards Yugoslavia, Iraq, Afghanistan, Libya, Syria, Russia over this fabricated Ukraine crisis so alarming; or the U.S. goading of China and its Asian neighbours over arcane territorial disputes that really should be none of Washington's business. The system has thus reached the historical point where war is once again being recklessly contemplated. But if a world war breaks out this time, there will likely be no world left to rebuild. That is the madness of capitalism and those who largely run it — the ruling elite all over the world.

The Crisis Is Systemic

Capitalism has a tendency to even ignore the boldest of writings on the wall. Marx had once said that capitalism 'has conjured up such gigantic means of production and of exchange, it is like the sorcerer who is no longer able to control the powers of the nether world whom he has called up by his spells'. It is not because of the greed or avarice of individuals. The only true liberation for humanity can come with the overthrow of this system. As world has witnessed that we have seen powerful *'Occupy Wall Street'* people's movements against poverty, inequality, unemployment and inflation not only in America, but entire world — Canada, Europe and Asia recently.

'Occupy Wall Street' call is popular, and almost 186 countries (all over the world) have witnessed the same protest march. American poor and jobless working people gathered around Wall Street and other 70 cities, and protested against big corporate sectors (as MNCs controlled more than 2 trillion dollars/US$200,000 million). Due to financial recession, the Bank of America announced 30,000 job cuts, and recently the American army has announced 212% job cuts. According to the latest 2011 population statistics, one American in each six is poor, and almost 46 million people live below the poverty line in America. Global capitalism is not able to solve problems like poverty, inequality, malnutrition, unemployment, illiteracy, economic-social-cultural backwardness and even environmental issues.

Mahathir Mohamed, former prime minister of Malaysia for 22 years from 1981 — years of reform in South Asia — invokes a Malaysian saying (similar wisdom can be found in almost all civilisations) which means that when you lose your way, go back to the beginning and start again.[2] Global capitalism is, however, obdurate in not learning from such wisdom. Instead, the neo-liberal prescriptions advocate the imposition of austerity. This, as

2. *Source*: International Conference on Trade, Investment, and Production Function in Asia organised by Nottingham University Malaysia, Kuala Lumpur in January 2012.

we have seen in these columns in the past, will only aggravate the situation and further accentuate the crisis.

Economic Justice and Environmental Sustainability

Most people are aware that we live in an unequal world. Few realise, however, just how extreme the inequality has become or how fast the gap between the poor and the super-rich is growing. Evidence is mounting that economic growth and free trade are not leading us towards social justice and environment sustainability. To the contrary, they are taking in the direction of increasing economic injustice and environmental unsustainability. The debates over jobs versus the environment miss a basic point. Assuring everyone the means to meet their basic needs and achieving a sustainable balance with the environment are mutually supportive goals. Indeed, there are powerful theoretical arguments why, in a resource-scarce world, neither is possible without the other. There is, however, an irreconcilable conflict between the goals of creating economically just and environmentally sustainable societies and embracing sustained economic growth, unregulated markets and free trade in the organising principle of public policy. The resulting policies are well suited to producing more millionaires and billionaires. They are ill suited to achieving justice and sustainability. That is real face of crony capitalism today which we can see everywhere.

Socialising Costs and Privatising Gains

The well-known American linguist Prof. Noam Chomsky says 'A basic principle of modern state capitalist is that costs and risks are socialized to the extent possible, while profit is privatized'.

Under crony capitalism — a deregulated global market economy global corporations are accountable to only one master, a rogue global financial system with one investment demand — keep your stock price as high as possible by maximising short-term returns. One way to do that is to shift as much of the cost of the corporation's operations as possible onto the community. The pressure involved makes it almost impossible to manage a corporation in the larger community interest. Indeed, any publicly traded corporation that attempts to manage its assets responsibly will almost certainly be bought out by a corporate raider.

Once upon a time local communities looked to corporations not only as source of jobs, but also as tax revenues to help cover the cost of essential local infrastructure and public services. Indeed, governments are now forced by the dynamics of global competition not only to give large corporations tax breaks, but also to directly subsidise their operations with public funds. For example, Indian government Rs. 12,000 billion tax rebate, and Rs. 60,000 billion's subsidies to the corporate sectors. In the past 20 years, corporate profits quadrupled, while the corporate tax rate has dropped by half and the payroll tax, paid by workers, has doubled. On the one hand government has increased gas and diesel prices, but on the other hand, there is increase in high corporate and stock profits. The world's 500 largest industrial companies control 25% of the world's economic output. The top 300 transnationals, excluding financial institutions, own some 25% of the world's productive assets. Of the world's 100 largest economies, 50 are now corporations — not including banking and financial institutions. The combined assets of the world's 50 largest commercial banks and diversified financial companies amount to nearly 60% of the *Economist*'s estimate of a US$20 trillion global stock of productive capital.

This book is divided into two parts: First, the current global economic depression, 'Theoretical Investigation', and second, 'Empirical Investigation' of the global economy includes the new emerging economies such as China, India and other BRICS nations.

2

The Great Recession and the Great Depression

The recession is a term used to describe the general economic decline observed in world markets. We need to first be clear on the difference between a recession and a depression. A recession is related to the word 'recede', meaning to fall back. An economic recession is a fall in total output of legally produced goods, falls during two consecutive quarters, that is, for six months. An economy is depressed when output falls below the long-run trend. Therefore, a depression begins during a recession, when GDP falls below the long-run trend, and ends in the recovery, when GDP rises above that trend. Generally, in the media, 'recession' is often used to refer to 'depression', but here I will be precise and use the definitions indicated. In the long-run, national income grows with an increasing population, so if the population grows by 1% and economy grows by half a percent, the economy is not regarded as a recession, but the average person has suffered a drop in income.

The global recession that followed resulted in a sharp drop in international trade, rising unemployment and slumping commodity prices. Several economists predicted that recovery might not appear until 2018. It has been as large as in the 'Great Depression' of the 1930s.

Recession and Business Cycle

A recession or a depression is caused by business cycle. There are two causes of business cycle: one is financial and the other is real. The financial cause is the expansion of money and credit by the banking systems. This monetary expansion lowers interest rates so that banks can loan out the extra money. Low interest rates induce a greater investment. The real side of the business cycle is the increase in construction and real estate speculation. At the peak of the economic boom, real estate prices are high and interest rates are rising. These higher costs choke off further construction and buying, so the rate of growth of the economy falls. The continuing slowdown stops the expansion, and as investment falls, the demand for goods also falls, and the whole economy then falls into a recession, and then into a depression. Economic investment drives the business cycles. While a financial investment can include stocks, bonds, real estate and mutual funds, an economic investment means an increase in the stock of capital goods, such as machines, buildings and inventory. (Education is also an economic investment, but 'human capital' does not affect business cycles.) The rate of increase in economic investment falls when entrepreneurs and investors expect lower profits. Pessimistic expectations are caused by either increased costs or an expected fall in overall demand. Since the fall in demand occurs after the recession starts, the expectations must be an increase in costs not matched by an increase in expected revenues.

The most important investment costs that change are interest rates and the cost of real estate. Interest rates are important for two reasons: First, much of investment is made with borrowed money. Second, even if the money is not borrowed, investors compare the expected rate of return relative to risk of the various financial alternatives, and choose the highest return. So, for example, if an investment in trees grows at 3% but bonds pay 5%, the investor will buy bonds. So, at a higher rate of interest, projects with lower returns are avoided.

All economic activity requires space and location. A big increase in the cost of using or buying real estate will reduce profit, and therefore, reduce investment. The high cost of renting an office, store or farmland, or the high cost of buying land, eats up much of the revenue and leaves less as profit. At the peak of the boom, both interest rates and real estate costs are rising, and so investment begins to slowdown. The amount of new economic investments keeps going down as costs keep rising, without any matching increase in expected revenues.

Economist Paul Krugman once commented on this as seemingly the beginning of 'a second Great Depression'. Paul Krugman wrote in 2009 that the run on the shadow banking system as the 'core of what happened' to cause the crisis. As the shadow banking system expanded to rival or even surpass conventional banking in importance, politicians and government officials should have realised that they were re-creating the kind of financial vulnerability that made the Great Depression possible — and they should have responded by extending regulations and the financial safety net to cover these new institutions.[1]

The financial crisis and the recession have been described as a symptom of another, deeper crisis by a number of economists. For example, Ravi Batra argues that growing inequality of financial capitalism produces speculative bubbles that burst and result in depression and major political changes. Feminist economists Alisa McKay and Margunn Biornholt argue that the financial crisis and the response to it revealed a crisis of ideas in mainstream economics and within the economics profession, and call for reshaping of the economy, economic theory and the economics profession.[2] There are two senses of the word 'recession': a less precise sense, referring broadly to 'a period of reduced economic activity', and the academic sense used most often in economics, which is defined operationally, referring specifically to the contraction phase of a

1. http//en.wikipedia.org/global_recession/cite_note%209.
2. *Ibid*.

business cycle, with two or more consecutive quarters of negative GDP growth. If one analyses the event using the economics-academic definition of the word, the recession ended in the United States in June or July 2009. However, in the broader, lay sense of the word, many people use the term to refer to the ongoing hardship (in the same way that the term 'Great Depression' is also popularly used).[3]

The crisis in Europe generally progressed from banking system crises to sovereign debt crises, as many countries elected to bailout their banking systems using taxpayer money. Greece was different in that it faced large public debts rather than problems within its banking system. Several countries received bailout packages from the 'troika' (European Commission, ECB, IMF), which also implemented a series of emergency measures. Many European countries embarked on austerity programs, reducing their budget deficits relative to GDP. For example, according to the *CIA World Factbook*, Greece improved its budget deficit from 10.4% GDP in 2010 to 9.6% in 2011. Iceland, Italy, Ireland, Portugal, France and Spain also improved their budget deficits from 2010 to 2011 relative to GDP. However, with the exception of Germany, each of these countries had public-debt-to-GDP ratios that increased (i.e., worsened) from 2010 to 2011. Greece's public-debt-to-GDP ratio increased from 143% in 2010 to 165% in 2011. This indicates that despite improving budget deficits, GDP growth was not sufficient to support a decline (improvement) in the debt-to-GDP ratio for these countries during this period. Eurostat reported that the debt-to-GDP ratio for the 17 euro area countries together was 70.1% in 2008, 79.9% in 2009, 85.3% in 2010 and 87.2% in 2011.

According to the *CIA World Factbook*, from 2010 to 2011, the unemployment rates in Spain, Greece, Italy, Ireland, Portugal and the United Kingdom increased. France had no significant changes, while in Germany and Iceland the unemployment rate declined.

3. *Ibid*.

Eurostat reported that eurozone unemployment reached record levels in September 2012 at 11.6% up from 10.3% the prior year. Unemployment varied significantly by countries.

Economist Martin Wolf analysed the relationship between cumulative GDP growth from 2008 to 2012 and total reduction in budget deficits due to austerity policies in several European countries during April 2012. He concluded that: 'In all, there is no evidence here that large fiscal contractions [budget deficit reductions] bring benefits to confidence and growth that offset the direct effects of the contractions. They bring exactly what one would expect: small contractions bring recessions and big contractions bring depressions.' Changes in budget balances (deficits or surpluses) explained approximately 53% of the change in GDP, according to the equation derived from the IMF data used in his analysis.

Economist Paul Krugman analysed the relationship between GDP and reduction in budget deficits for several European countries in April 2012 and concluded that austerity was slowing growth, similar to Martin Wolf. He also wrote: '... this also implies that 1 euro of austerity yields only about 0.4 euros of reduced deficit, even in the short run. No wonder, then, that the whole austerity enterprise is spiraling into disaster.'

However, the financial crisis did not affect developing countries to a great extent. Experts see several reasons: Africa was not affected because it is not integrated in the world market. Latin America and Asia seemed better prepared, since they experienced crisis before. In Latin America for example banking laws and regulations are very stringent.

What Does the Great Recession Mean?

There is no commonly accepted definition of the Great Recession. Most of us have an intuitive idea of what a recession entails — job losses, plant closures and tough times for families. But what exactly is a recession? There are a few similar, but not identical definitions. In economics, a recession is a business cycle contraction, a general slowdown in economic activity. During recessions, many macroeconomic indicators vary in a similar way. Production, as measured by GDP, employment, investment spending, capacity utilisation, household incomes, business profits and inflation all fall during recessions; while bankruptcies and the unemployment rate rise. Recessions generally occur when there is a widespread drop in spending often followed by an adverse supply shock or the bursting of an economic bubble. Governments usually respond to recessions by adopting expansionary macroeconomic policies, such as increasing money supply, increasing government spending and decreasing taxation.

As Nagle (2009) explains how the recession is perceived by the average citizen identifies recession as a period whereby jobs are limited and bills are hard to pay. Though the definition may not be limited to this particular way of thinking, Nagle identifies this to be the main train of thought. However, through basic definitions and illustrating causes of inflation, the readers' mind is able to fully evaluate what a recession means. Through the literary works of Nagle (2009), this research is fully able to relate correctly on the average citizens concepts on recession. Furthermore, through illustrations of real-world recessions and offering ways to deal with recessions, Nagle's work helps to further research through insights as to how future recessions may be predicted by the average citizen. King and Cushman's (1997) suggest that recessions are no longer caused by market forces but rather depend on the country in question being competitive globally. King and Cushman's work contributes to our research in that it helps further our understanding on other possible causes of inflation as well as providing adequate illustrations of situations in which companies are able to handle economic recessions.

Rhodes and Stelter (2010) indicate that one of the main reasons for the recurring recessions in the economic history of the United States is the current monetary policy in place at the time of the recession. Their contribution to this research is through this fact as well as providing means for companies to avoid being caught up in the inflation. Hetzel's (2010) article identifies one of the major causes for the economic recessions both in the past and in the present as changes in monetary policy that is placed into effect as the recession wears off. Through 'what–if' arguments and deductions based on past recessions, Hetzel seeks to help the public understand the relation between cyclic inflation and monetary policy.

The IMF defines a global recession as 'a decline in annual per-capita real world GDP (purchasing power parity weighted), backed up by a decline or worsening for one or more of the seven other global macroeconomic indicators: Industrial production, trade, capital flows, oil consumption, unemployment rate, per-capita investment, and per-capita consumption'. According to this definition, since the Second World War there were only four global recessions (in 1975, 1982, 1991 and 2009), all of them only lasting a year (although the 1991 recession would have lasted until 1993 if the IMF had used normal exchange rate weighted per-capita real-world GDP rather than the purchasing power parity weighted per-capita real-world GDP). The 2009 global recession, also known as the Great Recession, was by far the worst of the four post-war recessions, both in terms of the number of countries affected and the decline in per-capita real-world GDP. Before April 2009, the IMF argued that a global annual real GDP growth rate of 3% or less was 'equivalent to a global recession'. By this measure, there were six global recessions since 1970: 1974–1975, 1980–1983, 1990–1993, 1998, 2001–2002 and 2008–2009.

Informally, a national recession is a period of declining economic output. In a 1974 *New York Times* article, Julius Shiskin suggested several rules of thumb to identify a recession, which included two successive quarterly declines in GDP, a measure of the nation's output. This two-quarter metric is now a commonly held definition of a recession. In the United States, the National Bureau of Economic Research (NBER) is regarded as the authority which identifies a recession and which takes into account several measures in addition to GDP growth before making an assessment.

In many developed nations (but not the United States), the two-quarter rule is also used for identifying a recession.[4]

Whereas a national recession is identified by two quarters of decline, defining a global recession is more difficult, because developing nations are expected to have a higher GDP growth than developed nations. According to the IMF, the real GDP growth of the emerging and developing countries is on an uptrend and that of advanced economies is on a downtrend since late 1980s. The world growth was projected to slow from 5% in 2007 to 3.75% in 2008 and to just over 2% in 2009. Downward revisions in GDP growth vary across regions. Among the most affected are commodity exporters and countries with acute external financing and liquidity problems. Countries in East Asia (including China) have suffered smaller declines because their financial situations are more robust. They have benefited from falling commodity prices, and they have initiated a shift towards macroeconomic policy easing.

In intermediate macroeconomics textbook, Gregory Mankiw (Mankiw, 2003) distinguishes between the two: There are repeated periods during which real GDP falls, the most dramatic instance being the early 1930s. Such periods are called recessions if they are mild and depressions if they are more severe.

As Mankiw pointed out, perhaps the most famous economic downturn in the U.S.'s (as well as the world's) economic history was the Great Depression, often described as starting in 1929 and lasting at least through the 1930s and into the early 1940s, a period that actually includes two severe economic downturns. Using the NBER business cycle dates, the first downturn of the Great Depression started in August 1929 and lasted 43 months, until March 1933, far longer than any other twentieth-century contraction. The economy then expanded for 21 months, from March 1933 until May 1937, before suffering another downturn: from May 1937 until June 1938, a period of 13 months, the economy again contracted.

4. *Source*: http//en.wikipedia.org/global_recession/cite_note%209.

The IMF Prediction

The IMF estimates that global recessions seem to occur over a cycle lasting between eight and ten years. During what the IMF terms the past three global recessions of the last three decades, global per-capita output growth was zero or negative. Economists at the IMF state that a global recession would take a slowdown in global growth to 3% or less. By this measure, four periods since 1985 qualify: 1990–1993, 1998, 2001–2002 and 2008–2009. In other words, generally, the IMF considers a global recession as a period where GDP growth is at 3% or less.

In addition to that, the IMF looks at declines in real per-capita world GDP along with several global macroeconomic factors before confirming a global recession. However, Global Recession is defined slightly differently than national recession. A nation would be considered in a recession when GDP declines for two consecutive periods. A global recession has to take into account developing nations as well as developed nations, therefore requiring a benchmark for growth comparison which is set at around 3%.

In early 2009, the IMF and the World Bank predicted the global GDP growth rate to decrease to approximately 0.5%, meaning they expect a global recession to persist through 2009. In other words, economic depression is the result of reduction in the demand of products in the global market. Recession can also be associated with falling prices known as deflation due to lack of demand of products. Again, it could be the result of inflation or a combination of increasing prices and stagnant economic growth in the West. In a 1975 *New York Times* article, economic statistician Julius Shiskin suggested several rules of thumb for defining a recession, one of which was 'two down quarters of GDP'. In time, the other rules of thumb were forgotten.

Some economists prefer a definition of a 1.5% rise in unemployment within 12 months. In the United States, the Business Cycle Dating Committee of the NBER is generally seen as the authority for dating U.S. recessions. The NBER defines an economic recession as: 'a significant decline in the economic activity spread across the country, lasting more than a few months, normally visible in real GDP growth, real personal income, employment (non-farm payrolls), industrial production, and wholesale-retail sales'.

Almost universally, academics, economists, policymakers and businesses defer to the determination by the NBER for the precise dating of a recession's onset and end. A recession has many attributes that can occur simultaneously and includes declines in component measures of economic activity GDP such as consumption, investment, government spending and net export activity. These summary measures reflect underlying drivers such as employment levels and skills, household savings rates, corporate investment decisions, interest rates, demographics and government policies. Economist Richard C. Koo wrote that under ideal conditions, a country's economy should have the household sector as net savers and the corporate sector as net borrowers, with the government budget nearly balanced and net exports near zero.

When these relationships become imbalanced, recession can develop within the country or create pressure for recession in another country. Policy responses are often designed to drive the economy back towards this ideal state of balance. A severe (GDP down by 10%) or prolonged (three or four years) recession is referred to as an economic depression, although some argue that their causes and cures can be different. The economists sometimes refer to different recession shapes, such as V-shaped, U-shaped, L-shaped and W-shaped recessions.

Type of Recession or Shape

Recessions and subsequent growth periods may have distinctive shapes when graphed. In the United States, V-shaped, or short-and-sharp contractions, followed by rapid and sustained recovery, occurred in 1954 and 1990–1991; U-shaped (prolonged slump) in 1974–1975; and W-shaped, or double-dip recessions, in 1949 and 1980–1982. Japan's 1993–1994 recession was U-shaped, and its 8-out-of-9 quarters of contraction in 1997–1999 can be described as L-shaped. Korea, Hong Kong and South-east Asia experienced U-shaped recessions in 1997–1998, although Thailand's eight consecutive quarters of decline should be termed L-shaped.

Psychological Aspects

Recessions have psychological and confidence aspects. For example, if the expectation develops that economic activity will slow; firms may decide to reduce employment levels and save money rather than invest. Such expectations can create a self-reinforcing downward cycle, bringing about or worsening a recession. Consumer confidence is one measure used to evaluate economic sentiment. The term 'Animal Spirits' has been used to describe the psychological factors underlying economic activity. Economist Robert J. Shiller wrote that the term '... refers also to the sense of trust we have in each other, our sense of fairness in economic dealings, and our sense of the extent of corruption and bad faith. When animal spirits are on ebb, consumers do not want to spend and businesses do not want to make capital expenditures or hire people.'

Balance Sheet Recession

The bursting of a real estate or financial asset price bubble can cause a recession. For example, economist Richard Koo wrote that Japan's 'Great Recession' that began in 1990 was a 'balance sheet recession'. It was triggered by a collapse in land and stock prices, which caused Japanese firms to become insolvent, meaning their assets were worth less than their liabilities. Despite zero interest rates and expansion of the money supply to encourage borrowing, Japanese corporations in aggregate opted to pay down their debts from their own business earnings rather than borrow to invest as firms typically do. Corporate investment, a key demand component of GDP, fell enormously (22% of GDP) between 1990 and its peak decline in 2003.

Japanese firms overall became net savers after 1998, as opposed to borrowers. Koo argues that it was massive fiscal stimulus (borrowing and spending by the government) that offset this decline and enabled Japan to maintain its level of GDP. In his view, this avoided a U.S.-type Great Depression in which U.S. GDP fell by 46%. He argued that monetary policy was ineffective because there was limited demand for funds while firms paid down their liabilities. In a balance sheet recession, GDP declines by the amount of debt repayment and unborrowed individual savings, leaving government stimulus spending as the primary remedy.

Liquidity Trap

A liquidity trap situation can develop in which interest rates reach near zero yet do not effectively stimulate the economy. In theory, near-zero interest rates should encourage firms and consumers to borrow and spend. However, if too many individuals or corporations focus on saving or paying down debt rather than spending, lower interest rates have less effect on investment and consumption behaviour; the lower interest rates are like 'pushing on a string'. Economist Paul Krugman described the United States in 2007–2010 and Japan's lost decade as liquidity traps. One remedy to a liquidity trap is to expand the money supply via QE or other techniques in which money is effectively printed to purchase assets, thereby creating inflationary expectations that cause savers to begin spending again. Government stimulus spending and mercantilist policies to stimulate exports and reduce imports are other techniques to stimulate demand. He estimated in March 2010 that developed countries representing 70% of the world's GDP were caught in a liquidity trap.

Predictors

Although there are no completely reliable predictors, the following are regarded to be possible predictors.

I. Inverted Yield Curve, the model developed by economist Jonathan H. Wright, uses yields on 10-year and three-month Treasury securities as well as the Fed's overnight funds rate. Another model developed by Federal Reserve Bank of New York economists uses only the 10-year/three-month spread. It is, however, not a definite indicator.

II. The three-month change in the unemployment rate and initial jobless claims.

III. Index of Leading (Economic) Indicators (includes some of the above indicators).

IV. Lowering of asset prices, such as homes and financial assets, or high personal and corporate debt levels.

Government Responses

Most economists believe that recessions are caused by inadequate aggregate demand in the economy, and favour the use of expansionary macroeconomic policy during recessions. Strategies favoured for moving an economy out of a recession vary depending on which economic school the policymakers follow. Monetarists would favour the use of expansionary monetary policy, while Keynesian economists may advocate increased government spending to spark economic growth. Supply-side economists may suggest tax cuts to promote business capital investment. When interest rates reach the boundary of an interest rate of zero per cent, conventional monetary policy can no longer be used and government must use other measures to stimulate recovery. Keynesians argue that fiscal policy, tax cuts or increased government spending will work when monetary policy fails. Spending is more effective because of its larger multiplier but tax cuts take effect faster.

Stock Markets

Some recessions have been anticipated by stock market declines. In stocks for the long-run, Siegel mentions that since 1948, 10 recessions were preceded by a stock market decline, by a lead time of 0–13 months (average 5.7 months), while 10 stock market declines of greater than 10% in the DJIA were not followed by a recession. The real estate market also usually weakens before a recession. However, real estate declines can last much longer than recessions. Since the business cycle is very hard to predict, Siegel argues that it is not possible to take advantage of economic cycles for timing investments. Even the NBER takes a few months to determine if a peak or trough has occurred in the United States.

During an economic decline, high-yield stocks such as fast-moving consumer goods, pharmaceuticals and tobacco tend to hold up better. However, when the economy starts to recover and the bottom of the market has passed (sometimes identified on charts as a Moving Average Convergence Divergence [MACD]), growth stocks tend to recover faster. There is significant disagreement about how health care and utilities tend to recover. Diversifying one's portfolio into international stocks may provide some safety; however, economies that are closely correlated with that of the United States may also be affected by a recession in the United States. There is a view termed the *halfway rule* according to which investors start discounting an economic recovery about halfway through a recession. In the 16 U.S. recessions since 1919, the average length has been 13 months, although the recent recessions have been shorter. Thus if the 2008 recession followed the average, the downturn in the stock market would have bottomed around November 2008. The actual U.S. stock market bottom of the 2008 recession was in March 2009.

Reagan–Volcker–Carter Recession

Generally an administration gets credit or blame for the state of the economy during its time. This has caused disagreements about when a recession actually started. In an economic cycle, a downturn can be considered a consequence of an expansion reaching an unsustainable state, and is corrected by a brief decline. Thus it is not easy to isolate the causes of specific phases of the cycle. The 1981 recession is thought to have been caused by the tight-money policy adopted by Paul Volcker, chairman of the Federal Reserve Board, before Ronald Reagan took office. Reagan supported that policy. Economist Walter Heller, chairman of the Council of Economic Advisers in the 1960s, said that 'I call it a Reagan-Volcker-Carter recession'. The resulting taming of inflation did, however, set the stage for a robust growth period during Reagan's administration.

Economists usually teach that to some degree recession is unavoidable, and its causes are not well understood. Consequently, modern government administrations attempt to take steps, also not agreed upon, to soften a recession.[5]

Although the views of the authors towards the causes of Great Recession of 2008–2011 vary depending on their findings and other factors, it is agreed by many economists that the main factor that led to financial crisis in 2008 was liberalisation of financial markets and lack of control and regulations over the financial institutions and their activities towards risk taking. Stiglitz (2008) states that one of the main causes of financial recession was failure of policymakers in tightening the regulations and dishonesty of financial institutions.

According to Tropeano (2010) the roots of the financial crisis and main causes that led to recession were low interest rates that encouraged excessive borrowing by the investors worldwide. Investors were highly involved in excessive borrowing in low interest rates and investing in lucrative businesses.

Due to high demand for funds by the investors, banks could no longer provide loans to their clients until a new financial innovation, sub-prime mortgages were introduced. American banks started to sell mortgage packages to the investors worldwide in order to generate as much funds as possible. However, banks were not directly responsible for default cases by the mortgage holders and did not have incentive for proper checking of the credibility of the mortgage holders. The author states that the default cases on mortgage payments were the points where the financial crisis flamed.

Massive pressure and encouragement and greediness to earn more money accounting firms and credit rating agencies did not

5. Mishkin (2009).

check the credibility of the borrowers properly. As the authors concern, it is obvious that lending excessively without checking the credibility of the borrowers was the clear fact that resulted in higher rates of default cases. McKay (2011) states in his work where he compared the views of Stiglitz and Harvey that one of the obvious factors that led to global financial crisis was failure of Federal Reserve towards regulating the risk-taking activities of financial institutions.

A negative belief that some of the financial institutions can never fail due to their massive significance to the worldwide economy was another reason in formulation of the recent financial crisis. The government support for saving these 'too big to fail' financial institutions has been taken negatively by those institutions and led to formulation of view that they can take as much risk as possible, if they are successful then they end up making billions but if they fail, they believe that the government bails them out (Crotty, 2009). We shall discuss in detail on collapse of neoliberalism in Chapter 3.

What Does the Great Depression Mean?

First, Robert Lucas says about the Depression:

> If you look back at the '29 to 33' episode; there were a lot of decision made that, after the fact, people wished that they had not made. There were a lot of jobs people quit that they wished they had hung onto; there were job offers that people turned down because they thought the wage offer was crappy. Then three months later they wished they had grabbed [them]. Accounts who lost their accounting jobs passed over a cab driver job, and now they're sitting on the street while their pal's driving a cab. So they wish they'd taken the cab driver job. People are making this kind of mistake all the time. Anybody can look back over the '30's and think of decisions he could have taken to make a million. Stocks

> I would have bought. All kinds of things. I don't see what's hard about this question of people making mistakes in the business cycle.[6]

Robert Barro also sees monetary and other government policies as key factors in the 1929–1933 experience: 'The unprecedented monetary collapse over this period accords quantitatively with the drastic decline in economic activity.'[7] In addition to the effects that the rapid decline in the money supply may have had, Barro points to a real (or supply-side) effect from the collapse of much of the banking system during this period. (Nine thousand banks failed between 1929 and 1933.) As banks failed, for example, crops might not be produced because farmers could not get loans to buy farm machinery. In general, a decline in the availability of financial services may have reduced overall output supply in the 1929–1933 period.[8]

As a further alternative to Keynesian explanations of the Depression, Barro suggests that 'the government interventions associated with the New Deal, including the volume of public expenditures and direct price regulations, retarded the recovery of the economy, which was nevertheless rapid after 1933'.[9] But both Barro and Lucas still find parts of the Depression phenomenon puzzling and would, at least in some respects, agree with new classical economist Thomas Sargent that:

> I do not have a theory, nor do I know somebody else's theory that constitutes satisfactory explanations of the Great Depression. It's really a very important, unexplained event and process, which I would be very interested in and would like to see explained.[10]

6. Klamer (1983, p. 41).
7. Barro (1979, p. 58).
8. Barro (1984, p. 180).
9. Barro (1979, p. 57).
10. Klamer (1983, p. 69).

3

Collapse of Neo-Liberalism: The Debate

> Market economic system failed to provide full employment and equally distribution of wealth and income, and control inflation. Our analysis shows ... that long-run development is not inherent in the capitalist economy. Thus, 'specific development factors' are required to sustain a long-run upward movement. What is the fact that mature capitalist economies tend towards stagnation.
>
> — Keynes (1934)

Everybody agreed that capitalism is undergoing a serious crisis, but different people read this crisis differently. The progressive economists like Paul Krugman and Joseph Stiglitz view that the crisis is entirely a consequence of the collapse of the housing 'bubble'; since in this situation of crisis, private expenditure, whether on consumption or on investment, is unlikely to increase in the foreseeable future; a revival is possible only through an increase in state expenditure, which means that both in the United States and in Europe, far from adopting austerity measures, the state should instead be increasing its expenditure. The fact that this panacea for crisis is not being adopted is then explained by the 'bad economics' of the opinion makers, the 'bad faith' of the Republicans, the callousness of the Right and so on. This view, in short, sees the crisis exclusively as an isolated, one-off phenomenon, a predicament to which the U.S. economy and hence the world economy happens to have fallen because of the collapse of a 'bubble'-based boom, which the earlier irresponsible monetary policy of the Federal Reserve Board under the chairmanship of Alan Greenspan had connived to stimulate.

Structural Crisis

The problem with this view is that it is extremely limited; it does not see the whole truth. The crisis caused by the collapse of the housing 'bubble' is only a part of the story; it is itself located within a fundamental structural crisis of capitalism. Indeed the 'dotcom' and housing 'bubbles' had kept this structural crisis *hidden*; with their collapse we not only have the crisis caused by this collapse itself, but its superimposition upon the basic structural crisis which now gets revealed as well. Since this structural crisis is embedded in the logic of the capitalist system, what we have is a systemic crisis, not a sporadic or a cyclical one, from which there is no easy way out. In short, we have entered a period of protracted crisis of capitalism, reminiscent of the 1930s, which will open up not immediately but through a whole chain of political developments that it will unleash as in the 1930s and the 1940s, real revolutionary possibilities of transcending the system.

Let us begin by asking the question: why is there so much opposition to state expenditure as a means of overcoming the crisis both in the United States and Europe? Why is there a persistent demand for 'austerity' which is bound to aggravate the crisis? To say that it is only 'bad economics' is not enough. The 'economics' that acquires hegemony at any time is the one that the hegemonic class endorses (a proposition that is particularly true of economics because it has such a direct bearing on state policy). The 'bad economics' is one of the mechanisms through which the corporate-financial interests that dominate contemporary capitalism exert their pressure. 'Austerity' is being imposed because finance capital is opposed to large-scale state expenditure to stimulate the economy. It is not opposed to state activism as such, but it wants that activism to take the form of providing incentives to itself, of promoting its own interests, as the means of reviving the economy. It does not want direct state action for this purpose through larger public expenditure.

Any state action that operates independently of finance capital, that seeks to work directly instead of working through the promotion of corporate-financial interests, undermines the social legitimacy of capitalism, and especially of the corporate-financial interests. For it raises the question: if the state is required to fix the system, then why do we need the system at all, why not have state ownership itself? Finance capital in the United States therefore has no objections to $13 trillion of state support for stabilising the financial system; but the moment the question of state expenditure for reviving the economy is raised, it begins to preach the virtues of 'austerity'. *The era of hegemony of finance therefore is an era where 'state intervention in demand management'* a la *Keynes recedes to the background.*

Now, capitalism always requires some exogenous stimuli for sustaining its growth. It can sustain growth purely on its own steam, that is, purely because growth had been occurring, for some time, but if growth peters out for any reason, including the emergence of bottlenecks because of growth itself, then an opposite spiral of lower and lower investment and declining growth sets in which carries it towards a stationary state, that is, towards a state of simple reproduction. Extricating the system out of simple reproduction and ensuring that growth does not lose steam and collapse back into a state of simple reproduction is something that is ensured by the operation of a set of exogenous stimuli.

External Stimuli

Historically, two sets of exogenous stimuli have played this role. The first is the entire colonial system that played this role right until the First World War. The term 'colonial system' is used here not just to refer to colonial and semi-colonial possessions like India and China, but also to the so-called settler colonies from where the 'native population' was driven away to accommodate immigrants from the capitalist core. The 'colonial system' propped up growth under capitalism in the following manner: along with migration of population to the 'settler colonies' or the temperate regions of white settlement, there was also a parallel migration of capital to these regions from the capitalist core, but this 'export of capital' from the core was made possible through an appropriation of surplus from the colonial and semi-colonial possessions.

So the 'drain' of surplus without any *quid pro quo* from India and other colonies financed the capital exports from the capitalist core to the settler colonies. But underlying these movements in 'value' magnitudes there were also important changes relating to commodity composition: Britain, the leading capitalist country and also the leading capital-exporting country, did not produce goods which were in high demand in the settler colonies like the United States. The demand there was substantially for raw materials, that is, minerals and primary commodities, which were produced in the colonial possessions. Hence Britain's capital exports were made possible first by British goods like textiles being sold in the Indian and other eastern markets, and goods from the latter countries being exported to a matching, or, where 'drain' occurred, to an even greater, extent from these countries. British goods could be sold in the colonial and semi-colonial countries because they were markets on 'tap': their markets could be used for unloading British goods, to the extent required, any time.

This entire pattern of global movement of capital and commodities, which was very convenient from the point of view of the capitalist core, underlays the prolonged boom that capitalism witnessed from the mid-nineteenth century until the First World War. After the First World War, this pattern collapsed. Domestic bourgeoisies in colonies wanted their own space; Japan emerged as a rival to Britain in Asian markets; the scope for investment in the 'new world' got exhausted with the 'closing of the frontier'; and the scope for further de-industrialisation in economies like India also began to get more and more limited. The Great Depression of the 1930s was an expression of the fact that the old mechanism for stimulating buoyancy in capitalism could no longer function.

The Depression ended only when the second major exogeneous stimulus for capitalism, namely state expenditure, came into effect, initially for war preparations, and after the war, under the impact of working-class pressure and the threat of socialism, for introducing some 'welfare state' measures. But 'state intervention in demand management' has also now run its course: the emergence of international finance capital as the hegemonic force under capitalism has, for reasons mentioned earlier, attenuated the scope for it. *Capitalism, in short, now lacks any mechanism for imparting sustained growth to it.*

Falling Real Wages

This, moreover, is happening in a context when the need for such a mechanism is becoming ever more acute. Let us see why. With globalisation there has been much freer flow of capital, including in the form of finance, and also of goods and services, across countries than ever before in the history of capitalism. As a result, capital from the metropolis (and domestic big capital as well) can locate production in the third world countries, where wages are low because of the existence of massive labour reserves, and export to the metropolitan markets. This in turn makes the wages of workers in the metropolitan countries vulnerable to the downward drag exerted by the labour reserves existing in the third world countries. In the United States, for instance, in the last three decades the real wage rate of workers has fallen in absolute terms by nearly 30%.

In third world countries, in turn, it is not as if the real wage rate increases; on the contrary, the immiserisation and displacement of petty producers, including peasants, that is another hallmark of globalisation, entails a swelling of the reserve army of labour which also exerts a downward drag on the real wage rate of workers that constitute the active army of labour for capitalism. Taking the world economy as a whole, therefore, there is a tendency for the real wage rate of the workers to decline, or at the very least, not to increase. At the same time, however, there is a steady rise in labour productivity, which means that the share of surplus value in total output increases.

Now, since a rupee of output coming to the workers gives rise to a much larger amount of consumption than a rupee coming to the capitalists, any rise in the share of surplus value in output has, other things remaining the same, a demand-depressing effect. If capitalists' investment increased when the extra rupee came to them, then this demand-depressing effect could be overcome, and the entire produced output could be realised. But, we have already seen that the tendency for capitalists' investment, far from rising, is to remain subdued or depressed in the absence of any mechanism for sustained growth. The net result therefore is a pronounced tendency towards overproduction crises. The capitalist state that could have provided an antidote to this tendency towards overproduction by stepping up its expenditure, and thereby absorbing a larger share of surplus value and helping its realisation, cannot do so because of the opposition of finance capital to larger state expenditure.

It follows therefore that the incapacitation of the capitalist state as a provider of demand at will not only leaves world capitalism without the requisite exogenous stimulus for the maintenance of sustained growth, but also pushes it further into stagnation for an additional reason, namely the tendency for the share of surplus value to rise in world output. World capitalism is thus caught in a deep structural crisis from which there are no obvious escape routes. This is not to say that capitalism will collapse, for that never happens. But, as in the 1930s, a new conjuncture is emerging that is pregnant with historic possibilities for the transcendence of the system.

The Immediate Causes of the Economic Recession

The collapse of a global housing bubble, which peaked in the United States in 2006, caused the values of securities tied to real estate pricing to plummet, thereafter damaging financial institutions globally. Questions regarding bank solvency, declines in credit availability and damaged investor confidence had an impact on global stock markets, where securities suffered large losses during late 2008 and early 2009. Economies worldwide slowed during this period as credit tightened and international trade declined. Critics argued that credit rating agencies and investors failed to accurately price the risk involved with mortgage-related financial products, and that governments did not adjust their regulatory practices to address twenty-first-century financial markets. Governments and central banks responded with unprecedented fiscal stimulus, monetary policy expansion and institutional bailouts.

The immediate cause or trigger of the crisis was the bursting of the United States housing bubble which peaked in approximately 2005–2006. High default rates on 'sub-prime' and adjustable rate mortgages (ARMs) began to increase quickly thereafter. An increase in loan packaging, marketing and incentives such as easy initial terms and a long-term trend of rising housing prices had encouraged borrowers to assume difficult mortgages in the belief they would be able to quickly refinance at more favourable terms. However, once interest rates began to rise and housing prices started to drop moderately in 2006–2007 in many parts of the United States, refinancing became more difficult. Defaults and foreclosure activity increased dramatically as easy initial terms expired, home prices failed to go up as anticipated and ARM interest rates reset higher.

Low Interest Rates and Large Inflows of Foreign Funds

Low interest rates and large inflows of foreign funds created easy credit conditions for a number of years prior to the crisis, fuelling a housing construction boom and encouraging debt-financed consumption. The combination of easy credit and money inflow contributed to the U.S. housing bubble. Loans of various types (e.g., mortgage, credit card and auto) were easy to obtain and consumers assumed an unprecedented debt load. As part of the housing and credit booms, the amount of financial agreements called mortgage-backed securities (MBS) and collateralised debt obligations (CDO), which derived their value from mortgage payments and housing prices, greatly increased. Such financial innovation enabled institutions and investors around the world to invest in the U.S. housing market. As housing prices declined, major global financial institutions that had borrowed and invested heavily in sub-prime MBS reported significant losses. Falling prices also resulted in homes worth less than the mortgage loan, providing a financial incentive to enter foreclosure. The ongoing foreclosure epidemic that began in late 2006 in the United States continues to drain wealth from consumers and erodes the financial strength of banking institutions. Defaults and losses on other loan types also increased significantly as the crisis expanded from the housing market to other parts of the economy. Total losses are estimated in the trillions of U.S. dollars globally.

While the housing and credit bubbles built, a series of factors caused the financial system to both expand and become increasingly fragile, a process called financialisation. Policymakers did not recognise the increasingly important role played by financial institutions such as investment banks and hedge funds, also known as the shadow banking system. Some experts believe these institutions had become as important as commercial (depository) banks in providing credit to the U.S. economy, but they were not subject to the same regulations. These institutions as well as certain regulated banks had also assumed significant debt burdens while providing the loans described above and did not have a financial cushion sufficient to absorb large loan defaults or MBS losses. The parties that created the MBS and CDO were compensated with bonus pools that had no link to the quality of the instruments created, these risks were rated by rating agencies and no risk was assumed by the creators of the assets that were being bundled.

The compensation based on the creation of more profitable and commissionable MBS and CDOs was a key driving force in accelerating the issuance of these products. These losses impacted the ability of financial institutions to lend, slowing economic activity. Concerns regarding the stability of key financial institutions drove central banks to provide funds to encourage lending and restore faith in the commercial paper markets, which are integral to funding business operations. Governments also bailed out key financial institutions and implemented economic stimulus programs, assuming significant additional financial commitments.

Between 1997 and 2006, the price of the typical American house increased by 124%. During the two decades ending in 2001, the national median home price ranged from 2.9 to 3.1 times median household income. This ratio rose to 4.0 in 2004 and 4.6 in 2006. This housing bubble resulted in quite a few homeowners refinancing their homes at lower interest rates, or financing consumer spending by taking out second mortgages secured by the price appreciation.

In a Peabody Award winning programme, National Population Register (NPR) correspondents argued that a 'Giant Pool of Money' (represented by US$70 trillion in worldwide fixed income investments) sought higher yields than those offered by U.S. Treasury bonds early in the decade. Further, this pool of money had roughly doubled in size from 2000 to 2007, yet the supply of relatively safe, income-generating investments had not grown as fast. Investment banks on Wall Street answered this demand with the MBS and CDO, which were assigned safe ratings by the credit rating agencies. In effect, Wall Street connected this pool of money to the mortgage market in the United States, with enormous fees accruing to those throughout the mortgage supply chain, from the mortgage broker selling the loans, to small banks that funded the brokers, to the giant investment banks behind them. By approximately 2003, the supply of mortgages originated at traditional lending standards had been exhausted. However, continued strong demand for MBS and CDO began to drive down lending standards, as long as mortgages could still be sold along the supply chain. Eventually, this speculative bubble proved unsustainable.

The CDO in particular enabled financial institutions to obtain investor funds to finance sub-prime and other lending, extending or increasing the housing bubble and generating large fees. A CDO essentially places cash payments from multiple mortgages or other debt obligations into a single pool, from which the cash is allocated to specific securities in a priority sequence. Those securities obtaining cash first received investment-grade ratings from rating agencies. Lower priority securities received cash thereafter, with lower credit ratings but theoretically a higher rate of return on the amount invested. By September 2008, average U.S. housing prices had declined by over 20% from their mid-2006 peak. As prices declined, borrowers with ARMs could not refinance to avoid the higher payments associated with rising interest rates and began to default. During 2007, lenders began foreclosure proceedings on nearly 1.3 million properties, a 79% increase over 2006. This increased to 2.3 million in 2008, an 81% increase versus 2007. By August 2008, 9.2% of all U.S. mortgages outstanding were either delinquent or in foreclosure. By September 2009, this had risen to 14.4%.

Lower interest rates encourage borrowing. From 2000 to 2003, the Federal Reserve lowered the federal funds rate target from 6.5% to 1.0%. This was done to soften the effects of the collapse of the dotcom bubble and of the September 2001 terrorist attacks, and to combat the perceived risk of deflation. Additional downward pressure on interest rates was created by the U.S.'s high and rising current account (trade) deficit, which peaked along with the housing bubble in 2006. Ben Bernanke explained how trade deficits required the United States to borrow money from abroad, which bid up bond prices and lowered interest rates.[1]

Bernanke explained that between 1996 and 2004, the U.S. current account deficit increased by US$650 billion, from 1.5% to 5.8% of GDP. Financing these deficits required the United States to borrow large sums from abroad, much of it from countries running trade surpluses, mainly the emerging economies in Asia and oil-exporting nations. The balance of payments identity requires that a country (such as the United States) running a current

1. http://en.wikipedia.org/wiki/Financial_crisis_of_2007

account deficit also has a capital account (investment) surplus of the same amount. Hence large and growing amounts of foreign funds (capital) flowed into the United States to finance its imports. This created demand for various types of financial assets, raising the prices of those assets while lowering interest rates. Foreign investors had these funds to lend, either because they had very high personal savings rates (as high as 40% in China), or because of high oil prices. Bernanke referred to this as a 'saving glut'. A 'flood' of funds (capital or liquidity) reached the U.S. financial markets. Foreign governments supplied funds by purchasing U.S. Treasury bonds and thus avoided much of the direct impact of the crisis. The U.S. households, on the other hand, used funds borrowed from foreigners to finance consumption or to bid up the prices of housing and financial assets. Financial institutions invested foreign funds in MBS.

The Fed then raised the Fed funds rate significantly between July 2004 and July 2006. This contributed to an increase in 1-year and 5-year ARM rates, making ARM interest rate resets more expensive for homeowners. This may have also contributed to the deflating of the housing bubble, as asset prices generally move inversely to interest rates and it became riskier to speculate in housing. The U.S. housing and financial assets dramatically declined in value after the housing bubble burst.

Sub-prime Lending

The term 'sub-prime' refers to the credit quality of particular borrowers, who have weakened credit histories and a greater risk of loan default than prime borrowers. The value of U.S. sub-prime mortgages was estimated at $1.3 trillion as of March 2007, with over 7.5 million first-line sub-prime mortgages outstanding. In addition to easy credit conditions, there is evidence that both government and competitive pressures contributed to an increase in the amount of sub-prime lending during the years preceding the crisis. Major U.S. investment banks and government sponsored enterprises like Fannie Mae played an important role in the expansion of higher-risk lending. Sub-prime mortgages remained below 10% of all mortgage originations until 2004, when they spiked to nearly 20% and remained there through the 2005–2006 peak of the U.S. housing bubble. A proximate event to this increase was the April 2004 decision by the U.S. Securities and Exchange Commission (SEC) to relax the net capital rule, which permitted the largest five investment banks to dramatically increase their financial leverage and aggressively expand their issuance of MBS. This applied additional competitive pressure to Fannie Mae and Freddie Mac, which further expanded their riskier lending. Sub-prime mortgage payment delinquency rates remained in the 10–15% range from 1998 to 2006, then began to increase rapidly, rising to 25% by early 2008.

Some, like American Enterprise Institute Fellow Peter J. Wallison, believe the roots of the crisis can be traced directly to sub-prime lending by Fannie Mae and Freddie Mac, which are government sponsored entities. On 30 September 1999, the *New York Times* reported that the Clinton Administration pushed for sub-prime lending: 'Fannie Mae, the nation's biggest underwriter of home mortgages, has been under increasing pressure from the Clinton Administration to expand mortgage loans among low and moderate income people. In moving, even tentatively, into this new area of lending, Fannie Mae is taking on significantly more risk, which may not pose any difficulties during flush economic times. But the government-subsidised corporation may run into trouble in an economic downturn, prompting a government rescue similar to that of the savings and loan industry in the 1980s.' In 1995, the administration also tinkered with President Jimmy Carter's Community Reinvestment Act of 1977 by regulating and strengthening the anti-redlining procedures.

The result was a push by the administration for greater investment, by financial institutions, into riskier loans. A 2000 U.S. Department of the Treasury study of lending trends for 305 cities from 1993 to 1998 showed that $467 billion of mortgage credit poured out of CRA-covered lenders into low and mid-level income borrowers and neighbourhoods. Nevertheless, only 25% of all sub-prime lending occurred at CRA-covered institutions, and a full 50% of sub-prime loans originated at institutions exempt from CRA. Others have pointed out that there were not enough of these loans made to cause a crisis of this magnitude. In an article in *Portfolio Magazine*, Michael Lewis spoke with one trader who noted that 'There weren't enough Americans with [bad] credit taking out [bad loans] to satisfy investors' appetite for the end product'. Essentially, investment banks and hedge funds used financial innovation to synthesise more loans using derivatives. 'They were creating [loans] out of whole cloth. One hundred times over! That's why the losses are so much greater than the loans.'

Economist Paul Krugman argued in January 2010 that the simultaneous growth of the residential and commercial real estate pricing bubbles undermines the case made by those who argue that Fannie Mae, Freddie Mac, CRA or predatory lending were primary causes of the crisis. In other words, bubbles in both markets developed even though only the residential market was affected by these potential causes.

Predatory Lending

Predatory lending refers to the practice of unscrupulous lenders, to enter into 'unsafe' or 'unsound' secured loans for inappropriate purposes. A classic bait-and-switch method was used by Countrywide, advertising low interest rates for home refinancing. Such loans were written into extensively detailed contracts, and swapped for more expensive loan products on the day of closing. Whereas the advertisement might state that 1% or 1.5% interest would be charged, the consumer would be put into an ARM in which the interest charged would be greater than the amount of interest paid. This created negative amortisation, which the credit consumer might not notice until long after the loan transaction had been consummated. Countrywide, sued by California Attorney General Jerry Brown for 'Unfair Business Practices' and 'False Advertising', was making high cost mortgages 'to homeowners with weak credit, adjustable rate mortgages (ARMs) that allowed homeowners to make interest-only payments'. When housing prices decreased, homeowners in ARMs then had little incentive to pay their monthly payments, since their home equity had disappeared. This caused Countrywide's financial condition to deteriorate, ultimately resulting in a decision by the Office of Thrift Supervision to seize the lender. Former employees from Ameriquest, which was United States' leading wholesale lender, described a system in which they were pushed to falsify mortgage documents and then sell the mortgages to Wall Street banks eager to make fast profits. There is growing evidence that such mortgage frauds may be a cause of the crisis.

De-Regulation

Critics have argued that the regulatory framework did not keep pace with financial innovation, such as the increasing importance of the shadow banking system, derivatives and off-balance-sheet financing. In other cases, laws were changed or enforcement weakened in parts of the financial system. Key examples include: In October 1982, President Ronald Reagan signed into Law the Garn-St. German Depository Institution Act, which began the process of Banking de-regulation that helped contribute to the savings and loan crises of the late 1980s/early 1990s, and the financial crises of 2007–2010. President Reagan stated at the signing, 'all in all, I think we hit the jackpot'. In November 1999, President Bill Clinton signed into Law the Gramm-Leach-Bliley Act, which repealed part of the Glass-Steagall Act of 1933. This repeal has been criticised for reducing the separation between commercial banks (which traditionally had a conservative culture) and investment banks (which had a more risk-taking culture). In 2004, the SEC relaxed the net capital rule, which enabled investment banks to substantially increase the level of debt they were taking on, fuelling the growth in MBS supporting sub-prime mortgages. The SEC has conceded that self-regulation of investment banks contributed to the crisis.

Financial institutions in the shadow banking system are not subject to the same regulation as depository banks, allowing them to assume additional debt obligations relative to their financial cushion or capital base. This was the case despite the Long-Term Capital Management debacle in 1998, where a highly leveraged shadow institution failed with systemic implications. Regulators and accounting standard-setters allowed depository banks such as Citigroup to move significant amounts of assets and liabilities off-balance sheet into complex legal entities called structural investment vehicles, masking the weakness of the capital base of the firm or degree of leverage or risk taken. One news agency estimated that the top four U.S. banks will have to return between US $500 billion and US$1 trillion to their balance sheets during 2009. This increased uncertainty during the crisis regarding the financial position of the major banks. Off-balance-sheet entities were also used by Enron as part of the scandal that brought down that company in 2001.

As early as 1997, Fed Chairman Alan Greenspan fought to keep the derivatives market unregulated. With the advice of the President's Working Group on Financial Markets, the U.S. Congress and President allowed the self-regulation of the over-the-counter (OTC) derivatives market when they enacted the Commodity Futures Modernization Act of 2000. Derivatives such as credit default swaps (CDS) can be used to hedge or speculate against particular credit risks. The volume of CDS outstanding increased 100-fold from 1998 to 2008, with estimates of the debt covered by CDS contracts, as of November 2008, ranging from US $33 to US$47 trillion. Total OTC derivative notional value rose to US$683 trillion by June 2008.

Warren Buffett famously referred to derivatives as 'financial weapons of mass destruction' in early 2003. The U.S. households and financial institutions became increasingly indebted or overleveraged during the years preceding the crisis. This increased their vulnerability to the collapse of the housing bubble and worsened the ensuing economic downturn. Key statistics include: Free cash used by consumers from home equity extraction doubled from US $627 billion in 2001 to US$1428 billion in 2005 as the housing bubble built, a total of nearly US$5 trillion dollars over the period, contributing to economic growth worldwide. The U.S. home mortgage debt relative to GDP increased from an average of 46%

during the 1990s to 73% during 2008, reaching US$10.5 trillion. The U.S. household debt as a percentage of annual disposable personal income was 127% at the end of 2007, versus 77% in 1990.

I. In 1981, U.S. private debt was 123% of GDP; by the third quarter of 2008, it was 290%.

II. From 2004 to 2007, the top five U.S. investment banks each significantly increased their financial leverage, which increased their vulnerability to a financial shock. These five institutions reported over US$4.1 trillion in debt for fiscal year 2007, about 30% of U.S. nominal GDP for 2007. Lehman Brother was liquidated, Bear Steams and Merrill Lynch were sold at fire-sale prices, and Goldman Sachs and Morgan Stanley became commercial banks, subjecting themselves to more stringent regulation. With the exception of Lehman, these companies required or received government support.

III. Fannie Mae and Freddie Mac, two U.S. government sponsored enterprises, owned or guaranteed nearly US$5 trillion in mortgage obligations at the time they were placed into conservatorship by the U.S. government in September 2008.

These seven entities were highly leveraged and had US$9 trillion in debt or guarantee obligations, an enormous concentration of risk; yet they were not subject to the same regulation as depository banks.

Financial Innovation and Complexity

The term 'financial innovation' refers to the ongoing development of financial products designed to achieve particular client objectives, such as offsetting a particular risk exposure (such as the default of a borrower) or to assist with obtaining financing. Examples pertinent to this crisis included: the ARM; the bundling of sub-prime mortgages into MBS or CDO for sale to investors, a type of securitisation; and a form of credit insurance called CDS. The usage of these products expanded dramatically in the years leading up to the crisis. These products vary in complexity and the ease with which they can be valued on the books of financial institutions. Certain financial innovation may also have the effect of circumventing regulations, such as off-balance-sheet financing that affects the leverage or capital cushion reported by major banks. For example, Martin Wolf wrote in June 2009: 'An enormous part of what banks did in the early part of this decade — the off-balance-sheet vehicles, the derivatives and the "shadow banking system" itself — was to find a way round regulation'.

The pricing of risk refers to the incremental compensation required by investors for taking on additional risk, which may be measured by interest rates or fees. For a variety of reasons, market participants did not accurately measure the risk inherent with financial innovation such as MBS and CDOs or understand its impact on the overall stability of the financial system. For example, the pricing model for CDOs clearly did not reflect the level of risk they introduced into the system. The average recovery rate for 'high-quality' CDOs has been approximately 32 cents on the dollar, while the recovery rate for mezzanine CDOs has been approximately five cents for every dollar. These massive, practically unthinkable, losses have dramatically impacted the balance sheets of banks across the globe, leaving them with very little capital to continue operations. Another example relates to AIG, which insured obligations of various financial institutions through the usage of CDS.

The basic CDS transaction involved AIG receiving a premium in exchange for a promise to pay money to party A in the event party B defaulted. However, AIG did not have the financial strength to support its many CDS commitments as the crisis progressed and was taken over by the government in September 2008. The U.S. taxpayers provided over US$180 billion in government support to AIG during 2008 and early 2009, through which the money flowed to various counterparties to CDS transactions, including many large global financial institutions. The limitations of a widely used financial model also were not properly understood. This formula assumed that the price of CDS was correlated with and could predict the correct price of MBS. Because it was highly tractable, it rapidly came to be used by a huge percentage of CDO and CDS investors, issuers and rating agencies. Cracks started appearing early on, when financial markets began behaving in ways that users of Li's formula had not expected. The cracks became full-fledged canyons in 2008 — when ruptures in the financial system's foundation swallowed up trillions of dollars and put the survival of the global banking system in serious peril. Li's Gaussian copula formula will go down in history as instrumental in causing the unfathomable losses that brought the world financial system to its knees.

As financial assets became more and more complex, and harder and harder to value, investors were reassured by the fact that both the international bond rating agencies and bank regulators, who came to rely on them, accepted as valid some complex mathematical models which theoretically showed the risks were much smaller than they actually proved to be in practice. George Soros commented that 'the super-boom got out of hand when the new products became so complicated that the authorities could no longer calculate the risks and started relying on the risk management methods of the banks themselves. Similarly, the rating agencies relied on the information provided by the originators of synthetic products. It was a shocking abdication of responsibility.'[2]

Boom and Collapse of the Shadow Banking System

In a June 2008 speech, President and CEO of the NY Federal Reserve Bank Timothy Geithner, who in 2009 became Secretary of the United States Treasury, placed significant blame for the freezing of credit markets on a 'run' on the entities in the 'parallel' banking system, also called the shadow banking system. These

2. Ibid.

entities became critical to the credit markets underpinning the financial system, but were not subject to the same regulatory controls. Further, these entities were vulnerable because they borrowed short term in liquid markets to purchase long-term, illiquid and risky assets. This meant that disruptions in credit markets would make them subject to rapid deleveraging, selling their long-term assets at depressed prices. He described the significance of these entities: 'In early 2007, asset-backed commercial paper conduits, in structured investment vehicles, in auction-rate preferred securities, tender option bonds and variable rate demand notes, had a combined asset size of roughly US$2.2 trillion. Assets financed overnight in tri-party repo grew to US$2.5 trillion. Assets held in hedge funds grew to roughly US$1.8 trillion. The combined balance sheets of the then five major investment banks totalled US$4 trillion. In comparison, the total assets of the top five bank holding companies in the United States at that point were just over US$6 trillion, and total assets of the entire banking system were about US$10 trillion.' He stated that the 'combined effect of these factors was a financial system vulnerable to self-reinforcing asset price and credit cycles'.

Paul Krugman described the run on the shadow banking system as the 'core of what happened' to cause the crisis. 'As the shadow banking system expanded to rival or even surpass conventional banking in importance, politicians and government officials should have realised that they were re-creating the kind of financial vulnerability that made the Great Depression possible — and they should have responded by extending regulations and the financial safety net to cover these new institutions. Influential figures should have proclaimed a simple rule: anything that does what a bank does, anything that has to be rescued in crises the way banks are, should be regulated like a bank.' He referred to this lack of controls as 'malign neglect'.

Commodity Bubble

A commodity price bubble was created following the collapse in the housing bubble. The price of oil nearly tripled from US$50 to

US$140 from early 2007 to 2008, before plunging as the financial crisis began to take hold in late 2008. Experts debate the causes, which include the flow of money from housing and other investments into commodities to speculation and monetary policy or the increasing feeling of raw materials scarcity in a fast growing world economy and thus positions taken on those markets, such as Chinese increasing presence in Africa. An increase in oil prices tends to divert a larger share of consumer spending into gasoline, which creates downward pressure on economic growth in oil importing countries, as wealth flows to oil-producing states.

Systems Failure

The current crisis of the capitalist world is commonly explained as resulting from 'a lack of government regulation of the financial sector', 'insufficient supervision allowing reckless lending by financial institutions', 'the unbridled greed of the financiers' in short a series of mistakes and aberrations. These have contributed to a 'systems failure' in the words of Joseph Stiglitz, the distinguished economist and Nobel Laureate. This entire line of reasoning however misses the point. The crisis is not a 'failure' of the system; it is central to the mode of functioning of the system itself. It is not the result of some 'mistakes' or 'aberrations'; it is inherent to the logic of the system. If indeed government regulation in the United States had prevented 'reckless lending' by the financial institutions, if indeed there had been no 'sub-prime lending', then the housing boom would have been truncated much earlier.

Mass unemployment would have reared its ugly head much earlier, and even the entire world economy would have got into a state of recession much earlier. The fact that these things did not happen, the fact that the boom was kept going by sustaining the bubble in the housing market through enlarging the disbursement of credit, is precisely because the policy of the U.S. Federal Reserve was to make the financial system accommodative. And this is now being called 'irresponsible' and 'reckless'. It is precisely this so-called irresponsibility and recklessness that underlies booms in capitalism. Or, putting it differently, growth in conditions of modern capitalism is caused by financial, or more generally asset price, bubbles. And crises, such as what the capitalist world is experiencing today, are the necessary sequel of the bursting of such bubbles. What Stiglitz calls a 'system failure' is actually the 'system' itself.

Centralisation of Capital

Capitalism has reached a certain level of centralisation of capital that cannot be compared to the situation, even 50 years ago. At this stage, where a mere 5000 odd oligopolies control every production and organisation of exchange in the world. This is a terrific level of centralisation of capital, very different from the scenario prevalent in the early twentieth century, dominated by monopolies. That these oligopolies have the capacity to control not merely the economic, but the political sphere is striking. This centralisation is the basis on which unequal distribution of incomes has become possible. But it has led a shift in gravity from the productive sector to the redistribution of profit among the oligopolies through the means of financial investment. This is the secret behind the financialisation of the global capitalism. The emergence of new forms of global integration of production processes via direct investment, combined with the re-emergence of older forms via financial flows, has consolidated rather than undermined the fundamental difference in the material conditions of class formation that separates the north from the south.

The implications for processes of class formation on a world scale of this remarkable geo-political stability of the global hierarchy of wealth are straightforward. In the new phase of globalisation, the worldwide social linkage in an internal one springing from the globalisation of production process itself and the supranational integration of national productive structure are the most fundamental transformations from the past where the world was linked together via commodity and financial flows were an integrated international market. The other thing is the increasing class-consciousness of the Tactical Command Center (TCC), as witnessed by the rise of a transnational state (TNS) apparatus. A transnational working class 'is increasing a reality as a class in-itself'. But it is not yet for itself. It has become conscious of its transnationality, and has been pursuing a class project of capitalist globalisation, as reflecting by the rise of TNS under its auspices. Some African governments were still incapable of managing their natural resources in order to accumulate the reserves they need to resist the global economic downturn.[3] It is the fact that some African countries seem to have been left behind and marginalised by globalisation, and they are poorer today (i.e., their average real per capita income is lower today) than they were two or three decades ago.

Keynes' Ideas on Depression

John Maynard Keynes had been perceptive enough to realise this had therefore suggested an alternative source of growth itself, an alternative to the phenomenon of 'bubbles-led growth'. This was through what he had called the 'socialisation of investment', that is, the capitalist State, as the representative of society at large (being a Liberal he held this theory of the State) should always ensure enough aggregate demand to keep the economy as close to full employment as possible. A necessary condition for such activism on the part of the State according to him was 'the euthanasia of the rentier', that is, the 'mercy-killing' of the financial interests, which, he knew, would always oppose such activism. Keynes in other words did not just call for the regulation of capitalism, but its transformation in a manner that would ensure near-full employment and hence undermine a major argument for socialism.

Keynes' ideas, though meant to defend capitalism, were repugnant to finance capital and met with immediate rejection. The capitalist world came out of the 1930s Depression not because of Keynesian measures, but because of military spending in the run up to the Second World War. It is only after the war that the

3. Stiglitz (2010).

increase in the political weight of the working class, expressed through the rise to power of Social Democracy, and the temporary setback suffered by finance capital, allowed the adoption of Keynesian measures of 'demand management' by the capitalist States, which both kept employment rates consistently high and prevented financial crises (as would have occurred if 'bubbles' had been allowed to develop as the means for stimulating growth). But the emergence of finance capital to a position of hegemony all over the capitalist world, in the new garb of 'globalised finance', which pushed for neo-liberal policies everywhere, put an end to Keynesianism, and the resumption of the process of 'bubbles-led growth'.

The Great Crash we are currently witnessing is the necessary outcome of this process. Three conclusions follow: first, as already mentioned, such Great Crashes reflect not the failure of the system, but the system itself; second, the system they reflect is the system of contemporary capitalism, which is necessarily marked by the hegemony of finance capital, and sustained, because of this hegemony, by a process of 'bubbles-led growth'. And third, the specific policy measures adopted in such crisis situations depend not only upon the 'wisdom' of such measures, but also upon the balance of class forces or the state of class struggle. In short, what measures the capitalist economies are going to adopt in the face of this crisis today depend upon the extent to which the hegemony of finance capital can be confronted.

Two broad approaches have come to the fore among the governments in capitalist countries for tackling the crisis: the first of these emphasises fiscal expansion by the capitalist States. But expansion by any single capitalist State, if undertaken in isolation, will have its effects largely 'leaking' out of the economy (to a point where the benefits accruing to other countries would be greater than to it). Because of this the expansion will have to be a coordinated one among several capitalist States, or else the fiscally expanding economy will be tempted to put up protectionist barriers which will exacerbate conflicts and compound the problem. But any such coordinated fiscal expansion, or indeed any fiscal expansion for that matter, will have to be based on control over cross-border financial flows, that is, on the mobility of globalised finance, since, otherwise, large-scale and speculative shifts of finance from one country to another can easily destabilise fiscal policy. The second approach is to avoid doing anything positive, to avoid fiscal expansion, merely to support the financial system, and to wait for the next 'bubble' to come along. This is the approach that Herbert Hoover the American president before Franklin Roosevelt had adopted, which had the effect of prolonging and worsening the crisis, and the approach that George Bush has been inclined towards.

Not surprisingly, the first of these approaches is opposed by finance capital while the second of these is favoured by it. And again, not surprisingly, the first approach has been mooted by European Social Democracy in general and by the British Labour government, while the second is the favoured one among all Right-wing governments. At one point of time it appeared that the capitalist world was veering around towards a coordinated fiscal expansion, and even Bush started talking about it. That was in the immediate aftermath of the collapse of investment banking on the Wall Street, when the reputation of finance capital was down in the dumps and an anti-finance capital sentiment was sweeping the capitalist world. Since then however the Right (representing the interests of finance capital) has managed to regroup itself. Germany has debunked talk of fiscal expansion; and the British Tories, after initially supporting it, have opposed Gordon Brown's fiscal expansion plans. Fiscal expansion prospects in other words have again receded to the background, and it has become obvious once more that the world will remain steeped in crisis (until some new 'bubble' comes) unless the power of finance is broken. But that in effect would mean going beyond contemporary capitalism to a new and humane order.

John Maynard Keynes had rightly said,

> Our analysis shows ... that long-run development is not inherent in the capitalist economy. Thus, 'specific development factors' are required to sustain a long-run upward movement.

What is the fact that mature capitalist economies tend towards stagnation. What happens is that the rate of return on investment begins to dwindle as overcapacity builds. That causes declining profits which lead to belt tightening, rising unemployment and falling demand. As investment drops off further, growth slows correspondingly and the economy dips into a protracted slump. This corrosive stagnation is the challenge that all advanced capitalist economies face. The solution — as Keynes notes — lies in 'specific development factors', which in today's terms means 'financial innovations'.

Financial innovations, like derivations contracts and securitisation, have created vast new opportunities for investment and profit making. This complex nether world of highly leveraged debt instruments and off-balance-sheet operations constitutes a shadow — artificial unrealistic economy where the process of capitalist accumulation persists despite pervasive inertia in the underlying economy. This is why the Fed and the Treasury have been doing their best to stitch the system back together without changing its basic structure. John Maynard Keynes, though bourgeois in his outlook, was a remarkably insightful economist, whose book *Economic Consequences of the Peace* was copiously quoted by Lenin at the Second Congress of the Communist International to argue that conditions had ripened for the world revolution. But even Keynes' insights could not fully comprehend the paradox that is capitalism. In a famous essay 'Economic Possibilities for our Grandchildren', written in 1930, Keynes had argued: 'Assuming no important wars and no important increase in population, the economic problem may be solved, or be at least within sight of solution, within a hundred years'.

This means that the economic problem is not, if we look into the future, the permanent problem of the human race. He had gone on to ask: 'Why, you may ask, is this so startling? It is startling because, if instead of looking into the future, we look into the past, we find that the economic problem, the struggle for subsistence, always has been hitherto the most pressing problem of the human race ... If the economic problem is solved, mankind will be deprived of its traditional purpose.' He had then proceeded to examine how mankind could fruitfully use its time in such a world.

True, after Keynes had written there has been the Second World War, but thereafter mankind has had six and a half decades without any 'important war' of the sort that could interrupt what he had called the 'era of progress and invention'. And the rate of population growth has also not accelerated to a point that can be considered to have invalidated Keynes' premise. And yet if we take mankind as a whole, it is as far from solving the economic problems as it ever was. True, there has been massive accumulation of capital, and with it an enormous increase in the mass of goods available to mankind; and yet, for the vast majority of mankind, the 'struggle for subsistence' that Keynes had referred to has continued to remain as acute as ever, perhaps in some ways even more acute than ever before. To say that this is only because not enough time has passed, that over a slightly longer time period Keynes' vision will indeed turn out to be true, is facile. The fact that the bulk of mankind continues to face an acute struggle for subsistence is not a matter of degree; it is not as if the acuteness of this struggle for this segment of mankind has been lessening over time, or that the relative size of this segment has been lessening over time. We cannot therefore assert that the passage of more time will lift everybody above this struggle.

Dichotomy Structurally Inbuilt in Capitalism

Likewise, to say that while enormous increases have taken place in the mass of goods and services available to mankind (the increase in this mass being more in the last hundred years than in the previous two thousand years, as Keynes had pointed out), its distribution has been extremely skewed and hence accounts for the persistence of the struggle for subsistence for the majority of the world's population, is to state a mere tautology. The whole point is that there is something structural to the capitalist system itself, the same system that causes this enormous increase in mankind's capacity to produce goods and services, which also ensures that, notwithstanding this enormous increase, the struggle for subsistence must continue to be as acute as before, or even more acute than before, for the bulk of mankind. Keynes missed this structural aspect of capitalism. His entire argument in fact was based on the mere logic of compound interest, that is, on the sheer fact that 'if capital increases, say, 2 per cent per annum, the capital equipment of the world will have increased by a half in twenty years, and seven and a half times in a hundred years'. From this sheer fact it follows that output too would have increased more or less by a similar order of magnitude, and mankind, with so much more of goods at its disposal, would have overcome the struggle for subsistence.

The reason Keynes assumed that an increase in the mass of goods would eventually benefit everyone lies not just in his inability to see the antagonistic nature of the capitalist mode of production (and its antagonistic relationship with the surrounding universe of petty producers), but also in his belief that capitalism is a malleable system which can be moulded, in accordance with the dictates of reason, by the interventions of the State as the representative of society. He was a liberal and saw the state as standing above, and acting on behalf of, society as a whole, in accordance with the dictates of reason. The world, he thought, was ruled by ideas; and correct, and benevolent, ideas would clearly translate themselves into reality, so that the increase in mankind's productive capacity would get naturally transformed into an end of the economic problem. If the antagonism of capitalism was pointed out to Keynes, he would have simply talked about state intervention restraining this antagonism to ensure that the benefit of the increase in productive capacity reached all.

The fact that this has not happened, the fact that the enormous increase in mankind's capacity to produce has translated itself not into an end to the struggle for subsistence for the world's population, but into a plethora of all kinds of goods and services of little benefit to it, from a stockpiling of armaments to an exploration of outer space, and even into a systematic promotion of waste, and lack of utilisation, or even destruction, of productive equipment, only underscores the limitations of the liberal world outlook of which Keynes was a votary. The state, instead of being an embodiment of reason, which intervenes in the interests of society as a whole, as liberalism believes, acts to defend the class interests of the hegemonic class, and hence to perpetuate the antagonisms of the capitalist system.

Antagonisms in Three Distinct Ways

These antagonisms perpetuate in three quite distinct ways the struggle for subsistence in which the bulk of mankind is caught. The first centres on the fact that the level of wages in the capitalist system depends upon the relative size of the reserve army of labour. And to the extent that the relative size of the reserve army of labour never shrinks below a certain threshold level, the wage rate remains tied to the subsistence level despite significant increases in labour productivity, as necessarily occur in the 'era of progress and innovation'. Work itself therefore becomes a struggle for subsistence and remains so. Secondly, those who constitute the reserve army of labour are themselves destitute and hence condemned to an even more acute struggle for subsistence, to eke out for them an even more meagre magnitude of goods and services. And thirdly, the encroachment by the capitalist mode upon the surrounding universe of petty production, whereby it displaces petty producers, grabs land from the peasants, uses the tax machinery of the State to appropriate for itself, at the expense of the petty producers, an amount of surplus value over and above what is produced within the capitalist mode itself, in short, the entire mechanism of 'primitive accumulation of capital', ensures that the size of the reserve army always remains above this threshold level.

There is a stream of destitute petty producers forever flocking to work within the capitalist mode but unable to find work and hence joining the ranks of the reserve army. The antagonism within the system, and vis-à-vis the surrounding universe of petty production, thus ensures that, notwithstanding the massive increases in mankind's productive capacity, the struggle of subsistence for the bulk of mankind continues unabated. The growth rates of world output have been even greater in the post-war period than in Keynes' time. The growth rates particularly in capitalist countries like India have been of an order unimaginable in Keynes' time, and yet there is no let-up in the struggle for subsistence on the part of the bulk of the population even within these countries. In India, precisely during the period of neo-liberal reforms when output growth rates have been high, there has been an increase in the proportion of the rural population accessing less than 2400 calories per person per day (the figure for 2004 is 87%).

This is also the period when hundreds of thousands of peasants, unable to carry on even simple reproduction have committed suicide. The unemployment rate has increased, notwithstanding a massive jump in the rate of capital accumulation; and the real wage rate, even of the workers in the organised sector, has at best stagnated, notwithstanding massive increases in labour productivity. In short our own experience belies the Keynesian optimism about the future of mankind under capitalism. But Keynes wrote a long time ago. He should have seen the inner working of the system better (after all Marx who died the year Keynes was born, saw it), but perhaps his upper-class Edwardian upbringing came in the way. But what does one say of people who, having seen the destitution-'high growth' dialectics in the contemporary world, still cling to the illusion that the logic of compound interest will overcome the 'economic problem of mankind'?

Neo-liberal ideologues of course propound this illusion, either in its simple version, which is the 'trickle-down' theory, or in the slightly more complex version, where the State is supposed to ensure through its intervention that the benefits of the growing mass of goods and services are made available to all, thereby alleviating poverty and easing the struggle for subsistence. But this illusion often appears in an altogether unrecognisable form. Jeffrey Sachs, the economist who is well-known for his administration of the so-called shock therapy in the former Soviet Union that led to a veritable retrogression of the economy and the unleashing of massive suffering on millions of people, has come out with a book where he argues that poverty in large parts of the world is associated with adverse geographical factors, such as drought-proneness, desertification and infertile soil. He wants global efforts to help these economies which are the victims of such niggardliness on the part of nature.

The fact that enormous poverty exists in areas where nature is not niggardly, but on the contrary bounteous; the fact that the very bounteousness of nature has formed the basis of exploitation of the producers on a massive scale, so that they are engaged in an acute struggle for existence precisely in the midst of plenitude; and hence the fact that the bulk of the world's population continues to struggle for subsistence not because of nature's niggardliness but because of the incubus of an exploitative social order are all obscured by such analysis. Keynes' faith in the miracle of compound interest would be justified in a socialist order, but not in a capitalist one. The forces of production are the technology used by the society in producing material goods; manifested in labour skills, scientific knowledge, tools and capital goods, they are inherently dynamic. The relations of production are the rules of the game. There are relations between one person and another, or social relations, and relations between people and things, or property relations. Neo-liberal economist simply accepted markets and did not consider the nature of private property and the effect that the existence of markets had on people.

It was necessary to study the connection between private property, avarice and the separation of labour, capital and landed property; between exchange and competition, value and the devaluation of men, monopoly and competition, etc., the connection between this whole estrangement and the money system. Neo-liberal economists did not consider how the forces of production would undermine the relations of production, once the market had created the forces of production that could meet people's material needs, the alienation inherent in property rights and markets would lead individuals to free themselves from the markets and create a society that would eliminate private property and the alienation associated with it. In my opinion, one of the main characteristics of capitalism was the separation of labour from the ownership of the means of production. Under capitalism, labour no longer owns its workshops, its tools or the raw materials of the production process.

Capitalism is therefore essentially a society of two classes, and one of the most important aspects of this society is the exchange, the wage bargain, that takes place between the capitalist and the proletariat. In classical analysis this theory had been essential to explain the existence of profits. The classical economists maintained that capital accumulation leads to an increased demand for labour and a rise in the real wage of labour. If wages continued to rise with capital accumulation, the level of profits would fall. It is true that there is always an excess supply of labour in the market, which has the effect of depressing wages and keeping surplus value and profits positive.

The reserve army of the unemployed is being recruited from several sources. Direct recruitment occurs when machines replace humans in production processes. The capitalists' search for profits leads them to introduce new machines, thereby increasing the capital intensity in the economy. The workers displaced by the new technology are not absorbed into other areas of the economy. One of the important contradictions between the forces and relations of production would lead ultimately to the destruction of capitalism is the falling rate of profit. Competition in commodity and labour markets would lead to a fall in profits in the following way: There is a strong drive, for the capitalist to accumulate capital. Capital accumulation means that more capital will bid for labour, forcing up wages and reducing the size of the reserve army of the unemployed, and the rate of profit will fall. Competition in commodity markets will also result in a continuous decrease in the rate of profit because the capitalist will keep trying to reduce the costs of production in order to sell final output at lower prices.

Joseph Stiglitz (former Director of World Bank) said that the current financial crisis, which began in the United States and then spread to Europe, has now become global and requires a global response by an institution that is inclusive and that has political legitimacy. He indicated that any response should be based on social justice and solidarity that goes beyond national boundaries.

He stressed the need to reflect on the role of financial markets in the economy, said they should be evaluated on how they serve citizens and added that they were not an end in themselves — they were a means to economic growth and prosperity for all, including homeowners, ordinary people and the poor. He explained that the underlying doctrine of the current system is flawed and said that this was the root cause of the problem. 'What is good for Wall Street is not necessarily good for all', he said, and added that 'trickle-down economy' had been consistently rejected as a means to provide prosperity for all. He also indicated that, in the past, the global financial system often worked to the disadvantage of developing countries.

Banks in developed countries, for instance, were encouraged to lend short term to developing countries — while this provided greater liquidity to the former, it led to greater instability in the latter. He noted that pro-cyclical monetary and fiscal policies were often foisted on developing countries, while developed countries followed countercyclical policies. That situation must change, he said.

Creation of an external shock facility was a good idea, as was creating a multilateral reserve system with greater stability. There must also be more cooperation in setting macroeconomic policies, and the creation of a financial regulatory commission should be studied urgently. He stressed that the international community must commit itself to developing the institutions and instruments for increasing the stability and equity of the global financial system, and called for a reform in the governance of the international economic institutions and standard setting bodies. The reforms undertaken, for example, in IMF governance, so far have been inadequate. Unless far more fundamental reforms are taken, it will not be possible for these institutions to play the role they should — decision making must reside with international institutions with broad political legitimacy, and with adequate representation of both middle income countries and the least developed countries (LDCs). He concluded by saying that the only institution that currently has broad legitimacy is the UN. (Prof. Joseph Stiglitz, a Noble Laureate and Professor at Columbia University, was a panellist at UN General Assembly on Causes and Solutions to the Global Financial Crisis, 3 November 2008.)

According to Prof. Prabhaht Patnaik (Ex-member of Planning Commission of India), the cause of the problem was located in the fundamental defect of the free market system regarding its capacity to distinguish between 'enterprise' and 'speculation' and hence, in its tendency to become dominated by speculators, interested not in the long-term yield assets but only in the short-term appreciation in asset values. He said John Maynard Keynes wanted this link to be severed through what he called a comprehensive 'socialisation' of investment, whereby the State, acting on behalf of society, always ensured a level of investment in the economy, and hence, a level of aggregate demand that was adequate for full employment. In the process of globalisation, the role of nation-State has been undermined. As a result, fiscal intervention, as a means of sustaining growth, was replaced by globalised finance and de-regulation and an alternative paradigm was adopted whereby 'bubbles lead to booms' instead of financial and economic stability ensured by sound long-term macroeconomic policies. He noted that the response measures had also been inadequate because injection of liquidity alone is not the answer; it has to be accompanied by injecting demand into the market through State investment in infrastructure and social services.

The financial crisis will impact developing countries because of the ensuing recession which will contract demand for commodities, as well as sources of credit and financial flows. Even during the economic boom, the conditions of the poor worsened. Part of the response lies in supporting the livelihoods of peasants and small producers in developing countries through greater fiscal pro-activeness and expenditure for the revival of agricultural production. (Patnaik, 2009, Professor at the Centre for Economic Studies and Planning at India, was a panellist at UN General Assembly on Causes and Solutions to the Global Financial Crisis, 3 November 2008.)

Noam Chomsky argues that Smith supported markets in the belief that they would lead to equality, and that Smith opposed wage labour and corporations. Unfortunately, the current new liberal globalisation of course creates wealth but also inequality and poverty. Samir Amin (a noted Marxist economist) said, the global financial crisis is a system crisis of capitalism. Capitalism has reached a certain level of centralisation of capital that cannot be compared to the situation, even 50 years ago. At this stage, where a mere 5000 odd oligopolies control every production and organisation of exchange in the world. This is a terrific level of centralisation of capital, very different from the scenario prevalent in the early twentieth century, dominated by monopolies. That these oligopolies have the capacity to control not merely the economic, but the political sphere is striking. This centralisation is the basis on which unequal distribution of incomes has become possible. But it has led a shift in gravity from the productive sector to the redistribution of profit among the oligopolies through the means of financial investment. This is the secret behind the financialisation of the global capitalism.[4]

The IMF's Capital Control Regimes

On 19 February 2010, the IMF published a policy note that reversed its long-held position on capital controls. Taxes and other restrictions on capital inflows, the IMF's economists' comments can be helpful, and they constitute 'legitimate part' of policymakers' toolkits. The IMF's policy note makes clear that controls on cross-border financial flows can be not only desirable but also effective. This is important, because the traditional argument of last resort against capital controls has been that they cannot be made to stick. Financial markets would always outsmart the policymakers. One justification for capital controls is to prevent inflows of 'hot money' from boosting the value of the home currency excessively, thereby undermining competitiveness.

4. *Source*: System Crisis, South Centre, Geneva.

Another is to reduce vulnerability to sudden changes in financial market sentiment, which can wreak havoc on domestic growth and employment. To its credit, the IMF not only acknowledges this, but also provides evidence that developing countries with capital controls were hit less hard by the fallout from the sub-prime mortgage meltdown. The taboo that has been attached to capital controls has discouraged practical, policy-oriented work that would help governments manage capital flows directly. There is some empirical research on the consequences of capital controls in countries such as Chile, Colombia and Malaysia but very little systematic research on the appropriate menu of options. The IMF can help to fill in the gap. Emerging markets have resorted to a variety of instruments to limit private sector borrowing abroad-taxes, unremunerated reserve requirements, quantitative restrictions and verbal persuasion. In view of the sophisticated nature of financial markets, the devil is often in the details, and what works in one setting is unlikely to work well in others. For example, Taiwan's use of administrative measures that are rarely heavy on close monitoring of flows may be inappropriate in settings where bureaucratic capacity is more limited. Similarly, Chilean style unremunerated reserve requirements may be easier to evade in countries with extensive trading in sophisticated derivatives. With the stigma on capital controls gone, the IMF should now get to work developing guidelines on what kind of controls work best and under what circumstances.

The IMF provides countries with technical assistance in a wide range of areas — monetary policy, bank regulations and fiscal consolidation. It is time to add managing capital accounts to this list. With this battle won, the next worthy goal is a global financial transaction tax. Set at a very low level zero per cent is a commonly mentioned rate. Such a tax would raise hundreds of billions of dollars for global public goods while discouraging short-term speculative activities in financial markets. In the coming days, the financial industry will have a much harder time preventing the fetish of free finance from being tossed into the dustbin of history.

Structural Inequality among the People and between the Nations

Capitalist mode of production creates a wide structural inequality among the people and between the nations. The high-income economies control 78.3% of world GDP with only 15% of world population, their share in world exports has reached at 76.2%. The developing countries constitute 85% of the world population, enjoying only 21.7% of world GDP, their share in world exports have been diminishing. The low-income economies constitute 59.6% of world population and control only 6.3% of world GDP, their share in world exports was only 6.2%, and a vast country like India, their share in world exports was only 0.6%. The United States is the single largest economy of the world, accounting 28.5% of world GDP and 12.6% of world exports with only 4.6% of the world population. Over 75% of the world population lives in underdevelopment, and extreme poverty has already reached 1.2 billion people in the Third World. The 5% population currently earns 114 times as much as the poorest 5% in the world. The top 500 richest people currently own US$1.54 trillion, which is more than the entire GDP of Africa.

More than fifty thousand multinational corporations, the largest of these, General Motors and Exxon, each have assets totalling more than the gross national products of countries such as Australia, Denmark, Argentina, Norway, Hungry and Greece. The assets of the 200 richest people are more than the combined income of 41% of the world people. The assets of the three richest people are more than the combined GNP of all 48 LDCs, which have a population of more than 600 million people. The top 1% of Americans has doubled their share of national wealth since the 1970s, and now they own more than 40% of the total wealth. The top 1% now has more wealth than the entire bottom 95%.

The developed countries, with only one-fifth of global population, account for four-fifth of world output, more than four-fifth of world trade and almost all exports of capital and technology. Developing countries constitute 85% of the world population, enjoying only 21.7% of world GDP. Due to free trade and *laissez faire* global economic order based on international division of labour, international finance capital has come under pressure. However, the developed countries are still maintaining their economic status. On the basis of country's GDP, the rank of America is top with US$12.46 trillion where as India ranks 12th with US $785.47 billion GDP.

Some Theoretical Understanding

During the last two decades of the end of the Cold War, when the international correlation of forces moved in favour of imperialism following the dismantling of the USSR and the socialist countries in Eastern Europe, imperialism unleashed an all-round offensive — political, economic, military, cultural and ideological — to strengthen its global hegemony.

The emergence of international finance capital following unprecedented huge levels of capital accumulation unleashed a new re-ordering of the world economic order. This is to further facilitate profit maximisation — the *raison d'tre* of capitalism. By virtually drawing all the countries of the world into its vortex, imperialist globalisation under the dictates of international finance capital pressurises all countries to remove all restrictions for the flow of this capital in its pursuit of profit maximisation. The consequent package of economic reforms include financial liberalisation, the prising open of the markets of independent countries through trade liberalisation, the privatisation of State-owned assets, the conversion of public utilities (electricity, water, sanitation, civic amenities, etc.) and services (education, health, etc.) into areas of profit generation. Neo-liberalism is the ideological and theoretical construct that defines such reforms.

Such a process of gigantic accumulation under the leadership of international finance capital is generating deep crisis imposing unprecedented burdens on the vast majority of world's population. In the efforts to resolve one crisis, the seeds of a more intense crisis are being sown. The global financial meltdown caused by the sub-prime credit crisis was sought to be overcome through humongous bailout packages to resurrect those very financial giants who caused the crisis in the first place. This resulted in converting corporate bankruptcies into sovereign bankruptcies. This, in turn, is being sought to be solved through the reduction in government expenditures by imposing 'austerity measures' and drastically reducing social sector expenditures that are mounting further economic onslaughts on the people. This, in turn, is leading to a further contraction of the purchasing power in the hands of the people, sowing the seeds of a deeper crisis of double-dip global recession that is, today, looming large.

4 Crony Capitalism

The term *crony capitalism* refers to forms of capitalism in which leading businessmen enjoy close personal relationships with key politicians. Crony capitalism is often associated with corruption, and many commentators have seen it as a major obstacle to Third World development. Commentators often contrast crony capitalism with highly idealised neo-classical models of capitalism. In actuality, however, significant linkages between political elites and business classes can be found in almost all capitalist regimes, past and present, and the real task is to identify the variety of ways in which such linkages either facilitate or hinder economic development.

In many underdeveloped countries crony capitalism may be perceived both as corrupt and as anti-national. Crony capitalists often belong to ethnic minority groups whose activities have been historically concentrated within the business or financial sector and who in some cases had enjoyed protection under earlier colonial regimes. As in the cases of the Lebanese in Sierra Leone, Indians in Kenya, South Africa, Fiji, Malaysia and Indonesia, and the Chinese throughout Southeast Asia, perceived government favouritism toward entrepreneurial minorities may lead to fierce ethnic conflicts and the shattering of polities.

Crony capitalism may result in corruption. But corruption's effects on economic development need not necessarily be lethal and corruption is certainly not unique to modern Third World nations. While the World Bank and the U.S. government have intervened to make aid conditional on struggles against corruption, relatively little attention has been given to historical studies of the effects of corruption on economic development. American civic life in the era of the Second Industrial Revolution between 1870 and 1914 was immensely corrupt, though the effect of this corruption on U.S. economic growth remains largely unexplored. In *The Shame of the Cities* (1902) the social reformer Lincoln Steffens documented many cases of corrupt ties between businessmen and politicians during the era of the so-called Robber Barons. Steffens condemned the 'shamelessness' of municipal politics in St. Louis, a politics characterised by 'government of the people, by the rogues and for the rich'. Recent examples of cronyism show that the spirit of the Robber Barons continues: In 2001 the Enron case revealed collusion between politicians and corporate executives, while 2006 saw the conviction of the lobbyist Jack Abramoff, who had served as an intermediary between businessmen and key congressmen.

Some sociologists and political scientists have even maintained that some forms of crony capitalism may be indispensable for capitalist development, particularly when those forms of cronyism help prevent untrammelled corruption. As modern China shows, personal political networks tying central government leaders to regional industrialists may be invaluable in combating entrepreneurial corruption. China's increased movement away from state-owned enterprise has greatly increased opportunities for corruption at the higher ranks of society. Interestingly, however, the emerging Chinese culture of corruption so far seems mainly limited to regional levels, as the political elite that rules China at the national level has resisted absorption into this culture. Much of the success of the current Chinese economy may be due to the combination of local businessmen adept at adapting laws to local conditions and uncorrupted political elite with ties to regional economic leaders that imposes limits on regional corruption and maintains a legal framework on which local and foreign businessmen can rely.

Cronyism has been an important element of capitalism everywhere, but the relationship between cronyism, business and politics and cronyism's effect on development vary greatly from nation to nation. Crony capitalist economies often result in unequal societies where there are a few very wealthy individuals and many poor people.

Survey of Literature

Crony capitalism is the inevitable result of *any* capitalist system. Jane Jacobs described it as a natural consequence of collusion between those managing power and trade, while a famous American linguist Professor Noam Chomsky has argued that the word 'crony' is superfluous when describing capitalism. Since businesses make money and money leads to political power, business will inevitably use their power to influence governments. Much of the impetus behind campaign finance reform in the United States and in other countries is an attempt to prevent economic power being used to take political power.

Ravi Batra argues that 'all official economic measures adopted since 1981, have devastated the middle class' and that the Occupy Wall Street movement should push for their repeal and thus end the influence of the super wealthy in the political process, which he considers a manifestation of crony capitalism.

Socialist economists, such as Robin Hahnel, have criticised the term as an ideologically motivated attempt to cast what is in their view the fundamental problems of capitalism as avoidable irregularities. Socialist economists dismiss the term as an apologetic for failures of neoliberal policy and, more fundamentally, their perception of the weaknesses of market allocation.

Laissez-faire economists oppose crony capitalism as well disparaging governmental favours as incompatible with a true free market. Laissez-faire advocates criticise the term as an ideologically motivated attempt to cast what is in their view the fundamental problem of government intervention or 'investments' as an avoidable aberration; free-market advocates refer to governmental favouritism as 'crony socialism', 'venture socialism' or 'corruption', a modern form of mercantilism to emphasise that the only way to run a profitable business in such systems is to have help from corrupt government officials. Even if the initial regulation was well-intentioned (to curb actual abuses), and even if the initial lobbying by corporations was well-intentioned (to reduce illogical regulations), the mixture of business and government stifle competition, a collusive result called regulatory capture. In his book *The Myth of the Robber Barons*, Burton W. Folsom, Jr. distinguished those that engage in crony capitalism — designated by him 'political entrepreneurs' — from those who compete in the marketplace without special aid from government, whom he calls 'market entrepreneurs' who succeed 'by producing a quality product at a competitive price'.

Crony Capitalism: An Overview

Crony capitalism consists of collusion among market players. While perhaps lightly competing against each other, they will present a unified front (sometimes called a trade association or industry trade group) to the government in requesting subsidies or aid or regulation. Newcomers to a market may find it difficult to find loans, acquire shelf space or receive official sanction (like the Medallion System of the Taxicabs of New York City created during the Great Depression) to sell their product or services; in technological fields, they may be accused of infringing on patents that the established competitors never assert against each other. Distribution networks will refuse to aid the entrant. In spite of this, some competitors will succeed when the legal barriers are light, especially where the old guard has become inefficient and is failing to meet the needs of the market. Of course, some of these upstarts may then join with the established networks to help deter any other new competitors. Examples of this have been argued to include the Keiretsu of post-war Japan, the print media in India, the chaebol of South Korea and the powerful families who control much of the investment in Latin America.

However, crony capitalism is generally associated with more virulent government intervention. Intentionally ambiguous laws and regulations are common in such systems. Taken strictly, such laws would greatly impede practically all business; in practice, they are only erratically enforced. The spectre of having such laws suddenly brought down upon a business provides incentive to stay in the good graces of political officials. Troublesome rivals who have overstepped their bounds can have the laws suddenly enforced against them, leading to fines or even jail time. Even in high-income democracies with well-established legal systems and freedom of the press, a larger state is associated with more political corruption (including crony capitalism).

States often said to exhibit crony capitalism include Hong Kong, China, India (especially up to the early 1990s when manufacturing was strictly controlled by the government, also known as 'License Raj'), Indonesia, Argentina, Brazil, United Kingdom (especially in the 1600s and 1700s), the United States, Malaysia, Israel, Russia, most former Eastern European countries, as well as the most well-known case of economic crisis due to cronyism, Greece. Wu Jinglian, one of China's leading economists and a long-time champion of its transition to free markets, says that it faces two starkly contrasting futures: a market economy under the rule of law and crony capitalism.

A Case Study of the United States

A 1824 landmark U.S. Supreme Court ruling overturned a New York State-granted monopoly ('a veritable model of state munificence') facilitated by one of the Founding Fathers, Robert R. Livingston for the then-revolutionary technology of steamboats. Leveraging the Supreme Court's establishment of Congressional supremacy over commerce, the Interstate Commerce Commission was established in 1887 with the intent of regulating railroad 'robber barons'. President Groves Cleveland appointed Thomas M. Coolev, a railroad ally, as its first chairman and a permit system was used to deny access to new entrants and legalise price fixing.

The military-industrial complex in the United States is often described as an example of crony capitalism in an industry.

Connections with the Pentagon and lobbyists in Washington are described by critics as more important than actual competition, due to the political and secretive nature of defence contracts. In the Airbus Boeing WTO dispute, Airbus (which receives outright subsidies from European governments) has stated Boeing receives similar subsidies, which are hidden as inefficient defence contracts. Several companies received expedited no-bid contracts for Hurricane Katrina and Iraq war and Afghanistan reconstruction purportedly due to having cronies in the Bush administration.

Gerald P. O'Driscoll, former vice president at the Federal Reserve Bank of Dallas, stated that Fannie Mae and Freddie Mac became examples of crony capitalism. Government backing let Fannie and Freddie dominate mortgage underwriting. 'The politicians created the mortgage giants, which then returned some of the profits to the pols — sometimes directly, as campaign funds; sometimes as "contributions" to favored constituents'.

Raymond Vernon, specialist in economics and international affairs, wrote that the Industrial Revolution began in England, because they were the first to successfully limit the power of veto groups (typically cronies of those with power in government) to block innovations. Unlike most other national environments, the British environment of the early nineteenth century contained relatively few threats to those who improved and applied existing inventions, whether from business competitors, labour, or the government itself. In other European countries, by contrast, the merchant guilds ... were a pervasive source of veto for many centuries. This power was typically bestowed upon them by government. For example, a Russian inventor produced a steam engine in 1766 and disappeared without a trace. Steam powered horseless carriage produced in France in 1769 was officially suppressed. James Watt began experimenting with steam in 1763, got a patent in 1769 and began commercial production in 1775.

Anthropologist David Graeber's book *Debt: The First 5000 Years* provides an even broader perspective: For as far back as we can see in the historical and archaeological record, argues Graeber, people with wealth and power, typically a monarch and cronies, have written the rules to benefit them at the expense of others.

The situation would deteriorate for common folk until it was interrupted by a peasant revolt. Then the cycle would start over again.

America's economy is awful. Unemployment is high, young people cannot find decent work, and according to a Wells Fargo survey 37% of middle-income Americans expect to work until they die. It is not a wonderful life — unless, you happen to have some friends in state government.

In a new report, Good Jobs First details the growing use of 'public–private partnerships' (PPPs) to promote economic development and the conflicts of interests they carry. Unlike traditional economic development which is run from a department of government (e.g., Commerce), PPPs allow private interests to borrow public authority to promote an economic agenda. Not surprisingly, that agenda often benefits the private interests that propose it. What was supposed to be a programme for economic development quickly devolved into the basest form of government corruption and crony capitalism?

Three years ago, newly elected governors in several states, most notably Wisconsin and Ohio, decided that the best way to create jobs was to transfer economic development of business-recruitment functions to 'public–private partnerships'. These experiments in privatisation have, by and large, become costly failures. Privatised development corporations have issued grossly exaggerated job-creation claims. They have created 'pay to play' appearances of insider dealing and conflicts of interest. They have paid executives larger salaries than governors. They have resisted basic oversight.

We document here again numerous cases in which the PPPs have become embroiled in scandals involving misuse of taxpayer funds, conflicts of interest, excessive executive pay and bonuses, questionable subsidy awards, exaggerated job-creation claims, lack of public disclosure of key records and other accountability abuses.

First we identify Governor Scott Walker of Wisconsin, Governor Jan Brewer of Arizona and Governor John Kasich of Ohio as the chief culprits. This may result from hostility among those Republican Governors to unions and civil servants which

PPPs bypass. Instead PPPs offer an opportunity for governors to pay their friends well above standard government rates for public service.

Consider Don Cardon, hired by Arizona governor Jan Brewer in 2011 to run the Arizona Commerce Authority with at least US $25 million of taxpayer and private funds to give away. Cardon's salary was US$300,000, triple of what the finger-wagging governor makes. He also got a US$50,000 signing bonus, a grand a month car allowance and the prospect of a US$75,000 performance bonus if he was really good at giving away money to companies. That was more than enough to put him well into the top half of 1% of all workers that year. But Cardon quit and thus had to give back part of his signing bonus. The theory behind PPPs is that by working so closely with the private sector the government will create jobs. Unfortunately, after all the goodies were handed out to businesses and their friends on the PPPs, no jobs were to be found. From Iowa to Florida to Ohio, none of the PPPs have proved themselves. After spending millions upon millions of taxpayer money, it seems the only jobs created were for those that ran the PPPs at public expense.

Crony Capitalism Index

The Economist benchmarks countries based on a calculated Crony Capitalism Index. Its 2014 Crony Capitalism Index ranked Hong Kong, Russia and Malaysia in the top three spots.

The FORBES Global 2000 is a comprehensive list of the world's largest, most powerful public companies, as measured by revenues, profits, assets and market value. In 2014, the Global 2000 companies hailed from 62 countries, up from 46 in our inaugural 2003 ranking. In total, they raked in revenues of US$38 trillion and profits of US$3 trillion, with assets worth US$161 trillion and a market value of US$44 trillion. All those totals are higher than a year ago, with the largest growth being in market value (up 13% year-over-year). These firms employ 90 million people worldwide.

For the first time, China is home to the world's three biggest public companies and five of the top 10. State-controlled Chinese bank ICBC holds onto its No. 1 spot for a second consecutive year, while China Construction Bank takes second place and Agricultural Bank of China moves up five spots to third. They're joined in the top 10 by the other member of the 'Big Four' Chinese banks, Bank of China, at No. 9.

As China gains ground, its best frenemy — the United States — accounts for the other half of the top 10 spots. Berkshire Hathaway and Wells Fargo WFC –0.51% both move up four spots to No. 5 and No. 9, respectively. J.P. Morgan slides to fourth place as its total composite score slipped behind Agricultural Bank of China. Say goodbye to the two Europe-based companies in top 10 last year, Royal Dutch Shell (No. 11) and HSBC Holdings (No. 14).

The list presents an annual snapshot of the ever-changing global business landscape. The United States holds onto its crown as the country with the most Global 2000 companies: 564. Japan trails the United States with 225 companies in aggregate, despite losing the most members (26) this year. China (mainland and Hong Kong) adds 25 to the list this year, more than any other country, for a total of 207. Two countries debut on the list this year: Mauritius and Togo.

North America (564 members) and Europe (506 members) are behind. That's a stark contrast from 11 years ago when North America dominated the list with over 50% more than Asia's total number. Emerging markets, especially Middle East and Central and South America, also gained significant shares in the past decade with 265% and 76% growth, respectively. While Africa still has the least Global 2000 members, the continent has made slow progress, adding five companies to the list. Four of the African newcomers are based in Nigeria, giving it a total of five.

Take a peek at the top of each metric, and you will find the best of the biggest. Apple AAPL — –0.42% which stays at No. 15 — is again the world's most valuable company. Wal Mart Stores WMT +0.65% remain the world's sales leader, despite a steep drop in profit. Six years after being bailed out in the financial crisis, mortgage giants Fannie Mae and Freddie Mac finally bring some good news to their investors. Fannie Mae not only consolidates its top spot in terms of total assets, but also has become the most profitable company. With a record US$84 billion in profit, its accumulated payments to the federal government have now exceeded the amount it received during the 2008 bailout. Its competitor, Freddie Mac, also shines as the second most profitable company thanks to a 345% jump in profit (US$49 billion).

There are 179 newcomers to this year's Global 2000. Many household names make their debut thanks to the steadily rising equity market, the return of corporate deals and a new wave of IPOs. With a 561% year-over-year surge of market value, investors' darling Tesla Motor is defying sceptics of its US$5 billion Gigafactory investment. Japanese beverage giant Suntory (No. 1083) stunned the world by buying Jim Beam BEAM +0.02% for US$13.6 billion in cash, creating the largest food and beverage company on this year's Global 2000. Quite a few notable newcomers have joined the list thanks to their successful IPOs, such as Hilton Worldwide (No. 700), Twitter (No. 1645) and Australia's Nine Entertainment (No. 1749).

14 Chinese Companies Going Global in 2014

Over the course of 2013, an American pork producer, a British luxury boat manufacturer and a Canadian oil and gas firm all found new owners from China. These are only the most recent examples of major cross-border mergers and acquisitions — one important path Chinese firms are taking to expand into international markets. Building on last year's ranking of the top 13 companies going global, this year's list demonstrates how Chinese overseas investment continues to diversify across industries and increase dramatically in magnitude. According to China's Ministry of Commerce, Chinese overseas investment totalled US$61.6 billion by the end of September 2013 — a 17.4% year-on-year increase. Chinese overseas investment is set to continue to grow at double-digit rates in 2014.

1. Lenovo maintains its No. 1 spot for the second year in a row on this list. Its previous acquisitions of IBM +0.62% PC line, Germany's Medion and Brazil's CCE helped bolster its growing international portfolio. 2014 will likely see Lenovo push beyond PCs and move aggressively into the mobile space, as it was rumoured to acquire Canada's Blackberry in late 2013.
2. Dalian Wanda (Entertainment and Commercial Real Estate). After 2012's record-breaking US$2.6 billion acquisition of AMC Entertainment, Dalian Wanda continued its international expansion. In June 2013, the firm purchased a controlling stake in U.K.-based yacht maker Sunseeker International. In December 2013, Wanda took AMC public on the New York Stock Exchange. Led by China's wealthiest man, Wang Jianlin, the firm will certainly be one to watch in 2014.
3. Huawei (Telecommunications). Huawei continues to have one of the largest global business operating footprints among Chinese firms. In April 2013, a series of reports suggested that Huawei was 'giving up' on the U.S. market after years of regulatory obstacles. However, deeper analysis reveals that such claims were likely taken out of context. Even excluding the United States, Huawei did exceptionally well overseas with approximately two-thirds of its revenues originating outside of China.
4. CNOOC (Oil and Gas). After first making headlines in 2005 with its failed $18.5 bid for Unocal Corporation in the United States, in 2013 CNOOC finally closed on its largest North American deal to date. The Chinese oil and gas firm acquired Canada's Nexen for an astounding $15.1 billion.
5. Shuanghui International (Consumer Goods). A new addition to the list of Chinese companies going global is Shuanghui International, a Henan-based producer of pork products. In 2013, the firm made its highest profile acquisition yet with its $4.7 billion acquisition of Virginia-based

Smithfield Foods. A few months later, Shuanghui was already bidding on a second acquisition for Spanish meat processor Compofrio.

6. Fosun Group (Conglomerate). *Key Highlights*: Pharmaceutical division purchased Israeli medical device producer Alma Lasers Ltd for $240 million. Purchased One Chase Manhattan Plaza in New York for $725 million.
7. Alibaba (Internet). Made headlines about its pending overseas IPO. Continued international expansion was driven by new channels such as AliExpress in addition to its core B2B platform Alibaba.com.
8. Bright Food (Consumer Goods). After its successful acquisition of U.K. breakfast cereal brand Weetabix in 2012, the firm was reported to be considering an acquisition of Israel's Tnuva Food Industries Ltd.
9. ZTE (Telecommunications). Often grouped with its much larger competitor Huawei, ZTE has recently restructured its organisation into three business segments: focusing on operators, mobile devices and enterprises. The new structure aims to develop both its traditional business lines and its emerging smartphone business overseas.
10. Sany (Diversified Industrial). In 2012, Sany acquired German industrial firms Putzmeister and Intermix. Sany, along with its Chinese competitors, continues to look overseas for growth as domestic competitors proliferate and the infrastructure market in China cools.
11. Tencent (Internet). Success spreading its popular WeChat messaging application internationally. Investing in American mobile app Snapchat and was rumoured to be seeking a future acquisition of the firm.
12. Geely (Automotive). After its purchase of Volvo cars in 2010, Geely made headlines again in 2013 when it acquired Manganese Bronze, maker of London 'black cabs' for more than 60 years.

13. Baidu (Internet). Predominantly a China-focused Internet company, Baidu is increasingly looking to markets such as Brazil, Thailand and Egypt for international growth.

14. Li-Ning (Consumer Goods). Li-Ning entered 2013 with high hopes for its international business, particularly focused on North America. But its subsidiary, Digital Li-Ning, saw key executives leave within the first year, and its American website has scaled back dramatically to focus exclusively on its flagship endorsement deal with NBA star Dwayne Wade.

Creation of Crony Capitalism in Developing Economies

In its worst form, crony capitalism can devolve into simple corruption, where any pretence of a free market is dispensed with. Bribes to government officials are considered *de rigueur* and tax evasion is common; this is seen in many parts of Africa, for instance. This is sometimes called plutocracy (rule by wealth) or kleptocracy (rule by theft).

Corrupt governments may favour one set of business owners who have close ties to the government over others. This may also be done with racial, religious or ethnic favouritism; for instance, Alawites in Syria have a disproportionate share of power in the government and business there. President Assad is an Alawite. This can be explained by considering personal relationships as a social network. As government and business leaders try to accomplish various things, they naturally turn to other powerful people for support in their endeavours. These people form hubs in the network. In a developing country those hubs may be very few, thus concentrating economic and political power in a small interlocking group.

Normally, this will be untenable to maintain in business; new entrants will affect the market. However, if business and government are entwined, then the government can maintain the small-hub network.

Development with Greater Inequality and Poverty

Americans, even many of those in full-time employment, are increasingly mired in poverty, while the top 5% of the population amass even more obscene wealth. There are now 46.5 million Americans classed as poor out of a total population of 311 million. The Economic Policy Institute noted last year that 'income and poverty trends paint a bleak picture' with the median wage of American workers having slumped by nearly 12% between the years 2000 and 2012. Workers in fast food restaurants are a case in point. It is reckoned that half of all employees in this sector are subsisting below the official poverty line, as a result of pittance wages.

The same can be said for other Western countries. Britain, for example, was recently reported as the world's primary residence for billionaires, with London boasting more super wealthy individuals (300 or so) than any other international city. Yet, like the United States, British figures for poverty are at record levels. Soup kitchens and food banks can hardly cope with the increasing needs in the same capital that has the world's largest number of residing billionaires.

Back in the United States, there are reportedly some 600,000 homeless people — at a time when the construction industry is stagnant and whole city areas lie vacant because no one can afford to buy or rent the properties. Amnesty International has calculated that the number of vacant homes in the United States is five times the number of homeless people. How is that there is a mammoth failure in supply and demand capitalism?

Of the U.S. homeless numbers, some 60,000 — 10% — of all those living on the streets are reported to be military veterans. Having fought America's wars of aggression in Afghanistan, Iraq and elsewhere, many of these veterans return to a civilian life of unemployment, family estrangement, mental breakdown and drug abuse, without a roof over their heads.

Oxfam International, a poverty fighting organisation, said at the World Economic Forum in Davos earlier this year in its report that the world's 85 richest people own assets as the same value as those owned by the poorer half of the world's population, or 3.5 billion people. In other words, the world's 1% people have 40% of the world's wealth. Both groups have US$1.7 trillion. That is US $20 billion on average if you are in the first group and US$486 if you are in the second group.

Oxfam's calculations of the richest individuals are based on the 2013 Forbes Billionaires list. They are by now a much wealthier group. The rich got richer. And it was quite fast and dramatic. For example, while last year it took US$23 billion to be in the top 20 of the world's billionaires, this year it took US$31 billion, according to Luisa Kroll, Forbes wealth editor, writing on Forbes.com. As a result, by the time Forbes published its 2014 Billionaires List in early March, it took only 67 of the richest peoples' wealth to match the poorer half of the world. This has recently been skewing strongly toward recognition of the importance of income distribution and its inequality, most recently with the publication of *Capital in the Twenty-First Century* by Thomas Piketty.

Each of the 67 is on average worth the same as 52 million people from the bottom of the world's wealth pyramid. Bill Gates, the world's richest man, with a net worth of $76 billion, is worth the same as 156 million people from the bottom. Who are the 67? The biggest group — 28 billionaires, or 42% of them — is from the United States. No other country comes close. Germany and Russia have the second-highest number, with six each. The rest are sprinkled among 13 countries in Western Europe, APAC and the Americas. That the biggest group of the super-rich comes from the United States should not be a surprise, as the country holds almost a third of the world's wealth (30%), significantly more than any other country, according to the Global Wealth Data book, from Credit Suisse Research Institute. However, Europe, with a slightly bigger chunk of the world's wealth (32%), produced substantially fewer of the richest. That is due to less dynamic economies, which do not equal the United States in how they foster innovation, on which many of the newest United States fortunes are based.

When comparing the ratio of the richest to the percentage of the world's wealth held by each country, it is Russia that comes out the most lopsided, with its holdings skewed to the super-rich. As a country, Russia holds only half a percent of the world's wealth, and yet it has 9% of the 67 richest.

In India, only 0.1% corporates are 90% of share/stock-holder. These 0.1% corporates are benefited from tax concessions at least Rs. 21 trillion during the last five years, now their income levels has increased from 6% of total India GDP in 1999–2000 to 21% in 2013–2014.

5 Overproduction and Underconsumption

The capitalist system produced an ever-expanding flow of goods and services, which an impoverished proletarianised population could not afford to buy. The difficulties of capitalism, especially in crisis conditions, is that there is a lack of demand in the economy. Capitalism has an inbuilt tendency to produce far more than can be absorbed by consumption. This 'under-consumption' theory was developed by John Maynard Keynes, who believed that the problem of the lack of 'effective' demand could be resolved by the intervention of the state through deficit financing. Theories of 'under-consumption' are often confused with Marx's ideas. But these are not the same as Marx explained long ago. While under-consumption certainly exists for the masses, as any worker can testify, it is not the direct cause of capitalist crisis.

Survey of Literature

The idea of 'under-consumption' as the cause of crisis pre-dates Keynes and even pre-dates Marx which can be found in the writings of the great utopian socialists, such as Robert Owen. However, the best known proponents of these views were Jean Charles Sismondi (1773–1842), Thomas Malthus (1766–1834) and

Johann Karl Rodbertus (1805–1875). The most consistent and developed version of the theory, as well as the least vulgarised, was put forward by Jean Charles Sismondi. As Engels pointed out: 'The "under-consumption" explanation of crises originated with Sismondi, and in his exposition it still had a certain meaning'.[1] This 'certain meaning' was also recognised by Marx, as can be seen from his writings on the subject.

Sismondi's chief work, *New Principles of Political Economy*, was published in 1819. In this book he maintained that general crises were due to excess capacity, which in turn was due to the separation of the exchange values of commodities from the needs and wants of society. According to Sismondi overproduction of commodities did not arise from the general over-fulfilment of human needs but from the maldistribution of income and the poverty of the masses, resulting in insufficient demand in the society. In short, the working class did not receive enough in wages to buy back the goods that they produced, which is always the case under capitalism.

Say's Law

Although one-sided, Sismondi was not entirely wrong in this supposition. Indeed, he made a whole number of correct observations, which also were accepted by Marx. It was Sismondi, for instance, who pointed out the error of Jean Baptiste Say (supported by James Mill and David Ricardo) that every seller meets a corresponding buyer ('Say's Law') and they therefore regarded generalised overproduction as impossible. According to them, the economy would always arrive at equilibrium, which was clearly not the case. This vulgar 'theory' of equilibrium is the real origin of the 'efficient market hypothesis', which stated that the economy left unaided would reach an optimum state. This was the Credo of modern political economy — until its falsity was exposed by the greatest collapse of capitalism today.

1. Lawrence and Wishart (1977).

Unlike the vulgar bourgeois economists who dismissed crises, such as J.B. Say, Sismondi understood that crisis was inherent in the process of commodity production. However, his understanding of the real nature of capitalist crisis, while more advanced, was limited and rather one-sided. The real nature and central contradictions of capitalism, while clearly present, nevertheless eluded him. Despite his shortcomings, Marx paid tribute to him and regarded him as an original thinker who, out of the classical economists, was striving towards an understanding of capitalism and its tendency to crisis. In this regard, he was head and shoulders above David Ricardo, the outstanding representative of bourgeois classical political economy.

Sismondi is profoundly conscious of the contradictions in capitalist production, Marx wrote, '*he is aware that, on the one hand, its forms — its production relations — stimulate unrestrained development of the productive forces and of wealth; and that, on the other hand, these relations are conditional, that their contradictions of use-value and exchange-value, commodity and money, purchase and sale, production and consumption, capital and wage-labour, etc., assume ever greater dimensions as productive power develops.*'[2]

Marx continues: '*He is particularly aware of the fundamental contradiction: on the one hand, unrestricted development of the productive forces and increase of wealth which, at the same time, consists of commodities and must be turned into cash; on the other hand, the system is based on the fact that the mass of producers is restricted to the necessities. Hence, according to Sismondi, crises are not accidental, as Ricardo maintains, but essential outbreaks — occurring on a large scale and at definite periods — of the immanent contradictions.*'[3]

While recognising the great contribution of Sismondi, Marx was still well aware of his shortcomings and limitations, as with all the classical economists:

> He [Sismondi] forcefully criticizes the contradictions of bourgeois production but does not understand them,

2. *Ibid.*
3. *Capital*, Vol. 2, p. 209, Penguin.

and consequently does not understand the process whereby they can be resolved. However, at the bottom of his argument is indeed the inkling that new forms of the appropriation of wealth must correspond to productive forces and the material and social conditions for the production of wealth which have developed within capitalist society; that the bourgeois forms are only transitory forms, in which wealth attains only an antithetical existence and appears everywhere simultaneously as its opposite.[4]

Malthus' Theory

Thomas Malthus added nothing new to what Sismondi had already written. Malthus, the arch-vulgariser and reactionary apologist attempted to crudely use these arguments to justify the interests of 'the aristocracy, Church, tax-eaters, toadies, etc.' Marx accused Malthus of plagiarising the weak side of Adam Smith and caricaturing Sismondi.

Marx developed his own ideas on capitalist crisis on the basis of a very thorough study and criticism of all the classical economists, especially its chief representatives, among others, Adam Smith and David Ricardo. While Marx did not manage to write a specific book on capitalist crisis, his theory of crisis is present throughout his economic writings, especially *Capital and Theories of Surplus Value.*[5]

Rate of Profit

Some people falsely attribute the tendency of the rate of profit to decline as the real cause of capitalist crisis, but this is not correct and Marx never recognised it as such. While it is without question an important tendency under capitalism, it operates as a long-term

4. *Capital*, Vol. 1, p. 407.

5. The Theory of Surplus-Value, Vol. 2, p. 541.

tendency that bears down upon the system. Marx expressed himself in very precise terms that countervailing factors transformed this law into a tendency, describing it uniquely as 'this double-edged law'. He went on to explain: 'The law operates therefore simply as a tendency, whose effect is decisive only under certain particular circumstances and over long periods'.[6]

There have been long periods where the rate of profit was falling. That was the case towards the end of the long period of capitalist upswing that followed the Second World War. But there were also long periods when the rate of profit was rising as in the last 30 years. We therefore have to look elsewhere for an explanation of crisis, which Marx reveals in his extensive writings on political economy.

In the Theories of Surplus Value, described by Engels as volume four of *Capital*, Marx gives a clear outline of the fundamental contradiction facing capitalism:

> The fact that bourgeois production is compelled by its own immanent laws, on the one hand, to develop the productive forces as if production did not take place on a narrow restricted social foundation, while, on the other hand, it can develop these forces only within these narrow limits, is the deepest and most hidden cause of crises, of the crying contradictions within which bourgeois production is carried on and which, even at a cursory glance, reveal it as only a transitional, historical form. This is grasped rather crudely but nonetheless correctly by Sismondi, for example, as a contradiction between production for the sake of production and distribution which makes absolute development of productivity impossible.[7]

Marx stated numerous times that the ultimate cause of capitalist crisis is overproduction. But this is not overproduction in relation

6. Grundrisse, pp. 748 and 754, Penguin.
7. *Ibid.*, p. 748.

to what people need or want. In a market economy overproduction refers only to what can be profitably sold. 'The English, for example, are forced to lend their capital to other countries in order to create a market for their commodities', explained Marx.

> Overproduction, the credit system, etc., are means by which capitalist production seeks to break through its own barriers and to produce over and above its own limits ... Hence crises arise, which simultaneously drive it onward and beyond [its own limits] and force it to put on seven-league boots, in order to reach a development of the productive forces which could only be achieved very slowly within its own limits.[8]

Marx reiterates this point again and again throughout his writings. 'Overproduction is specifically conditioned by the general law of the production of capital: to produce to the limit set by the productive forces, that is to say, to exploit the maximum amount of labour with the given amount of capital, without any consideration for the actual limits of the market or the needs backed by the ability to pay'.[9]

Reproduction Process

Again, in volume two of *Capital*, Marx explains,

> The volume of the mass of commodities brought into being by capitalist production is determined by the scale of this production and its needs for constant expansion, and not by a predestined ambit of supply and demand, of needs to be satisfied. Besides other industrial capitalists, mass production can have only wholesale

8. *Ibid.*, pp. 762–763.
9. *Capital*, Vol. 3, p. 319, Penguin.

> merchants as its immediate purchasers. Within certain bounds, the reproduction process may proceed on the same or on an expanded scale, even though the commodities ejected from it do not actually enter either individual or productive consumption. The consumption of commodities is not included in the circuit of the capital from which they emerge. As soon as the yarn is sold, for example, the circuit of the capital value represented in the yarn can begin anew, at first irrespective of what becomes of the yarn when sold. As long as the product is sold everything follows its regular course, as far as the capitalist producer is concerned. The circuit of the capital value that he represents is not interrupted.[10]

Marx then goes on to explain that this expansion allows the whole reproduction process to be completed. However, they pile up and lie unsold in the hands of retail traders and remain on the market. 'One stream of commodities', writes Marx, 'now follows another, and it finally emerges that the earlier stream had only seemed to be swallowed up by consumption. Commodity capitals now vie with each other for space on the market. The late-comers sell below the price in order to sell at all. The earlier streams have not yet been converted into ready money, while payment for them is falling due. Their owners must declare themselves bankrupt, or sell at any price in order to pay. This sale, however, has absolutely nothing to do with the real state of demand. It has only to do with the demand for payment, with the absolute necessity of transforming commodities into money. At this point the crisis breaks out. It first becomes evident not in the direct reduction of consumer demand, the demand for individual consumption, but rather in a decline in the number of exchanges of capital, in the reproduction process of capital.'[11]

The same point is again reiterated in volume three of *Capital*, where (once again) Marx emphasises the fundamental contradiction

10. *Ibid.*, p. 317.
11. *Ibid.*, p. 331.

of the capitalist mode of production: 'The ultimate reason for all real crises always remains the poverty and restricted consumption of the masses as opposed to the drive of capitalist production to develop the productive forces as though only the absolute consuming power of society constituted their limit'.

Theory of Overproduction

Some 'clever' people have tried to get round this clear explanation of crisis by claiming that this statement of Marx was an isolated phrase, a 'description', or 'simply a throw-away remark'. But, even the most cursory examination of his writings shows that this is not the case. Far from being an isolated and accidental remark, this explanation is, in fact, absolutely central to Marx's theory of crisis. This is a theory based not on 'under-consumption' theory, which is at best completely one-sided, but on the central contradiction of overproduction under capitalism. Marx and Engels had already alluded to this cause in *The Communist Manifesto*, where overproduction is described as an epidemic, 'that, in earlier epochs, would have seemed an absurdity — the epidemic of overproduction'.[12]

It was none other than the revisionist Eugene Dühring who borrowed and vulgarised the 'under-consumptionist' explanation of crisis, which he put forward in opposition to Marx's theory of overproduction. Engels pointed out: 'Rodbertus took it from Sismondi, and Herr Dühring has in turn copied it, in his usual vulgarizing fashion, from Rodbertus'.

It was left to Engels, assisted by Marx, to rebut the false ideas of professor Dühring, including the idea of 'under-consumption'. The reply was so comprehensive that the series of articles published in the German party press soon became a book entitled *Anti-Dühring*, which first appeared in 1878, and has become established as one of the fundamental classics of Marxist theory.

---

12. *Ibid.*, p. 331.

It is significant that when dealing with capitalist crisis, the explanation in *Anti-Dühring* contains not a single reference to the tendency of the rate of profit to fall. Yes, not one single solitary word — not even a 'throw-away remark' is to be found on the subject. Some academic 'Marxists' are extremely irritated by this silence. They are so irritated that have even tried to argue that Engels' views did not coincide with those of Marx, in other words, that Engels was not really a Marxist!

Typical in this respect are Professor M.C. Howard and Senior Lecturer in Economics, J.E. King, who informed us in their *History of Marxian Economics* that Engels 'interpreted Marx's ideas in his own distinctive manner' and 'came no closer than Marx to providing a coherent theory of economic crisis'. We are then told by these learned critics: 'Indeed, by neglecting the tendency of the rate of profit to decline he renounced a major strand in Marx's crisis theory, though he was followed in this by almost all Marxian economists before 1929'. They conclude that 'Controversy still rages as to whether his [Engels] own later thought constitutes a distinct "Engelsism" which, with its determinism and its application of natural scientific reasoning to the study of human history, is separate from and antagonistic towards Marx's own philosophy and methods of analysis ... It is conceivable that Engels took a conscious decision to suppress those of Marx's writings with whose humanist orientation he had (by the 1880s) very little sympathy.'[13]

These are unfounded trumped-up allegations, which have no bearing in truth but are peddled around the universities like so much cheap gossip. They are part of the academic world, which is divorced from Marxism but attempts to make its mark by manufacturing differences between Marx and Engels. They may have read all the right books, but their views are not of much use to Marxists or anybody else seeking a scientific explanation.

But can it really be true, as suggested, that Engels misunderstood or misrepresented Marx's views on economics — in this

13. *Ibid.*, p. 323.

case in his classic work *Anti-Dühring*? No, it is not true, and for a very good reason: Although this book was written by Engels, the completed drafts were read, and approved, by Marx, who also contributed a whole section to it. Which section did Marx write? While Engels concentrated on philosophy, history and science, it was Marx himself, as Engels admitted, who wrote a long section on economic theory in *Anti-Dühring*.

Since this book was written more than a decade after the drafts for *Capital* had been completed, and since Marx died some five years after its publication, the section on economics in *Anti-Dühring* can be taken as Marx's final thoughts on capitalist crisis. Certainly these are the last things he wrote on the subject.

Anti-Dühring

Let us see what Engels (and Marx) wrote in *Anti-Dühring*.

> We have seen that the ever increasing perfectibility of modern machinery is, by the anarchy of social production, turned into a compulsory law that forces the individual industrial capitalist always to improve his machinery, always to increase its productive force, explains the author. The bare possibility of extending the field of production is transformed for him into a similar compulsory law. The enormous expansive force of modern industry, compared with which that of gases is mere child's play, appears to us now as a necessity for expansion, both qualitative and quantitative, that laughs at all resistance.[14]

Having described the relentless growth of the productive forces under capitalism, driven by compulsory laws, the author then goes on to explain the fundamental contradiction that plagues the

14. Engels (1969).

capitalist system, namely, the continuous outpouring of commodities which eventually crash into the limits of the market.

'Such resistance is offered by consumption, by sales, by the markets for the products of modern industry', explains Engels. 'But the capacity for extension, extensive and intensive, of the markets is primarily governed by quite different laws that work much less energetically.'

Here Engels (and Marx) describes a gap opening up between production and consumption, which operate by different laws, some more vigorous than others. 'The extension of the markets cannot keep pace with the extension of production. The collision becomes inevitable ... Capitalist production has begotten another "vicious circle",' explains Engels.[15] He makes the same point in the November 1886 Preface to *Capital*: 'While the productive power increases in a geometric, the extension of markets proceeds at best in an arithmetical ratio.'

So, what is the character of crises under capitalism? Engels explains, 'the character of these crises is so clearly marked that Fourier hit [the nail on the head] when he described the first as crise plethorique, a crisis of super-abundance'.[16] In other words, they were crises of overproduction. This simply repeats what Marx had explained elsewhere. For instance, in volume one of *Capital*: 'The enormous power, inherent in the factory system, of expanding by jumps, and the dependence of that system on the markets of the world, necessarily beget feverish production, followed by over-filling of the markets, whereupon contraction of the markets brings on crippling of production. The life of modern industry becomes a series of periods of moderate activity, prosperity, over-production, crisis and stagnation.'[17]

In explaining the Marxist theory of crisis, Engels demolishes Eugene Dühring's attempt to explain crises by the 'underconsumption of the masses'. Engels draws the clear distinction

15. *Ibid.*, p. 339.
16. *Ibid.*, pp. 341–342.
17. *Ibid.*, pp. 344–345.

between 'under-consumption' (which has always existed in class society, as a result of the poverty of the masses) and the phenomenon of overproduction, which is applicable to capitalism alone.

A recent online article published by The *Economist* (June 2013) entitled 'The Mismatch', highlighting the continued rise in profits for big business, say, 'although the economy has been weak, American corporate profits are high relative to GDP.' It says that 'an increasing share of the wealth produced within the USA — the biggest and richest economy in the world — is falling into the hands of the capitalists in the shape of profits.' In another recent article, The *Economist* (10 August 2013) outlines a similar picture for the United Kingdom, stating:

> By some measures, the economy is moving from 'rescue to recovery'... Yet the wallets of many, particularly those on lower and middle incomes, bear little evidence of it. Inflation is relatively modest, but wages lag far behind. A recent government funded study found that 52 percent of Britons are struggling to keep up with the bills ...

The article says: 'The popular explanation is that the economic background has shifted firmly in favour of capital and away from labour.' In other words, the growing inequality that we have seen in society in the past few years is not the result of the current crisis, but is part of a long-term process of decades, in which the capitalist class has increased their profits at the expense of workers — both in the advanced capitalist countries and in emerging economies — who have faced increasing levels of exploitation.

An Inherent Contradiction

The same article goes further still, referencing Marx and pointing out that it is not the crisis that has caused this rising inequality between capital and labour, but the rising inequality that has caused the crisis:

> Karl Marx thought this would eventually cause capitalism's collapse — industry would become concentrated in a few hands with monopoly power and workers would be unable to afford to buy the goods they made.

We come to the crux of the issue with the capitalist system — an issue that the reformists consistently miss. The inequality we see today — with declining living standards for workers and youth alongside increasing corporate profits — is not simply the product of the crisis, but is the logic of capitalism itself. The gap between capital and labour is not a mere symptom of the crisis, but is also its cause — and the disease is the capitalist system itself.

Capitalism is a system with an unquenchable thirst for profits. Each capitalist must continually accumulate, invest and expand or face losing their share of the market. Yet in this chase for ever-increasing profits, competition forces each capitalist to invest in labour-saving machinery, attack workers and cut wage costs. And by all doing so at the same time, the capitalist class as a whole are cutting away at the wages of the working class as a whole — that is to say, cutting away at the very demand for the goods that capitalism produces; cutting away at the branch that they, the capitalists, are sitting on.

This process, as Marx explained, is not a crisis of under-consumption — that is, a crisis due to workers not consuming enough that can be easily resolved by taxing the rich and paying workers more, or by stimulating the economy through government investment, as the reformists and Keynesians idealistically imagine — but a crisis of overproduction: the result of an inherent contradiction arising from a system in which the means of production are privately owned and where production is only for profit. It is not that workers are merely paid too little; in a system where production is for profit, the working class — as a whole — will never be able to afford to buy back the commodities that they produce.

It is not simply that there is inequality — that is, a gap between capital and labour — that crises occur; this inequality is a necessary part of the capitalist system: the exploitation of the many is the prerequisite for the wealth of the few; the mere simultaneous existence of these opposites — of the capitalist and the worker — necessarily implies an inequality. And it is the logic of this system that each side will try to increase their share of the wealth — the capitalist to increase profits and widen this inequality; the worker to increase wages and reduce inequality — and this is precisely the meaning of class struggle: the struggle between the capitalist and the worker for the surplus produced in society. Thus, as the reformists continually fail to comprehend, to eliminate inequality is to eliminate the capitalist system itself.

The same article in The *Economist* then asks an important question:

> But one doesn't need to be a Marxist to perceive that the share of capital might be cyclical; surely high returns should be competed away? A high return on capital [i.e. high profits] should attract more entrepreneurs or should encourage existing business to invest more, bringing the return on capital back down. So why isn't that happening?

The article then goes on to present statistics demonstrating that corporate profits in the United States (as a share of GDP) are at an over 30 year high (of over 12%), whilst business investment (also as a share of GDP) is at a record low over the same period (at around 10%). Figures elsewhere demonstrate the same phenomena — that big businesses are not investing. For example, Gillian Tett in the *Financial Times* (17 January 2013) comments that:

> In recent years, commentators and politicians have often bewailed the fact that American companies are sitting on oodles of spare cash. Some studies calculate this to be about $2tn. Others put it even higher ... Either way,

> what is crystal clear is that this cash hoard has been rising …
>
> … Logic might suggest this is not an ideal development. After all, if companies are hanging on to cash, rather than investing it in machinery or hiring workers, that will not create growth.

Meanwhile, Tony Jackson, also writing in the *Financial Times* (11 March 2012), provides similar figures for European and British companies, who have cash hoards of €2 trillion and £750 billion, respectively. Jackson bluntly states that, 'It is a notorious truth that western companies are hoarding cash. They are not hiring or investing as they should.' Statistics for Canadian firms talk of a cash hoard of over US$500 billion, up by 43% since 2009. Apple — the giant multinational consumer electronics firm — alone is sitting on a cash pile of US$100 billion.

The UK GDP is approximately £1570 billion and its total accumulated government debt currently stands at around £1200 billion. Big businesses in the United Kingdom, therefore, are sitting on cash piles (of £750 billion) — idle money that could be spent straight away — equivalent to about half of everything the British economy produces each year; also equivalent to over 60% of the national government (public) debt. This £750 billion of idle cash in the banks of big business is greater than the annual UK public spending, which stands at around £700 billion per year.

Meanwhile, the US$2 trillion (US$2000 billion) worth of money that U.S. corporations are sitting on is double the value of the U.S. Federal budget deficit (i.e., the shortfall between government spending and government income from taxes), which currently stands at around US$1 trillion. This US$2 trillion in the pockets of U.S. big business is also equivalent to about 12% of U.S. Federal debt (around US$17 trillion), whilst the €2 trillion in the hands of European corporations is equivalent to around 18% of total eurozone debt (which stands at around €11.1).

Just imagine what a tremendous boost to the economy it would mean to invest all this idle money! The UK economy could be given a one-off annual boost of almost 50%, with annual public spending — on education, health care, transport, etc. — more than doubling. So why are not businesses across the world investing? Why sit on piles of cash when profit rates are high and there is money to be made? The *Economist* tries to answer their own question:

> In other words, the lack of investment on a world scale is due to the enormous existing excess capacity — i.e. overproduction — in the system. Why would any capitalist invest more — in new production; in jobs, machinery, factories, infrastructure, etc. — when businesses cannot sell what they already produce?

Use-Values

Pre-capitalist societies were natural economies, mainly based on the production of use-values. The phenomenon of overproduction was unknown in these societies, which suffered from the opposite problem, namely the problem of underconsumption arising from the scarcity of use-values, as a result of the low level of the productive forces and the natural disasters (drought, plague, pestilence, etc.) as well as war, to which these societies were prone.

Overproduction, then, is peculiar to capitalism, and exists in no other society. It arises from the anarchic laws of the market economy and commodity production. Under capitalism, the productive forces have been revolutionised to such an extent that they could, if production was rationally planned and organised, completely satisfy the basic needs of society. They have completely outgrown the capitalist system and private ownership.

On the basis of a rational plan of production, the productivity of labour, and with it the living standards of the overwhelming majority, could be vastly increased in a relatively short space of time. The problem is that under capitalism production is not rationally planned, but geared to the maximisation of profit and dominated by blind market forces. Here we are faced with the contradiction between social production and individual appropriation, where the capitalists appropriate the wealth produced by the social labour of the working class.

Overproduction arises under capitalism because the unlimited drive to expand production periodically comes into collision with the limited confines of the market economy. Plenty of people want and need things, but do not have the money to buy them. They lack 'effective demand', according to the bourgeois economists. This strange phenomenon of overproduction, where excess commodities, goods produced for sale, cannot be sold, arises ultimately from the fact that the working class cannot buy back the full value of what it produces. Profit is the unpaid labour of the working class. This state of affairs is irrational from any sane point of view, but arises out of the anarchy of the market economy and the class structure of capitalist society.

'Under-consumption' also exists under capitalism, as any working-class person will testify. Surplus value cannot come from machines or buildings, which simply transfer their own value to the commodities. Only human labour is able to produce new value. The working class receives in wages less value than they produce. This unpaid labour is the source of surplus value, and is appropriated by the capitalist. The workers can never buy back what they produce as they only receive enough to maintain themselves and their families. As Marx explained, the problem is not to explain why there is crisis, but why, as a result, there is no permanent crisis under capitalism, starting from day one.

However, the capitalist system gets around this problem of insufficient 'demand' with the division of the economy into two main sectors: department one, which produces consumer goods, and department two, which produces capital goods (means of production).

'One section of capitalists produce goods which are directly consumed by the workers', explained Marx, 'another section produce either goods which are only indirectly consumed by them, insofar, for example, as they are part of the capital required for the production of necessities, as raw materials, machinery, etc., or commodities which are not consumed by the workers at all, entering only into the revenue of the non-workers.'[18]

As long as the capitalist class, which appropriates the surplus value, takes the surplus and reinvests it in more new machinery, buildings and general infrastructure, the system can develop, but only at the cost of preparing the way for a new crisis of overproduction. In other words, the capitalist system creates its own market through the interaction between the two departments of production and temporarily overcomes this inherent contradiction. The only problem is that this increased capacity produces even more consumer goods, which eventually cannot be sold, and we have a new crisis. However, the slaughter of the values of capital arising from the slump lays the basis for a new period of boom, but, in turn, reproduces the contradictions on a higher level. This takes the form under capitalism of a boom and slump cycle.

Unlimited Expansion

The lack of purchasing power of the working class is therefore only one side of the equation. More significant is the capitalist's continual drive for unlimited expansion by ploughing back the surplus extracted from the unpaid labour of the working class. This dialectical contradiction lies at the heart of the capitalist system. This uncontrolled drive to accumulate and produce will sooner or later hit the limits of consumption. Here we have a system of production for production's sake, and accumulation for accumulation's sake, as Marx explained. To sell this flood of commodities, the capitalist is forced to reduce his prices below the price of production, resulting in losses, falling profits, and likely bankruptcy. This drives out the weaker capitalists and prepares the ground for a new boom, based upon a higher rate of profit.

'The under-consumption of the masses, the restriction of the consumption of the masses to what is necessary for their maintenance and reproduction, is not a new phenomenon', explains

18. *Capital*, Vol. 1, p. 347.

Engels. 'It has existed as long as there have been exploiting and exploited classes'. The crisis of overproduction is however a new phenomenon, which has arisen only under the capitalist mode of production. 'Therefore, while under-consumption has been a constant feature for thousands of years', continues Engels, it nevertheless 'tells us just as little why crises exist today as why they did not exist before'.[19]

He then goes on to explain the reason in the capitalist form of production, characterised by 'the general shrinkage of markets which breaks out in crises as the result of a surplus of production [which] is a phenomenon only of the last fifty years'.

The Marxist theory of crisis is based upon a dialectical contradiction: the unlimited drive to produce, which is unique to the capitalist mode of production, combined with the limited consumption of the masses arising from their social position. As a consequence, capitalism is like a man sawing away the branch on which he is sitting. It creates and destroys the market at the same time, by squeezing more and more surplus value out of the working class, while attempting to hold down wages to the bare minimum. 'The part falling to the share of the working class (reckoned per head)', explains Engels, 'either increases only slowly and inconsiderably or not at all, and under certain circumstances may even fall.'[20] This in turn becomes a barrier to the expansion of the market and therefore the realisation of surplus value, as we are witnessing in this present period of prolonged austerity.

Push Down Wages

The capitalists as a whole naturally want to see an expanding market. Each individual capitalist would be delighted to see all competitors increase the wages of their workers to boost demand. Yet when it comes to their own workers, they are determined to keep down wages in order to reduce costs and increase profits. So the

19. *Capital*, Vol. 3, p. 346.
20. The Economics of Global Turbulence (1998).

capitalists, driven by competition, all end up attempting to push down wages and therefore demand. 'The product governs the producers', explains Engels. They are all caught up in this contradiction of capitalism.

In a kick against Dühring, Engels remarks: 'It requires a strong dose of deep-rooted effrontery to explain the present complete stagnation in the yarn and cloth markets by the under-consumption of the English masses and not by the overproduction carried on by the English cotton mill owners'.

Such a view, it should be noted, has nothing in common with the positions of various schools of bourgeois economists known as 'under-consumptionists', most notably the Keynesians.

Marx himself had criticised the concept of 'under-consumption' as the cause of crisis in volume two of *Capital*, written some 10 years before *Anti-Dühring*. Consumption alone (or rather the lack of it) is not the fundamental cause, he explained. If this were the case, the problem could be solved by increasing the purchasing power of the masses. This is precisely the false argument of the Keynesians. Marx answers this as follows:

> It is a sheer tautology to say that crises are caused by the scarcity of effective consumption, or effective consumers. The capitalist system does not know [of] any other modes of consumption than effective ones. Those commodities are unsaleable means only that no effective purchasers have been found for them, i.e., consumers (since commodities are bought in the final analysis for productive or individual consumption).[21]

He continues:

> But if one were to attempt to give this tautology the semblance of a profounder justification by saying that the working class receives too small a portion of its own

21. *Ibid.*, p. 95.

> product and the evil would be remedied as soon as it receives a larger share of it and its wages increase in consequence, one could only remark that crises are always prepared by precisely a period in which wages rise generally and the working class actually gets a larger share of that part of the annual product which is intended for consumption. From the point of view of these advocates of sound and 'simple' (!) common sense, such a period should rather remove the crisis.

In other words, wages tend to rise at the peak of a boom, where labour tends to be in short supply, shortly before a slump in the economy. Therefore, lack of demand cannot be considered the real cause of the crisis of overproduction.

It is precisely the Keynesians who believe that crises are caused by a lack of 'effective demand' ('under-consumption') and that wages or state spending should be raised in order to fix the problem. Left reformists frequently put this Keynesian argument forward as a solution to the present crisis. While we are certainly in favour of increasing wages, the idea that this will solve the crisis of capitalism is completely wrong. In fact, increased wages will simply eat into profits and push the capitalists to cut back on investment and production, thereby cancelling out the effects of this measure. It is impossible to create demand from thin air. The laws of capitalism are determined by a system of commodity production, including labour power. To call for the state to 'create' demand is also utopian. The attempt to use the printing press to 'create' money, not backed by extra production, will only serve to fuel inflation and reduce workers' income. The only other way for the state to increase spending is to take a further slice of the surplus value through taxation. Again, this will either mean cutting into profits, which will stop the capitalists investing, or taxing the working class, which will cut consumption, thereby reducing demand. If they borrow (deficit financing), they will have to pay it back with interest. At the end of the day, such solutions simply intensify the problems of capitalism, not solve them.

'The whole mechanism of the capitalist mode of production breaks down under the pressure of the productive forces, its own creations,' states Engels. 'It is no longer able to turn all this mass of means of production into capital. They lie fallow, and for that very reason the industrial reserve army must also lie fallow. Means of production means of subsistence, available labourers, all the elements of production and of general wealth, are present in abundance. But "abundance becomes the source of distress and want" (Fourier), because it is the very thing that prevents the transformation of the means of production and subsistence into capital.'[22]

Towards the end of his life, Engels once again returned to the fundamental contradictions of capitalism in his 1891 introduction to Marx's Wage Labour and *Capital*. It could have been written to describe the situation in the world today. We therefore leave him the last word on the subject of crisis:

> This productivity of human labour which rises day by day to an extent previously unheard of, finally gives rise to a conflict in which the present-day capitalist economy must perish. On the one hand are immeasurable riches and a superfluity [super-abundance] of products which the purchasers cannot cope with; on the other hand, the great mass of society proletarianised, turned into wage-workers, and precisely for that reason made incapable of appropriating for themselves this superfluity [super-abundance] of products. The division of society into a small, excessively rich class and a large, propertyless class of wage-workers results in a society suffocating from its own superfluity [super-abundance], while the great majority of its members is scarcely, or even not at all, protected from extreme want. This state of affairs becomes daily more absurd and — more unnecessary. It must be abolished, it can be abolished.[23]

22. *Ibid.*, p. 246.
23. *Ibid.*, p. 252.

Marx, Keynes, Hayek and the Crisis of Capitalism

In this third part of the chapter on Keynes, Hayek and Marx, the author deals with the shortcomings of Hayek's economic analysis and shows the utopian character of modern Keynesianism. Only socialism can provide a positive way out of the present crisis.

Hayek on Credit and the Crisis

Keynes saw the problem as one of effective demand during the crisis, Hayek saw the problem as one of loose monetary policy in the period before the crisis. In particular, Hayek argued that it was government interference in the money supply — for example, through setting low interest rates, printing too much money and encouraging the expansion of credit — that created bubbles and distorted the market, leading to crisis when the bubbles burst and the boom were seen to be largely based on fictitious capital.

Like Keynes, Hayek only sees one side of the problem — that is, that of supply, as opposed to Keynes and the problem of demand. And also like Keynes, Hayek does not follow through his analysis to its logical conclusion and ask the obvious question: what would happen if governments had not intervened by setting low interest rates and encouraging the expansion of credit? First, however, one must ask the even simpler question of: what is credit?

Marx explains the role of credit under capitalism in *Capital*, explaining that credit serves a dual function. On the one hand, relatively short-term credit is required to overcome bottlenecks in production and maintain the flow and circulation of capital. For example, businesses need to borrow money to pay for wages and raw materials whilst they wait for previous produced good to reach the market and be sold. Alternatively, credit may be used to allow firms to expand production when they don't have the upfront capital to pay for it.

On the other hand, credit also plays the role of artificially expanding the market — that is, effective demand — and thus helping to delay a crisis. As explained earlier, under capitalism, the working class can never buy back the full value of the commodities it creates, due to the fundamental nature of capitalism as production for profit. As was also explained earlier, capitalism traditionally overcomes this contradiction of overproduction by reinvesting the surplus value created into new means of production in the search for greater profits. This, however, only serves to create even greater productive forces, and thus an even greater mass of commodities that must find a market, and thus — rather than resolving the contradiction — only exacerbates overproduction.

Credit — formed by the concentrated savings and deposits of individuals and firms in the banks — is used to artificially increase the consumptive capacity of the masses, and thus to temporarily overcome overproduction, allowing the productive forces to continue expanding. As we have explained elsewhere, the expansion of credit over the past 20 years — and particularly since the turn of the century — created the largest credit bubble in history and was the primary factor in delaying the onset of crisis.

This expansion of credit was required to overcome the growing proportion of wealth going to capital rather than labour, which became increasingly unequal with the attacks on the working class that followed the crisis of the 1970s and continued in the 1980s with the policies of Reagan, Thatcher and the other political representatives of capitalism. This ever-increasing exploitation of the working class continued into the 1990s and the twenty-first century though the intensification of the working week and the increase in overtime, attacks on wages and conditions, and with many workers being forced to take two jobs in order to just get by. Alongside this increasing exploitation, credit was massively expanded through the use of mortgages, credit cards, student loans, etc.

Hayek's ideas contain an element of truth in saying that the expansion of credit causes crisis. In reality, however, the expansion of credit does not cause the crisis; rather it delays the crisis by artificially expanding the market in the short term, at the expense of exacerbating the problem of overproduction, leading to an even bigger crisis in the future. Similarly, low interest rates were used to fuel the boom beyond its limits by encouraging investment and consumer spending — consumption that was, again, reliant on credit.

The expansion of credit, however, is a dialectical process: the expansion of credit allows the productive forces to grow; the growth of the productive forces fuels the expansion of credit. As Marx explains:

> Credit is, therefore, indispensable here; credit, whose volume grows with the growing volume of value of production and whose time duration grows with the increasing distance of the markets. A mutual interaction takes place here. The development of the production process extends the credit, and credit leads to an extension of industrial and commercial operations.[24]

During the boom, nobody questions this seemingly virtuous circle. The bourgeoisie are filled with a sense of optimism. All is for the best in the best of all possible worlds. But as with all dialectical processes, at a certain point there must be a transformation from quantity into quality: the vast lending of credit on one side appears now as a tremendous pile of debts on the other; the restricted consumption of the masses is once again apparent, and the limits of the productive forces to expand reassert themselves; overproduction is evident and crisis breaks out. As Marx explains, this overproduction is, in the final analysis, the cause of the crisis:

> The ultimate reason for all real crises always remains the poverty and restricted consumption of the masses as opposed to the drive of capitalist production to develop the productive forces as though only the absolute consuming power of society constituted their limit.[25]

Marx also long ago answered those who claim that it is the drying up of credit — familiarly known today as the 'credit

24. *Capital*, Vol. 3, chapter 30.
25. *Ibid.*

crunch' — that causes crisis, pointing out that it is, in fact, not the lack of credit that is responsible for the crisis but that it is the crisis that leads to a lack of credit:

> As long as the reproduction process is continuous and, therefore, the return flow assured, this credit exists and expands, and its expansion is based upon the expansion of the reproduction process itself. As soon as a stoppage takes place, as a result of delayed returns, glutted markets, or fallen prices, a superabundance of industrial capital becomes available, but in a form in which it cannot perform its functions. A great deal of commodity capital, but unsaleable. A great deal of fixed capital, but largely idle due to stagnant reproduction. Credit is contracted:
>
> I. because this capital is idle, i.e., blocked in one of its phases of reproduction because it cannot complete its metamorphosis;
>
> II. because confidence in the continuity of the reproduction process has been shaken;
>
> III. because the demand for this commercial credit diminishes …
>
> … Hence, if there is a disturbance in this expansion or even in the normal flow of the reproduction process, credit also becomes scarce; it is more difficult to obtain commodities on credit. However, the demand for cash payment and the caution observed toward sales on credit are particularly characteristic of the phase of the industrial cycle following a crash …
>
> … Factories are closed, raw materials accumulate, finished products flood the market as commodities.[26]

26. *Ibid*.

It is, therefore, neither the expansion of the credit during the boom nor the contraction of credit that is responsible for crisis. The expansion of credit merely delays the crisis of overproduction; the contraction of credit is simply a qualitative manifestation of this very same overproduction.

To return to Hayek and the original question that the Hayekians do not consider: what would happen if governments were not to intervene in the economy and credit was not expanded? Would crises be avoided by the magical invisible hand of the market? The modern-day Hayekians imagine that without government interference, the market forces of supply and demand, with their accompanying price signals, would have solved all problems; that a crisis may still have occurred, but it would have been a minor blip in comparison to the deep recession that we are now experiencing due to a vastly inflated credit bubble. But as we have explained above, credit does not create a crisis, but merely delays it. In the absence of the expansion of credit over, the crisis of the 1970s would simply have continued and developed onto a new plane. The expansion of credit was required to maintain the consumptive capacity of the working class in the face of attacks on the wages — that is, the purchasing power — of these very same workers, all in the name of maintaining profits for the capitalists. Without the expansion of credit, the expansion of the productive forces would have been met with a limited market — that is, a lack of effective demand — at a much earlier date. Companies would have ceased to expand production in the face of a falling demand for consumer goods; unemployment would have risen; the vicious cycle of recession would have set in.

Rather than finding a stable equilibrium, the solution of the Hayekians — to remove any interference in the market and to allow the money supply to regulate itself — would simply lead to an increasingly volatile and turbulent system; to an economy that spirals out of control; that is, to a situation that resembles that of the current period.

Once again we see that the fault of the Hayekians, as with the Keynesians, is their focus on only one side of a many-sided problem. In trying to resolve one contradiction, the capitalists merely create new contradictions elsewhere on a bigger scale.

In reality, despite his unbridled faith in the free market, Hayek was never really accepted by the political representatives of capitalism, who could not swallow his creed that there should be no government interference in the economy at all. In the face of crisis, bourgeois politicians have always buckled, throwing away all talk of the 'free market', and instead doing whatever it takes to save capitalism from its own contradictions. Hence the preference amongst the bourgeois politicians such as Thatcher and Reagan for Milton Friedman, a man who preached the virtues of the free market, but who was not afraid to advocate the strong arm of the state in guiding the invisible hand. Hence also we see the acceptance of Keynesian ideas in periods of crisis, such as now, by certain elements of the bourgeoisie, who, like Keynes, see the necessity for the state to intervene in the running and regulation of capitalism.

Keynesianism Today

Modern macroeconomics, based on Keynes' ideas in the General Theory, cite four main sources of output, demand and growth for a national economy: consumption; investment; government spending; and exports. In 'normal' times, a contraction of one section would hopefully be compensated for by another. But today all four of these sectors are held back.

Consumption is restrained by the enormous amounts of private debt, with even the so-called rich countries of northern Europe seeing huge household debts; for example, as a percentage of income the household debt in Denmark and the Netherlands is 268% and 249%, respectively, whilst the United Kingdom has a figure of 143%. A *Wall Street Journal* article entitled 'Private debt will likely weigh on growth for years' (13–15 April 2012) states that:

> Public debt has received most of the spotlight since the European debt crisis flared up more than two years ago.

> But private sector debt is arguably a more intractable problem …
>
> …The origin of the private debt problem is mortgages: real-estate prices soared in a number of European countries, and banks were willing to lend ever-larger sums for home purchases. The real-estate boom has since hit the rocks throughout much of Europe, but mortgage debt endures as an albatross handing around the necks of European consumers.
>
> Economists have found a strong link between consumption, credit booms and falling real-estate prices: countries that experienced a sharp rise in household debt will experience a sharper fall in consumption than nations where debt hasn't risen as fast. If you borrowed a lot of money to buy your house (and the land it rests on), and then prices fall soon afterwards, you are more likely to want to repay the debt than go out to dinner, buy a new car or renovate your house.

Meanwhile, the banks, which have equally large debts on their books, are attempting to 'deleverage' — that is, to reduce their debts. Hence the apparent mystery of why there has been so little inflation in recent times, despite the huge amounts of money that have been pumped into the global economy through QE and other similar policies; rather than going into the real economy and being spent, this money is simply being used by the banks to reduce their debts.

For similar reasons to households, governments in the advanced capitalist countries are restricted in their ability to increase spending, given their already vast public debts. Far from expanding government spending, the U.S. economy — the largest in the world — is facing a 'fiscal cliff', with cuts to public spending and increases in taxes worth a total of approximately 5% of GDP due to kick in at the end of 2012.

Given the desperate times, equally desperate measures have been proposed. Forgetting all the lessons of history, a number of commentators have suggested that governments with independent monetary policy can just print money to pay off their debts, and QE is the first step on a slippery slope towards this. At best, such policies do nothing to solve the crisis; at worst, they can lead to hyperinflation.

Investment, as we pointed out earlier, is at a historic low, with capitalists unwilling to invest in new production when there is already excess capacity — that is, overproduction — across the board. Finally, therefore, we are left with exports. But it is a basic truism that not every country can be a net-exporter. For every export that must be an equivalent value of imports, or, as in the case inside the eurozone at the current time, there will be a flow of exports from one country and an accumulation of debt elsewhere.

Trade Imbalances

Each nation's politicians promise to export their way out of the crisis. In an ideal world they would like to do this by making their country's exports more competitive by holding wages down, whilst simultaneously hoping that every other country increases their imports by paying their workers more. But every country's capitalists and political representatives are attempting to do the same thing. Hence we arrive at the general pattern of overproduction, but now seen on an international scale, with competition between the capitalists of different nations leading to wages being cut across the board, demand falling and the market shrinking.

We see this today reflected in the calls by the Keynesian commentators of various countries, who exclaim that 'we must be more like Germany and China!'; 'we must invest, be more competitive, and export!' But not everyone can be like Germany and China. One only needs to ask the simple question of: export to whom? At a time when governments everywhere are carrying out austerity, where is there the demand for increased imports? Hence the calls by politicians and political commentators for Germany and China to 'rebalance' their economies — that is, to increase wages, thus reduce the competitiveness of exports and providing the means for greater consumption of imports. But why would the bourgeoisie in Germany and China want to do this when they are doing very well out of the current situation?

In reality, such attempts by countries to export their way out of a crisis only lead to a race to the bottom; to trade wars, increasing protectionism; and to an exacerbation of the crisis for all. Keynes, in fact, understood the dangers of large trade imbalances in a global economy, and was keen to see an agreement within the post-war Bretton Woods system that would limit imbalances between countries. In a world where every economy is linked to every other by a thousand threads, crisis in one country affects all. We therefore end up at the situation today where the crisis in the peripheral countries of the eurozone has led to a slowing down of the economies in Germany and China, who were reliant on exports to Europe for their growth. In turn, countries such as Australia, Brazil and South Africa, who rely on exporting raw materials to China, have also seen a slowdown.

As we have pointed out elsewhere, China's export-led growth is no longer a reality. Instead, the Chinese government has been forced to embark on one of the largest Keynesian experiments in history, pouring government spending into housing, infrastructure and new means of production. But like all Keynesian experiments, this is only preparing the way for an even greater crisis of overproduction in the future.

At its root, trade imbalances — with deficits at one end and surpluses at the other — are not the cause of the crisis, but are yet another manifestation of it. The huge trade deficits of the peripheral countries in Europe — Greece, Spain, Portugal, etc. — are the other side of the coin to the trade surpluses in Germany. Wages have been held down in Germany and China, whilst the productive forces have expanded. The commodities produced cannot be sold at home, but have found a market abroad. The vast wealth of German and Chinese export is, therefore, simply an expression of the equally vast overproduction that exists within these countries.

Marx understood and explained this in *Capital*:

> It should be noted in regard to imports and exports, that, one after another, all countries become involved in a crisis and that it then becomes evident that all of them, with few exceptions, have exported and imported too much, so that they all have an unfavourable balance of payments. The trouble, therefore, does not actually lie with the balance of payments …
>
> Now comes the turn of some other country. The balance of payments was momentarily in its favour; but now the time lapse normally existing between the balance of payments and balance of trade has been eliminated or at least reduced by the crisis: all payments are now suddenly supposed to be made at once. The same thing is now repeated here … What appears in one country as excessive imports appears in the other as excessive exports, and vice versa. But over-imports and over-exports have taken place in all countries … that is over-production promoted by credit and the general inflation of prices that goes with it …
>
> The balance of payments is in times of general crisis unfavourable to every nation, at least to every commercially developed nation, but always to each country in succession, as in volley firing, i.e., as soon as each one's turn comes for making payments; and once the crisis has broken out … It then becomes evident that all these nations have simultaneously over-exported (thus over-produced) and over-imported (thus over-traded), that prices were inflated in all of them, and credit stretched too far. And the same break-down takes place in all of them. The phenomenon of a gold drain then takes place successively in all of them and proves precisely by its general character: (1) that gold drain is just a phenomenon of a crisis, not its cause; (2) that the sequence in which it hits the various countries indicates only when

their judgement-day has come, i.e., when the crisis started and its latent elements come to the fore there.[27]

The high public debts in the weaker economies of the eurozone, such as Greece and Portugal, are similarly a symptom of this same process. As we have explained elsewhere, the creation of the Euro was benefiting mostly to the German capitalists, who used the single currency as a means of economic domination over the rest of the Europe. German capitalism, which was (and still is) of greater competitiveness, due to a combination of low wages and high productivity, was able to use the Euro to increase the flow of exports to the weaker peripheral countries of the eurozone. But these countries had nothing to offer in return, and could only pay for these imports using credit — primarily supplied by German banks — which had become much cheaper thanks to the low interest rates that membership of the Euro provided. The result was rising profits in Germany and rising debts in Greece, Portugal and elsewhere.

Public debt, therefore, is not a cause of the crisis, but yet another symptom of the crisis of overproduction. This is highlighted by the example of Spain, a country that before the crisis had public debts of only 36% of GDP and consistently ran a budget surplus, and which still has a public debt of only 69% today. But yet Spain is in a deep economic crisis. Its pre-crisis boom was based on a massive housing bubble, which in turn was fuelled by cheap credit, and now these bubbles have burst leaving the contradiction of empty houses alongside mass homelessness.

The bourgeois commentators often refer to the Euro crisis as simply a problem of competitiveness. But as we have explained above regarding imports, exports and trade imbalances, international competitiveness is fundamentally no different from the competition between different capitalist firms: under capitalism there will always be winners and losers. Not everyone can be the most competitive. Competition is always relative. The main difference is

27. *Ibid.*

that in the competition between firms, weak firms will go under and will be subsumed by the stronger ones; on the international plane, less competitive national economies cannot be so simply assimilated — although that, in essence, is the proposal for a fiscal union inside the eurozone: for a single economic zone in which the weaker economies are placed under the direct control of the stronger ones — that is, of German capitalism.

But as with the competition between capitalist firms, the competition between capitalist nations is ultimately a race to the bottom in which the capitalists are cutting away at the very branch they are sitting on: in trying to gain competitiveness they must either cut the wages of the working class, and thus cut into the market for the commodities that are produced; or they must invest in productivity and thus expand the productive forces. In either case, the crisis of overproduction is exacerbated. Again, what makes sense from the perspective of a single national capitalism — to cut wages, increase productivity, gain competitiveness and export abroad — is ultimately destructive for the international economy as a whole.

This, once again, demonstrates the fundamental barriers to the growth of the productive forces: the private ownership of the means of production and the nation state, both of which have become the most monstrous of fetters on the development of science, technology, culture and society in general.

The Growth Fairy Does not Exist

It is clear today that neither the Keynesians nor the monetarists have any answers. Unlike the optimism felt by the bourgeoisie in the years of boom, now there is nothing but pessimism amongst the ruling class. The monetarists and Keynesians are both wrong and they are both right; but both only see one side of the problem. It is clear that austerity is not working, but yet there is no money left for governments to stimulate the economy, and the financial markets are demanding cuts. The real answer is that there is no solution under capitalism.

The dichotomy of 'austerity vs growth' is ultimately a false one. As the *Economist* highlighted (5 May 2012), 'Calling for growth is like advocating world peace: everybody agrees that it is a good thing, but nobody agrees how to do it.' To simplify: the pro-austerity camp believe that the private sector will step in to invest and create economic growth, but that debts and deficits must first be cut back and that structural 'reforms' must be carried out to remove any 'barriers' to labour market flexibility — for example, trade unions, workers' rights, health and safety regulations. The Keynesians believe that it is government that must step in to stimulate the economy with investment in new infrastructure and housing.

The Keynesians are quite correct when they point out that austerity is not the answer, and that cuts are simply exacerbating the recessions across Europe. However, the Keynesians' promises of 'growth' instead of cuts are equally utopian. As we have pointed out previously, growth under capitalism cannot be created out of thin air. As the *Economist* eloquently put it (12 May 2012), the 'growth fairy does not exist'.

François Hollande, the president of France, has positioned himself as the leader of the 'alternative to austerity', in contrast to Merkel, who is seen as the callous representative of cuts. Opposition parties across Europe have lined up to support Hollande's calls for a 'growth pact': Tsipras, the leader of SYRIZA in Greece, urges for a renegotiation of the memorandum; the United Left in Spain presents similar demands for 'investment' and 'growth'; Ed Miliband and the other Labour leaders in Britain have applauded the election of Hollande and his opposition to 'excessive' austerity.

But behind the platitudes and the pleasant sounding rhetoric, these very same leaders understand the true severity of the crisis and do, in fact, accept the need for austerity. For example, whilst presenting himself in opposition to cuts, Hollande has promised to reduce the French budget deficit to 3% by the end of 2013 and to eliminate the budget deficit altogether by 2017. Interestingly, these are the very same targets that the openly pro-austerity Tory party has committed to in Britain. Meanwhile, Miliband has admitted that the Labour Party cannot promise to reverse any of the Tory cuts if they win the next election in 2015.

These leaders are caught between a rock and a hard place; between the immense pressures of the financial markets and the masses of radicalised workers and youth. On the one hand they must offer some hope to the masses they are meant to represent, and who have turned to them looking for an alternative. But on the other hand, these same leaders make every attempt to reassure the markets that they are 'responsible' statesmen. At heart, they understand that the cuts are not ideological and that under capitalism there is no alternative. The need for cuts is not questioned, simply the scale and the speed of these cuts.

The result is the so-called Goldilocks economic policy, as advocated by the IMF and others: a little bit of cutting in short term (but not too much!), accompanied by government policies to stimulate growth, followed by longer term plans to reduce debts and deficits. As the *Economist* states:

> ... The myth of an expansionary fiscal contraction, the idea that deficit-cutting would boost growth, has been largely dispelled. The latest evidence is that in a downturn the multiplier effect of fiscal tightening can lead to deeper recession, making it even harder to cut the deficit. In the euro zone, moreover, countries cannot easily mitigate the impact through looser monetary policy or currency devaluation. Structural reforms may boost growth, but mostly in the medium term. Yet if high deficits were the answer, Greece and Spain should be booming. Many countries in the euro zone had no choice but austerity to try to calm bond markets that were pushing them into bankruptcy. Others cut for fear of suffering the same fate. Debt in advanced economies has reached levels exceeded only during the World War-II, and the evidence is that high debt can stifle long-term growth. Sooner or later, most European countries have to start working off their debt. So the choice is not really between austerity and growth, but over the timing and

> speed of deficit-cutting and the right mix of structural reforms. The Goldilocks policy, as the IMF calls it, urges countries to embark on a gradual fiscal adjustment in the short term, if the markets allow it, coupled with a credible medium-term debt-reduction plan.[28]

Such a 'plan' is completely utopian and merely emphasises the complete confusion and pessimism of the bourgeoisie who, in the absence of a proper analysis of the crisis and of capitalism, are forced to react empirically to events, stumbling from one disaster to another along the way.

The trade union leaders are equally enamoured with talk of 'jobs, investment, and growth'. Keynesian policies are put forward, but are cloaked and sugar-coated with the language of socialism. Len McCluskey, the General Secretary of Unite, Britain's largest trade union, has called for 'socialism of the 21st Century', but is purposefully vague about what this means. These are hollow phrases with no real meaning, acting as an empty bottle, into which any content can be poured.

McCluskey is right to call for socialism. The labour movement in all countries is in need of a socialist programme. But this socialism must be clearly defined: the nationalisation of the banks and the other commanding heights of the economy as part of a democratic plan of production. In short: the abolition of capitalism and the transformation of society.

The potential that could be achieved by such a plan of production is evident by the tremendous amounts of idle factories, empty houses and unemployed workers that sit unoccupied due to the crisis of overproduction and the limits of a system in which production is only for profit. If these human and material resources were put to use, there would be no talk of scarcity or poverty. Living standards could be improved dramatically; the working day could be reduced to mere hours; the material basis would be

28. The Economist (2012).

laid for everyone to fully participate in the democratic running of society.

The inspiring struggles in Greece, Spain and Portugal show the willingness to fight for an alternative. But yet, in each case, the leaders of the movement are not up to the challenge. The situation is like that before a wild forest fire breaks out: the ground is dry and a simple spark could ignite a rapid wave of flames. The workers and youth of all countries are watching each other. All that is needed is for one example to point the way forward for the rest. The call must be: neither austerity nor Keynesianism, but the socialist transformation of society.

The Tendency of the Rate of Profit to Fall

These days there is considerable confusion about the tendency for the rate of profit to fall, not least in academic circles. This confusion arises from a one-sided undialectical view, which isolates one element in Marx's economic theory and exaggerates its significance far beyond Marx's intention. During the 1960s, the defence of Marx's ideas about the falling rate of profit against bourgeois critics was no doubt necessary and progressive. Today however it has developed into a kind of infatuation, a veritable obsession of academic 'Marxists' who lack any knowledge of dialectics and are incapable of seeing the process as a whole.

In these circles, it has become fashionable to reduce the whole of Marx's theory of crisis to this one element. What Marx regarded as a tendency (he was very careful to use that term) has been elevated into an absolute principle, a kind of economic Philosopher's Stone that can seemingly explain everything. If things were as simple as that, one wonders why Marx took the trouble to write three (in reality four) hefty volumes to explain the workings of capitalism.

In reality, there are a host of interacting causes of crisis, some fundamental, others secondary, one of which can be the falling rate of profit. However, for some, it has become a new orthodoxy; the unique reason for capitalist crisis, even to the point of claiming to be able to predict when, where and why a crisis beaks out!

Seemingly, armed with a knowledge of profit rates, one can predict almost anything. When profits are up, we are in a boom; when profits are down, we are in a slump! But nothing is that simple or mechanical. Today's recovery in profit rates is accompanied by deepening crises and collapsing demand in Europe. This in turn has produced a global slowdown, especially in China, Japan, India and South Korea. This is a reflection of the organic crisis of capitalism as we experienced in the 1930s.

Strangely enough, even Marx himself, with years of study behind him was unable to accurately predict crises. This was not Marx's method or intention. Clearly he should have waited a hundred years so as to be educated by the 'Prophets of the Falling Rate'. Sadly, however, every attempt to predict capitalist crises by this nostrum has been wide of the mark, including this latest crisis. Some say they predicted the 2008 slump, but they have been making the same prediction every year for 20 years! Such 'predictions' are two a penny. Needless to say, a stopped clock is normally correct twice in every 24 hours.

Today, we have the sorry spectacle of different schools of academic 'Marxists', established to argue over their rate of profit, based upon their interpretations and calculations. But as Mark Twain said, 'there are lies, damned lies, and statistics'. Like the medieval Schoolmen arguing over the sex of angels they squabble over the minutiae of statistics to prove that they, and not the other side, are correct. Needless to say, we are none the wiser after this 'debate' than we were beforehand. The whole thing has become quite sterile and reveals a mechanical undialectical approach to this as well as other subjects.

Let us try to put Marx's idea in its proper context. Although the law of the tendency of the rate of profit to decline was important to Marx, it was not regarded by either him or Engels as the main cause of crisis or focus of Marxist economics.

Labour Theory of Value

In volume one of *Capital*, Marx shows how surplus value is produced. He explains that the capitalist finds in the market place a particular commodity, which, unlike all other commodities, is the source of values greater than its own value. This commodity is labour power. Marx defined it as the 'aggregate of those mental and physical capabilities existing in a human being'.[29] The purchase and use of these 'mental and physical capabilities', the physical and mental muscle of the labour process, constitutes the exploitation of the working class. In contrast, labour — or the labour process — is the work that adds value to the raw materials.

After purchasing labour power for a wage intended to keep the worker and his or her family going, the capitalist proceeds to put his hired hands to work. While the worker has a contract to work for let us say 8 hours, he covers the value of his wage in perhaps 4 hours. This initial period Marx describes as necessary-labour-time. But once covering the value of his wage, he does not stop work but continues until the end of his 8-hour shift. This extra period beyond the necessary part is where the worker produces surplus value for the capitalist, and is described by Marx as surplus labour-time. This is unpaid labour and is where capitalists' profits come from.

The value of the raw materials and the power used up in the production of the commodity do not create new value, but simply transfer their existing value to the new product. This includes the wear and tear of the machines, which only gradually transfer their value, known as depreciation. Labour (combined with nature) is the source of all new value, including surplus value. A plant containing machines and raw materials, if left idle, will simply rust away and eventually ruin. However, as soon as human labour is applied to these things, new commodities and new values are created. This is the source, and the only source of surplus value. A machine simply increases the productivity of human labour and allows the labour power to be consumed at a greater intensity.

All the existing value from past labour contained in the raw materials, etc., is transferred to the new commodities. This Marx calls 'dead labour', as opposed to the new value added, which

29. www.marxist.com. The Tendency of the Rate of Profit to Fall.

Marx describes as 'living labour'. He compares it to a blood-sucking vampire. 'Capital is dead labour', explains Marx, 'that vampire-like, only lives by sucking living labour, and lives the more, the more labour it sucks'.[30]

The driving force of capitalism is the production of surplus value. The capitalist is determined to squeeze the last drop of profit from the unpaid labour of the working class. He does this through a combination of ways: lengthening the working day, speeding up the machines, introducing labour-saving machines, rationalisation, productivity deals, new shifts, time and motion studies, lean production techniques, etc. These are techniques workers have become very familiar with, especially over the last 30 years or so.

The total capital invested by the capitalist was considered by Marx as follows. The capital made up of means of production, raw materials, power, etc., is deemed constant capital, as it simply transfers its value to the new commodities. The value they impart is fixed. However, the capital represented by labour power (wages) is regarded as variable capital, as it is the source of all new value. The amount of value it imparts is not fixed, but expanding. Therefore, total capital can be presented as $c + v$, where c is the constant part and v is the variable. It follows that the total value of all commodities is made up of $c + v + s$, where s represents the surplus value. As the surplus value is 'locked up' inside the commodity, the capitalist can only realise this surplus value when the commodities are sold. Thus, surplus value is created only in production, but only realised in exchange, in the market place.

The Greater the Surplus, the Greater the Rate

If the working day is divided between necessary-labour and surplus labour, the rate of surplus value is the ratio between the two portions of the working day. It is exactly the same ratio as

30. *Ibid.*

between surplus value and variable capital, namely s/v. In simple terms, the rate of surplus value is the rate of exploitation of labour by capital, or the worker by the capitalist. The capitalist class forces the working class to perform more labour than required to cover their means of subsistence, thus producing surplus value.

Of course, the capitalists attempt to conceal this exploitation. They say they buy the workers' labour rather than the workers' labour power. But this is not true. The capitalists would not employ workers unless they could make a profit, and the unpaid labour of the workers is the source of this profit. While exploitation is transparent under feudalism, as the serf labours on the lord's land for free for so many days, under capitalism, surplus and necessary-labour performed by the workers are not separated in time and space. It is therefore not so obvious.

'The essential difference between the various economic forms of society, between, for instance, a society based on slave labour, and one based on wage labour', explained Marx, 'lies only in the mode in which this surplus labour is in each case extracted from the actual producer, the labourer.'[31]

Of course, such categories are rejected by bourgeois economists, whose role it is to disguise the exploitation that exists. The concepts of Marx are therefore an anathema to them. Through competition, the capitalist is forced to invest to produce commodities more cheaply than his rivals. *Capital* is therefore a self-expanding value. Accumulation is a compelling law of capitalism. Capitalism had become 'accumulation for accumulation's sake', explained Marx.

Production for Production's Sake

Those industries where the productivity of labour lags behind the average are driven out of business by those using the most up-to-date methods. In this way, the introduction of machinery increases the productivity of labour, and reduces the necessary-labour-time

31. *Ibid.*

(thereby increasing surplus labour time). It allows those who introduce new techniques to sell their products above their individual value (the labour time it costs to produce them) but less than the average cost, thereby gaining super profits.

Competition leads to a concentration and centralisation of capital. This process results in bigger and bigger factories with the most modern equipment and technique. Whereas in the past the chemical giant ICI would spend £2 million for a plant, these days it would pay around £600 million. This accumulation of capital is a key characteristic of capitalism, and constitutes the historic mission of capitalism to develop the productive forces. The driving force of capitalist production is not the satisfaction of human need but the production of surplus value at an ever-increasing rate, a large part of which must be accumulated and incorporated into new means of production.

This drive to introduce labour-saving machines leads, however, to a relative decrease in variable capital (labour power) to constant capital (means of production, raw materials, etc.). While there is a relative decrease in labour power to that invested in constant capital, this nevertheless results in more investment being placed at the elbow of every worker employed. Ultimately, however, the amount of surplus value obtained by the capitalists depends upon two things: the rate of surplus value and the number of workers employed.

Clearly, the introduction of machinery tends to reduce the number of workers and therefore changes the ratio between variable and constant capital, the relationship between dead and living labour. Marx described this process as a rising organic composition of capital. This inevitably leads, all things being equal, to a declining rate of profit. 'Hence, the application of machinery to production of surplus value', explains Marx, 'implies a contradiction which is immanent in it.'[32]

32. *Ibid.*

The Grundrisse

Marx was not the first to discover the tendency of the rate of profit to fall. The founders of classical political economy, most notably Adam Smith and David Ricardo, had already been aware of it. Ricardo, in particular, was very worried about its implications. However, their explanations were deficient and undeveloped.

According to Ricardo's theory of rent, the rate of profit has a tendency to fall, as a result of the accumulation of capital and the growth of the population, because the necessary means of subsistence rise in value, or agriculture, becomes less productive.

> Consequently accumulation has the tendency to check accumulation, and the law of the falling rate of profit — since agriculture becomes relatively less productive as industry develops — hangs ominously over bourgeois production. On the other hand, Adam Smith regards the falling rate of profit with satisfaction. Holland is his model. It compels most capitalists, except the largest ones, to employ their capital in industry, instead of living on interest, and is thus a spur to production. The dread of this pernicious tendency assumes tragi-comic forms among Ricardo's disciples.[33]

'It is a law which, despite its simplicity, has never before been grasped and, even less, consciously articulated', explained Marx. Ricardo in particular mixes up the rate of surplus value with that of profit. He made the fall in the rate of profit dependent on the so-called diminishing returns from land, which led Marx to quip, 'He (Ricardo) flees from economics to seek refuge in organic chemistry'![34]

It was left to Marx to undertake a thorough study of this law — or tendency as he preferred to call it. At one point, Marx describes

33. *Ibid.*
34. *Ibid.*

this tendency for the rate of profit to fall in his notebook as 'in every respect the most important law of modern political economy, and the most essential for understanding the most difficult relations. It is the most important law from the historical standpoint.'[35]

This phrase is constantly repeated by the fans of the Transposition Form (TRPF) as positive proof that Marx considered this as the most important element in his economic theory. However, this bold assertion does not stand up to even the most cursory scrutiny. In the first place, if Marx really believed this to be the most important question, he would certainly have repeatedly emphasised it. Yet, apart from the unpublished Grundrisse, the expression was only ever again used in another unpublished work called the Economic Manuscripts of 1861–1863. These are the only two references where Marx uses this expression in the entire 50-volume Marx and Engels Collected Works.

It does not appear in any of the published works, and there is not a mention of it in any of the three volumes of *Capital or the Theories of Surplus Value*. Nor is it ever mentioned in the voluminous correspondence of Marx and Engels. If Marx had discovered that the tendency of the rate of profit to fall was 'the most important law of modern political economy', one might well ask why he never mentioned this 'eureka' moment in any of his detailed correspondence with Engels, his closest collaborator, or anyone else for that matter.

The Grundrisse, a collection of rough notebooks, was only published after Marx's death. They contain only the 'first cut' of his ideas, so to speak. These ideas were as yet not fully worked out and were written only as notes for self-clarification. Because of this, Marx apparently contradicts himself on the tendency of the rate of profit to fall. Only a few pages after referring to it as 'the most important' law, he then describes it as 'the second great law', among the 'two immediate laws'.

35. *Ibid.*

The first law he describes as 'surplus value expressed as profit always appears as a smaller proportion than surplus value in its immediate reality actually amounts to'. He underlines this sentence, by which to emphasise that the rate of profit is always smaller than the rate of surplus value. Consequently, 'the rate of profit never expresses the real rate at which capital exploits labour, but always a much smaller relation'.[36]

The falling rate of profit is then referred to as the second great law. These apparent contradictions can only be explained by the fact that the Grundrisse was not a finished expression of Marx's economic theories but a work in progress. Marx's ideas were not yet completely crystallised. His final thoughts on the subject were expressed later in *Capital* in a far more complete form. But here, the reference to 'the most important law of modern political economy' is dropped altogether. In other words, it is an isolated comment that has been taken out of context to prove something that cannot be proved. It was a casual remark, which Marx made in his preparatory writings for *Capital*. These represent his initial thoughts on the subject, which he later modified.

While the Grundrisse contains very valuable thoughts on many questions, they cannot be considered to represent the final expression of Marx's economic theories. These are contained in *Capital*, especially in the third volume, where the theory of the falling rate of profit is explained at some length and in great detail. To tear out of context one isolated remark made in Marx's notebooks and attempt to elevate it above the finished version of the theory in *Capital* volume three is neither scientifically rigorous nor particularly honest.

Marx's *Capital*

By the time Marx writes *Capital*, he writes not about the most important law, but rather of the law being of 'great importance' for capitalist production.[37] The emphasis had clearly changed.

36. *Ibid.*
37. *Ibid.*

Despite its undoubted importance, out of 52 chapters in volume three of *Capital*, only three are devoted to the tendency of the rate of profit to fall. Again, this is hardly the space you would expect to squeeze in 'the most important law of modern political economy'. If Marx had regarded it as such, he would have written a whole book on the subject. Instead, one chapter deals with 'The Law Itself', followed by a chapter on 'Counteracting Factors' and finally one on 'The Development of the Laws's Internal Contradictions'.

He explains the tendency in the third volume of *Capital* by the following example:

> Once wages and the working day are given, a variable capital, which we can take as 100, represents a definite number of workers set in motion; it is an index of this number. Say that £100 provides the wages of 100 workers for one week. If these 100 workers perform as much surplus labour as necessary labour, they work as much time for the capitalist each day, for the production of surplus value, as they do for themselves, for the reproduction of their wages, and their total value product would then be £200, the surplus value they produce amounting to £100. The rate of surplus value s/v would be 100 per cent. Yet, as we have seen, this rate of surplus value will be expressed in very different rates of profit, according to the differing scale of the constant capital c and hence the total capital C, since the rate of profit is s/C. If the rate of surplus value is 100 per cent, we have:
>
> If $c = 50$ and $v = 100$, then $p' = 100/150 = 66\ 2/3$ per cent;
>
> If $c = 100$ and $v = 100$, then $p' = 100/200 = 50$ per cent;
>
> If $c = 200$ and $v = 100$, then $p' = 100/300 = 33\ 1/3$ per cent;
>
> If $c = 300$ and $v = 100$, then $p' = 100/400 = 25$ per cent;
>
> If $c = 400$ and $v = 100$, then $p' = 100/500 = 20$ per cent.

> The same rate of surplus value, therefore, and an unchanged level of exploitation of labour, is expressed in a falling rate of profit, as the value of the constant capital and hence the total capital grows with the constant capital's material volume.[38]

In other words, a rising organic composition of capital, assuming that the rate of exploitation remains the same, must bring about a fall in the rate of profit. This is a permanent tendency under capitalism as the system expands and the productivity of labour grows. In other words, the relative decrease in variable capital relative to constant capital is but another expression for greater productivity of labour. Every capitalist is striving to increase the productivity of his workforce, namely the amount produced in a given period of time. If this is so, why is there not a permanent fall in the rate of profit? Marx explains that the TRPF is a 'double-edged law' which produces its own counteracting tendencies, which, under certain conditions, can even result in the rate of profit to rise.

The tendency can also bring about a decline in the profit rate with a simultaneous increase in the mass of profit. For example, a capital of £1 million at 40% rate of profit produces £400,000, but a capital of £5 million at 8% also produces £400,000 — all things being equal. While the capitalists are concerned about the falling rate of profit, and they will do everything to combat it, it is manageable as long as the mass of profit is increasing. This is a vital point to grasp. The absolute mass of profit can continue to grow despite the tendency of the rate of profit to fall as a result of larger investments of capital. Paradoxically the same causes that produce a growth in the mass of profit also produce the tendency for the rate of profit to decline. In the long term, the capitalists are caught in a vicious circle.

38. *Ibid.*

As Marx explained:

> the same reasons that produce a tangential fall in the general rate of profit also bring about an accelerated accumulation of capital and hence a growth in the absolute magnitude or total mass of the surplus labour (surplus value, profit) appropriated by it. Just as everything is expressed upside down in competition, and hence in the consciousness of its agents, so too is this law — I mean this inner and necessary connection between two apparently contradictory phenomena.[39]

He goes on to add:

> It is evident that, on the figures given above, a capitalist controlling large capital will make more profit in absolute terms than a smaller capitalist making apparently high profits. The most superficial examination of competition also shows that, under certain conditions, if the bigger capitalist wants to make more room for himself on the market and expel the smaller capitalists, as in times of crisis, he makes practical use of this advantage and deliberately lowers his profit rate in order to drive out the smaller ones from the field.[40]

Tendency Always Applies?

The tendency does not mean that the absolute mass of exploited labour falls. In fact, historically the direction is for the scale of production to increase with a rise in the labour force and for production to become ever more concentrated into fewer but larger units. The concentration of capital is far greater today than in Marx's time, but the working class has never been so numerous. 'The fall

39. *Ibid.*
40. *Ibid.*

in the rate of profit does not arise from an absolute decline in the variable component of the total capital but simply from a relative decline, from its decrease in comparison with the constant component.'[41]

Nevertheless, the falling rate of profit is not absolute, applicable to all periods. The capitalists are constantly looking for ways around it. In practice, the rate of profit does not always fall, but can actually rise for a considerable period of time, as we have witnessed over the last 30 years, which does not contradict the process as some so-called Marxists seem to fear. We must base ourselves not only on the theory, but also on the facts and how the different tendencies and counter-tendencies work themselves out in practice. It is a tendency and not a law, as Marx emphasised. 'The rate of profit could even rise', states Marx, 'if a rise in the rate of surplus value was coupled with a significant reduction in the value of elements of constant capital, and fixed capital in particular.'[42] This is what has happened in the last three decades, but this could not last indefinitely, or 'in the long run', to use the exact words of Marx.

However, Marx points out that the problem is rather to explain why the rate had not fallen far more, and more rapidly. 'Counteracting influences must be at work', he explains, 'checking and cancelling the effect of the general law and giving it simply the character of a tendency, which is why we have described the fall in the general rate of profit as a tangential fall.'[43] In fact, Marx also points out that all economic laws have the nature of tendencies, affected by forces pulling in different directions. He then goes on to explain the factors that serve to counteract the law of the falling rate of profit and transform it into a tendency, all of which incidentally have been operating in the recent period.

The first counteracting tendency explained by Marx is a more intense exploitation of labour, an increase in relative surplus value.

---

41. *Ibid.*
42. *Ibid.*
43. *Ibid.*

That has been happening on a massive scale over the last period. In Britain, manufacturing industry produces the same level of output with a million less workers. This is a reflection of the squeeze that has taken place across the workforce, not only in Britain, but worldwide.

Labour's share in national income has been in decline across the main capitalist economies (OECD) since 1980. The gap has been especially wide in the United States, where productivity rose by 83% between 1973 and 2007, but male median real wages increased by just 5%. The share of the U.S. national income that goes to wages has fallen to its lowest level since records began after the Second World War. The production of relative surplus value is a process of progressively cheapening commodities, with the new commodities containing less value than before. A larger mass of use-values will be expressed in a smaller total value.

Alternatively, the working day can be prolonged, resulting in greater absolute surplus value. The working week has been increasing everywhere in the past period. The working class has been squeezed by deskilling, the introduction of part-time work, just-in-time production, short-term contracts and other regressive measures to extract more unpaid labour out of the working class. If you increase the rate of surplus value, you will increase the mass of surplus value, everything being equal. This then serves to push up the rate of profit. 'It does not annul the general law', he explains. 'But it has the effect that this law operates more as a tendency, i.e. as a law whose absolute realisation is held up, delayed and weakened by counteracting factors.'[44]

The driving down of wages below their value is another factor that serves to counteract a falling rate of profit. Again this has become a feature especially in the developing world where labour is viciously exploited without limit. The exploitation of women and children is part of this process. In addition, the cheapening of commodities, which has been a very important feature over the past period, serves to cheapen the cost of labour power.

---

44. *Ibid.*

Marx now refers to the cheapening of constant capital as a key factor in this process. If the rate of profit tends to fall with a greater proportion invested in constant capital as opposed to variable capital, then a cheapening of constant capital will serve to counteract the falling rate of profit. The increasing productivity of labour serves to cheapen the constant capital transferred to the product in the bargain, despite the continued rise in its volume.

Thus the same influences that tend to cause a fall in the rate of profit would serve to moderate this tendency. The value of constant value would depend on which of these two tendencies is stronger. If productivity of labour doubles, then the value of constant capital will be halved. If productivity is less than the rising value of constant capital, there will be a falling rate of profit. Therefore, we need to see the net effect of these conflicting forces. In practice, however, over the last 30 years we have seen a dramatic decrease in the value of components of constant capital, especially with the advance of new technology.

The falling price of computer chips, for example, has cheapened computers, which are part of constant capital used extensively in the economy. China has been a source of cheap goods flooding the world market, which have taken the increasing form of constant capital, and has assisted the rising rate of profit for the past three decades.

Relative surplus population is another factor. We can see the growth of mass unemployment everywhere, which has now become a permanent feature. This has served to drive down wage levels and to cheapen the cost of labour power, thereby increasing the surplus labour time for the capitalists. The reduction of 'wage costs' has been the main character of the past period, as the capitalists seek to push up their profits.

Foreign trade is also a means of cheapening elements of constant capital as well as introducing cheaper commodities from abroad, which again serve to reduce the cost of labour power. This was why the capitalists in the nineteenth century fought to abolish the Corn Laws that prevented the importation of cheap wheat that would reduce the cost of bread. The lower cost of living for the workers could allow the capitalists to depress wages, thereby increasing their profits. Foreign trade could also cheapen the elements of constant capital.

Capital invested in foreign countries, where the organic composition is lower, will also yield a higher rate of profit and will increase the average rate of profit of those engaged in foreign trade. 'Capital invested in foreign trade can yield a higher rate of profit, firstly, because it competes with commodities produced by other countries with less developed production facilities, so that the more advanced country sells its goods above their value, even though still more cheaply than its competitors', explains Marx.[45]

The privileged country receives more labour in exchange for less, continues Marx, a reference to the adverse terms of trade. The benefit is the same as for the capitalist who introduces new machinery that allows him to sell below his competitors but reap a surplus profit. This notion of foreign cheap labour points to a theory of imperialism, which was later developed by Lenin.

The expansion of the world market ('globalisation') has allowed a massive increase in investment, production and sales. There has been a massive increase in the export of capital. The collapse of the Soviet Union and the restoration of capitalism in Russia, Eastern Europe and China have provided capitalism with new markets and areas of exploitation. This allowed some 2 billion people to enter the world capitalist market. The 'liberalisation' of the developing countries, including privatisation of basic utilities, also opened up possibilities for new investment, all of which allowed the rate of profit to increase during this period.

The final point that Marx mentions, but says will need more detailed consideration later, is that with the development of capitalism 'one portion of capital is considered simply to be interest-bearing capital'.[46] He feels that this does not affect the level of the general rate of profit as such capitalists are content with a lower rate of interest, for instance, investments in railways, which do not enter into the general rate of profit.

---

45. *Ibid.*
46. *Ibid.*

In other words, what we are dealing with is only a tendency which manifests itself over the whole history of capitalist development. 'The law operates therefore simply as a tendency, whose effect is decisive only under certain particular circumstances and over long periods', explains Marx.[47] Thus, there can be long periods, even decades, where the tendency of the rate of profit to fall is cancelled out by the above counteracting tendencies. These can cut across the process and even reverse it, but not indefinitely. Eventually, this downward tendency will reassert itself and act as a further barrier to the development of capitalism.

The TRPF in Practice

The Current Crisis written in 1987 by Mark Glick published the following figures for the long-term rate of profit in the United States (Table 5.1).

Table 5.1: The TRPF in Percentage.

Year	Percentage
1899	22
1914	18
1921	18
1929	12
1932	2
1939	7
1945	23
1948	17
1965	18
1983	10

47. *Ibid.*

So, from an historical point of view, we see that, leaving aside the inevitable cyclical fluctuations, the rate of profit in 1983 was lower than it was a hundred years ago. However, for whole periods this tendency has been reversed. In the post-war period, the rate of profit began to fall roughly from the mid-1960s to its low-point in 1983. Then, with the onslaught against the working class, coupled with a whole host of the counteracting tendencies described above, the rate of profit began an ascent, with various ups and downs, that was to last approximately 30 years, up until the emerging crisis of 2007.

The rate of profit in the major G-7 economies peaked in 1997; it fell sharply in 2001 and then recovered up to 2007, states Michael Roberts in January 2009. The slump of 2000–2001 had hit the United States particularly hard. But by 2005, profits had dramatically recovered almost to 1997 levels, which 'was the highest level of profits reached since the 1960s', explained Roberts (September 2005). This process was confirmed by figures produced by Robert Brenner. 'Between 1965 and 1973, US manufacturers sustained a decline in the rate of return on their capital stock of over 40 per cent', states Brenner.[48]

In the same period, the rates of profit in the manufacturing and private business sectors fell by 40.9% and 29.3%, respectively. 'Profitability in the US economy thus began a downward trajectory that would not bottom out until the early 1980s'.[49] Thus we saw a reversal. 'It is true', states Brenner, 'that the profit picture has improved significantly for US firms in recent years — between 1989 and 1997, corporate profits increased about 82 per cent and the corporate rate of profit by 27.8 per cent.'

During the decade of the 1990s, 'profitability has rebounded significantly', states Brenner. Despite the weakness of the cyclical upturn, the rate of profit in the private business sector has increased steadily over the course of the 1990s. By 1996, it had, for the first time since the start of the long downturn, decisively

48. *Ibid.*
49. *Ibid.*

surpassed its level of 1973, achieving its level of 1969, 20–25% below its boom time peaks. By 1997, it had almost certainly come back even further, for in that year, profitability in the corporate sector (for which the most recent data is available) had returned to within 15% of its 1960s highs. Making this recovery possible was, in part, the resiliency of the non-manufacturing sector, where profitability had never fallen all that greatly, had made significant recoveries in both the late 1970s and early to mid-1980s, and had risen over the course of the 1990s above its 1969 level, to within 15–20% of its heights in the boom.

But the truly dynamic element was obviously the manufacturing sector: rising by 25% above its average for the second half of the 1980s, 100% above the terrible lows of the early 1980s and about a third above the levels registered at the end of the Keynesian 1970s, the manufacturing profit rate managed by 1995 and 1996 to exceed its level of 1973 for the first time and to come to within about 30% of its level at the peak of the boom.[50]

Brenner concludes: 'the US profitability recovery has been very major and its positive economic effects very real'.[51]

Rise in Profitability

According to Andrew Kliman: 'Finally there was a sharp rise in profitability in the middle years of this decade [2000s]. As we know, however, it was driven by an asset bubble and was not a sustained recovery. Revised and updated Bureau of Economic Affairs data indicate that the rate of profit fell from a peak of 25 per cent in 2006 to 17.9 per cent in 2008.'[52] Clearly in 2008, there was a massive fall in production, which drove down profit rates. The rate of profit peaked in 2006 and then began to fall in 2007 with the onset of the financial and banking crisis following the bursting of the U.S. housing bubble in 2005.

50. *Ibid.*
51. *Ibid.*
52. *Ibid.*

Fred Moseley, the author of *The Falling Rate of Profit in the Post War United States Economy*, states in an interview in March 2008 that 'there has not been a complete recovery of the rate of profit in recent years. I don't want to overstate it. There are different measures of profit rates, but according to my estimates, which are for the total business sector of the economy; by 2006 the rate of profit was within ten per cent of its earlier post-war peak. Mid-2006 was the peak of its current profit cycle. The profit share and profit rate have declined a bit in the last year or so, and the trajectory seems to be down right now. But there was a substantial recovery in the rate of profit. The rate of profit had declined roughly 50 per cent from the peak of the sixties to the trough of the 80s. At least half of that previous decline — I would say, more than half of the previous decline — was reversed.'

Today, profits are, by almost any measure, a lot better than they were in the 1970s and 1980s. Bear in mind also a couple of additional considerations. One is that these statistics are for the domestic U.S. economy. They do not include foreign profits; and foreign profits are an increasing share of total U.S. corporate profits. Thirty or 40 years ago they were less than 10%, today they are 30%. None of that gets counted in the official U.S. government estimates of profit rates.

In sum, there has been a substantial recovery of profit rates. Maybe not complete, and we may disagree a few percentage points on the extent, but a substantial recovery. He goes on to argue that this increase in the rate of profit has been mainly due to the holding down of wages and an increase in productivity. 'In Marxist terms, that reduced necessary labour time and increased surplus labour time, and therefore increased the rate of surplus value. Over the three decades, we're talking about the rate of surplus value has approximately doubled ...'

Another author who analyses the present crisis, Graham Turner, also recognises that 'profits rose strongly after the dotcom recession. They did not quite reach the dizzying heights of 1950 during the long post-war boom, but they were not far short.' He goes on to say that 'much of this was due to rising profits from overseas', a counteracting factor that Marx talks about in *Capital*. 'Domestic non-financial profits rose slowly during the boom.'[53]

'Globalization was a classic countervailing force, but it subsequently turned from being virtuous to vicious', explains Turner. 'It led to a stunning collapse in production and output, and the sudden emergence of enormous excess capacity. And it triggered a wave of job cuts, as companies reacted with a vengeance to the inevitable slump in profits by exporting more capital and squeezing labour costs.'[54]

He correctly adds that, falling output and such huge excess capacity destroyed profit margins, even as raw material costs fell. In Japan, the decline was seismic. Profits fell by more than two-thirds. Within manufacturing, profits disappeared altogether, as industry recorded a loss for the first time on record ...

> Across the West, the decline in profits was initially driven by the rise in raw material costs, as commodity prices soared in the early months of 2008. But the biggest drop came after the credit crunch hit consumer demand. Falling demand, when firms had already been struggling to use their available capacity, caused profits to implode ...[55]

'Not surprisingly, one of the most heavily impacted industries was capital goods. With so much excess capacity, there was little need to expand existing facilities. That is why Japan and Germany, both major exporters of capital goods, were hit so hard by the credit crisis of 2008. In Germany, foreign demand for capital goods tumbled by nearly half. In Japan, foreign demand for machinery fell by nearly three-quarters in the year to February 2009.' What Turner, not being a Marxist, is describing is a classic crisis of overproduction, but uses the term 'excess-capacity' instead.[56]

---

53. *Ibid*.
54. *Ibid*.
55. *Ibid*.
56. *Ibid*.

He says the following about profits: 'Data published by the Bureau of Economic Analysis in the US strongly supports the argument by those who claim the economic crisis of 2008 was attributable to a declining profit rate.'[57] But this conclusion is not supported by the facts as laid out by Turner. He goes on:

> Superficially (!), it would appear (!) That US companies have seen a secular improvement in their profits during recent years. Looking at total profits in relation to the economy, it is hard to see why there was such a collapse into a deep recession in 2008. The ratio of profits to GDP fell sharply during the dotcom recession, dropping to 7.0 percent in the third quarter of 2001. But aggressive central bank reflation, the rapid rise in house prices and a determination to keep a lid on labour costs, partly through outsourcing, saw the profits to GDP climb steadily. It reached a high of 12.9 percent in the third quarter of 2006. This was far short of the post-war high, when the profits to GDP ratio hit 13.3 percent in the fourth quarter of 1950. Since 2006, the collapse of house prices has precipitated a swift drop in the profits to GDP ratio. It fell to 8.9 percent by the fourth quarter of 2008, before rebounding to 9.3 percent in Q1 2009. But there is nothing in any of this to connect profits or the over-accumulation of capital to the current credit crisis. Profits appear not to have been under pressure during the upswing. And even in the downturn, they remain above their historic low reached in the fourth of 1982, when the profits to GDP ratio dropped to 6.3 percent.[58]

He continues: 'the ratio of profits to investment spending did rise during the housing boom, climbing from a cyclical low of 61.2 percent in the third quarter of 2001 to 19.6 percent five years later. The profit rate has since fallen, but again, the decline is not

57. *Ibid*, pp. 130–131.
58. *Ibid*.

particularly striking. It was down to 84.1 percent by the end of 2008, but that was still above the dotcom low. And again it rebounded in Q1 2009, to 98.4 percent.'[59]

Turner admits that these profit rate figures are not the way Marx would have calculated them. These are bourgeois statistics which do not define figures in Marxist categories, such as constant capital or variable capital. There have been various attempts to do so, but this is an impossible task given the way such statistics are compiled, including the Bureau of Economic Analysis. In addition, companies, for different reasons, either attempt to inflate or deflate their profits to avoid taxes or increase the values of their shares. General Electric, the biggest U.S. manufacturing company, was fined several million dollars in August 2010 for falsely inflating its profit figures. There are many things these days that distort profit figures, rendering a precise picture impossible. Nevertheless, despite all these massive problems and disparities, the figures produced by different sources can provide a rough guide to the situation.

Turner continues, 'Looking at domestic profits is an entirely different matter. At the top of the housing boom, more than a third of US company profits were being earned abroad. Indeed, by the fourth quarter of 2008, overseas profits had risen to a record 45.6 percent of domestic profits.'[60]

Turner's argument centres on the figures of U.S. domestic profits and those earned abroad. But this is not an appearance, but a fact. It also represents a misunderstanding of Marx. As we saw earlier, Marx never made this distinction between domestic and foreign-earned profits. In fact, he stated that foreign trade would serve as a counteracting tendency in regard to a falling rate of profit. It was for him an important addition to the process. And this was clearly the case in the past period with the intensification of so-called globalisation and the exploitation of new markets.

59. *Ibid.*
60. *Ibid.*

Furthermore, a growing share of domestic profits came from the financial sector. During the 1950s and 1960s, an average of 31.1% of domestic profits derived from the finance sector. That grew to a peak of 45.3% in the fourth quarter of 2001. Finance was responsible for a third of domestic profits at the end of 2006, before the slide in house prices began to take its toll on bank earnings.[61]

The problem is that Turner and many others besides have accepted consciously or unconsciously capitalist definitions of costs. They view rent (for the landlords) and interest (for the bankers) as costs, when for Marxists these are part of the surplus value produced by the working class. These should be included in the real rate of profit and not excluded. The massive increase in the share of profit going to the banks and financiers only means that the division of surplus value between the ruling class has changed. Finance capital has become increasingly dominant and is now taking an increasing proportion of the surplus value. In addition, the banks are involved in all kinds of investments, not only lending to industry, but also investing heavily in the property market, at least up until the crash. The attempt to exclude 'financial' profits from the equation in order to depress figures for the rate of profit is therefore wrong.

In any case, non-financial corporations like General Electric, Ford and General Motors have increasingly engaged in financial operations from the 1990s onwards. The tentacles of finance capital and industrial capital have become entwined.

Turner nevertheless makes the point that 'it is worth stressing again that the crisis has not been caused by falling profit rates per se. The profit rate does not actually fall until after the crisis has manifested itself in the finance sector.' In his opinion, 'it is the desperate attempt by companies to try and drive profit rates higher — back to levels not seen since the 1950s and 1960s — that leads to the crisis'.[62] If he means by this the squeezing of the

---

61. *Ibid.*
62. *Ibid.*

working class through relative and absolute surplus value, then he has a point. But this, as we have explained, is only one side of the picture.

Rather than explaining crisis in terms of the rate of profit, Marx explains that 'the market expands more slowly than production ... there comes a moment at which the market manifests as too narrow for production. This occurs at the end of the cycle. But it merely means the market is glutted. Over-production is manifest.'[63] And again, 'Over-production is specifically conditioned by the general law of production of capital: to produce to the limit set by the productive forces, that is to say, to exploit the maximum amount of labour with the given amount of capital, without any consideration for the actual limits of the market or the needs backed by the ability to pay; and this is carried out through continuous expansion and reproduction and accumulation ...'[64]

Lowering Profitability

This explanation of crisis is repeated again and again throughout Marx's works. The present crisis was not caused by a crisis of profitability, but certainly resulted in one. When there is a slump in production, this will mean a fall in sales, which in turn, cuts into profits. The rate of profit falls, as does the mass of profit. The crisis, however, was a result of a massive overproduction of consumer and capital goods which the market could not profitably absorb. When the capitalists cannot sell their products, the rate of profit is zero. In fact, it is less than zero as the total value of the commodity is written off. At best, they slash their prices to below their cost of production in an attempt to shift them. It was this that had its impact in lowering profitability. In fact, the mass of profit collapsed as a consequence of the collapse in output. 'Excess capacity' grows as the big corporations attempt to stem overproduction and curtail their losses. As a consequence, factories and

63. *Ibid.*
64. *Ibid.*

production lines are closed, workers are put on short-time and machines are left idle. Giant blast furnaces and plant are shut or 'mothballed'. As explained, once overproduction occurs, sales fall, the market shrinks, production is cut back and profits tumble. It was as a consequence of an inability to sell the commodities that relentlessly poured onto the market as the market collapsed, which in turn led to a collapse in the mass of profit. It produced what Marx described as a problem of realisation of surplus value, an inability of the capitalists to turn commodities into money, the real aim of their activity.

Overproduction, the fundamental cause of crisis, was beginning to manifest itself at the height of the boom in 2005–2006, where supply was outstripping demand. In general, as Marx explained, overproduction develops precisely at the height of a boom when profitability is high ('at the end of the cycle', to use his words) and appears well before a fall in the mass of profit that accompanies a slump. This capitalist crisis not only drives down the rate of profit, which started to slide, but more importantly, drives down the mass of profit as the economy comes to a standstill.

By 2008, the massive crisis of overproduction had produced a big fall in the rate and eventually the mass of profit by the last quarter of that year. This is, however, hardly the long-term trend that Marx talked about, and the fall in the rate of profit is very much a consequence of the crisis of overproduction. This crisis was certainly not due to a single factor, but a whole series of factors that were to culminate is a massive crisis of overproduction. 'In world market crises', explained Marx, 'all the contradictions of bourgeois production erupt collectively.'[65]

Today's capitalist crisis can only be really understood, not in reference to this or that secondary aspect, including the rate of profit, but through an appreciation of its contradictions in its wider historical context. The present crisis is not a cyclical crisis, but an organic crisis rooted within the system itself. It is a reflection of the epoch of capitalist decline, where the system has

65. *Ibid.*

exhausted itself. The productive forces have been strangled by private ownership and the nation state, a fundamental contradiction ignored by our academic 'Marxists'. The decline of capitalism will not be a straight line, but affected by intermittent ups and downs, crises and convulsions, which has nothing to do with the episodic movements in the rate of profit and everything to do with the inherent barriers to capitalism in its old age. Capitalism has now reached its limits. This essential character, together with all its implications, is ignored by all those who are mesmerised by a mechanical explanation of crisis, simply reducing the cause of crisis to this or that particular aspect.

The capitalist system was able to put off deep crisis for a whole historical period. Now all the contradictions have risen to the surface. While there are many reasons for capitalist crisis, the overriding reason is overproduction. This was explained by Ted Grant long ago, who underlined what Marx had written:

> The fundamental cause of crisis in capitalist society, a phenomenon peculiar to capitalist society alone, lies in the inevitable over-production of both consumer and capital goods for the purposes of capitalist production. There can be all sorts of secondary causes of crisis, particularly in a period of capitalist development — partial over-production in only some industries; financial juggling on the stock exchange; inflationary swindles; disproportions in production; and a whole host of others — but the fundamental cause of crisis lies in over-production. This, in turn, is caused by the market economy, and the division of society into mutually conflicting classes.[66]

However, what is striking about the last 30 years, despite the successful attempt to drive up the rate of profit by a whole range of means, as explained above, the capitalists were never able to

66. *Ibid.*

restore the profit rate to the levels of the post-war upswing. Despite all their attacks and efforts over this period, they failed in this regard.

Today, there has been a recovery in the rate of profit since 2009 following the destruction of capital and its values arising from the crisis. Profits in the U.S. corporate sector are 25–30% greater than before the recession. But despite this fact, there has been no return to 'normality'. Those who regard profitability simply as a gauge to the health of capitalism must be scratching their heads. Despite the boost to profits, there has been no investment and no recovery. 'Profit margins are not only very high today', states Andrew Smithers, who runs a London consultancy, 'but [companies'] behaviour has been very unusual'.[67]

What he means by 'unusual' is that there is no investment and without this there can be no boom. The reason for this is the massive over-hang of personal, corporate and government debt, which kept capitalism afloat in the past period, but has now undermined demand. Without potential sales and an expanding market, there will be no incentive to produce or invest. That is why large parts of the world are either slowing down or in recession, while mass unemployment is growing. Once again, this is a reflection of a structural crisis of capitalism and nothing to do with the normal boom and slump cycle.

---

67. *Ibid.*

6

Technology and Economic Growth

The main motor force in history is the need for society to develop the productive forces: to increase our knowledge of and mastery over nature; to reduce the socially necessary labour time needed to produce and reproduce the conditions of life; to improve lifestyles and raise the standards of living. As Marx wrote in his preface to 'A Contribution to the Critique of Political Economy':

> In the social production of their life, men enter into definite relations that are indispensable and independent of their will, relations of production which correspond to a definite stage of development of their material productive forces. The sum total of these relations of production constitutes the economic structure of society, the real foundation, on which rises a legal and political superstructure and to which correspond definite forms of social consciousness.[1]
>
> The mode of production of material life conditions the social, political and intellectual life process in general. It is not the consciousness of men that determines their being, but, on the contrary, their social being that determines their consciousness.[2]

---

1. *Capital*, Vol. 1, chapter 25, p. 929, Penguin Classics edition.
2. *Ibid*.

Marx goes on to explain that it is precisely in those periods when society can no longer develop the productive forces — when science, technology and industry stagnate; when economic growth, employment and rising living standards cannot be guaranteed — that revolutions occur, in order to remove the barriers standing in the way of progress:

> At a certain stage of their development, the material productive forces of society come into conflict with the existing relations of production, or — what is but a legal expression for the same thing — with the property relations within which they have been at work hitherto. From forms of development of the productive forces these relations turn into their fetters.[3]

The epoch of social revolution has clearly arrived: from the Bolivarian revolution in Venezuela, to the Arab revolutions and the marvellous movements of the masses in Spain, Greece, Brazil and Turkey, all of these are a clear symptom of the current crisis and the inability of capitalism to provide a future for the vast majority of workers and youth across the world. But now even the serious bourgeoisie are worried, not only because of the social turmoil caused by the crisis, which increasingly threatens their own privileged position within this system, but also because of evidence of a longer term inability for this same system to provide growth, jobs and a decent standard of living — that is, to develop the productive forces.

Technology is a motor force and always plays an important role in socio-economic-cultural activities of human life. Any debates on how best to promote sustainable and inclusive development are incomplete without a full consideration of issues of STI. Access to new and appropriate technologies promotes steady improvements in living conditions, which can be lifesaving for the most vulnerable

3. *Ibid.*

populations, and drives productivity gains which ensure rising incomes.[4]

Historically, we have seen in the first Industrial Revolution, starting in the late eighteenth century, and the second one, around 100 years later, victims who lost their jobs to Cartwright's power loom and later to Edison's electric lighting, Benz's horseless carriage and countless other inventions that changed the world. But those inventions also immeasurably improved many people's lives, sweeping away old economic structures and transforming society. They created new economic opportunity on a mass scale, with plenty of new work to replace the old. A third great wave of invention and economic disruption, set off by advances in computing and information and communication technology in the late twentieth century, promises to deliver a similar mixture of social stress and economic transformation. It is driven by a handful of technologies including machine intelligence, the ubiquitous web and advanced robotics capable of delivering many remarkable innovations: unmanned vehicles; pilotless drones; machines that can instantly translate hundreds of languages; mobile technology that eliminates the distance between doctor and patient, teacher and student. Whether the digital revolution will bring mass job creation to make up for its mass job destruction remains to be seen.[5]

Recently machines have found it difficult to 'understand' written or spoken language, or to deal with complex visual images, but now they seem to be getting to grips with such things. Apple's Siri responds accurately to many voice commands and can take dictation for e-mails and memos. Google's translation programme is lightning-fast and increasingly accurate, and the company's computers are becoming better at understanding just what its cameras (as used, for instance, to compile Google Maps) are looking at.[6]

4. Prabhakar, Ahmad, and Khan (2015).

5. *Ibid*.

6. *Ibid*.

At the same time, hardware, from processors to cameras to sensors, continues to get better, smaller and cheaper, opening up opportunities for drones, robots and wearable computers. And innovation is spilling into new areas: in finance, for example, crypto-currencies like Bitcoin hint at new payment technologies, and in education the development of new and more effective online offerings may upend the business of higher education. This wave is likely to bring vast improvements in living standards and human welfare, but history suggests that society's adjustment to it will be slow and difficult. At the turn of the twentieth century writers conjured up visions of a dazzling technological future even as some large, rich economies were limping through a period of disappointing growth in output and productivity. Then, as now, economists hailed a new age of globalisation even as geopolitical tensions rose. Then, as now, political systems struggled to accommodate the demands of growing numbers of disappointed workers.

Technology is empowering talented individuals as never before and opening up yawning gaps between the earnings of the skilled and the unskilled, capital-owners and labour. At the same time, it is creating a large pool of underemployed labour that is depressing investment. The effect of technological change on trade is also changing the basis of tried-and-true methods of economic development in poorer economies. More manufacturing work can be automated and skilled design work accounts for a larger share of the value of trade, leading to what economists call 'premature deindustrialisation' in developing countries. No longer can governments count on a growing industrial sector to absorb unskilled labour from rural areas. In both the rich and the emerging world, technology is creating opportunities for those previously held back by financial or geographical constraints; yet new work for those with modest skill levels is scarce compared with the bonanza created by earlier technological revolutions.[7]

7. *Ibid.*

Workers in America, Europe and Japan have been through a difficult few decades. Some economists are offering radical thoughts on the job-destroying power of this new technological wave. Carl Benedikt Frey and Michael Osborne, of Oxford University, recently analysed over 700 different occupations to perceive how easily they could be computerised, and concluded that 47% of employment in America is at high risk of being automated away over the next decade or two. Messrs Brynjolfsson and McAfee ask whether human workers will be able to upgrade their skills fast enough to justify their continued employment.[8]

The digital revolution is opening up a great divide between a skilled and wealthy few and the rest of society. In the past, new technologies have usually raised wages by boosting productivity, with the gains being split between skilled and less-skilled workers, and between owners of capital, workers and consumers. The digital economy, far from pushing up wages across the board in response to higher productivity, is keeping them flat for the mass of workers while extravagantly rewarding the most talented ones. Between 1991 and 2012 the average annual increase in real wages in Britain was 1.5% and in the United States just 1%, according to the Organisation for Economic Co-operation and Development.

Innovation Pessimism

An increasing number of mainstream commentators are now seriously questioning whether our ability to innovate — to develop science and new technologies — has fundamentally slowed down. Exemplifying this 'innovation pessimism' was a leading article in the *Economist* (12 January 2013) with the title 'Has the ideas machine broken down?', which states that, 'a small but growing group of economists reckon the economic impact of the innovations of today may pale in comparison with those of the past'.

Such commentators claim that behind the obviously apparent and relatively recent 'Great Recession' lies a less obvious long-term

8. *Ibid*.

decline in the contribution made by technological progress and innovation towards economic growth — a so-called Great Stagnation. Indeed, evidence given in the *Economist*'s article shows that there has been a slowdown in the growth of productivity — that is, the economic and productive output per person — that precedes the crisis and goes back several decades to the 1970s.

The *Economist* explains how economic growth can primarily be broken down into two categories: extensive and intensive. Extensive growth refers to the increase in output due to an increase in the factors of production; for example, by expanding the workforce — as has happened in many periods in the history of capitalism through the growth in the population, the use of migrant labour, the introduction of women into the workforce or in modern times by increasing the retirement age — and increasing the amount of capital (e.g., machinery and factories) in proportion to this expanded workforce.

Intensive growth, by contrast, is the increase in output for a given size of the workforce. This reflects an increase in the productivity or intensity of labour — what Marx refers to as an increase in 'relative surplus value' in terms of capitalism. The difference between 'extensive' and 'intensive' growth, therefore, is a difference of quantity and quality: extensive growth merely increases the quantity of the productive forces; intensive growth increases their quality.

Capitalism and Growth

Marx explained how capitalism, in its early, progressive phase, gave a huge impetus to the development of the productive forces. Competition between different capitalists, in the pursuit of increased profits and greater markets, led not only to extensive growth — through accumulation and reproduction — but also to intensive growth, as the capitalists reinvested profits into the development of new machinery, technologies and productive techniques. Those who could not keep up with the application of the latest technology and technique produced at a higher cost and were undercut by their competitors. The weak went under and were consumed by the strong, leading over time to a concentration and centralisation of capital in the hands of the few, as Marx describes in *Capital*:

> Hand in hand with this centralisation, or this expropriation of many capitalists by few, other developments take place on an ever-increasing scale, such as the growth of the co-operative form of the labour process, the conscious technical application of science, the planned exploitation of the soil, the transformation of the means of labour into forms in which they can only be used in common, the economising of all means of production by their use as the means of production of combined, socialise labour, the entanglement of all peoples in the net of the world market, and, with this, the growth of the international character of the capitalist regime.[9]

This then was the historical role of capitalism: to concentrate the previously scattered means of production into giant monopolistic firms; to establish an interconnected capitalist world market; to develop the means of production and thus lay the material basis for socialism — that is, the creation of a society not of scarcity, but of superabundance.

The laws of capitalism, in its heyday, were a powerful force in the development of innovation and industry. Marx and Engels themselves spoke in the *Communist Manifesto* of how capitalism 'has accomplished wonders far surpassing Egyptian pyramids, Roman aqueducts, and Gothic cathedrals'. The invention and application of the steam engine was, without exaggeration, an 'industrial revolution'.

Many other qualitative leaps have followed under capitalism, from the invention of trains and telegrams, to the application and generation of electricity. But by the early twentieth century, such

9. *Capital*, Vol. 1, chapter 25, p. 929, Penguin Classics edition.

leaps were few and far between. By this stage, the productive forces had far outgrown the market; the imperialist nations could expand no further without re-dividing up the world. Thus began a period of two world wars, with the Great Depression in-between.

The Impetus of War

It is notable that the main development in technology and innovation from this period came not from capitalism and the competition of the free market, but from the state control over industry and the planning that capitalist nations were forced to adopt for the purposes of war. Nationalisation and public control of the key sectors of research and development were introduced in the advanced capitalist countries during the Second World War in order to innovate and develop new technologies. Aircraft, plastics, synthetic rubber, medicines, telecommunications, nuclear energy, etc., all of these technologies and many more were either invented or given an enormous boost due to Second World War, alongside a general development of industry and the introduction of new production techniques for the purpose of the war.

This rapid period of development in terms of the research and application of new technologies and techniques, along with the destruction caused during the war itself and the expansion of world trade that followed, in turn led to the post-war economic boom — the so-called Golden Age of capitalism. Suddenly, whole nations, whose industrial base had been flattened during the war, were given Marshall Aid from the United States — which came out of the war greatly strengthened with its industry and economy almost untouched — and were able to import and implement the most modern industrial methods, providing a great leap forward in terms of productivity.

This, the tremendous qualitative development of the productive forces as a result of state control and planning during the war, and not the Keynesian policies of the reformists, was the real secret behind the post-war boom. Since the war, the military-industrial complex — both in terms of the war machine and the

Apollo programme — continued to play an important role; today, total global military spending (at almost US$1.8 trillion), outstripping estimates for total spending on R&D (between US$1.0 and US$1.4 trillion). This is not to mention the important research that takes place in universities — publically funded and nominally not for profit, although big business is increasingly dictating research agendas.

During the same interwar period, whilst capitalism was experiencing its greatest crisis in history, the planned economy in the Soviet Union, despite all the deformations introduced by the cancerous fetter of the Stalinist bureaucracy, was developing at lightning speed, going from being a backward, mainly peasant-based economy before the 1917 Revolution to putting the first man in space 44 years later.

What this all demonstrates is that, for almost a century now, the motor force of innovation has not been capitalist competition, but planning and public ownership. Capitalism, far from developing science and technology, has become an enormous fetter on the development of the productive forces. Private ownership over the means of production has become a gigantic barrier to innovation and ingenuity and must be replaced by a plan of production under the democratic control of society itself.

Stagnation and Decline

At its post-war peak, economic output per person — a measure of productivity — in America was growing at over 3% per year. In the 1970s, with the collapse of the boom, this figure dropped to around 2%, and today this figure is under 1%. All of this slowdown in productivity has occurred despite tremendous technological advances, most notably the introduction of personal computers, mobile phones and the Internet. Hence, the talk of 'innovation pessimism' by the bourgeois commentators today.

The *Economist* importantly notes that there is a difference between innovation and technology: innovation is the actual development of science and 'know-how'; technology is the application of this 'know-how' in terms of production and society. It is the latter that matters when it comes to actual increases in productivity and economic growth. Today there is innovation everywhere, but the actual impact of this on society is not dramatic.

As the *Economist* points out, whilst great advances have been made in some areas, in many respects society is still the same today as it was 40 years ago, domestic lifestyles are largely unchanged; we still travel around on the same trains, planes and automobiles; and average life expectancy in the United States has risen by less than five years since 1980, compared to a rise of 25 years between the turn of the twentieth century and 1980. There are more people today involved in research and development than ever before, and yet it is estimated that technology and innovation contribute seven times less towards growth than in 1950.

Again, it is the existence of private ownership, not only over the material means of production, but also over the ideas and knowledge generated by society (i.e., patents and intellectual property), that is stifling the actual development and implementation of technology. Rather than co-operating and sharing knowledge to produce the best phone possible, companies such as Apple and Samsung instead embroil themselves in an endless series of legal cases over the infringement of various patents. Rather than investing in education and applying the most modern techniques in the advanced industrial countries, the capitalists instead take advantage of the abundant supply of cheap labour in Asia and elsewhere; or simply choose to speculate parasitically in the financial markets. And rather than employing the most advanced production techniques, such as 3D printers, which have the potential to provide another industrial revolution, such technologies are held back for fear of exacerbating the already existing excess capacity — that is, overproduction — in the system and generating yet more unemployment by replacing workers with machines.

Why invest in real production when there is already excess capacity and when you could make billions on the stock exchange or in various financial derivatives instead? Why spend on R&D in Britain and the United States when you could simply employ hundreds of low-paid workers in China? It should be noted that for many years, growth in China was largely of the extensive kind, fuelled by a move from agriculture to industry, with millions migrating from the countryside to the city, and by the importing of modern production techniques from abroad via joint-ventures between Chinese state-owned enterprises and multinational firms. Nowadays, there has been genuine innovation in China (think of companies such as Huawei and Lenovo) and investment in greater automation as Chinese workers become increasingly militant and more organised, demanding and winning wage increases and better conditions.

The increasingly parasitic nature of capitalism and the use of off-shoring in terms of industry have not helped innovation and technology. On the one hand, they have created greater inequality everywhere, with profits accumulating in the hands of the big multinationals at one end and with an ever more impoverished working class at the other. But on the other, they have also helped to create the largest and most interconnected working class that has ever existed.

Race against the Machine

Alongside 'innovation pessimism', there exists amongst other bourgeois commentators the opposite tendency: the fear that rapid technological progress in the modern age could potentially lead to mass unemployment, with machines replacing workers in a vast range of jobs in terms of both manual and mental labour, particularly with the advent of advanced computing techniques, such as machine learning and voice recognition. As the *Economist* (25 May 2013) comments:

> There is a good chance that technology may destroy more jobs than it creates. There is an even greater chance that it will continue to widen inequalities. Technology is creating ever more markets in which innovators, investors and consumers not workers get the lion's share of the gains. It

is not, as many on the Right would have us believe, foreigners or immigrants who are taking our jobs — it is the machines! Such fears of mass unemployment due to technological progress, however, are nothing new, as economist Michael Stewart discusses back in 1985:

> In the 1830s the hand-loom weavers of Lancashire were put out of business by the new power looms. In the same way, in the 1980s, semi-skilled car workers are being put out of business by robots.

Because the scope for the displacement of labour by the chip (computer micro-chip) is so vast, and the pace of change so great, it is difficult to see what kind of jobs large numbers of semi-skilled and unskilled workers are going to be needed to do.[10] Meanwhile, John Maynard Keynes, the famous British economist, remarked in an essay in 1930 that:

> We are being afflicted with a new disease of which some readers may not yet have heard the name, but of which they will hear a great deal in the years to come—namely, technological unemployment. This means unemployment due to our discovery of means of economising the use of labour outrunning the pace at which we can find new uses for labour. (Economic Possibilities for Our Grandchildren, John Maynard Keynes)

Today, this tendency has been expressed within recent books such as *Race against the Machine* by two academics from MIT university's Sloan Business School. The authors, Erik Brynjolfsson and Andrew McAfee, state:

> The stagnationists [those who argue that innovation and productivity has been stagnating for several decades] correctly point out that median income and other important

10. See Keynes and Michael Stewart.

> measures of American economic health stopped growing robustly some time ago, but we disagree with them about why this has happened. They think it's because the pace of technological innovation has slowed down. We think it's because the pace has sped up so much that it is left a lot of people behind. Many workers, in short, are losing the race against the machine ...

'It may seem paradoxical that faster progress can hurt wages and jobs for millions of people, but we argue that's what's been happening ... How can so much value creation and so much economic misfortune coexist? How can technologies accelerate while incomes stagnate?'[11] In other words, improved technology and increased productivity, rather than raising living standards, have actually lowered them for the vast majority, creating stagnant wages and permanent structural unemployment. As Brynjolfsson and McAfee point out:

> There have been trillions of dollars of wealth created in recent decades [in the US economy], but most of it went to a relatively small share of the population ... over 100 percent of all the wealth increase in America between 1983 and 2009 accrued to the top 20 percent of households. The other four-fifths of the population saw a net decrease in wealth over nearly 30 years ...
>
> There has been no stagnation in technological progress or aggregate wealth creation as is sometimes claimed. Instead, the stagnation of median incomes primarily reflects a fundamental change in how the economy apportions income and wealth. The median worker is losing the race against the machine.

The authors of *Race against the Machine*, however, are only half correct when arguing that technological development is

11. Brynjolfsson and McAfee, *Race against the Machine.*

responsible for unemployment and inequality. The problem is not technology, but the application of technology under capitalism.

Artificial Surplus Population

Marx long ago explained how the laws of capitalism — the anarchic competition between capitalists for greater profits — force each capitalist to try and reduce their costs, in order to sell at a lower price, by increasing productivity through the replacement of labour with machinery. This in turn creates an 'artificial surplus population' of the unemployed:

> The fall in prices and the competitive struggle, on the other hand, impel each capitalist to reduce the individual value of his total product below its general value by employing new machinery, new-and-improved methods of labour and new forms of combination. That is, they impel him to raise the productivity of a given quantity of labour, to reduce the proportion of variable capital [wages] to constant [machinery, tools, equipment, raw materials, etc.] and thereby to dismiss workers, in short to create an artificial surplus population ...
>
> The same causes that have raised the productivity of labour, increase the mass of commodity products, extended markets, accelerated the accumulation of capital, in terms of both mass and value, and lowered the rate of profit, these same causes have produced, and continue constantly to produce, a relative surplus population, a surplus population of workers who are not employed by this excess capital on account of the low level of exploitation of labour at which they would have to be employed, or at least on account of the low rate of profit they would yield at the given rate of exploitation.[12]

12. See *Capital*, Vol. 3, chapter 15, pp. 363–364, Penguin Classics edition.

> It is capitalist accumulation itself that constantly produces, and produces indeed in direct relation with its own energy and extent a relatively redundant working population, i.e. a population which is superfluous to capital's average requirements for its own valorisation, and is therefore a surplus population.[13]

It is, therefore, not technology itself, but the use of technology under capitalism, implemented in an anarchic and unplanned way, which leads to mass unemployment, and which in turn places pressure on those still in work to accept lower wages, as competition for the remaining jobs increases.

Alongside the creation of an 'artificial surplus population', therefore, there exists also a super-exploitation of those remaining in work, again in the name of increasing profits for the capitalists. Thus arises the contradiction in which mass unemployment can sit side-by-side with millions who must work 50–60 hours per week or take multiple jobs just in order to scrape by:

> The over-work of the employed part of the working class swells the ranks of its reserve, while, conversely the greater pressure that the reserve by its competition exerts on the employed workers forces them to submit to over-work and subjects them to the dictates of capital. The condemnation of one part of the working class to enforced idleness by the over-work of the other part, and *vice versa*, becomes a means of enriching the individual capitalists, and accelerates at the same time the production of the industrial reserve army on a scale corresponding with the progress of social accumulation.[14]

The existence of such a contradiction emphasises the fact that such a surplus population is entirely 'artificial'. Those who are unemployed are not 'surplus' to the needs of society, but merely

---

13. See *Capital*, Vol. 1, chapter 25, p. 782, Penguin Classics edition.
14. *Ibid.*, pp. 789–790.

'surplus' to the needs of capital. Capitalism is unable to use the human resources available, and instead consigns millions to forced idleness. Big business refuses to invest and factories, shops and offices lie empty, all because of the already existing excess capacity — that is, overproduction. The productive forces outgrow the 'effective demand' of the market; commodities cannot be sold at a profit, or even sold at all; the economy grinds to a halt, not for any lack of 'needs' in society, but simply because there is no profit to be made for the capitalists.

In addition, capitalism cannot even use the knowledge and technology that society has discovered and invented over millennia of history: innovation is not realised in any practical application because of the private ownership over ideas themselves, whilst new technologies are not introduced for fear of the further excess capacity, unemployment and fall in demand that they would generate.

Under capitalism, the individual capitalist introduces technology and improves productivity in order to increase their own individual profit, without any regard for the living standards of workers or the needs of society. Hence the fear of bourgeois commentators, such as the authors of *Race against the Machine*, that it is technology that is responsible for unemployment and inequality.

Under socialism, the anarchy of competition and the market would be replaced by a rational plan of production, allowing technology to be introduced, and productivity to be raised. Man and the machine could coexist in harmony rather than in competition. Rather than generating the contradiction of unemployment alongside extreme toil, work could be shared out equally and the hours of the working day could be reduced for all, with further investment and improvement leading to an ever-increasing amount of leisure time.

We see, once again, that it is not technology that is the source of social ills, but the capitalist system itself, and the enormous barrier to progress that this system imposes due to private ownership and production for profit. But how can these two separate tendencies amongst bourgeois economists and commentators exist side-by-side? How can there be both too much innovation and technology, and yet apparently also too little?

This contradiction between 'innovation pessimism' and the 'race against the machine' is a reflection of the contradictions of capitalism itself: the barrier of private ownership; the tendency for the productive forces to outgrow the market; and the juxtaposition of extreme planning of production within firms alongside anarchy between firms.

The paradox of both too much and too little innovation at the same time simply expresses the dialectical laws of capitalism — laws based on the 'rational' pursuit of profit by the individual capitalist, which in turn leads to an outcome that is wholly *irrational* for the capitalist class as a whole.

The individual capitalists invest in research and technology to improve their company's productivity and undercut their rivals, reducing wages and replacing workers with machinery in the process. But each capitalist is pursuing the same 'rational' aim, and in doing so the capitalist class as a whole cuts away at the very market that it is trying to sell to. With commodities unable to be sold, the crisis of overproduction reveals itself and production stops. The individual capitalist benefits, in the short term, from technological innovation; but the capitalist class as a whole ends up generating unemployment and crisis.

With a glut of excess capacity in the system and no effective demand for further goods and services, there is no incentive for any capitalist to invest in the development and implementation of new technologies. Innovation and productivity, in turn, therefore slow down also. Capitalism, in other words, cuts away at the very branch it is sitting on: competition drives investment; investment creates unemployment; and unemployment leads to a vicious cycle of no demand, no investment and further unemployment.

Capitalism whilst creating mass unemployment on the one hand is unable to create the conditions for innovation on the other. Innovation is not an exogenous manna from heaven; it does not simply fall from the sky. Innovation requires certain material conditions, above all, the ability for the system to be able to divert and dedicate labour towards science, research and development.

In this respect, we can see how the crisis forces capitalism to eat away at the very source of its own growth. For example, across the advanced capitalist countries, spending on higher education is being slashed and students are being asked to take on a tremendous burden of debt, all because of the crisis, which has forced governments to cut public expenditure. Meanwhile, these same governments have to cut military 'defence' budgets, another traditional source of innovation under capitalism.

In addition, the application of technology also requires certain material conditions in terms of the socio-economic system present and the ability of new technology to meet the interests of the ruling class in a given system. For example, the concept of steam power was known to the ancient Greeks, and yet this potentially revolutionary technology was not implemented since the economy was based on the labour of the abundant supply of cheap slaves. Labour-saving machinery was, therefore, of little use. Similarly, there was little incentive to develop technology under feudalism, a system based on the labour of the serfs who were tied to the land of their lords.

It is only with capitalism, a system in which competition and the profit motive provides an incentive to invest in new machinery and technology, that we see the Industrial Revolution and the development and application of steam power on a mass scale. Suddenly, society is given an enormous boost and the productive forces are rapidly developed as labour-saving technology is discovered and used.

But now these same forces that were once progressive have turned into their opposite. What incentive is there for the capitalists to invest in labour-saving technology when there is an abundance of cheap labour across the globe? Why develop and apply technology to increase productivity when there is already excess capacity and piles of unsold goods? Why should private firms spend on research and development when they can piggy-back on the successes of publically funded research?

Far from being an 'incentive', therefore, competition and the profit motive — arising due to the private ownership of production — have become an enormous barrier to the development of science and technology. The need to transform society and overthrow the rotting social relations of capitalism has never been more evident.

Creative Destruction

We see, therefore, that 'innovation pessimism' and the 'race against the machine' are two sides of the same coin; a dialectical unity of opposites that reflect the contradictory, anarchic and irrational nature of capitalism — a system in which progress and development of the productive forces can only occur in an extremely chaotic and destructive way.

Remarkably, the capitalists do not deny the destructiveness of their system — rather they revel in it, coining phrases such as 'creative destruction' to make the boom-and-slump of capitalism seems not just necessary, but desirable. According to such theories, crises are needed to rid society of old industries and obsolete jobs, which must first be destroyed before new-and-improved — that is, more efficient and productive — industries and technologies can be created.

In this respect, the ruling class — and in particular the monetarist, neo-liberal wing of the capitalists — consistently pushes for 'supply-side' measures, for example, the abolition of trade unions, the elimination of the minimum wage and the 'labour market flexibility'. According to such monetarist theory, these measures are required to ensure the free movement of labour and encourage workers to retrain in search of more productive jobs. The truth, however, is that 'labour market flexibility' is simply a euphemism for 'exploitation flexibility' and an excuse for the mass unemployment that capitalism creates.

Importantly, the preachers of such dogma should check their theories against reality! One can see plenty of destruction from the 'supply-side' policies of Thatcher, Reagan, the IMF, etc., but where is the creation? And where destruction has paved the way for growth, as discussed previously in terms of the Second World War and the subsequent post-war boom, the creation of new, more productive technologies was not led by the private sector, but by the state, which took control over the main levers of scientific research and development.

The so-called creative destruction of Thatcherism in Britain has destroyed industry and unbalanced the economy in favour of a reliance on speculation, financial gambling and credit-fuelled growth; it has destroyed vital skills, but provided no training in order to help people develop any new skills, leaving millions without any hope of a job. As Marx says:

> Capital demand more youthful workers, fewer adults. This contradiction is no more glaring than the other contradiction, namely that a shortage of 'hands' is complained of, while, at the same time, many thousands are out of work, because the division of labour chains them to a particular branch of industry.[15]

Today, such complaints are more common than ever, with the spokesmen of industry and their bourgeois mouthpieces constantly talking of the need for more engineers, more scientists, more computer programmers, etc. But what do these same ladies and gentlemen do about such a shortage? Retrain those who they have previously made unemployed? Provide more money to higher education? No — the complete opposite! Unemployment increases; educated graduates stack shelves; and those looking for a future are denied an education due to larger cuts and higher fees.

Capitalism, due to its anarchic nature, based on competition and the individual pursuit of profit, is inherently unable to introduce new technologies and innovative methods except in an unplanned, chaotic and destructive way, in which new conditions of production and life are imposed upon society, as if by a force from above. Under socialism, a system based on a rational and democratic plan of production, society can make a harmonious and smooth transition to new technologies and techniques, with lifelong education and training available to everyone, and with the latest labour-saving methods used to create not forced idleness, but voluntary leisure.

15. *Ibid.*, p. 795.

Not Liberating, but Enslaving

Marxists are not against technological progress; we are not luddites who believe in the 'lump of labour' fallacy — that is, that there is a given amount of work in society and that the application of labour-saving technology must *necessarily* result in unemployment. Marxists are fully in favour of innovation and technology — in fact, we are the most consistent and ardent supporters of new technologies, which are vital for the development of the productive forces and thus of society in general.

The problem is that under capitalism, such technological progress is riddled with contradictions. The result is that the vast majority are alienated from the fruits of society's innovation. Technology, far from liberating us, is used to enslave us. Mass unemployment exists alongside those working 50–60 hours per week; meanwhile, the rich get even richer. Inequality widens, with a greater accumulation of profits at one end and increasing misery and toil at the other:

> Within the capitalist system all methods for raising the social productivity of labour are put into effect at the cost of the individual worker; all means for the development of production undergo a dialectical inversion so that they become means of domination and exploitation of the producers; they distort the worker into a fragment of a man; they degrade him to the level of an appendage of a machine, they destroy the actual contact of his labour by turning it into a torment; they alienate from him the intellectual potentialities of the labour process in the same proportion as science is incorporated in it as an independent power; they deform the conditions under which he works, subject him during the labour process to a despotism the more hateful for its meanness; they transform his life-time into working-time, and drag his wife and child beneath the wheels of the juggernaut of capital. But all methods for the production of surplus-value are at the same time methods of accumulation,

> and every extension of accumulation becomes, conversely, a means for the development of those methods. It follows therefore that in proportion as capital accumulates, the situation of the worker be his payment high or low must grow worse.

Finally, the law which always holds the relative surplus population or industrial reserve army in equilibrium with the extent and energy of accumulation rivets the worker to capital more firmly than the wedges of Hephaestus held Prometheus to the rock. It makes an accumulation of misery a necessary condition, corresponding to the accumulation of wealth. Accumulation of wealth at one pole is, therefore, at the same time accumulation of misery, the torment of labour, slavery, ignorance, brutalisation and moral degradation at the opposite pole, that is, on the side of the class that produces its own product as capital.[16]

This rising inequality is aptly demonstrated by the graph below, which shows the change in household income and GDP (economic output) per person for the United States, with 1975 as the baseline reference year.

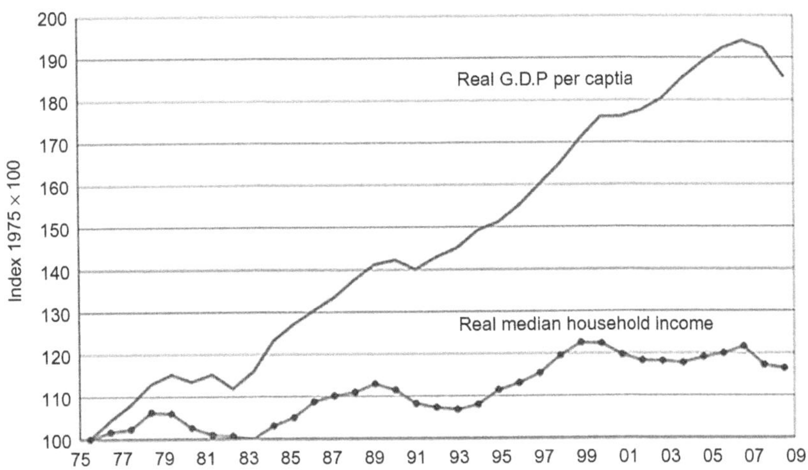

16. *Ibid.*, p. 799.

In the passage above from *Capital*, Marx refers to the 'industrial reserve army' — the unemployed workers whose ranks swell and subside with the boom–slump cycle of capitalism. But with the Great Depression of the 1930s and today's even greater crisis, we see a new phenomenon: no longer that of a reserve army of labour, but permanent mass unemployment due to the organic crisis of capitalism.

In particular, young people today have suffered from the crisis. The *Economist* (27 April 2013) estimates that, 'Around the world almost 300m 15- to 24-year-olds are not working ... almost a quarter of the planet's youth', with advanced capitalist countries such as Spain and Greece seeing youth unemployment rates of over 60%.

The *Economist* recognises the crisis as being a factor in this high youth unemployment, but again points to 'supply-side problems', complaining about 'the mismatch between the skills that young people offer and the ones that employers need'. But the question must be asked: who is providing training? Which governments are increasing the funding for education? And what problems are there in terms of 'labour flexibility'? In Britain, where the youth unemployment rate is over 20%, more than double the national average across all age groups, real wages have been stagnant at best and even business leaders state that the country has one of the most flexible labour markets.

The reality is that capitalism has nothing to offer the youth of today except a future, as Marx said, of 'misery, the torment of labour, slavery, ignorance, brutalisation and moral degradation'. A system that cannot provide a future to young people is a system that has outlived itself; a system that needs to be overthrown.

Innovation and technological progress are not a linear march onwards and upwards. Like all developments in history, the development of the productive forces — of science, industry and technique — moves in ebbs and flows.

In certain periods, technological progress and economic growth can feedback upon each other to create a virtuous circle of development: economic growth fuels the demand for labour, absorbing the 'surplus population'; the demand for labour strengthens the working class and their demands for better wages; the increased cost of wages creates a greater incentive for labour-saving techniques; and new machinery boosts productivity and thus economic growth also.

But as explained earlier, these same forces that propel the economy forward in one period can turn into their opposite and cause the virtuous circle to become a vicious one: investment in labour-saving technologies creates unemployment, putting downward pressure on wages; effective demand is cut; profit rates decline; the system, driving with pedal-to-the-metal, hurtles itself over a cliff. Thus growth and progress under capitalism can only develop in an anarchic and contradictory way.

In periods of ebb in history, it is typical for pessimism of all kinds to be expressed in the ideas expressed by the ruling class. In such times, the whole concept of progress in general is denied, and the possibility of further development is refuted on the grounds of this-or-that insurmountable barrier.

The 'innovation pessimism' of certain bourgeois economists is a reflection of this: rather than seeing the slowdown in innovation as a temporary phenomenon arising from the limits of the current social relations — that is, private ownership of the means of production — society's lack of technological progress is painted as the inevitable result of having reached a certain level of development, of having 'picked all the low-hanging fruit'. But this innovation slowdown is only 'inevitable' within the confines of capitalism, which, having reached a certain level in the development of the productive forces, is no longer able to utilise these very same forces that it has created.

The current pessimism of this tendency within the bourgeoisie is idealistic, imagining that innovation simply falls from the sky and failing to see the material, economic basis required for technological progress. The current lack of progress, like all ebbs in history, reflects the fact that the forces of production have come into contradiction with the relations of production — in other words, the ability for society to produce has come into conflict with the laws of production itself, that is, of private ownership and production for profit.

But like all previous ebbs, the barriers to further development of the productive forces can be removed and will be removed. This is the meaning of social revolution. And, as in all previous epochs, such a revolution will be accompanied by great advances, not just in science and technology, but in all areas of life — in ideas, art and culture — which are currently held back by the absolute fetter of capitalism.

Far from having 'picked all the low hanging fruit', there is a whole world of possibilities and potential awaiting humanity. In this sense, socialism will not be the end of history, but merely the beginning. One only has to think of all the potential Einsteins, Picassos and Beethovens, who are currently forced to a lifetime of drudgery in factories and fields, to imagine the potential for science, art and culture under socialism, a society in which billions would, for the first time, be able to develop and apply their individual creativities to the maximum. As Engels explains:

> With the seizing of the means of production by society, production of commodities is done away with, and, simultaneously, the mastery of the product over the producer. Anarchy in social production is replaced by systematic, definite organisation. The struggle for individual existence disappears. Then, for the first time, man, in a certain sense, is finally marked off from the rest of the animal kingdom, and emerges from mere animal conditions of existence into really human ones. The whole sphere of the conditions of life which environ man, and which have hitherto ruled man, now comes under the dominion and control of man, who for the first time becomes the real, conscious lord of nature, because he has now become master of his own social organisation.

The laws of his own social action, hitherto standing face-to-face with man as laws of Nature foreign to, and dominating him, will then be used with full understanding, and so mastered by him. Man's own social organisation, hitherto confronting him as a necessity imposed by Nature and history, now becomes the result of his own free action. The extraneous objective forces that have, hitherto, governed history pass under the control of man himself. Only from that time will man himself, more and more consciously, make his own history — only from that time will the social causes set in movement by him have, in the main and in a constantly growing measure, the results intended by him. It is the ascent of man from the kingdom of necessity to the kingdom of freedom.

A Society of Superabundance

Marxists are fully in support of developing technology: replacing labour with machinery; producing more wealth for society with less work; and reducing the hours of the working day. In the science fiction of the past — influenced by the rise of automation in production at the beginning of the twentieth century — writers imagined a future utopia in which the biggest problem facing humanity would be what to do with all our leisure time whilst machines did all the work!

Such a society has been made entirely possible by capitalism, which played a most revolutionary and progressive role in the past in terms of its development of the productive forces. But now capitalism is unable to use these productive forces and has become an absolute fetter on further progress. Rather than realising the dream of a life of leisure for all, millions are consigned to forced idleness by a system that cannot create jobs, whilst millions of others work round the clock in order to feed themselves and their families.

What's more, those increases in living standards that have been seen under capitalism — of better incomes and increased leisure time — have not been benevolently granted by the ruling class, but have been struggled for by the masses. The welfare state and the minimum wage; the weekend and the eight-hour working day; healthcare and education all of these were fought for by the working class, and are now under attack from the ruling class due to the crisis of their system.

The potential for a society of superabundance is more real now than ever. One only has to look at the official economic statistics of the bourgeoisie to see what would be possible with a socialist plan of production. The figures below show 'capacity utilisation' in Britain — that is, the percentage of the productive forces that are utilised at any time. It can be seen that even in the best of times over the past five years only 76% of our productive capability was used. In the worst periods, this falls to 50%. In other words, capitalism is only able to produce half as much as it could!

To put this into perspective, the UK's GDP is currently around £1.5 trillion. Assuming this represents, on average, only around 60% capacity utilisation, this means that under a socialist plan of production, where society's ability to use the productive forces is not held back by the need to only produce for profit, and where now 100% capacity utilisation would be possible, we could overnight increase the national economic output to £2.5 trillion.

What could we do with an extra £1 trillion (i.e., £1000 billion)? To put this in context, £1000 billion is double the combined amount that the UK government spends on pensions (£130 billion), healthcare (£121 billion), education (£87 billion), welfare (£114 billion), transport (£20 billion) and other public services (£47 billion). In other words, we could double pensions for the elderly, double spending on hospitals and schools, double the budget for infrastructure, etc., overnight by adopting a rational plan of production and utilising society's full productive capabilities.

Suddenly the so-called problem of old-age would disappear. No longer would the elderly be painted as a burden on society. Proper care and a decent pension could be provided for all. A massive programme of construction could be implemented immediately to build council homes and improve the country's creaking infrastructure. Schools and hospitals, rather than being closed and privatised, could be built and renovated. And green energy could be rolled out across the country to provide a clean environment for future generations.

The figures above in fact *underestimate* the actual potential, as in reality the unemployed would now be able to find work; the welfare bill would thus plummet, and all these extra working hands would create yet more wealth for society. And with a plan of production in place, the surplus in society could be ploughed back into further production; for example, the £800 billion worth of accumulated cash that currently sits in the bank accounts of big business in Britain — wealth that is idle due to the 'excess capacity' that exists under capitalism — could now be put to use and invested in new industry and infrastructure.

To put these figures in a different context, by increasing the capacity utilisation from 60% to 100%, society could produce the same amount of wealth using less than two-thirds the amount of labour. This means that the working day could be slashed from (a nominal length of) eight hours to less than five hours, creating an enormous amount of leisure time for all. In addition, under a rational plan of production, work would be shared out equally, eliminating unemployment and reducing the working day yet further. Meanwhile, with further investment in research, technology and productivity, further labour-saving methods could be applied, reducing the hours of the working day even further still.

Part 2
Empirical Investigation

7

Global Economy — An Enquiry

The World Bank's economic forecasts are significantly lower than those in June 2011. The fears articulated in 2011 seem to have already materialised. The global economy is likely to grow by 2.5% in 2012 and 3.1% in 2013 compared with the forecasts of 3.6% for both years. The eurozone economy is expected to contract no longer in individual countries but as a whole, that is, decline in real terms in 2012. The other advanced countries can at best register a 2.1% growth rate. The growth rate in the United States has stalled at 1.3% in the second quarter of this year. The rate of growth has slowed in five out of the last six quarters. In Britain, the growth rate has been dismal with the economy registering only 0.2% growth in the second quarter of this year. Year on year the UK economy grew by 0.7% which was the lowest rate of growth since the first quarter of 2010.

The IMF predicts the global economy will grow by 3.25% in 2012, down from an earlier forecast of 4%. The growth forecast for the UK economy has been cut to 0.6% from 1.6%. But the eurozone is set for a 'mild recession' in 2012, with GDP expected to shrink by 0.5%, compared with a previous forecast of 1.1% growth. Shadow chancellor Ed Balls called for the government to rethink its austerity plan in the light of the IMF estimates. Last year the IMF was clear that if growth undershot expectations, then the

British government should reconsider the pace of spending cuts and tax rises which choked off recovery well before the recent eurozone crisis, pushed up unemployment and has seen borrowing forecasts soar. Now the IMF has slashed their growth forecasts and confirmed that growth in Britain will indeed be much lower than they expected. And they have called on countries with low interest rates, like the United Kingdom, to reconsider the speed of their spending cuts and tax rises. World trade was slowing sharply, with growth seen at only 4.7% for this year compared with an estimated 6.6% in 2011. It also noted that oil supplies could be disrupted amid potential political tensions in the Middle East and North Africa. High deficits and debts in the United States and Japan, as well as a slow-trend GDP, or economic output, in other high-income countries, 'could trigger sudden adverse shocks'.

Recently, the Indian Commerce and Industry Ministry has released a report on the performance of industrial production and trade, says that 'industrial production growth rate has sharply declined from 6.1% to 1.9% between Septembers 2010 and 2011. India's trade deficit increased 19.6 billion dollars. Indian export has been declining from 82% in July 2011 to 44.25% in August, 36.36% in September and 10.8% in October 2011 against imports from 21.7% to 39.5% in the same year (Tables 7.1–7.4).

Table 7.1: GDP Growth Estimates and Projections: IMF and World Bank (in Percentage).

	2008	2009	2010	2011
World output	2.8	−0.6	4.8	4.2
Developed countries	0.2	−3.2	2.7	2.2
Developing countries	6.0	2.5	7.1	6.4

Source: IMF World Economic Outlook, October 2010.

Table 7.2: World Bank Global Economic Prospects, June 2010 (in Percentage).

	2008	2009	2010	2011
World output	1.7	−2.1	3.3	3.3
Developed countries	0.4	−3.3	2.3	2.4
Developing countries	5.7	1.7	6.2	6.0

Note: Figures for 2008 and 2009 are estimates, while that for 2010 and 2011 are forecasts.

Global economic growth started to decelerate on a broad front in mid-2011 and is estimated to have averaged 2.8% over the last year. This economic slowdown is expected to continue into 2012 and 2013. The United Nations baseline forecast for the growth of world gross product (WGP) is 2.6% for 2012 and 3.2% for 2013, which is below the pre-crisis pace of global growth.[1]

Persistent high unemployment in the United States and low wage growth are holding back aggregate demand and, together with the prospect of prolonged depressed housing prices, this has heightened risks of a new wave of home foreclosures. Growth in the eurozone has slowed considerably since the beginning of 2011 and the ever-simmering sovereign debt crisis heavily weighs on consumer and business confidence across Europe. The failure of policymakers in developed countries to address unemployment and prevent sovereign debt distress and financial sector fragility from escalating has posed the most acute risk for the global economy in the outlook for 2012–2013, with renewed global recession being a distinct possibility.

1. World Economic Situation and Prospects (WESP) is a joint product of the Department of Economic and Social Affairs, the United Nations Conference on Trade and Development and the five United Nations regional commissions. It provides an overview of recent global economic performance and short-term prospects for the world economy and of some key global economic policy and development issues. One of its purposes is to serve as a point of reference for discussions on economic, social and related issues taking place in various United Nations entities during the year.

Table 7.3: Global Outlook for Growth of GDP in Percentage, 1996–2012 (January 2012).

		1996–2005		2006–2011		2011		2012	
	Distribution of world output 2011	GDP growth	Contribution to world GDP growth[a]	Projected GDP growth	Contribution to world GDP growth[a]	Projected GDP growth	Contribution to world GDP growth[a]	Projected GDP growth	Contribution to world GDP growth[a]
United States	18.6	3.3	0.7	0.9	0.2	1.8	0.3	1.8	0.3
EU-15[b]	17.9	2.3	0.5	0.8	0.2	1.4	0.3	0.2	0.0
Japan	5.7	1.0	0.1	0.2	0.0	–0.5	0.0	1.5	0.1
Other advanced[c]	8.2	3.8	0.3	2.9	0.2	3.2	0.3	2.8	0.2
Advanced economies	*50.4*	*2.7*	*1.6*	*1.1*	*0.6*	*1.6*	*0.8*	*1.3*	*0.7*
China	15.8	8.1	0.6	10.9	1.3	9.2	1.4	8.0	1.2
India	5.7	6.5	0.2	8.3	0.4	7.5	0.4	6.9	0.4
Other developing Asia	5.1	3.9	0.2	5.1	0.2	5.1	0.3	5.0	0.3
Latin America	7.8	2.8	0.2	3.8	0.3	4.1	0.3	3.6	0.3

Middle East	3.5	4.5	0.1	4.8	0.2	4.8	0.2	4.0	0.1
Africa	3.3	4.5	0.1	4.9	0.2	3.8	0.1	4.8	0.2
Central and Eastern Europe	3.9	3.8	0.1	3.3	0.1	4.2	0.2	2.5	0.1
Russia and other CIS[d]	4.4	4.0	0.2	4.0	0.2	4.4	0.2	4.2	0.2
Emerging market and developing economies	*49.6*	*4.9*	*1.9*	*6.5*	*2.9*	*6.2*	*3.0*	*5.6*	*2.7*
World	*100.0%*	*3.6*		*3.5*		*3.9*		*3.5*	

Source: The Conference Board Global Economic Outlook, January 2012.
[a]The percentage contributions to global growth are computed as log differences and therefore do not exactly add up to the percentage growth rate for the world economy.
[b]EU-15 refers to states that joined the EU before 2004.
[c]Other advanced economies include Canada, Switzerland, Norway, Israel, Iceland, Cyprus, Korea, Australia, Taiwan Province of China, Hong Kong, Singapore, New Zealand and Malta.
[d]CIS is Commonwealth of Independent States which includes all former republics of the Soviet Union, excluding the Baltic states.

Table 7.4: Comparison of Base Scenario with Optimistic and Pessimistic Scenarios, 2012–2025.

	2012–2016			2017–2025			
	GDP growth in optimistic scenario	GDP growth in base scenario	GDP growth in pessimistic scenario	GDP growth in optimistic scenario	GDP growth in base scenario	GDP growth in pessimistic scenario	Distribution of world output 2025
United States	3.6	2.3	1.5	3.1	2.3	1.5	18.3
EU-15[a]	2.8	1.5	0.4	2.4	1.7	1.0	16.1
Japan	2.3	1.1	−0.1	2.0	1.5	0.9	4.9
Other advanced[b]	3.0	2.6	2.3	2.0	1.7	1.4	7.8
Advanced economies	*3.0*	*1.9*	*1.1*	*2.6*	*1.9*	*1.3*	*47.2*
China	9.6	6.9	3.9	4.9	3.5	3.1	21.8
India	7.7	6.2	4.6	5.6	4.6	4.2	8.4
Other developing Asia	5.5	4.6	3.9	4.5	3.8	3.1	4.3
Latin America	4.1	3.6	3.2	3.7	3.2	2.8	7.4

Middle East	4.8	3.9	3.0	3.9	3.2	2.5	2.7
Africa	5.4	4.6	3.9	4.7	4.1	3.7	2.7
Central and Eastern Europe	3.2	2.7	1.9	2.3	2.0	1.7	2.7
Russia and other CIS[c]	3.6	3.4	3.2	2.2	1.1	0.0	2.9
Emerging market and developing economies	*6.5*	*5.1*	*3.6*	*4.3*	*3.3*	*2.8*	*52.8*
World	*4.8*	*3.6*	*2.3*	*3.6*	*2.7*	*2.1*	*100*

Source: The Conference Board Global Economic Outlook, January 2012 † due to a calculation error in our November 2011 release for the estimates for some of the major emerging economy regions, the 2012 and 2013 are adjusted in January 2012.[2]

[a]EU-15 refers to states that joined the EU before 2004.

[b]Other advanced economies include Canada, Switzerland, Norway, Israel, Iceland, Cyprus, Korea, Australia, Taiwan Province of China, Hong Kong, Singapore, New Zealand and Malta.

[c]CIS is Commonwealth of Independent States which includes all former republics of the Soviet Union, excluding the Baltic States.

Meanwhile, developing countries and economies in transition are expected to continue to stoke the engine of the world economy, growing on average by 5.4% in 2012 and 5.8% in 2013 in the baseline outlook. Among the major developing countries, growth in China and India is expected to remain robust. GDP growth in China slowed from 10.3% in 2010 to 9.3% in 2011 and is projected to further slow to below 9% in 2012–2013. India's economy is expected to expand by between 7.7% and 7.9% in 2012–2013, down from 8.5% in 2010.

Low-income countries have experienced only a mild slowdown. In per capita terms, income growth slowed from 3.8% in 2010 to 3.5% in 2011 and, despite the global downturn; the poorer countries may see average income growth at or slightly above this rate in 2012 and 2013. The same holds for average growth among the United Nations category of LDCs.

Against this background, the report discusses several policy directions which could avoid a double-dip recession, including: optimal design of fiscal policies to stimulate more direct job creation and investment in infrastructure, energy efficiency and sustainable energy supply and food security; stronger financial safety nets; better coordination between fiscal and monetary policies; and the provision of sufficient support to developing countries in addressing the fallout from the crisis and the coordination of policy measures at the international level (Figures 7.1–7.4).

2. The Conference Board Global Economic Outlook 2012 provides projections for the output growth of the world economy for 2012, 2013–2016 and 2017–2025, including 12 major regions and about 50 advanced and emerging economies. Most forecasters only focus on the next year or two, while the IMF provides an outlook that projects six years ahead. By extending projections based on a growth accounting model, looking at the contributions of labour, capital and productivity, over more than a decade. The Conference Board outlook can identify underlying structural changes in the economy.

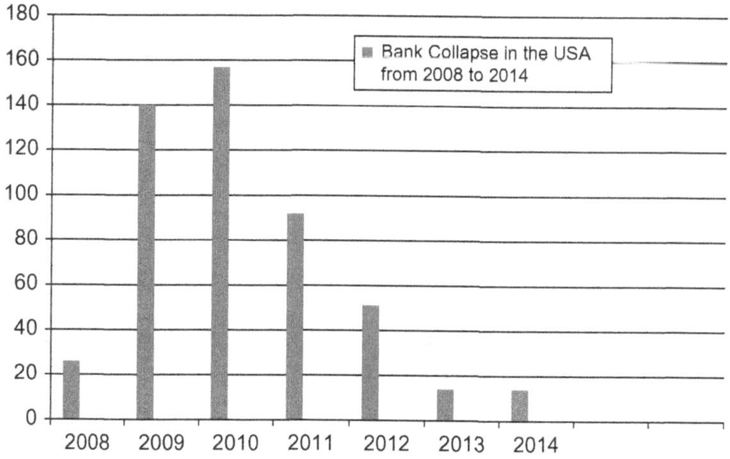

Figure 7.1: Bank Collapse in the United States (2008–2018).

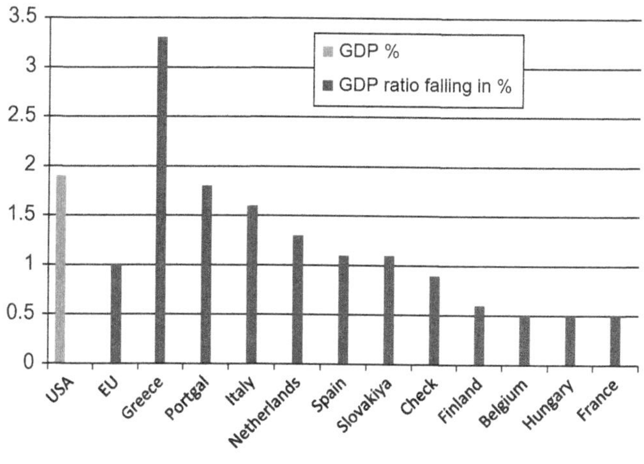

Figure 7.2: GDP Falling per Year (in Percentage). In the EU, the GDP ratio is negatively growing with 12% unemployment rate. Unemployment rates in Greece are 52% and Spain are 25%, respectively.

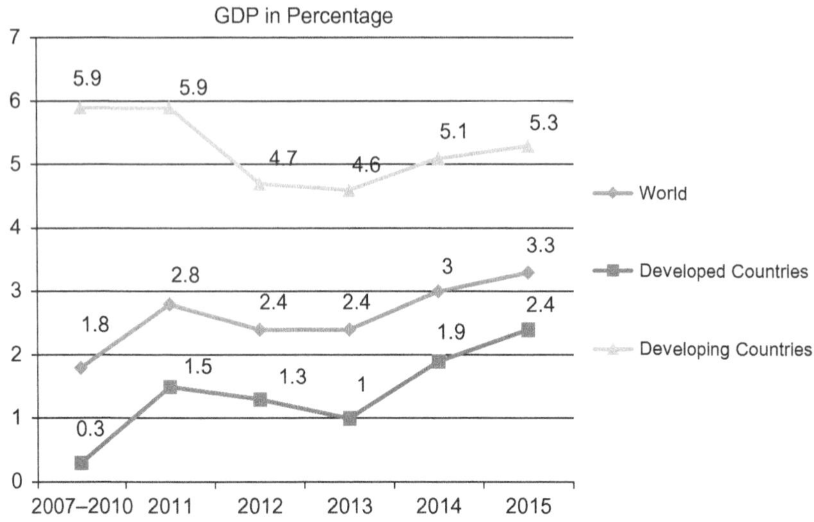

Figure 7.3: World GDP (in %).

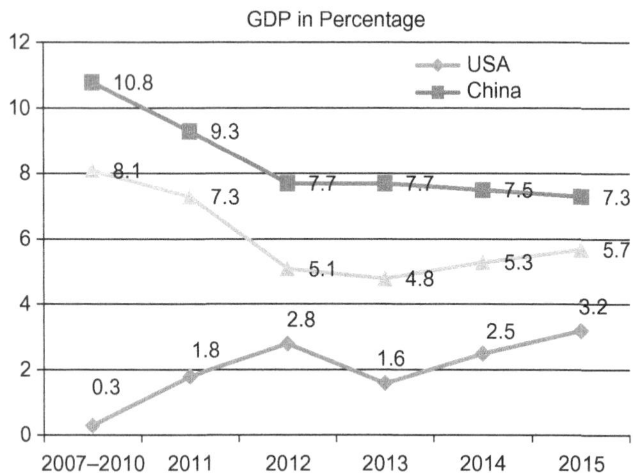

Figure 7.4: GDP of United States, China and India (in %).

Global Economic Outlook 2012

Until at least the middle of the next decade, global growth is likely to slow to approximately 3% per year on average — a rate

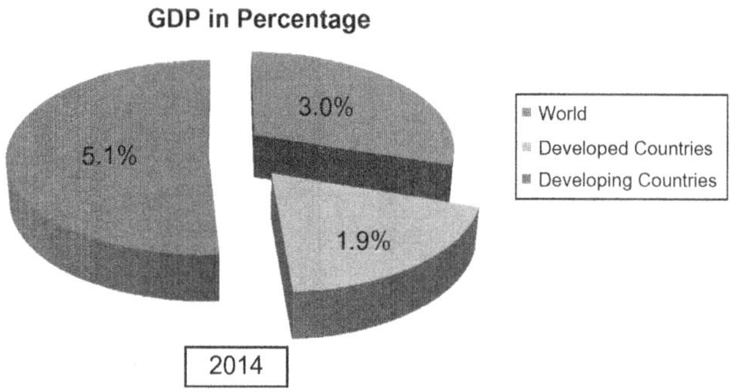

Figure 7.5: GDP of World, Developed and Developing Countries (in %).

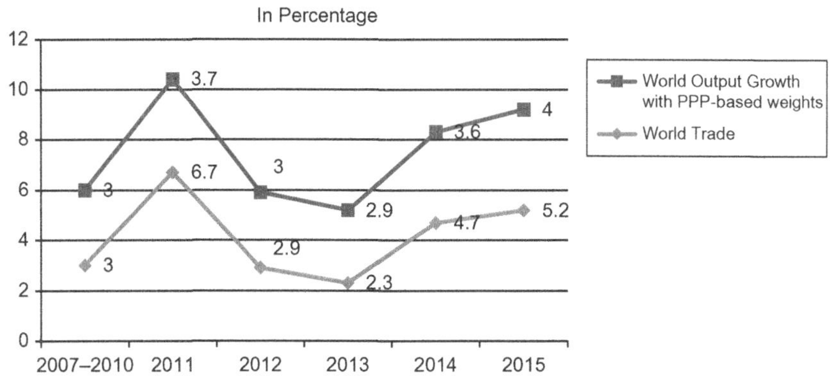

Figure 7.6: World Output Growth and World Trade (in %).

somewhat below the average of the last two decades. A recovery in advanced economies will be more than offset by a gradual slowdown in emerging ones as they mature, with the net result that global growth will slow. But the biggest risk ahead for the global economy is not this slower overall growth in output but a slowdown in average output per capita, which will determine how fast living standards can be supported and raised (Figures 7.4–7.8).

Main results:

I. Global growth is projected to grow at 3.5% in 2012, then accelerate somewhat to 3.6% from 2013 to 2016 and then

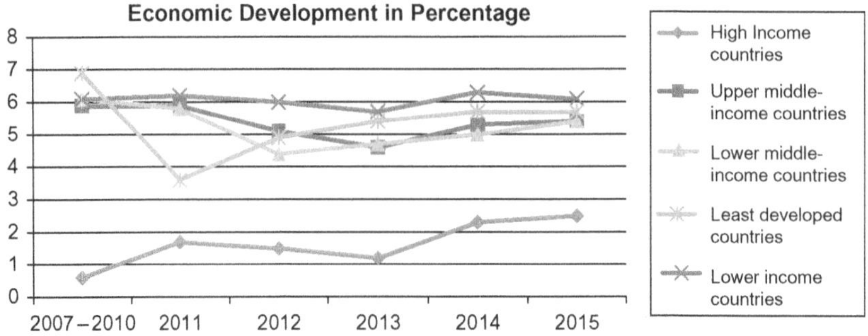

Figure 7.7: Economic Development (in %).

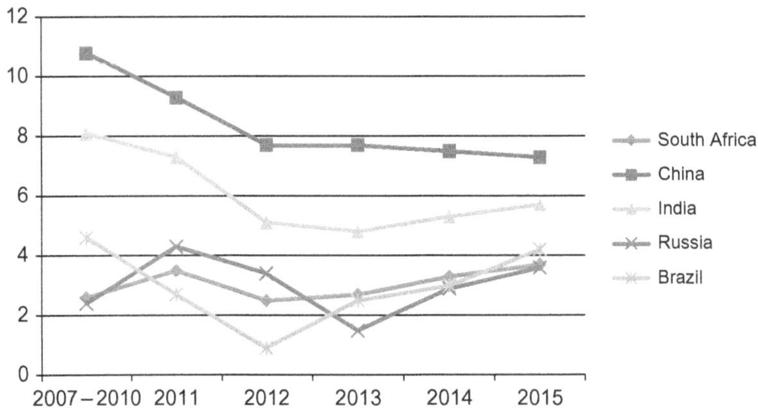

Figure 7.8: BRICS' Economic Performance in Terms of GDP (in %).

show a further slowdown to 2.7% from 2017 to 2025. At 3%, on average, global growth will still be somewhat higher than the period 1980–1995 but between half and a full percentage point below the growth rate from 1995 to 2008.

II. Advanced economy growth is expected to slowdown from an already meagre 1.6% in 2011 to 1.3% in 2012. For 2013–2016, the outlook suggests some recovery in advanced economies, bringing these countries back to the pre-recession growth trend of a little more than 2%.

III. In 2012 emerging economies will slow in growth by 0.7 percentage points on average, going from 6.3% growth in 2011 to 5.6% in 2012, partly as a result of slower export growth and partly because several of them have been growing above trend. From 2017 to 2025 emerging and developing countries are projected to grow at 3.3%. Many economies will begin to show signs of maturing, at which point the rapid catch-up growth abates.

IV. The greatest challenge for the global economy in this slow growth environment is to raise productivity without losing job opportunities for the millions who are looking for reasonably paid jobs to support their living standards. The growth rate of per capita income globally has been around 2.5% since the beginning of the century but sometime between 2017 and 2025, this rate will fall below 2%. In contrast to the past half century, that slowdown will also be accompanied by slower growth in population (Tables 7.5–7.7).

WGP is estimated to have grown by 2.1% in 2013, lower than the baseline forecast of 2.4% in 2013, but still better than the alternative pessimistic scenario presented in that report. Underperformance in the world economy was observed across almost all regions and major economic groups. Most developed economies continued struggling in an uphill battle against the lingering effects of the financial crisis, grappling in particular with the challenges of taking appropriate fiscal and monetary policy actions. A number of emerging economies, which had already experienced a notable slowdown in the past two years, encountered new headwinds during 2013 on both international and domestic fronts.

Some signs of improvements have shown up more recently: the euro area has finally come out of a protracted recession, with GDP for the region as a whole returning to growth; a few large emerging economies, including China, seem to have backstopped a further slowdown and are poised to strengthen. Premised on a set

Table 7.5: Growth of World Output 2007–2015.

Annual Percentage (%) Change								Change from WESP 2013 Forecast	
S. No.	Region/Country	2007–2010	2011	2012	2013	2014	2015	2013	2014
1.	World	1.8	2.8	2.4	2.4	3.0	3.3	0.3	–0.2
2.	Developed economies	0.3	1.5	1.3	1.0	1.9	2.4	–0.1	–0.1
3.	United States	0.3	1.8	2.8	1.6	2.5	3.2	–0.1	–0.2
4.	Japan	0.0	–0.6	1.9	1.9	1.5	1.2	1.3	0.7
5.	EU	0.2	1.7	–0.4	–0.3	1.4	1.9	–0.7	–0.3
6.	EU15	0.1	1.5	–0.5	–0.1	1.4	1.8	–0.6	–0.2
7.	New EU members	2.0	3.0	0.6	0.5	2.1	2.7	–1.5	–0.8
8.	Euro areas	0.2	1.6	–0.7	–0.5	1.1	1.6	–0.8	–0.3
9.	Other European countries	1.1	1.6	1.9	1.7	2.6	2.9	0.2	0.7
10.	Other developed countries	1.6	2.4	2.5	2.0	2.6	2.9	0.0	–0.4
11.	Economies in transition	2.9	4.6	3.2	2.0	3.3	4.0	–1.6	–0.9

12.	South-Eastern Europe	2.6	1.9	–0.9	1.8	2.6	3.1	0.6	0.0
13.	CIS and Georgia	2.9	4.8	3.4	2.0	3.4	4.1	–1.8	–1.0
14.	Russian Federation	2.4	4.3	3.4	1.5	2.9	3.6	–2.1	–1.3
15.	Developing economies	5.9	5.9	4.7	4.6	5.1	5.3	–0.5	–0.5
16.	Africa	4.8	0.8	5.7	4.0	4.7	5.0	–0.8	–0.4
17.	North Africa	4.6	–6.1	7.2	2.3	3.3	4.3	-	-
18.	East Africa	6.5	6.5	6.0	6.0	6.4	6.4	-	-
19.	Central Africa	4.8	3.9	5.8	4.2	4.8	4.1	-	-
20.	West Africa	6.0	6.1	6.7	6.7	6.9	6.8	-	-
21.	Nigeria	6.9	6.8	6.5	6.5	6.9	6.7	–0.3	–0.3
22.	Southern Africa	3.9	4.0	3.5	3.6	4.2	4.4	-	-
23.	South Africa	2.6	3.5	2.5	2.7	3.3	3.7	–0.2	–0.5
24.	East and South Asia	7.6	7.0	5.5	5.6	5.8	6.0	–0.4	–0.5
25.	East Asia	7.7	7.1	5.9	6.0	6.1	6.1	–0.4	–0.4
26.	China	10.8	9.3	7.7	7.7	7.5	7.3	–0.2	–0.5
27.	South Asia	6.9	6.4	4.2	3.9	4.6	5.1	–0.2	–1.1

Table 7.5: (*Continued*)

Annual Percentage (%) Change								Change from WESP 2013 Forecast	
S. No.	Region/Country	2007–2010	2011	2012	2013	2014	2015	2013	2014
28.	India	8.1	7.3	5.1	4.8	5.3	5.7	–1.3	–1.2
29.	Western Asia	4.0	6.9	3.9	3.6	4.3	3.9	0.3	0.2
30.	Latin America and the Caribbean	3.4	4.4	3.0	2.6	3.6	4.1	–1.3	–0.8
31.	South America	4.5	4.6	2.5	3.2	3.4	4.1	–0.8	–1.0
32.	Brazil	4.6	2.7	0.9	2.5	3.0	4.2	–1.5	–1.4
33.	Mexico and Central America	1.4	4.1	4.0	1.5	4.0	4.2	–2.4	–0.6
34.	Mexico	1.2	4.0	3.9	1.2	4.0	4.2	–2.6	–0.6
35.	Caribbean	3.5	2.7	2.8	2.4	3.3	3.8	–1.3	–0.5
By level of development									
36.	High-income countries	0.6	1.7	1.5	1.2	2.3	2.5	–0.3	–0.1

37.	Upper middle-income countries	5.9	5.9	5.1	4.6	5.3	5.4	–0.8	–0.5
38.	Lower middle-income countries	6.1	5.8	4.4	4.7	5.0	5.4	–0.8	–1.0
39.	Low-income countries	6.1	6.2	6.0	5.7	6.3	6.1	–0.2	0.2
40.	Least developed countries	6.9	3.6	4.9	5.4	5.7	5.7	–0.3	0.2
41.	World trade	3.0	6.7	2.9	2.3	4.7	5.2	–2.0	–0.2
42.	World output growth with PPP-based weights	3.0	3.7	3.0	2.9	3.6	4.0	–0.4	–0.4

Source: UNCTAD 2014/UN/DESA.

Table 7.6: Total 474 Banks Collapse in the United States in the Last Five Years, and It Is Continued.

	2008	2009	2010	2011	2012	2013	Until July 2014 (within Six Months)
United States	26	140	157	92	51	14	14

Source: Interview of Dr. Raghuram Rajan (Governor of Indian Reserve Bank), with Central Banking Journal (Financial Magazine, London on 6 August 2014).

of assumptions, WGP is forecast to grow at a pace of 3.0% and 3.3% for 2014 and 2015, respectively.

While the average growth of middle-income countries continues to be the highest, growth for the LDCs is expected to strengthen in 2014–2015. Among developed countries, the United States of America is estimated to grow at a meagre pace of 1.6% in 2013, significantly lower than the 2.8% growth of the previous year. Fiscal tightening and a series of political gridlocks over budgetary issues during the year have weighed heavily on growth. Monetary policy has been extremely accommodative, but it has had greater effect on boosting equity prices than on stimulating the real economy. Expectations arising in mid-2013 about the possible tapering of the QE programme caused some jitters in financial markets, pushing up long-term interest rates. A moderate improvement earlier in 2013 in such areas as housing and employment lost momentum towards the end of the year.

In the outlook, assuming that the future unwinding of the monetary easing will be smooth, GDP is expected to increase 2.5% and 3.2% for 2014 and 2015, respectively. Risks remain on the downside, however, particularly because political wrangling over the budget may linger for several years. Western Europe emerged from recession in the second quarter of 2013, led by net exports and, to a lesser extent, private and public consumption, but investment remained weak and unemployment stood elevated. GDP is expected to grow by 1.5% and 1.9% in 2014 and 2015, respectively.

Table 7.7: GDP Falling (in Percentage).

Country	GDP (in Percentage)	GDP (in Percentage) Falling Ratio/ Year in the Last Five Years
United States	1.90	
EU	Negative growth rate	1
Greece	–	3.30
Portugal	–	1.80
Italy	–	1.60
Netherlands	–	1.30
Spain	–	1.10
Slovakia	–	1.10
Czech	–	0.90
Finland	–	0.60
Belgium	–	0.5
Hungary	–	0.5
France	–	0.5

Source: Interview of Dr. Raghuram Rajan (Governor of Indian Reserve Bank), with Central Banking Journal (Financial Magazine, London on 6 August 2014).

Growth remains weak due to a number of factors: fiscal austerity programmes, while reduced in intensity, remain a drag; intraregional demand is still exceptionally low; and extra regional demand has slowed. Lending conditions remain tight for some countries, particularly for small- and medium-sized enterprises (SMEs).

Considerable diversity is found across countries, with the United Kingdom and Northern Ireland showing relatively strong growth, followed by Germany, while the crisis countries remain in very weak positions, with Cyprus, Greece and Portugal expected to stay in recession in 2014. Many of the new EU members in Eastern Europe remained in a sustained recession in the first half of 2013, but the situation improved in the second half of the year, with business sentiment and household confidence strengthening in response to the return to growth in Western Europe. For example, the automotive industry in Central Europe showed signs of an upturn and retail sales also increased in the Czech Republic and Poland. The aggregate GDP growth for the region is estimated to be 0.5% in 2013, and is forecast to strengthen moderately to 2.1% in 2014 and further to 2.7% in 2015.

Japan is estimated to grow by 1.9% in 2013, boosted by a set of expansionary policy packages, including fiscal stimulus and large-scale purchases of assets by the central bank. Fixed investment has been a key driver of growth, as a number of public construction projects have been financed by the supplemental budget. The Government is also expected to introduce another package targeting structural reforms soon, but the effects are not certain. Meanwhile, the anticipated increase in the consumption tax rate over the next two years is expected to curb growth. GDP is forecast to moderate to 1.5% in 2014. Regarding other developed countries, GDP in Canada is estimated to grow at 1.6% in 2013, and is expected to grow by 2.4% and 2.8% for 2014 and 2015, respectively. Residential construction was a positive contributor to GDP growth in 2013, but the pace of construction is near a maximum. GDP in Australia is estimated to grow by 2.6% in 2013 and is forecast to grow by 2.8% in 2014.

While export growth will remain solid, investment in the mining sector is expected to peak in 2014. Growth in government consumption and public investment will decelerate. GDP in New Zealand is estimated to grow by 2.6% in 2013 and is forecast to grow by 2.8% in 2014, driven by growth of exports to Asian markets.

Among developing countries, growth prospects in Africa remain relatively robust. After an estimated growth of 4.0% in 2013, GDP is projected to accelerate to 4.7% in 2014. Growth prospects are expected to be supported by improvements in the global economic and regional business environment, relatively high commodity prices, easing infrastructural constraints and increasing trade and investment ties with emerging economies. Other important factors for Africa's medium-term growth prospects include increasing domestic demand — especially from a growing class of new consumers associated with urbanisation and rising incomes — and improvements in economic governance and management. A moderate growth recovery in 2014 in emerging and developing countries, led by China, and projected improvement in major developed economies should also stimulate growth in Africa, through increased trade, investment and capital flows. After a notable slowdown in 2011–2012, economic growth in East Asia stabilised at a moderate level in 2013. The region continues to be adversely affected by relatively weak external demand from developed economies, as well as an adjustment to slower growth in China. The average growth of the region is estimated to average 6.0% in 2013, almost the same pace as 2012. A moderate pickup to 6.1% is forecast for 2014 and 2015, mainly driven by a gradual recovery in export growth amid improving conditions in developed countries. In most East Asian economies, private consumption and investment will continue to expand at a solid pace, supported by stable labour market conditions, low inflation and fairly accommodative monetary policies. Fiscal policies will remain moderately expansionary and continue to provide support for growth.

Growth in South Asia remains lacklustre as a combination of internal and external factors hamper activity, particularly in the region's largest economies, such as India, Iran and Pakistan. Growth is estimated to be 3.9% in 2013, nearly the slowest pace in two decades. Growth is forecast to pick up moderately to 4.6% in 2014 and 5.1% in 2015, supported by a gradual recovery in domestic demand in India, an end to the recession in Iran and an upturn in external demand. However, in most economies, growth will likely remain well below the level prior to the global financial crisis. Private consumption and investment are held back by a wide range of factors, including energy and transport constraints, volatile security conditions and macroeconomic imbalances.

Western Asia is estimated to grow by 3.6% in 2013, and will accelerate to 4.3% in 2014. While the member countries of the Gulf Cooperation Council (GCC) have been on a stable recovery path, continuing political instability, social unrest, security incidents and geopolitical tensions have hampered a number of other economies in the region. The Syrian crisis has been impacting the neighbouring countries in a multifaceted way. The subdued cross-border economic activities — including trade, investment and tourism — between GCC countries and the rest of Western Asia continued to fail to bring intraregional positive spillover effects. The stagnation of private capital inflows put Jordan, Lebanon and Yemen under moderate foreign exchange constraints. Turkey continued to face financial pressures, with its currency depreciating and interbank interest rates rising as a result of the decline in international capital inflows.

Growth in Latin America and the Caribbean decelerated in 2013, to a pace of 2.6%, but is forecast to improve to 3.6% and 4.1% in 2014 and 2015, respectively. In South America, Brazil is still growing at a subdued pace, curbed by weak external demand, volatility in international capital flows and tightening monetary policy. The expected improvement in the outlook will depend on strengthening global demand. Private consumption has been supportive of growth in many South American economies. Growth in Mexico and Central America is expected to accelerate in 2014–2015, supported by better performance of manufacturing exports and stable domestic demand, as well as structural adjustment. Growth in the Caribbean has been hampered by weak external demand for the tourism sector in particular and weaker commodity prices, but is expected to strengthen in the outlook.

Among economies in transition, growth in most economies of the CIS decelerated in 2013, curbed by weak exports and external financing constraints, supply-side bottlenecks and weak consumer and business confidence. Growth in the Russian Federation weakened further in the first half of 2013, as industrial output remained weak and investment became a drag on growth. The economic slowdown eventually affected previously resilient consumer confidence and led to weakening retail sales growth. The weakness in the Russian Federation has had a negative impact on its neighbours in the CIS through trade, investment and remittance channels. In the outlook, structural problems such as sluggish energy sector expansion, capacity constraints and weak investment will prevent an acceleration of growth to pre-crisis levels.

Growth in South-Eastern Europe has improved in 2013, but growth is expected to remain marginal in the near term, fluctuating between 1% and 2%, which is insufficient to address the region's long-standing needs for reindustrialisation, increased labour force participation and reduction of excessively high unemployment rates. In the outlook, the external environment for those countries is expected to improve, including the terms of access to external finance. With easing credit conditions, investment is set to recover gradually in 2014–2015, along with strengthening private consumption. GDP growth is projected to accelerate to 2.6% in 2014 and 3.1% in 2015.

Inflation Outlook

Inflation remains tame worldwide, partly reflecting output gaps, high unemployment and a continued financial deleveraging in major developed economies. Among developed economies, inflation decelerated in the United States during 2013 and is expected to remain below 2% in 2014 and 2015. Inflation has similarly decelerated in the euro area, but has dipped below 1.0%, which has raised some deflationary concerns. In Japan, the large expansionary policies aiming to reflate the economy managed to end the decade-long deflation in 2013, as the consumer price index (CPI) is estimated to increase by 0.3%, and is forecast to hit the target of 2.0% in 2014.

Among developing countries and economies in transition, inflation rates are above 10% in only about a dozen economies scattered throughout different regions. Several economies in South Asia and Africa, plus a few in the CIS, will continue to face high inflation rates, mainly owing to elevated inflationary expectations, rapid credit growth, localised food price pressures and structural bottlenecks such as energy shortages. On the other hand, most economies in East Asia continue to face benign inflation.

High Unemployment Remains a Key Challenge

The global employment situation remains challenging, as long-lasting effects from the financial crisis continue to weigh on labour markets in many countries and regions. How much of the unemployment is structural and how much is cyclical is still under debate. The answer appears to differ by region, with some countries, such as the United States facing mainly cyclical unemployment, whereas others, such as Spain, face more structural issues.

Among developed countries, the unemployment rate in the United States has continued its slow decline, down to 7.0% in late 2013, from a peak of 10% in 2010. A significant portion of this decline, however, is owing to a retreat in labour force participation. The unemployment rate is expected to decline further and reach the U.S. Federal Reserve's (Fed) critical threshold of 6.5% sometime in mid-2015. Unemployment in the euro area appears to have stabilised during 2013, at the historical high of 12.2%. In the euro area, while the unemployment rate in Germany is near historical lows of about 5%, Greece and Spain are facing extraordinarily high unemployment rates of about 27%, with the youth unemployment at twice this rate. These high rates in the euro area are expected to come down only slightly, as GDP growth will not be strong enough to make significant progress over the forecast period.

In addition, there will be lasting damage to the labour market from discouraged workers who have been unemployed for significant periods of time. The unemployment rate in Japan is relatively low, while the labour force participation rate continues to decline as the working-age population shrinks. The unemployment situation is mixed across developing countries and economies in transition, with extremely high structural unemployment in North Africa and Western Asia, particularly among youth. The unemployment rates remain low across much of East Asia, estimated at below 3% in Malaysia, Singapore, Thailand and Vietnam. In the outlook period, little change is expected, based on the comparatively modest growth forecast for the coming two years. Slowing growth in South Asia appears to have had a considerable adverse impact on employment. Reported unemployment still remains relatively low in India, but has deteriorated somewhat over the past fiscal year.

In some of these economies, changes in employment due to structural issues have affected women to a greater degree, aggravating already significant gender gaps, with high female unemployment rates in Pakistan and low female participation in Bangladesh. Modest growth in the outlook period combined with population pressures is likely to exacerbate pressures on the labour market. Positive growth in many African countries has had a limited impact on employment; the informal sector is still large and opportunities remain limited for many of those seeking to enter the labour market, as manifested in high youth unemployment rates and wide gender disparities in earnings.

In addition, continual pressure on labour markets from a steady stream of new entrants has meant that even solid GDP growth rates have not been sufficient to make measurable impacts. Even as growth slowed down in major economies in South America, such as Brazil and Mexico, unemployment remained at about 6% or below. Labour market indicators are likely to remain solid over the remainder of the year for the region; however, there may be no further improvement in the near future, despite improvements in growth, due to the fact that unemployment growth is barely equal to the growth of the labour force for a number of countries. The unemployment rate remains at historical lows in the Russian Federation, between 5% and 6%, despite a noticeable slowdown and in-migration from surrounding countries in the CIS.

A number of countries are making concerted efforts at addressing labour market issues, such as aligning macroeconomic policies appropriately with domestic conditions, promoting training for youth and other excluded segments of the labour force and taking steps to induce advances in productivity and innovation.

The expectation is that these measures will be enacted through a coordinated and integrated policy framework that will balance labour demand and labour supply, with sufficient efforts to ensure sustainable social protection. This also includes promoting an environment that is conducive to job creation with access to finance, necessary infrastructure and support for SMEs. Further steps to activate labour through skills training and upgrading will be necessary to integrate those groups that have been excluded or that have been forced to subsist through intermittent and vulnerable employment.

Trends in International Finance and Trade

Capital inflows to emerging economies are declining. Net private capital inflows to emerging markets, a subgroup of developing countries and the economies in transition have shown a measurable decline during 2013. At the same time, volatility in the financial markets of emerging economies has increased significantly, featuring equity market sell-offs and sharp depreciations of local currencies — both partly triggered by the Fed announcement that it might taper the amount of its monthly purchases of long-term assets later in the year. Waning growth prospects for emerging economies have also played a role in triggering the decline of capital inflows.

The unconventional monetary policies, or so-called QE, adopted by major central banks in the aftermath of the global financial crisis have had a significant influence on the net capital inflows to emerging economies. The QE programmes injected substantial liquidity into global financial markets and at the same time repressed long-term interest rates in developed countries. As a result, in a search for higher yields, a significant amount of capital flows was driven to markets of primary commodities and markets of equities and bonds in emerging economies in the period 2009–2012. However, in late 2012 and early 2013, as systemic risks associated with the sovereign debt crisis in the euro area abated and the prospects for economic recovery in the United States and Japan improved, international capital flows started to move away from emerging markets back to developed markets, particularly developed equity markets.

More recently, on the expectation that major central banks will taper their purchases of long-term assets and eventually sell their assets back to the markets, international investors have ratcheted up the re-pricing of assets and rebalancing of portfolios. This has led to the latest wave of declines in capital inflows to emerging economies. Given the prodigious size of the assets accumulated by major central banks through QE in the past few years, and the challenges for determining the timing and magnitude for unwinding these assets, more volatile movements of capital inflows to emerging economies are expected to occur in the next few years.

Among emerging economies, declines and volatility in capital inflows have been most pronounced in Asia. While growth in FDI inflows to China seems to have resumed some strength recently, portfolio equity inflows to India and Korea and non-bank credit flows to Indonesia have registered significant falls. Latin America has also seen a notable retrenchment of inflows, mostly in portfolio equities. In contrast, Africa, Western Asia and emerging European countries continue to see increases in capital inflows. For example, in the past year Nigeria has registered significant increases in capital inflows to both its equity and bond markets. Egypt has, however, witnessed sharp declines in net private capital inflows due to continued political instability.

External financing costs for developing countries and transition economies have also risen in the second half of 2013, triggered by the anticipation of QE tapering. The spreads between yields on sovereign bonds issued by emerging economies and the benchmark yields on government bonds of major developed countries surged by more than 100 basis points in the two weeks immediately following the Fed's announcement in May 2013 of the possibility for reducing the size of its QE purchases. By taking into account that the benchmark yields on government bonds in major developed countries also increased by about 100 basis points, the costs of external financing for emerging economies, in terms of the yields, actually increased 200 basis points on average. Among emerging economies, the spreads for Latin America are wider than others.

Outward capital flows from emerging economies have continued to increase. In addition to a continued increase in official foreign reserves, which are counted as part of outward capital flows and stood at about US$7.5 trillion by mid-2013 for emerging and developing countries as a whole, private outward capital flows of emerging economies have increased in the past few years at a robust pace, reaching an estimated amount of about US$1000 billion in 2013, almost to the same level as the net capital inflows to these countries.

Among emerging economies, China has significantly increased its outward direct investment in recent years, supported by more encouraging government policies promoting its enterprises to 'walk abroad'. After registering a total of US$88 billion in outward direct investment in 2012, available data have indicated another increase of about 20% in 2013. Many economies in Latin America, such as Brazil, Chile, Colombia, Mexico and Peru, have also increased outward capital flows, mostly in the form of portfolio investments, reflecting the need by companies, banks and pension funds in Latin America to internationally diversify their assets.

Official development assistance (ODA) flows to developing countries contracted in the past two years, falling cumulatively 2% in 2011 and 2012, down to US$126.4 billion. Of the 25 Development Assistance Committee (DAC) members, 16 decreased their ODA, mainly owing to fiscal austerity measures. Preliminary data show that bilateral aid from DAC donors to sub-Saharan Africa fell for the first time since 2007, with assistance totalling US$26.2 billion in 2012, a decline of 7.9% in real terms. Aid to landlocked developing countries and Small Island developing States also fell. In 2012, the combined DAC donors' ODA was equivalent to 0.29% of their combined gross national income, far from the United Nations target of 0.7%. ODA flows in 2013 are estimated to remain at the same level as in 2012. Slight increases are expected for 2014–2015, as more DAC members see improvement in their economies and fiscal situations. A strengthening of political commitment in the international community spurred by the United Nations campaign for accelerating progress in the Millennium Development Goals (MDGs) is also expected to support increases.

Currencies of Developing Countries under Depreciation Pressures

Foreign exchange markets experienced two distinctive episodes during 2013: the early part of the year was highlighted by a dramatic depreciation of the Japanese yen, and in May–June, a number of emerging and developing countries saw the sharp devaluation of their currencies. In the outlook for 2014–2015, major uncertainties and volatility in foreign exchange markets will still be associated with the currencies of emerging economies. Among major currencies, the yen devalued significantly vis-à-vis the U.S. dollar, from 80 yen per dollar by the end of 2012 to about 100 yen per dollar in March 2013, partly reflecting a set of drastically expansionary policies adopted by the new Japanese Administration. The yen has since stabilised within a small range of about 98 yen per dollar. The euro-to-dollar exchange rate saw some fairly wide swings, between 1.28 and 1.34, but with no clear direction during the first half of 2013, and followed by a period of appreciation in the third quarter (reaching 1.38 before dropping to 1.34 during November). Changes in relative risk perceptions were an important driving force. For the last few years these have been evenly balanced between eruptions of the euro area debt crisis and U.S. fiscal impasses. As the year progressed, however, risks stemming from the European debt crisis subsided significantly, while those in the United States remained in play.

In addition, the euro area current-account surplus began to widen notably, but stronger growth in the United States provided some counterbalance. Going forward, however, the shifting balance of monetary policies is expected to play an important role. The ECB cut its policy rates in November (the second time in 2013) leading to a sharp drop in the euro. In terms of unconventional policies, the United States is expected to taper its QE programme soon, while the ECB is still entertaining new forms of stimulus. The balance of expected policies in the three areas, coupled with the stronger growth outlook in the United States, leads to an expectation of the dollar appreciating moderately against both the yen and the euro.

Currencies in many developing countries and economies in transition have depreciated vis-à-vis the U.S. dollar and other major currencies in 2013. Currencies in a number of emerging economies depreciated by the greatest amount in May–June 2013, particularly in Brazil, India, Indonesia, South Africa and Turkey, at the same time that capital inflows to these economies declined. In contrast, the renminbi of China continued to appreciate gradually against the U.S. dollar and other major currencies. The difference between the trends in the exchange rates of China and other large emerging economies can be accounted for by a number of factors, including much larger foreign reserves, a less open capital account, higher domestic savings and more concentration of FDI in the capital inflows to China (when compared with the other emerging economies). Given the remaining current-account surplus of China vis-à-vis the United States, the renminbi is expected to further appreciate slightly against the dollar in 2014–2015, unless China liberalises its capital and financial accounts soon, which could trigger more capital outflows and renminbi depreciation. The currencies of other emerging economies are likely to remain under depreciation pressures.

Foreign Currency Reserve in Emerging Countries

The total of foreign exchange reserves held by governments around the world stood at a record $11.8646 trillion at the end of March, up $178.7 billion from the end of last year, according to the IMF. Much of the increase was due to the build-up of reserves by China and other Asian export 'tigers'.

China's foreign reserves, the world's largest, reached a record $4 trillion at the end of June. The assets in foreign currencies held by South Korea and Taiwan have also hit record highs.

The foreign reserves of even India and Indonesia, which were hit by a currency crisis due to outflows of foreign capital last summer, are also on the rise.

A net total of $44.3 billion of foreign capital flowed into emerging countries in July 2014, the highest level since September 2012, according to the Institute of International Finance, an association of major financial institutions around the world.

Such massive inflows of capital inevitably put strong upward pressure on the currencies of these emerging countries. In early July, the South Korean won, for instance, reached its highest level against the dollar in six years.

Some 60% of the world's foreign reserves are dollar assets, according to the IMF. As the flow of funds into the financial markets of emerging countries increases, the foreign reserves of their governments also grow because of currency interventions. Long-term interest rates in the U.S. have fallen to around 2.5% from the 3% level at the end of last year.

One key factor behind the decline of U.S. interest rates has been growing foreign reserves in emerging countries, said Shogo Fujita, chief Japanese-bond strategist at Merrill Lynch.

Lower interest rates in major industrial nations give a boost to capital flows into emerging countries. But the easy credit climate in industrial nations could change.

If market players become convinced that a U.S. rate hike is in the offing, foreign exchange may start pouring out of emerging countries. That's because investors are putting their money into these countries on the assumption that interest rates in the United States, Europe and Japan will remain low. Currently, money is again flowing from industrial nations into emerging nations.

There is also the possibility that the current money flow from the foreign reserves of emerging countries into U.S. government bonds may be keeping the levels of U.S. interest rates lower than where they should be from the viewpoint of the country's economic fundamentals.

Prices of Primary Commodities on a Moderate Downtrend

The prices of most primary commodities have declined moderately during 2013, mainly driven by generally weak global demand as global economic growth remained anaemic. Different patterns continue to be evident across different commodity groups, as prices are also determined by various factors on the supply side. In the outlook, with global demand expected to pick up moderately in 2014–2015, commodity prices are expected to stabilise, though they are still subject to changes in supply-side factors, such as weather conditions (for agricultural commodities) and geopolitical tensions (for oil).

Oil prices were on a downward trend in the first half of 2013, as global demand for oil weakened along with the deceleration in world economic growth overall. Geopolitical tensions can entail a large risk premium on oil prices, particular when oil supply is also tight. Most recently, global oil supply has been declining modestly: increased oil supply in North America has been offset by declines in the North Sea, while high Saudi output only partly counterbalanced a collapse in Libyan production. In the outlook, by assuming no further significant eruptions in geopolitical tensions, the Brent oil price is expected to be around US$108 per barrel (pb) for 2014–2015, compared with an estimated average of US $108.1 pb for 2013 and US$111.6 pb in 2012.

As production is expected to increase by a large margin in 2013–2014, food prices declined steadily during 2013, with prices for wheat, maize and rice declining by about 5–10%. In the outlook, food prices are projected to moderate further in 2014–2015 based on the assumption of continued increases in the global production of these grains.

Prices of minerals, ores and metals strengthened in early 2013 but fell markedly in the latter part of the year, owing to weaker than anticipated global growth — the deceleration in the growth of emerging economies being particularly notable. For example, price indices for aluminium, copper, nickel and zinc registered a steady decline during 2013, while the price of iron ore also declined significantly. In the outlook for 2014–2015, the prices of minerals, ores and metals are projected to stabilise and register modest gains as global demand improves.

International Trade Flows Remain Sluggish

International trade as the engine for global growth has shifted to a low gear over the past two years. After growing at a sluggish pace of less than 3% in 2012, as measured by the volume of world exports, international trade flows are estimated to have grown by 2.3% during 2013. Notably, the ratio between the growth of world trade and the growth of global output is at a historical low. While protracted anaemic import demand from major developed countries can explain part of the cyclical downturn in trade activity, the lack of any progress in multilateral trade negotiations over the past decade may have reduced the momentum in creating new trade flows in the world economy.

On the other hand, South-South trade is still demonstrating more dynamic patterns and becomes a major driver for the growth of international trade as a whole. The feedback effects of slow international trade growth have in turn dragged down the growth of global output. In the outlook, international trade is expected to pick up the momentum gradually, growing at 4.7% and 5.2% in 2014 and 2015, respectively.

Global Imbalances

Global imbalances, namely, the current-account imbalances across major economies, continued to narrow to a benign level in 2013. Such narrowing is not considered to be an imminent threat to the stability of the world economy, although efforts to strengthen international policy coordination should continue in order to prevent the imbalances from widening to excessive levels again in the longer run.

The United States remained the largest deficit economy, with an estimated external deficit of about US$410 billion (2.4% of GDP) in 2013, down from US$450 billion in 2012, and substantially lower than its peak of US$800 billion (6.0% of GDP) registered in 2006. The external surpluses in China, the euro area, Japan and a group of fuel-exporting countries, which form the counterpart to the U.S. deficit, have narrowed accordingly, albeit to varying degrees. China, for instance, is estimated to register a surplus of just above 2% of GDP in 2013, a sharp decline from a high of 10% of GDP in 2007.

Japan is expected to register a surplus of about 1% of GDP in 2013, also a significant reduction from its peak level of 5% of GDP reached in 2007. The current account for the euro area as a whole is in surplus of 2.5% of GDP, with Germany's surplus remaining above 5% of GDP. Large surpluses relative to GDP are still present in oil-exporting countries, reaching 20% of GDP or more in some of the oil-exporting countries in Western Asia. These countries plan to share the wealth generated by the endowment of oil with future generations through a continued accumulation of surpluses in the foreseeable future.

While some of the adjustment of the imbalances in major economies reflects certain improvements in the unbalanced domestic structure of these economies, a large part of the adjustment reflects a cyclical downturn — that is, a weakening in external demand from the deficit countries, rather than a strengthening of external demand from the surplus countries. In the United States, a corresponding narrowing of the saving-investment gap reflects a slight decline in the savings rate in 2013 and a large moderation in investment.

In the outlook for 2014–2015, the current-account deficit in the United States is expected to remain at the same level relative to GDP. In the surplus countries, the narrowing in the external surplus of China reflects a confluence of a more flexible exchange rate, and the policy measures to move the economy towards greater reliance on domestic demand. Global imbalances are not expected to widen by a significant margin in the next two years.

Uncertainties and Risks

The baseline outlook presented above is subject to a number of uncertainties and risks, mostly on the downside. In WESP 2013, three major downside risks were identified, namely, a much more detrimental adjustment in the euro area, a 'fiscal cliff' in the United States, and a hard landing in some large emerging economies. All three risks manifested themselves to some extent during 2013 and entailed certain costs for the global economy, although not to the full scale that was presented in the downside scenarios. In the outlook for 2014–2015, these risks remain relevant. While the systemic risks in the euro area abated, owing to a number of policy measures adopted over the past year, the real economy in the euro area, particularly in those member countries under debt distress, remains fragile. The United States averted a fiscal cliff in 2013, but fell into fiscal sequestration, and uncertainties remain high about the debt ceiling and the budget for 2014. The slowdown in a number of emerging economies in 2013 was 'hard' enough, and many of these emerging economies remain vulnerable in the outlook.

In addition to these remaining risks, new risks are also emerging. One of them is the risk associated with the unwinding of the unconventional monetary policies by the central banks of major developed countries over the course of 2014–2015. As indicated by the mini-financial crisis of mid-2013, sparked by the Fed simply mentioning the possibility of tapering its purchases of assets (tapering should have far less impact than unwinding, as the former continues to add liquidity while the latter withdraws liquidity), this risk could cause substantial instability for the world economy. Moreover, beyond economic risks, geopolitical tensions in Western Asia and elsewhere in the world might spiral out of control. Such tension could lead to economic disruptions directly, or indirectly through rising oil prices. These and other risk factors, unfolding unexpectedly, could derail the world economy far away from the projections outlined in the baseline forecast.

Uncertainties and Risks Associated with QE

Great uncertainties and risks for global economic growth and the financial stability of the world in the coming years are inextricably associated with the unconventional monetary policies adopted in major developed countries, or, more precisely, with the process in which the central banks of these countries start to change their stances on these policies. Since the eruption of the global financial crisis in 2008, central banks in major developed countries have implemented QE policies to purchase and hold increasingly large amounts of long-term assets. These policy measures have played a critical role in stabilising financial markets, injecting liquidity to the beleaguered banks and providing necessary support for economic recovery in general, although the significance of these positive effects is still in question. However, by moving a prodigious amount of financial assets from markets to their own balance sheets, these central banks have also created non-trivial market distortions that repress the risk premiums for certain classes of financial assets and generate moral hazard for commercial banks (allowing them to delay the clean-up of the balance sheets).

Certain side effects generated by QE have already manifested themselves in the past few years. For example, developing countries have repeatedly complained about the spillover effects of QE on their macroeconomic stability, seeing it lead to increases in volatility in capital inflows, in prices of primary commodities, and in their exchange rates. The extra liquidity injected through QE turned out to be beyond the control of the central banks that issued it. From the first round of QE occurring in late 2008 to the current open-ended, ongoing QE, international capital flows have been moving erratically back and forth across developed equity markets, emerging markets and international commodity markets.

During the summer of 2013, the Fed signalled the possibility of tapering the size of its monthly purchases of long-term assets and triggered global financial turmoil. Both equity and bond markets worldwide experienced a sharp sell-off. While equity prices in developed countries recuperated, bond yields remain elevated relative to the level before May 2013. For instance, the yield on the 10-year U.S. Treasury bond soared by about 100 basis points, reaching the highest level since late 2011. By this measure, all the efforts by the Fed to lower long-term interest rates through the latest round of QE that began in late 2012 were completely undone by the market reaction in just a few weeks. The shocks to emerging markets were more pronounced, leading to substantial declines of capital inflows for the first time since 2009. Equity prices in emerging markets plummeted by about 20% in two months and in the same period, the risk premia, as measured by the spreads of the bond yields, increased by 30% on average. Declines of capital inflows were found to be more acute in such countries as Brazil and India because of the relatively high degree of liquidity in these markets, accompanied by sharp depreciations of the local currencies.

Even in China, a seize-up of interbank lending in late June — although rooted mainly in the problems of its own banking system — was to some extent also related to the global financial turmoil. Both policymakers and financial markets are aware that, in the future, when the central banks start to taper the pace of their asset purchases and eventually unwind the process (by selling the assets back to markets), investors will inevitably have to reprise the assets and rebalance their portfolios. The hope is that, by then, banks, investors and the economy at large will be in a more robust position to endure such adjustments and the central banks will be able to engineer a smooth exit.

However, the market reaction — or over-reaction — in the summer of 2013 to the mere possibility of tapering QE in the United States has dimmed this hope and provided a vivid and timely alert to the risks for a bumpy rather than smooth exit. A bumpy exit from QE programmes could lead to a number of problematic developments: a surge in long-term interest rates, not only in developed economies but also in developing countries; a sell-off in global equity markets; a sharp decline of capital inflows to emerging economies; and a spike in the risk premia for external financing in emerging economies. Exactly because of the large scale of the assets the major central banks have accumulated in the past few years through QE, the magnitude of these shocks from the unwinding could be equally significant. For example, the QE programmes have led to a broad-based shift into fixed-income assets with longer durations; the increased duration has significantly increased the potential losses to the holders of those portfolios when interest rates rise.

Moreover, as QE moved a large proportion of the long-term bonds out of the markets, it reduced market liquidity, which in turn could intensify the shocks and lead to an overshooting of long-term interest rates. More importantly, those first-round shocks in international financial markets could transmit quickly to the domestic real economic sectors of both developed and developing countries. For example, in major developed countries, such as the United States, a marked increase in long-term interest rates would be detrimental not only to banks, in terms of funding challenges, but also to households and businesses, in terms of higher financial costs. This could stifle the fledgling recovery in private consumption and business investment. In fact, the 100-basis-point increase in benchmark long-term interest rates during the financial turmoil of May–June 2013 has already left a measurable imprint on the housing sector in the United States. As mortgage interest rates spiked, the recovery in the housing sector weakened notably.

In emerging economies, higher benchmark interest rates, rising risk premium on external financing and the decline in capital inflows would exacerbate the challenges they are already facing — that is, a slowdown in GDP growth and a further narrowing of policy space — especially for those economies with large twin deficits and elevated inflation.

Vulnerability of Emerging Economies to External Shocks

Many large developing countries, including Brazil, China, India and the Russian Federation, saw a significant deceleration in GDP growth in the past two years, due to a combination of challenging external conditions and domestic impediments. In the baseline outlook discussed earlier, growth in these economies is expected to strengthen in some cases, such as Brazil and India, and to stabilise in others, such as China. Risks remain, however, for a hard landing for some of these economies.

The financial turbulence encountered by many emerging economies during 2013 has reminded the world of the Asian financial crisis of 1997–1998. Several aspects prompt comparison between the vulnerability facing emerging economies today and the situation in the run-up to the Asian financial crisis. A few indicators are selected from three Asian economies involved in the Asian financial crisis (Indonesia, Republic of Korea and Thailand) to compare with five economies most affected by the current episode (Brazil, India, Indonesia, South Africa and Turkey).

Growth Slowdown in the BRICS

In many large developing countries, including the BRICS (Brazil, the Russian Federation, India, China and South Africa), economic growth has weakened considerably over the past two years and is now well below the pre-crisis level. For 2013, weighted GDP growth in the BRICS is projected at 5.6%, down from an annual average of about 8% during the period 2000–2008.

An important question is how much of the recent slowdown in these emerging economies is cyclical and temporary, and how much is structural and longer-term. The former implies that growth in these economies could return to the same high growth paths they enjoyed prior to the global financial crisis, once the cyclical conditions (such as external demand from developed countries) improve. The latter, on the other hand, suggests that these economies would, in the longer-term, face a 'new normal' growth path that is notably slower than before the crisis.

A standard growth decomposition exercise for the BRICS for the period 1996–2012 can reveal some interesting features about the growth deceleration in these countries. By a production function approach, GDP growth can be decomposed into the contributions from three sources: growth in labour inputs, accumulation in capital and increase in total factor productivity (TFP) — a catch-all category that measures the overall efficiency of the economy in transforming labour and capital into output. As illustrated in the figure below, most of the decline in GDP growth triggered by the eruption of the global financial crisis of 2008 can be attributed to a drop in the growth of TFP. However, the contributions from growth in labour (measured as total employment (quantity) adjusted for changes in the composition of labour) and capital have also been on a downward trend in recent years. One caveat about this exercise is that since TFP is estimated as the residual, a large part of its fluctuation in the aftermath of the financial crisis may reflect a cyclical movement caused by changes in aggregate demand, rather than a structural change in technological advance or other supply-side factors.

A number of recent studies, with various more sophisticated approaches, including structural modelling and time-series analysis techniques, have offered more information. Estimates of potential output and output gaps (the gap between actual GDP growth and potential growth) in the BRICS suggest: First, prior to the crisis, from 2005 to 2008, actual GDP grew faster than potential output, resulting in a significant positive output gap at the onset of the crisis. The rising output gap was associated with a marked increase in inflation in all of these economies, except Brazil. The output gap was probably largest in the Russian Federation and South Africa. Second, potential GDP growth seems to have declined in the aftermath of the crisis in all five economies, with the decline most pronounced in China and India. And third, small negative output gaps are currently estimated for these economies, with the largest gap in India.

The estimated decline in the potential growth, combined with relatively small negative output gaps, suggests that the pace of economic expansion in the BRICS will remain notably below the pre-crisis period. A moderate cyclical upturn is expected in the near term, particularly in India, but more lasting progress will depend on policies and reforms to remove supply-side bottlenecks to growth. In most economies, this will require increased efforts to stimulate capital accumulation, promote technological advances, strengthen human capital and improve the functioning of labour markets.

Volatility of Capital Inflows

As in the Asian financial crisis, the latest financial turmoil experienced by emerging economies has also been driven by pro-cyclical movements in fickle international capital flows. In the run-up to the Asian financial crisis, net private capital inflows to emerging economies increased by about 90% from 1994 to 1996, followed by a sharp decline of 50%. Currently, net private capital inflows to emerging economies increased by 85% from the trough of 2008 to 2012, followed by an estimated decline of 12% in 2013.

Current-Account Balances

In the three years before the Asian financial crisis, the three selected economies all experienced increases in their current-account deficits, with Thailand registering the greatest increase, from 5.4% of GDP in 1994 to 8% in 1996. In comparison, all five sampled economies have been running current-account deficits in the past few years, with the largest deficit in Turkey, at 9.7% of GDP in 2011. India's deficit was also sizeable at more than 5% of GDP.

External Debt

Measured by the ratio of foreign debt to GDP, among the three selected economies for the Asian financial crisis, Thailand had the highest external debt ratio of 50% in 1996. In the current episode, India and Turkey have the highest external debt-to-GDP ratio of about 20%. In addition, currency and maturity mismatches in emerging markets' balance sheets (particularly of the private sector) played a central role in the Asian financial crisis, but are less pronounced this time. In South Africa, for instance, approximately two-thirds of the total external debt is in domestic currency and only about 10% of total external debt is short-term debt denominated in foreign currency. Similarly, India's short-term external debt accounts for only about 5% of GDP.

Exchange-Rate Regimes

In the 1990s, most emerging economies adopted a fixed exchange-rate regime, pegging their currencies to the U.S. dollar, or other major currencies. The fixed exchange-rate regime caused at least two types of problems. First, in the run-up to the financial crisis, the fixed exchange-rate regimes tended to lead to overvaluation of the local currencies when these countries experienced higher inflation than that in the United States, and/or when they encountered adverse shocks to their exports. Second, when the crisis erupted, the fixed exchange-rate regime also obligated these countries to defend their currencies by selling their foreign reserves, only to watch those hard-earned reserves quickly drain away.

In contrast, most emerging economies have recently adopted floating, or managed floating exchange-rate regimes. A sharp devaluation of the local currency in a short period is still harmful for emerging economies, in terms of the adverse effects on inflationary pressures and losses on the balance sheets of businesses. But a flexible exchange-rate regime can, to some extent, act as a relief valve — it offsets part of the external demand shocks on the domestic economy, through adjustments to relative prices between the external sector and the domestic sector. Because of the flexible regime, the authorities do not have to vigorously defend their currencies at any pre-set level, thus avoiding rapid exhaustion of their foreign reserves.

Foreign Reserves

Before the Asian financial crisis, foreign reserves in the Republic of Korea were at about percent of GDP, Indonesia about 8% and Thailand about 20%. When they began defending their currencies from depreciation, foreign reserves were rapidly depleted, forcing these economies to seek aid from international financial institutions. Currently, foreign reserves in most emerging economies are substantially higher. For example, even in the five economies that are under financial pressure, each of them has accumulated foreign reserves above 10% of GDP, not to mention a group of other emerging economies with much higher foreign reserves.

Since the Asian financial crisis of the 1990s, as well as a few financial crises in other emerging economies in the late 1990s and the early 2000s, these economies have made a number of improvements. There is a greater transparency in the disclosure of financial information, including data on foreign reserves and non-performing loans; banking supervision and regulation has been strengthened so as to reduce mismatches in currencies and terms of debt; policy measures in managing capital inflows are more flexible; and better macroeconomic positions, in terms of more prudent fiscal and monetary policies and lower government debt-to-GDP ratios, have been achieved. In the outlook, as major central banks (particularly the Fed) are expected to taper and eventually unwind their QE programmes, emerging economies are bound to face more external shocks, especially marked declines of capital inflows. Some of these economies, particularly those with large external imbalances, remain vulnerable. Nevertheless, economic fundamentals and the policy space in these economies are better than when the Asian financial crisis erupted.

Remaining Risks in the Euro Area

The crisis in the euro area has cooled significantly but remains a significant risk factor for the world economy. The Outright Monetary Transactions (OMT) programme adopted by the ECB and other policy initiatives since late 2012 have significantly reduced sovereign risks and the risk of a euro area break-up. The OMT in particular has acted as a circuit breaker between the eruption of country-specific crises and sovereign bond markets. This explains why the political impasse in Italy and the Cypriot bank bailout during 2013 caused only limited disturbances. Despite this progress, considerable banking and fiscal risks remain.

A large number of banks still have weak balance sheets, particularly in the southern region, and could face insolvency. The Cypriot bailout in March 2013 actually raised risks in the banking sector by bailing in additional classes of creditors, thus increasing the possibility of bank runs in the future. This has heightened the urgency to create a region-wide banking union. EU finance ministers have agreed on the first stage of a banking union, and the ECB will become the top bank supervisor in the euro area. However, in the continuing discussion over the form of the future banking union, the issue of bank resolution is far from resolved, so that the problem of weak banks remains a major concern. One side effect of the OMT policy has been that banks have added more sovereign debt to their balance sheets and would therefore be more vulnerable to sovereign instability if it were to return.

The dangerous feedback loop between fiscal consolidation and economic weakness remains a risk. The growth performance of the region is improving, but most of the crisis countries remain in recession. The pressure to enact austerity measures has been reduced somewhat, as the Economic and Financial Affairs Council granted some countries extensions on the deadlines for hitting their fiscal targets. But the targets remain challenging, and will continue to hinder recovery. Considerable risk remains that these targets will be missed, owing to growth shortfalls and/or political difficulties in implementation. This could lead to a return to crisis; and, as was seen during the Cypriot episode, the support for assistance to countries in crisis has weakened.

Uncertainties and Risks from Lingering Budget Issues in the United States

Over the course of 2013, the United States has experienced a series of small-scale fiscal crises caused by political divides over budget issues in Congress. At the beginning of the year, a full-scaled fiscal cliff was averted when an agreement was reached to permanently maintain a large part of the temporary tax cuts after they were due to expire. But Congress failed to agree on a long-term deficit reduction plan, triggering automatic, across-the-board spending cuts (sequestration) worth US$1.2 trillion over the next nine years, with a cut of US$85 billion for 2013. In early October, a failure in Congress to agree on the 2014 budget and to raise the debt ceiling led to a partial shutdown of the federal government and heightened the risk of a default on the U.S. debt. At the last minute, an agreement was reached to fund the government through 15 January 2014 and suspend the debt limit through 7 February 2014, merely postponing the issues.

There are two different types of economic costs associated with these uncertainties and risks. First, the recurrent uncertainties about the government budget, even if no large-scale crisis erupts, discourage business investment and hiring, thereby leading to lower growth and higher unemployment in the short run and damaging potential growth in the longer run.

Second, should a crisis occur if the debt ceiling were not raised, for example, the consequences would be devastating not only for the United States, but also for the world economy? With the federal government budget deficit at more than 4% of GDP, if no more net borrowing were allowed, the government would be forced to take actions which would entail a combination of defaulting on the debt and cutting expenditures. Given that the United States has never defaulted, that the dollar is the major international reserve currency and that half of the U.S. government debt is held by foreigners, including foreign central banks, it is difficult to make a plausible estimate for the costs of such a default. On the other hand, the impact of a cut in government spending can be estimated through model simulation (as the one simulating the fiscal cliff in WESP 2013, for example, which remains valid today).

Policy Challenges

Macroeconomic policy stances in the world economy have become more diverse across countries, and some critical transitions are expected to occur in 2014–2015. While policies in most developed countries, except Japan, will continue to feature a combination of tightening fiscal policy and accommodative monetary policy, the degree of fiscal tightening will be less restrictive and the extent of monetary easing will taper off. The central banks of major developed countries have the primary responsibility for providing adequate and stable global liquidity, as they are the issuers of the international reserve currencies. Managing a smooth tapering of the QE will be the key challenge for the monetary authorities in major developed countries, as the risks associated with this transition will pose a threat not only for developed economies, but also for the rest of the world. In developing countries and economies in transition, policymakers are facing a more challenging international economic environment, as well as more demanding domestic economic situations, that require tough trade-offs amid a confluence of different policy needs.

Moreover, some of the challenges facing developing countries and economies in transition may go beyond the reach of standard macroeconomic policies, requiring institutional and structural reforms. A number of developing countries, such as Brazil, China and India, have indeed embarked on various reforms, including reforms in social security, income distribution, the financial sector, taxation, energy, transportation, education and health care.

Fiscal Policy

Most developed economies, with Japan as the exception, have continued fiscal tightening during 2013 by reducing government spending, raising taxes and, in some cases, liquidating public assets. The average budget deficit of developed countries is estimated to have been reduced by 1.4% of GDP to 4.5% of GDP by 2013, compared with the peak of 8.9% in 2009 at the height of the financial crisis. The average debt stands at 108.5% of GDP. In the outlook, fiscal tightening will likely continue in most of these economies, but with a notably less acute stance.

In the United States, fiscal policy has tightened markedly in 2013, through increases in taxes and automatic spending cuts (sequestration). As a result, government spending in real terms is estimated to have declined by about 5% in 2013 from the previous year. The outlook for fiscal policy in 2014–2015 is clouded by uncertainties emanating from political wrangling. Fiscal policy is expected to remain restrictive, but less severe than in 2013. In Western Europe, fiscal policy remains dominated by the need to reduce deficits under the eurozone rules and was reaffirmed by the ratification of the new fiscal compact this year. Progress has been made, but 12 out of 17 euro area countries remain under the Excessive Deficit Procedure of the Stability and Growth Pact. The fiscal compact of the euro area entered into force in 2013, adding additional fiscal targets: the structural deficit should now be less than 0.5% of GDP, and remedial action will now be required for countries with debt-to-GDP ratios above 60%. Japan, despite facing the largest debt-to-GDP ratio in the world, has adopted expansionary fiscal policy during 2013, through a supplemental budget to increase government spending by about 2.2% of nominal GDP. The government decided to implement plans to raise the consumption tax rate from the current level of 5% to 8% in April 2014 and 10% in October 2015. A new complementary package of about 5 trillion yen was introduced to compensate the negative impacts of the higher consumption tax.

Compared with developed economies, most developing countries and economies in transition have a better fiscal position in terms of budget deficits and public debt. However, their fiscal position has deteriorated measurably in 2013, with a number of low-income countries experiencing high budget deficits. The fiscal deficit has deteriorated in much of Africa, as governments across the continent are under continuous pressure to increase spending on public services, wages in the public sector and provision of subsidies on food and fuel. The deterioration is largely due to lagging revenues in oil-importing countries, while oil-exporting and mineral-rich countries have sizeable fiscal surpluses. In East Asia, fiscal policy has remained generally expansionary, as a number of countries adopted various stimulatory measures, including tax relief, expenditures in support of job creation and infrastructure projects, to counter the slowdown in domestic demand. As a result, fiscal positions have worsened slightly in 2013. A similar stance is expected for 2014. Public finances in South Asia are under pressure, with governments increasing already large deficits and regularly missing deficit reduction targets by a wide margin. Given the weak growth momentum in the region and the difficulties in raising tax revenues and curbing expenditure growth, fiscal deficits will remain large in the near term. In Western Asia, the active fiscal policy employed by oil exporters will remain, in contrast to more pronounced fiscal constraints of the non-oil exporters. In Latin America and the Caribbean, the fiscal position has deteriorated slightly in the past two years, mainly due to higher public expenditures in South America, but public revenues are also vulnerable to a softening of the prices of the primary commodities that the region exports.

In the CIS, the Russian Federation has maintained a prudent fiscal stance as budget revenue increased less than anticipated. While Ukraine is restrained by high fiscal deficit, a few oil and natural gas exporting countries, such as Azerbaijan, Kazakhstan and Turkmenistan, continued massive fiscal spending on public wages and public infrastructure

Monetary Policy

Major developed countries share a number of common features in their monetary policy. In addition to maintaining policy interest rates at zero or near zero, and adopting large-scale purchases of long-terms assets, central banks in these countries have also increasingly turned to 'forward guidance' as a policy tool, thus providing additional stimulus by anchoring expectations that interest rates will remain low for an extended period. The Fed was the first central bank to adopt forward policy guidance; it stated publicly that it would keep the target range for the federal funds rate at exceptionally low levels as long as the unemployment rate remains above 6.5%, or inflation between one and two years ahead is projected to be no more than a half percentage point above the 2% longer-run target.

The Bank of England (BoE) has joined the Fed in framing its guidance as refraining from raising the bank rate from its 0.5% level at least until the unemployment rate has fallen to a threshold of 7%. The BoE also made it clear that the unemployment threshold is not expected to be breached until at least the second half of 2016. The Bank of Japan has announced that it will continue the Quantitative and Qualitative Monetary Easing until the CPI inflation rate reaches the target of 2%. In comparison, the forward guidance recently instituted by the ECB is to confirm that their current policy setting will stay in place for an extended period of time without specifying a numerical target for exiting this setting.

Enhanced guidance by the central banks is seen as necessary for increasing policy transparency and reducing uncertainties, thereby limiting the risk of financial market volatility that diminishes policy effectiveness. In reality, however, confusion can still occur. For example, when the Fed announced in May 2013 the possibility of tapering the amount of its purchases of long-term assets by late 2013, financial markets reacted immediately by pushing up long-term interest rates significantly. When the Fed did not reduce its purchases in September 2013, markets seemed to be confused again. Managing public expectations, if possible, remains a big challenge for policymakers. As delineated in box I.1 above, central banks in major developed countries are expected to maintain the policy interest rates at their current low levels at least until mid-2015, to be followed by a gradual increase in the rates. The Fed is expected to taper QE in 2014.

Among central banks in developing countries and economies transition there is no apparent common trend in monetary policy, as some of them are tightening while others are easing. In the outlook, the monetary authorities in these countries are expected to adopt appropriate monetary policy stances in accordance with the challenges they face, including the responses to spillovers from the changes in QE of major developed countries, fluctuations in exchange rates, volatility in capital inflows and the movements in inflation, unemployment and growth.

Policy Challenges in Managing the Risks Associated with the Unwinding of QE

The tapering and unwinding of the unconventional monetary policies in major developed economies in the next few years poses significant risks for global growth and the stability of the world economy. It is a challenge for policymakers in these countries to harness a smooth process for this transition. Central banks should develop a clear communication strategy to articulate the timing and the targets of the policy action, and avoid repeating the episodes resulting from the actions of the Fed in May–June and September of 2013. At the macroeconomic levels, the timing and the pace of the unwinding are crucial: a premature and rapid unwinding may risk choking off the economic recovery, but a delayed unwinding could risk creating financial bubbles. At the technical level, contingency plans are also needed to deal with the overreaction of financial markets and prevent contagion. Efforts are needed to enhance supervision, regulation and surveillance of financial markets, in order to be able to identify and mitigate risks and vulnerabilities associated with the liquidity of some assets, market structure and other problems in advance. For developing countries and emerging economies, the challenge is to shield themselves from the spillover effects of the unwinding of QE in major developed countries, which will be transmitted through international finance and trade. As shown by the financial market turmoil in the summer of 2013, the spillover shocks to these countries can be consequential and costly, particularly to those emerging economies that are highly exposed to international capital markets and have large external imbalances financed by short-term external capital flows. Before the next episode of shocks arrives, these economies need to address external and internal imbalances and build policy space. Supervision and regulation should also be strengthened to prevent a build-up of mismatches in foreign currency funding on bank balance sheets. Prudential oversight should be tightened, particularly for shadow banking activity.

Many emerging economies today have gained policy flexibility from adopting a more flexible exchange-rate regime, compared with the Asian financial crisis of the 1990s. However, central banks in these economies may still have to defend their currencies from sharp depreciation in case of a significant decline in capital inflows. How to do it effectively remains a challenge. During the most recent financial turmoil of mid-2013, some countries, such as Brazil, India and Indonesia, raised interest rates in an attempt to curb currency depreciation. Alternatively, the central bank of Turkey has adopted a different policy scheme by creating an interest rate corridor without increasing the policy interest rate. Individual countries can and should adopt measures that are most suitable to their institutional settings and policy targets.

International Policy Coordination

The multiple and complex challenges in the world economy call for strengthening of international policy coordination. While the primary focus of globally concerted and coherent policy actions should be a stronger recovery — particularly the recovery of jobs — increasing attention should also be given to mitigating the spillover effects emanating from the large-scale, unconventional monetary policies adopted by major developed countries regarding developing countries and economies in transition. Maintaining an open multilateral dialogue on the economic policy intentions of all countries, particularly the major economies, is a crucial element in international policy coordination to promote policy coherence and concerted action. Such dialogue has so far been frequently held in the context of the Group of 20 (G-20), but it should also be promoted to more broadly representative international forums, particularly the United Nations.

At the G-20 Summit held in St. Petersburg on 5 and 6 September 2013, members reaffirmed the framework for strong, sustainable and balanced growth. The G-20 has committed to undertaking further policy adjustments towards rebalancing global demand between surplus and deficit countries. The surplus countries will achieve stronger domestic demand while the deficit countries will increase savings, and countries are encouraged to make their exchange rates more flexible. The Summit also called for urgent action to increase the momentum of the global recovery and generate higher growth and better jobs. The effectiveness of the G-20 policy coordination, however, will still need to be enforced by compliance at the individual country level.

International policy cooperation and coordination are needed to advance the reforms of the international financial system on several fronts. Progress in financial regulatory reform has been slow, encountering growing resistance from the financial industry. Some progress has been made in amending the global financial safety standards for the banking sector. A dozen countries have issued final regulations to implement Basel III and more countries have committed to do so during 2013. Progress has also been made in implementing OTC derivatives reforms. On the other hand, the question of ending the 'too big to fail' approach is still pending, and recommendations from the Financial Stability Board for the oversight and regulation of the shadow banking sector have yet to be issued. More forceful efforts are needed to address the issues of international tax avoidance and evasion, particularly through tax havens.

The current phase of reforming both the IMF and the World Bank needs to be completed to make their governance structures more representative, responsive and accountable. While there has been progress in ratifying the 2010 IMF quota and governance reforms, the process has not been finalised. The new review of the IMF quota formula should be resolved quickly to enhance the voice and participation of developing economies.

International policy cooperation should ensure that sufficient resources are made available to developing countries — especially the LDCs — and countries that possess limited fiscal space and face large financing needs for sustainable development and poverty reduction. The decline in ODA flows over the past two years should be reversed. As the target date for the MDGs is approaching, international donors should redouble their efforts to deliver on existing commitments. These resources are greatly needed in order for developing countries to accelerate progress towards the achievement of the MDGs by the end of 2015, and to build a solid foundation for long-run sustainable development beyond 2015.

8

Income, Poverty and Inequality

The world's wealth reached a record US$263 trillion in mid-2014 (which is US$20.1 trillion more wealth, as increased with 8.3% ratio when compared to mid-2013). It has almost doubled since 2000. The top richest 1% people accumulated more wealth than 3.5 billion people who just survive with 1% wealth. The 500 richest people currently own $1.54 trillion, which is more than the entire GDP of Africa. The OXFAM International predicted that the wealth of 1% of the richest people in the world amounts to US$110 trillion, and if this trend continues then they can control more wealth than 99% people in 2016. The world's 85 richest people have more assets with the same value as those owned by the poorer half of the world's population, or 3.5 billion people. In other words, it is 65 times the total wealth of the bottom half of the world's population (3.5 billion people) who just survive with 1% wealth, resulting over 75% of the world population living in underdevelopment, and extreme poverty has already reached 1.2 billion people in the third world, as shown in international organisations' reports, including UN, World Bank, Forbes, Oxfam, etc. Unemployment continues at a high level of 8.4% in the developed capitalist countries, according to the World Economic Studies and Prospects of the United Nations.[1]

1. Prabhakar, Abidin, and Saha (2015).

The OECD report (2014) says, 'In the US, the average income of the richest 10 per cent is 16 times as large as the poorest ten per cent. The US has 481 billionaires, followed by China with 358 billionaires. The US and China now have half of all billionaires on the planet. The UK, Japan, Switzerland, India and Russia are growing fast in terms of billionaires.' However, Forbes claims that each of the 67 is on average worth the same as 52 million people from the bottom of the world's wealth pyramid. Bill Gates, the world's richest man, with a net worth of $76 billion, is worth the same as 156 million people from the bottom. Who are the 67? The biggest group — 28 billionaires, or 42% of them — is from the United States. No other country comes close. Five British families enjoyed with 1.7 trillion dollars whereas world's half population have 1% of the world's total resources or wealth. On the other hand, United Nations warned that approximately 805 million people are hungry in the world every day. In India, approximately 194 million people are hungry every day. More than 46.7% of children are underweight (between 5 and 10 years). Fifty-eight percent of children aged under two are not properly developed for their age. One child out of every two is malnourished. Nearly 3000 children die from malnutrition every day. India has a 24% child mortality rate for children under five. It is also observed that each day, approximately 30% of newly-born babies die. Each year the number of Indians dying of hunger is greater than the number of Indians dying of diseases like AIDS, Malaria, and TB.[2]

A staggering 75% of the world's poor live in rural areas. Most of the rural population depends, directly and indirectly, on small-scale food crop agriculture, fishery, pastoral animal husbandry or rural wage labour associated with plantations and ranches, and ancillary activities linked to rural townships. Many rural families need to diversify their sources of income and employment in view of increasingly smaller parcels of land, low agricultural productivity, volatile weather conditions and soil erosion. Mostly developing countries' large rural communities suffer from inadequate access to food and lack of employment opportunity.

2. *Ibid.*

Under capitalism profit and income rise, and poverty, unemployment and inequality also rise. World Bank's report suggested that inequality between the rich and the poor countries has become double in the last four decades. The 20 richest nations have increased 35 times more their average incomes than the poorest nations. On the other hand, the data from all corners show that approximately 54% people of the developed countries live in slum areas.[3]

In the United States and the EU, only 1% people controlled 90% of wealth/resources, and an eminent writer and economist Davis Coten has rightly said that capitalism is an alienated ideology. In America on one side when 3000 workers have lost not only their savings but jobs in a famous company, the top managers sold their bonus and stocks and get billions of dollars on the other. In 1980, CEOZ Company's ordinary employer's salary was 40 times more than the others, today becomes 400 times more in the United States on the cost of ordinary employees who have lost their jobs due to economic recession.

The advanced capitalist economies continue to witness sluggish and unstable growth and with unemployment persisting at very high levels, for instance, a person is unemployed out of three persons today in the world. The unemployment rate stood at 9.2% in the United States in June 2011 and 9.9% in the 17 countries of the eurozone in May 2011. Today, inequality, poverty and malnutrition are growing among the societies all over the world. For instance, 1% people controlled approximately 90% of wealth/resources in America.

In India, only 8700 rich people controlled 70% of Indian wealth/resources. Approximately 230 million people (one-fourth of Indian population) are in hunger and just sleep without food. More than 800 million people (three-fourth) live on Rs. 20–25 per day. Due to global economic recession, malnutrition increased to 80% in Africa but in India, around 42% of children are malnourished, where more than 421 million Indians are absolutely poor, living across several Indian states like Bihar, Jharkhand, Orissa,

3. *Source*: UN Survey (2011).

Uttar Pradesh, Madhya Pradesh, Chhattisgarh, Rajasthan, Assam and West Bengal. The surveyors reached more than 73,000 households in 112 districts across these nine states. To measure more than 1 lakh children and talk to 73,000 mothers is indeed an extraordinary accomplishment.[4]

The survey reports high levels of malnutrition, but it also indicates that one child in five has reached an acceptable healthy weight during the last seven years in 100 focused districts. However, what concerns me is that 42% of our children are still underweight. The health of country's economy and society lies in the health of its children, Manmohan Singh said: 'There are nearly 16 crore children in the country below the age of six years. In the years to come, these children will join our work force as scientists, farmers, teachers, data operators, artisans, service providers. Several of them will become social workers like many of you in this hall.' More than 250,000 farmers (from 1997 till date) committed suicide due to inability to deposit agriculture and allied sector's both public and private loans. The wide inequality gap among the people is worsening (Table 8.1).

Table 8.1: Income Inequality Gap in India (in %).

Population in Percentage	Income in Percentage
First top richest 20%	82.7
Second top richest 20%	11
Third 20%	2.3
Fourth 20%	2.4
Bottom line poorest 20%	0.2

Source: United Nations Human Development Report (2011).

4. Source: IANS, The Citizen's Alliance against Malnutrition, Nandi Foundation, Mahindra & Mahindra and other partners and supporters for carrying out the survey.

Jobless Growth Model Has Failed

In United States jobless rate has reached a new 17 year high. The number of Britons out of work reached its highest level in more than 17 years in November 2011. The Office for National Statistics stated that the total number of people unemployed (studied using the ILO measure) rose 118,000 in three months to November 2011 to 2.69 million, the highest since August 1994.[5]

More than 4.5 American workers may lose their jobs in the near future and almost its double ratio would be in the European countries. The capitalist system has failed at all levels such as policy, management, inspection and distribution of the roles and responsibilities of the financial institutions, said OECD General Secretary Mr. Khose Ankhel Gudia on 30 September 2011. Inflation increased at highest level (especially in food and basic commodities) all over the world. Unemployment ratio has increased from 10% to 40% everywhere. A jobless growth model is only responsible for increasing poverty, inequality among the society and between the nations, unemployment, malnutrition due to food unavailability, illiteracy and environment degradation. We find everywhere that job loss and inflation are common phenomena.

Biggest Lenders (the United States and EU) Shucking the World Economy

Advanced capitalist countries are facing two basic problems such as financial deficit and public debt which have reached 100% of their GDP. The United States, Greece and Italy are the biggest lenders. Approximately, Italy has taken €1.8 trillion which is more than that of Spain, Portugal and Ireland. It is more than 126% of Italian GDP. According to European banking authority, Spain has €326 billion which has been taken from 90 European

5. *Source*: Reuters.

banks. Italian economic growth ratio is only 0.1%, and Italian government recently announced to cut their government budget, at least 20 billion dollar in 2012 and 25 billion dollar in 2013. As a result of that, 50,000 public servants may lose their jobs in the near future. It's clear that workers are paying the heaviest cost for a crisis far beyond their control.

The impact of the crisis will go further than job and income losses, causing the incidence of informal work and working poverty to rise. Young people, migrant and women workers are the most vulnerable to the current downturn and are all faced with considerable difficulties in integrating in today's labour market. This trend stands to be exacerbated by the global crisis and if viable solutions are not found, personal development and future employment prospects are threatened for millions of young people. Compared to adults, youth are almost three times as likely to be unemployed, and although they make up only 24.7% of the total working-age population, youth make up as much as 40.2% of the world's total unemployed.

Investors Have Lost Confidence

World Bank Chief Robert Zoellick said on 14 August 2011 that investors have lost confidence in the economic leadership of several key countries, warning global markets were in a 'new danger zone' as a result. It's true that investors worldwide have lost confidence in economic leadership, driving markets into a 'new danger zone', the head of the World Bank has warned ahead of a crucial meeting that could shape the eurozone's future. In a clear shot across the bows of leaders in Europe and the United States, Robert Zoellick said the events of recent weeks had led 'many market participants to lose confidence in economic leadership of some of the key countries'. Speaking at a dinner in Sydney, Australia, he added: 'I think those events, combined with some of the other fragilities in the nature of recovery, have pushed us into a new danger zone. I do not say those words lightly ... so that policymakers recognize and take it seriously for what it is.' Mr Zoellick said that a trend of acting on issues 'a day late' had led to a situation where worry 'has accumulated and so we're moving from drama to trauma for a lot of the Eurozone countries'.

Two Basic Principles of Capitalism

Man is able to control the behaviour of markets was totally wrong, and

I. Prices of commodities and factors/resources are determined by the market forces; such as demand and supply forces, were also wrong.

History shows that exploitation of resources at massive levels at cheapest price on the one hand, and highest rate of selling their products in the open market on the other hand for profit maximisation by the big corporate sectors-led economies were the two basic principles of capitalism, are still being practiced from slavery, feudalism, colonialism, capitalism and imperialism.

In capitalist society, an economic minority (the bourgeoisie) dominates and exploits the working-class (proletariat) majority. Marx uncovered the interworking of capitalist exploitation, the specific way in which unpaid labour (surplus value) is extracted from the working class (the labour theory of value), extending and critiquing the work of earlier political economists on value. Although the production process is socialised, ownership remains in the hand of the bourgeoisie. This forms the fundamental contradiction of capitalist society. Without the elimination of the fetter of the private ownership of the means of production, human society is unable to achieve further development.

Crisis Impacts on the Rest of the World: An Overview

The eurozone crisis has had a massive impact on global markets, as investors nervously await a plan to ensure Italy's government can continue to support its enormous debts. The United States and Europe, including the United Kingdom, have also come to accept that it may be many years before their heavily indebted economies regain their former dynamism. The UK FTSE 100 fell 5.6% in 2011, while the French and German markets saw falls of 17% and 15% as growing fears for the survival of the euro took their toll. But U.S. stocks ended the year up. The Libyan revolution saw the oil price surge in the first half of the year, while the gold price set a new record high as investors sought its safety.

The IMF says the current economic depression will have adverse effects on the rest of the world, and especially strongest in central and eastern Europe, where there are strong trade and financial links with the eurozone. The report calls for decisive action by governments. It says most rich countries are now doing enough to strengthen their government finances, although it says that the United States and Japan do need credible plans. But it also calls for some countries to think again about how fast they are cutting. It doesn't name countries, but it does look like the IMF is suggesting that Germany is trying to curb government borrowing too quickly. Their expectations for UK growth are in line with those of the Office of Budgetary Responsibility, and stronger than for the other major European economies.

Eurozone Growth

EU economic affairs commissioner Olli Rehn said he expected a 'moderate recession' across Europe in the first half of this year. On Monday, IMF chief Christine Lagarde warned the global economy could fall into an economic spiral reminiscent of the 1930s unless action was taken on the eurozone crisis. In its update to its September report, the IMF warned that the 'United States and other advanced economies are susceptible to spillovers from a potential intensification of the Eurozone crisis'. Growth estimates have been reduced for the main eurozone countries, including Germany, which is widely seen as the powerhouse of the region. Germany is forecast to grow 0.3% in 2012, down from the 1.3% originally predicted in September. France is expected to show 0.2% growth in 2012, down from 1.4%. However, the IMF stands by its 1.8% growth prediction for the United States, based on recent strong domestic data on jobs and manufacturing.

Risk of 'Spillovers'

Emerging markets, such as central and Eastern Europe and Asia, could also be hit by the eurozone crisis. The IMF said: 'While these markets have been quite resilient to shocks and developments in major economies in the past year, recent indicators have weakened significantly and the general business climate has deteriorated'. The IMF said Europe's most pressing challenge was to restore confidence and put an end to the crisis in the euro area. It added that world economies needed 'decisive and consistent policy action' to improve the current financial environment. 'There are three requirements for a more resilient recovery: sustained but gradual adjustment, ample liquidity and easy monetary policy, mainly in advanced economies, and restored confidence in policymakers' ability to act.'

U.S. Debt Ceiling Crisis

The deadlock in the U.S. Congress over raising the debt ceiling of the government took the country to the brink of a debt crisis. The right-wing Republicans who dominate the House of Representatives wanted deep spending cuts and no raising of taxes. President Obama succumbed to the right-wing blackmail and the Democrats struck a deal with the Republicans for spending cuts. The debt ceiling has now been raised only against an equivalent deficit reduction of $2.4 trillion over the next 10 years, out of which $900 billion will be cut straightaway from public spending programmes. The Republicans are hell bent on ensuring that taxes on the rich are not raised to narrow the deficit, which would only imply a further $1.5 trillion across the board cuts on public spending in the years to come.

Coming at time when the U.S. economy is growing at less than 1% in 2011 and unemployment is over 9% these spending cuts would weaken the welfare programmes, worsen the economic slowdown and adversely impact the global economy. The downgrading of the credit rating of the United States by the rating agency Standard and Poor's after the debt ceiling standoff in the Congress will only add to the economic woes. Already there has been a crash in the stock markets around the world after this step was taken. The sovereign debt crisis afflicting European countries also continues unabated. Governments across Europe have witnessed a marked rise in their indebtedness, owing to falling revenues on account of the economic crisis and in some cases due to the takeover of the debts of failing banks. The IMF and EU have prescribed neoliberal austerity measures as a way out of the debt crisis. The profligacy of the bankers and the bailout for them by the governments has contributed to the debt crisis. The people, especially the working class, are being made to pay the price. These austerity measures — deficit reduction through sharp cuts in public spending, cuts in wages and salaries of government employees, freeze on new employment and raising of retirement age — are being implemented across Europe.

While the governments in Greece, Romania, Ireland and Portugal who had to be directly bailed out by the EU–IMF have implemented the most drastic austerity measures, all other European governments (right-wing or centre-right in most cases) like in Spain, Italy, United Kingdom, France, Germany, etc. are also implementing deep spending cuts. This is aggravating the unemployment scenario and evoking widespread protests by workers as well as students and youth.

Crisis in Greece

Greece is a prime example where the neoliberal austerity measures, far from alleviating the crisis, has led to further slowdown in growth and revenue earnings and increased the indebtedness of the government. Unemployment in Greece has crossed 16% and the number of unemployed has risen by 40% over 2010. The IMF has extended over €17 billion as loans to the Greek government out of the total agreed bailout amount of around €110 billion. As per the loan conditionalities, the Greek government has agreed to cut spending by €14 billion and raise another €14 billion in new taxes, besides an aggressive privatisation programme, which will raise €50 billion by 2015 through sale of state assets. The Greek parliament narrowly passed these austerity measures in a vote in June 2011 in the backdrop of massive protests by the trade unions and Left-wing parties.

In many of these countries, the social democratic governments are instituting the austerity measures and refusing to contemplate any alternate policies. The Papandreou government of the Socialist Party of Greece has been in the forefront in adopting the drastic austerity measures. In Spain and Portugal, it is the Socialist Party governments which instituted the austerity measures. In the face of crisis, the social democratic parties are shifting further to the Right. They are faced with mounting popular discontent and protests. In Spain there have been prolonged sit-ins in the public squares of many cities. Tens of thousands of young people have participated in these demonstrations.

The growing unemployment and economic difficulties are giving rise to extreme right-wing forces that whip up feelings against immigrant workers and foster Islam phobia. The horrific incident in Norway in which a right-wing fanatic killed 69 young people in a youth camp of the ruling Labour Party and planted a bomb in Oslo is an outcome of such extremist and neo-fascist ideology.

Europe's Four Big Dilemmas

In October 2011, Europe's leaders reached yet another wide-ranging deal to prevent economic problems from causing financial meltdown in the eurozone. For many onlookers, the issues they face may seem complicated and interconnected. But essentially they boil down to four big dilemmas. How these dilemmas are resolved will decide whether the eurozone stays together, or ultimately unravels despite the latest agreement. Like the United States and United Kingdom, Europe faces an enormous overhang of accumulated government and private-sector debt, much of which is now not repayable. So the question is, how much gets written off, and who picks up the tab? For the eurozone as a whole, the debt problem is comparable with that of the United States, and potentially manageable. The problem is that some eurozone countries are much more heavily indebted than others. In (2011) October's deal some private sectors lenders have already agreed to write down the value of Greek debt by half. Investors also think the Portuguese, Irish and even the Spanish and Italian governments may eventually follow suit. But when bad debts get written off, someone has to take a loss.

While some of those debts are held in the United States, United Kingdom or elsewhere overseas, most of it is held by the European banks, and increasingly by the ECB. This is the primary reason for the recent loss of confidence in the European banking system. But while Germany can afford to rescue its banks, as the Irish Republic has already demonstrated, other countries may not be able to rescue theirs. The October package calls for banks to invest more than €100 billion building up their capital, but it is not yet clear if they will be able to do so without intervention from governments. If other European countries join Greece in writing off their debts, banks may need even more money. Ultimately Germany and other less-indebted countries may have to bear much of the cost of rescuing the eurozone's banks as well as its weaker governments.

Austerity versus Growth

Like everywhere else, most European governments have seen their borrowing balloon during the recession and anaemic recovery. At the same time, fears over southern European governments' ability to repay their debts mean their borrowing costs have also gone through the roof. Under pressure from Germany and the ECB, all of these countries have been pushing through painful spending cuts and tax rises (Table 8.2).

To set a good example, Germany has even donned the hair shirt itself, promising to eliminate its own modest deficit by 2013. But here's the problem: austerity is killing growth throughout Europe. And with less profit to tax and more dole cheques to write, weak growth makes it even harder for governments to cut their borrowing and repay their debts. In order to turn the slowing eurozone economy around, the ECB now looks set to slash interest rates from their current 1.5%. The central bank considered buying up

Table 8.2: Rate at Which Markets Are Willing to Lend to Governments (in %) for 10 Years.

Germany	2.05%
France	2.83%
Spain	4.95%
Italy	5.56%
Irish	7.41%
Portugal	10.80%
Greece	22.14%

Source: Bloomberg, data as of 11 October 2011.

more Italian and Spanish debt, pumping cash into the financial system and easing the pressure on those countries to slash their borrowing. But this move has always been strongly opposed by German members of the ECB. Another option to stimulate growth is for the few other countries that markets are still willing to lend to borrow and spend more, offsetting spending cuts in southern Europe. Yet for Germany, who can currently borrow at unprecedentedly cheap interest rates, borrowing is anathema.

Discipline versus Solidarity

Germany's view on the eurozone crisis is simple. Southern European governments borrowed recklessly at the cheap interest rates available inside the euro. Now they are being punished by markets, and must learn discipline. Germany wants other governments to incorporate strict budget rules into their constitutions to stop such recklessness in future. A 20% unemployment rate helped spark Egyptian-style mass protests in Spain. But rules, with penalties attached, may not be credible. Imposing a fine on an over-indebted government is rather like kicking someone when they are down. Indeed, just such a 'stability pact' of budget rules, insisted on by Germany at the euro's creation, was quickly broken with impunity by Germany itself. Moreover, the focus on discipline misses a bigger point.

While Germany's view may be apt for Greece — whose government cheated on its borrowing statistics to qualify for the euro in the first place — it is grossly unfair for Spain. Before the financial crisis, Spain's government had lower debt levels than Germany's, and (unlike Germany) actually spent less than it earned in taxes. But the country experienced a property bubble that then burst spectacularly, leaving its economy high and dry. Wages, inflated during the good years, are now uncompetitive, and unemployment has shot up to 20%. Yet, inside the euro, Spain cannot devalue to regain a price advantage. Nor can it necessarily expect the ECB to cut interest rates or buy up its debts. Compare this with the U.S. state of Michigan, where the collapse of the U.S. car industry has spelled disaster. Unlike in Europe, the United States has a federal government that can tax other states in order to help out Michigan, by paying for unemployment benefits and rehabilitating the big car companies. If the euro is to function in the future, economists warn, and then a similar system of centralised fiscal transfers will be needed there too.

Europe versus the Nations

On the face of it, the big political standoff in Europe is one of paymaster Germany versus bankrupt southern Europe. For German voters, their country's post-War economic miracle was built on a hard currency, prudent finances, and strong exports. It is hard for German voters to fathom that these very virtues are at the heart of the current crisis. But Germany has everything to lose if it does not help the south out, and the eurozone unravels. If the Greeks, Italians and others default on their debts, German and French lenders would be the biggest losers. If they also leave the euro, it would be a legal and financial disaster for all concerned.

Moreover, German export success for the past decade has been built on the weaker, more competitive exchange rate that came with sharing a currency with southern Europe. Without the euro, safe haven Germany could expect its currency to shoot up, with devastating consequences for the country's export-driven industry. Southern Europeans meanwhile would see their currencies plummet outside the euro, leading to rises in inflation and their cost of living as painful as the austerity they are protesting against. Yet these stark realities are not widely appreciated in Germany or its neighbours. Because the real problem is that there is nobody who can credibly speak for the common interest of Europe.

Since its inception in the 1950s, the European project has been run and controlled by a club of national governments. The political process has been one of haggling behind closed doors, with issues presented to electorates as a matter of competing national interests. But such haggling is dangerous in a financial crisis. Any solution must be agreed by 17 governments, and ratified by 17 parliaments, an impossibly slow process. And the longer it takes, the more bitter each dispute risks become, and the greater the market's loss of confidence in the euro becomes, undermining Europe's fragile economy.

The European Commission president, Jose Manuel Barroso, has tried to speak for the common interest, pleading for the Commission to take the lead in solving Europe's problems. But he is a political appointee, and as such, he is easily ignored by national leaders and scarcely noticed by the wider public. Perhaps, if Mr Barroso were an elected leader, he could guide European public opinion towards a comprehensive solution to the crisis that balanced the interests of the different nations. But as it is, the European public is very far from understanding the issues, or agreeing to the greater economic and political integration that may be needed to save the euro. Sadly, this political dilemma is one that may not have a workable solution.

How did the credit crunch at the end of 2007 become a full financial meltdown by the middle of 2008, and finally turn into a global recession?

HSBC reveals huge losses at its U.S. mortgage arm Household Finance due to sub-prime losses, in one of the first signs that the U.S. housing market is turning sour, and that it could have a knock-on effect on the global financial sector.

Traders Are Nervous

It has been a volatile period for global markets, driven by almost unprecedented uncertainty amongst investors about the global economy and fears that politicians may be unable to fix economic problems. Recent economic data has suggested the recovery in the West may be petering out, feeding renewed worries about the eurozone debt crisis. This, it is feared, could in turn cause a second banking crisis if governments are unable to pay back their debts. And in the face of these twin concerns some investors say policy-makers have not done enough to provide certainty about how the crisis will be tackled.

Growth Fears

The key factor worrying investors is slowing growth in the United States and Europe. The best credit rating that can be given to a borrower's debts, indicating that the risk of borrowing defaulting is minuscule. The IMF has warned that the global economy has entered what it calls a 'dangerous new phase' of low growth and high public debt. It significantly reduced its growth forecast for the world's advanced economies, predicting GDP growth of just 1.5% this year.

The U.S. Federal Reserve has also painted a pessimistic picture of the economic outlook. 'There are significant downside risks to the economic outlook, including strains in global financial markets', said the U.S. central bank in a statement. The U.S. economy created 103,000 new jobs in September, ahead of many economists' expectations. But the jobless rate was stuck at 9.1%, according to latest data from the Department of Labor. And the U.S. Commerce Department said that the world's largest economy grew at an annualised rate of 1.3% between April and June.

The eurozone's manufacturing sector is still in the doldrums, with output in September falling at its fastest pace in two years, according to Market's Eurozone Manufacturing Purchasing Managers Index. Growth in the German economy also slowed sharply between April and June, growing by just 0.1% in the quarter. The French economy was flat during the same period.

Debt Crisis Spreading

The concerns about growth have also fuelled worries about the indebtedness of eurozone states. If economies are not growing, tax receipts fall, making it harder for governments to pay off their debts. So far Greece, Portugal and the Irish Republic have received international help to deal with their crippling debt problems.

In early October, Italy's credit rating was slashed by Moody's from Aa2 to A2, with the ratings agency blaming a 'material increase in long-term funding risks for the euro area' due to lost confidence in eurozone governments' debt.

Italy follows fellow eurozone countries Spain, the Republic of Ireland, Greece, Portugal and Cyprus in having its credit rating downgraded this year. In July 2011, eurozone leaders agreed a second bailout deal for Greece, and also agreed more powers for the European Financial Stability Fund to help countries struggling with indebtedness. This allowed the fund to buy government debt (bonds), offer credit to nations in difficulty and created a special facility for recapitalising banks.

It included an agreement by private banks to swap existing Greek debt with longer-term debt paying lower interest. The enlarged eurozone rescue fund was ratified in most of the 17 nations that use the single currency, including Germany. But Italy's problems in particular meant the July deal was soon seen as insufficient.

Following its role in the Greek bailout, the European Financial Stability Facility (EFSF) was estimated to have just €250 billion (US$350 billion, £219 billion) left, which was not enough to guarantee lending to a large economy like Italy for more than a year. In October 2011 European leaders agreed a series of new measures to try to prevent the debt crisis spreading.

The EFSF will be boosted to ensure it can insure loans made to governments such as Italy up to a value of €1 trillion. In addition banks will have to write off a larger portion of Greek debt.

To prepare them for this and any future losses they will have to increase the capital they hold by more than €100 billion between them, if necessary with intervention from national governments.

Vulnerable Banks

The changes are partly designed to tackle fears that worries over sovereign debt could spill over to the banking sector. When shares have fallen they have often been led by bank shares as investors worry about what level of eurozone government debt they are holding, and whether this will be repaid.

French banks have come under particular pressure as they hold more than €40 billion (£35 billion) of Greek debt, for example, almost four times more than any other country. The Institute of

International Finance, a global trade body representing big banks and their major lenders, has said the Greek debt swap deal implies a loss for Greek lenders equivalent to 21% of the market value of their debts. This will now increase to 50%. If banks were forced to accept similar or greater losses on the debts of other countries it could trigger a new banking crisis, further destabilising the global economy.

Meanwhile, there has also been concern about the U.S.'s ability to repay its debts, with Congress agreeing on a deficit reduction plan only at the 11th hour. This delayed deal also led to the credit-rating agency Standard & Poor's cutting the long-term U.S. rating by one notch from AAA to AA+ for the first time. The G20 group of leading economies has said it is ready to 'take action' to stabilise global markets. But there is disagreement as to what form that action would take. A statement is expected during its next meeting at the start of November. Any global action will be based on steps taken at a regional and national level. With deficits already at record highs, governments have very limited room to man oeuvre.

U.S. president Barack Obama unveiled a US$450 billion (£282 billion) package of tax cuts and spending plans aimed at creating jobs and bolstering the economy. But the plans have run into trouble in Congress.

European leaders are under particular pressure to provide long-term stability for the single currency. October 2011's expansion of the EFSF, recapitalisation of the banks and further write-off of private-sector Greek debt are designed to provide that sort of reassurance. EU leaders also agreed a further €130 billion bailout for Greece, some of which will be used to assist with the further write-off of Greek government debt. However, announcing the latest deal, European Commission President Jose Manuel Barroso admitted that this was unlikely to be the last package they provided. 'I have said it before and I shall say it again, this is a marathon not a sprint.'

While the package may reassure investors, questions remain about how it will be funded. It is not yet clear who will fund the expansion of the EFSF if the loans it insures are not paid back. The recapitalisation of the banks and the write-off of Greek debt have not yet been explained in detail.

World stock markets have rounded off a wild and difficult year. The UK FTSE 100 fell 5.6% in 2011, while the French and German markets saw falls of 17% and 15% as growing fears for the survival of the euro took their toll. But U.S. stocks ended the year up.

Meanwhile, the euro ended 2011 close to a 15-month low against the dollar. The eurozone crisis has had a massive impact on global markets, as investors nervously await a plan to ensure Italy's government can continue to support its enormous debts. The United States and Europe, including the United Kingdom, have also come to accept that it may be many years before their heavily indebted economies regain their former dynamism.

Financial Markets Crashed after Crashed

International finance capital is just like flying birds. Foreign investors do not like to invest in the real (physical) economic sectors, as they always prefer in sharing with the share markets. They are committed to make huge profits for short-term goals only.

U.S. Troubles

Financial markets started 2011 in an optimistic mood. But this was dramatically halted in the summer after the United States lost its top AAA credit rating, following political deadlock in Congress over raising the country's debt ceiling — the legal limit on the federal government's total borrowing. Much of the year has been dominated by the euro crisis, which came to the boil in August. The euro ended the year close to a 15-month low against the dollar after it shed more than 3% on 19 January 2012.

With fears over the future of the eurozone, many analysts say it could drop even further in 2012. Of the heavily indebted so-called PIIGS (Portugal, the Irish Republic, Italy, Greece and Spain) countries, Irish shares fared best. France and Germany look likely to bear the brunt of the bailout costs for the southern European states — and this was reflected in the performance of their equity markets.

German Falls

France's Cac 40 dropped 17% and Germany's Dax fell 14.7% over the year. By contrast, the German market was the best performer in Europe in 2010, so it marks a dramatic change in fortunes for the European 'powerhouse'. Overall, however, the UK FTSE 100 index is 5.6% lower on the year, having fallen from 5,899.94 to close at 5,572.28 over 12 months, with worries over the impact of the eurozone crisis doing much of the damage.

This is in marked contrast to previous years — 2010 saw a 9% rise, while 2009 saw stocks rise in value by 22% during the year. 'As traders say goodbye and probably good riddance to 2011, a year that saw most of the European and Asian indices recording double-digit losses, traders may not be so welcoming to 2012 either', said Jonathan Sudaria, a dealer at brokerage Capital Spreads. The one bright spark to 2011 has been the resilience of the United States, given the weak global economic backdrop.

U.S. Downgrade

The U.S. NASDAQ and Dow Jones were rocked by the Americans' own financial woes in July, when the United States rapidly approached its debt ceiling, risking default if agreement could not be reached by a polarised Congress to raise it. And despite ultimately raising the ceiling, rating agency Standard & Poor's lowered the credit rating of the United States from AAA to AA+, deciding that the budget plan that was passed did not go far enough to address the country's deficit — a move which wiped off 5.6% of the DJIA in a single day.

On 20 January 2012, the Dow Jones industrial average closed down 69 points at 12,218, but remained higher than at the start of the year. Japan's stocks lost 17% in 2011 in the wake of March's devastating tsunami, which saw 20,000 lives lost and affected manufacturing of some of the world's most vital component suppliers, not to mention severe damage to the country's energy sector, including a nuclear meltdown at the Fukushima Daiichi plant.

Japan's Nikkei index closed at 8,429.45 on Friday — its lowest year-end close since 1982.

Top and Bottom

Unsurprisingly, the two worst performing equity markets were in the eurozone. The Cyprus market fell 72% over the year, while the Greek market was the next worse performer, down 52%. But which world stocks were the best? Not what people may expect? Calculated in their respective currencies, Venezuela was top of the class, with gains of almost 79% in 2011, followed by Mongolia and Zambia. Very few other stock markets ended the year in positive territory. On commodity markets, both the Arab Spring and the eurozone crisis have taken their toll.

The price of oil surged to the highest in more than two years in May, after a popular uprising in Tunisia sparked similar protests across the Middle East and North Africa. Clashes in Libya between rebels and forces loyal to Colonel Gadaffi cut off more than 1.5 million barrels a day of oil exports from the country. Prices gave up the year's gains by August amid the concern that the U.S. economic recovery was stalling, and speculation that Libya would resume oil production faster than expected after Gadaffi's ousting that month. The price of Brent crude — Europe's main oil price benchmark — slipped in October to its lowest in a year, as Europe's escalating debt crisis sapped confidence in the health of the global economy.

Gold Standard

For precious metals, the year was affected by fears over the sustainability of debts in Europe and the United States, and speculation that the U.S. Federal Reserve's unprecedented money creation may ultimately lead to sharply higher inflation.

During the first few months of the year, the price of silver sharply outperformed gold and by the end of April the silver price rose by nearly 56%. Gold rallied in August as the eurozone crisis affected stock markets across the globe, but has fallen back at the end of 2011. It hit an all-time high of US$1921.15 per troy ounce in September.

The bank said there is a risk that turmoil in Europe could interact with the delayed effects of monetary tightening in Asia and Latin America, reinforcing each other in a 'downward overshooting of activity'.[6] The bank cut its global forecast from 3.4% to 2.5% for 2012, warning that the eurozone has already fallen into recession and is likely to contract by 0.3% this year. 'The possibility of much worse outcomes are real', he said. If Europe's financial system to seizes up, this could lop a further 4% of global GDP.[7] 'In the event of a major crisis' countries could be forced to cut spending, which would further deepen the negative cycle. Financial turmoil in both developing and high-income countries has slammed the brakes on global growth despite relatively strong activity in the United States and Japan.

Japan Posts First Annual Trade Deficit in 30 Years

Japan has announced its first annual trade deficit in more than 30 years, a setback for a country known for its exports including cars and electronics. The deficit came in at 2.49 trillion yen (US$32 billion; £20 billion) for 2011. Japan's imports rose 12% and its exports fell 2.7%, compared to the previous year.

Struggling Exporters

The deficit underscores the pressure that Japanese exporters have come under since the disaster. Factories were damaged and supply chains disrupted for major exporters including Toyota Motor and Sony. Exporters' problems have been exacerbated by further

6. 'The sovereign debt crisis in the eurozone appears to be contained', Justin Lin, the chief economist for the World Bank, told reporters in Beijing on 18 January 2012 (Wednesday).
7. *Source*: Reuters.

disruptions to production in some of their Thailand facilities due to flooding, as well by a rising yen, which makes Japanese products more expensive overseas. The uncertainty surrounding Europe and the United States has caused global investors to turn to the yen, as a safer investment, causing it to appreciate. This means that Japan's exporters face losing their competitiveness even as rivals in South Korea and other Asian nations compete in markets which Japanese companies had previously dominated.

Energy Demands

On the import side of the trade balance Japan has had to increase the amount of incoming energy supplies, as the Fukushima nuclear disaster saw many atomic power stations being taken offline. As a result, crude oil imports surged 21.3% by value, liquefied natural gas imports rose 37.5% and petrochemical imports were up 39.5% compared to 2010, government figures showed. Nuclear power previously accounted for about 30% of electricity generation in Japan. But since the accident, Tokyo Electric Power and other utilities have been trying to restart their conventional power plants to meet energy needs. Bank of Japan Governor Masaaki Shirakawa said on Tuesday that the trade deficit would not become a 'firmly established trend' attributing it to 'temporary factors' such as the increased demands after the earthquake.

However, given that Japan's major export markets, the United States and Europe are seen going into recession some analysts are forecasting that the trade deficit will continue. Takuji Okubo of Societe Generale in Tokyo said Japan would see a trade deficit till 2014 because of 'the combination of strong demand in Japan because of earthquake and reconstruction demand and weak demand outside of Japan in Europe and the US'.

Crisis Impact on the Developing Nations: Survey

Developing country growth was revised down to 5.4% from 6.2% in the June 2011 projections. High-income countries were expected to grow a tepid 1.4% this year, weighed down by a 0.3% contraction in the 17-nation eurozone. The World Bank projected the United States, the world's largest economy, would grow 2.2% this year as it slowly recovers from the Great Recession. The 30 developing countries with financing needs that exceed 10% of GDP should seek to refinance those needs 'now', the bank said. It also recommended prioritising social safety net and infrastructure programs that are key to longer-term growth. Noting a recent decline in commodity prices had eased inflation in most developing countries, the bank said that nonetheless 'food security for the poorest, including in the Horn of Africa, remains a central concern'.

Developing countries should prepare for further downside risks, as euro area debt problems and weakening growth in several big emerging economies are dimming global growth prospects, says the World Bank in the newly released *Global Economic Prospects* (GEP) 2012. The Bank has lowered its growth forecast for 2012 to 5.4% for developing countries and 1.4% for high-income countries (−0.3% for the euro area), down from its June estimates of 6.2% and 2.7% (1.8% for the euro area), respectively. Global growth is now projected at 2.5% and 3.1% for 2012 and 2013, respectively. Slower growth is already visible in weakening global trade and commodity prices. Global exports of goods and services expanded an estimated 6.6% in 2011 (down from 12.4% in 2010), and are projected to rise by only 4.7% in 2012. Meanwhile, global prices of energy, metals and minerals, and agricultural products are down 10%, 25% and 19%, respectively, since peaks in early 2011. Declining commodity prices have contributed to an easing of headline inflation in most developing countries. Although international food prices eased in recent months, down 14% from their peak in February 2011, food security for the poorest, including in the Horn of Africa, remains a central concern.

Developing countries need to evaluate their vulnerabilities and prepare for further shocks, while there is still time, said Justin Yifu Lin, the World Bank's Chief Economist and Senior Vice President for Development Economics. Developing countries have less fiscal and monetary space for remedial measures than they did in 2008–2009. As a result, their ability to respond may be constrained if international finance dries up and global conditions deteriorate sharply. To prepare for that possibility, Hans Timmer, Director of Development Prospects at the World Bank, said: 'Developing countries should pre-finance budget deficits, prioritize spending on social safety nets and infrastructure, and stress-test domestic banks.'

While prospects in most low- and middle-income countries remain favourable, the ripple effects of the crisis in high-income countries are being felt worldwide. Already, developing country sovereign spreads have increased 45 basis points on average and gross capital flows to developing countries plunged to US$170 billion in the second half of 2011, compared with US$309 billion received during the same period in 2010. An escalation of the crisis would spare no one. Developed- and developing-country growth rates could fall by as much or more than in 2008–2009 said Andrew Burns, Manager of Global Macroeconomics and lead author of the report. The importance of contingency planning cannot be stressed enough.

The economic crisis affected developing countries through declining private financial flows, trade and remittances. IMF expects ASEAN economies, including Malaysia, to slow because of the external headwinds and weakening internal demand. The updated World Economic Outlook out of Washington on 24 January 2012 has revised downwards its growth forecast for the ASEAN-5, which also includes Indonesia, the Philippines, Thailand and Vietnam, to 5.2% for 2012.

Compared to its outlook four months ago, it now expects these economies to grow by 5.6% in 2013. During 2012–2013, growth in emerging and developing economies is expected at an average 5.75%, a significant slowdown from the 6.75% growth registered during 2010–2011 and about 0.5 percentage point lower than projected in the September 2011 WEO. This reflects the deterioration in the external environment, as well as the slowdown in domestic demand in key emerging economies, the IMF said (Table 8.3).

Despite a substantial downward revision of zero percentage point, developing Asia, which includes China and India (and ASEAN-5), is still projected to grow most rapidly at 7.5% on

Table 8.3: Overview of the World Economic Outlook Projections (Percent Change Unless Noted Otherwise).

Year over Year					Q4 over Q4		
			Projections		Estimates	Projections	
	2010	2011	2012	2013	2011	2012	2013
Developing Asia	9.5	7.9	7.3	7.8	7.4	7.9	7.6
China	10.4	9.2	8.2	8.8	8.7	8.5	8.4
India	9.9	7.4	7.0	7.3	6.7	6.9	4.8
ASEAN-5	6.9	4.8	5.2	5.6	3.7	7.4	5.0

Source: IMF (2012).
Note: Real effective exchange rates are assumed to remain constant at the levels prevailing during 14 November–12 December 2011.
ASEAN-5: Indonesia, Malaysia, Philippines, Thailand and Vietnam.

average in 2012–2013. It said the recovery of the supply chain disruptions caused by the March 2011 Japanese earthquake was also stronger, while stabilising oil prices helped support consumption. But these developments, if added, are not expected to sustain significant momentum.

By contrast, growth in the emerging and developing economies slowed more than forecast, possibly due to a greater than expected effect of macroeconomic policy tightening or weaker underlying growth. The IMF said emerging and developing economies near-term policy should focus on responding to moderating domestic growth and to slowing external demand from advanced economies. Some emerging economies with low debt and deficits and declining inflationary pressure have room to make policy more supportive of economic activity. Emerging economies highly dependent on commodity revenues and external capital inflows also need to consider the risk of a large and protracted decline in these flows. In September 2013 the IMF revised down its growth projections for the Malaysian economy from 5.5% to 5.2% for 2011 and 5.1% for 2012.

Supported by domestic demand, it expects Malaysia's growth to be led by robust investment to offset the slowdown in export momentum. The IMF warned that the risks to stability have increased, despite the various policy steps taken to contain the euro area debt crisis and banking problems. The United States and other advanced economies will be impacted by spillovers from the euro area crisis. Developments in the euro area also threaten emerging Europe and may spill over to other emerging markets. Further policy actions are needed to restore market confidence.

China Slowdown

China's Shanghai Composite Index lost 22% in 2011 as tighter government curbs on lending and investment cooled the country's rapid economic growth. The flood of state spending and bank lending after the 2008 crisis had fuelled a surge in house and stock prices. In 2010, Beijing responded by clamping down on credit and property speculators to cool inflation and soaring housing prices. Beijing is trying to ensure economic growth remains at a more sustainable level after 2010's rate of 10.3%. Growth eased to an annual rate of 9.1% in the three months ending in September, down from 9.5% on the previous quarter.

India Slowdown

The Indian economy after a year of sluggish growth is now destined to bounce back from 6.7% in 2012 to 4.8% in 2013–14, the World Bank has issued an ominous warning that the developing countries, India in particular, should be prepared for a crisis that will be on par or worse than the 2008–09 global economic meltdown. In India that further financial liberalisation will attract an inflow of foreign funds providing an impetus for growth also appear remote with the World Bank warning that the rich countries had little monetary or fiscal ammunition available to stem any vicious circle of continuing recession.

In 2014 the Indian markets saw the second biggest fall in a decade. The Sensex, the Bombay Stock Exchange's benchmark equity index, ended trading at 15,543.93 on 27 January 2012, falling 24% during the year. But foreign investors would have been doubly burnt, as India's rupee was one of the worst performing currencies this year, down 16% against the dollar.

While the East Asia and Pacific region recovered quickly from the March 2011 Tohoku disaster in Japan, flooding in Thailand and the turmoil in Europe have started to affect regional growth. After expanding by 9.7% in 2010, regional GDP grew an estimated 8.2% in 2011, but growth is projected to ease to 7.8% for both 2012 and 2013. In China, which accounts for about 80% of regional GDP, growth eased from 10.4% in 2010 to an estimated 9.1% in 2011 and is expected to dip to 8.4% in 2012 as authorities continue to dampen 'overly-fast' growth in particular segments of the economy.

GDP growth in Europe and Central Asia increased marginally from 2010 outturns to 5.3% in 2011, despite the global financial turmoil since August 2011 and weakening external demand, especially from the euro area. However, the expected slowdown in high-income Europe, still troublesome inflationary pressures in the region and reduced capital flows due to the euro area crisis may slow regional growth to 3.2% in 2012, before firming to 4.0% by 2013. Close trade and financial ties to high-income Europe will make regional outturns particularly sensitive to developments in the euro area.

Latin America and Caribbean grew by an estimated 4.2% in 2011, but this is expected to ease to 3.6% growth in 2012, before picking up to 4.2% in 2013. Weaker global growth, uncertainty arising from the euro area debt crisis, slower growth in China, and a policy-induced deceleration in domestic demand are weighing on growth prospects. Brazil's economic growth came to a halt in the third quarter and growth is forecast to be 3.4% in 2012, up slightly on 2011 but well below the 2010 growth of 7.5%. Several countries in the region could be hard hit, if international commodity prices were to weaken sharply.

Dramatic political changes in the Middle East and North Africa have disrupted economic activity substantially, but selectively, across the region, while a deteriorating external environment is beginning to amplify adverse effects on trade, commodity prices, tourism and other revenues. Developing oil exporters and the high-income GCC economies benefitted substantially from the rise in oil prices but they remain vulnerable to a sudden fall in these prices. GDP for the developing countries of the region grew by an estimated 1.7% in 2011 and is expected to remain subdued in 2012 (2.3%), rising to an expected 3.2% gain by 2013.

GDP in South Asia slowed to an estimated 6.6% in calendar year 2011, from 9.1% in 2010, reflecting a sharp slowdown in the second half of the year in India as well as external headwinds. Exports are negatively affected by weaker foreign demand and remittances have grown only modestly. Domestic demand is down sharply due to rising borrowing costs, high input prices, worries over the global slump and delay in reforms. The region's GDP growth is projected to ease further to 5.8% in 2012, before strengthening to 7.1% in 2013. High inflation and fiscal deficits remain concerns going forward.

Growth in sub-saharan Africa remained robust in 2011 at 4.9%. Excluding South Africa, which accounts for over a third of the region's GDP, growth in the rest of the region was even stronger at 5.9% in 2011, making it one of the fastest growing developing regions. Increased investment flows, rising consumer spending, and the coming on stream of new mineral exports in a number of countries should accelerate sub-Saharan Africa's growth to 5.3% in 2012 and 5.6% in 2013. Nonetheless, merchandise exports, tourism receipts, commodity prices, FDI and remittances are all susceptible to a euro area recession.

Concluding Remarks

Asia's economies are set for a tough start to 2012 as both China and India expand at their weakest pace since the tail-end of the global financial crisis in 2009 before rebounding in the second half, a Reuters poll showed on 19 January 2012. Survey of more than 250 economists across Asia found slashing growth estimates, a sign that the once roaring region is feeling the heat from higher interest rates and a raging crisis in the eurozone that is dragging it into recession. But Asia's policymakers, unlike those in the developed world who have chopped interest rates to near zero and are resorting to bond purchases and extraordinary liquidity injections as stimulus, still have ammunition left in their arsenal.

They will act to stave off any sharp declines in growth, with rate cuts expected for India, Australia, Indonesia, Malaysia, the Philippines, Thailand and Vietnam, and fine tuning of policy in the world's second largest economy, China. Asia is somewhat insulated from, but not immune to, the eurozone debt crisis. With the focus now on how to contain—rather than prevent—an eventual Greek debt default, leaders are racing to stop any contagion that might to tip the world back into recession. The IMF is now seeking to more than double its war chest by raising US$600 billion to help struggling economies but that plan is already facing stiff resistance from the United States and other countries.

China's growth is set to slip to just under 9% in 2012 with its renewed softening in price pressures providing officials with the flexibility to favour even more accommodative policy setting in support of growth. Out of 34 economists polled on China, five thought growth would dip below 8% this year (2012), a level many consider marks the borderline between a severe slowdown and a mild one. In the Reuters poll conducted on 19 January 2012, not a single economist predicted China's growth would fall below 8%.

In spite of this economic backdrop, real estate in various parts of the world has shown different price movements. According to the Savills Insights World Cities Review Spring 2011/Summer 2012 report, the value of all properties owned by the Savills Executive Unit in all cities rose 77% on average between December 2005 and June 2011. There have been big differences in the performance of individual cities: Mumbai grew 154% over the last five and a half years while New York rose only 7% over the whole period. The price growth for various cities from December 2005 to June 2011 were: Shanghai 143%, Singapore 123%, Hong Kong 98%, Moscow 94%, Paris 49%, Tokyo 44%, London 32% and Sydney 27%. The biggest difference in performance can be seen between what might be called the old economies of Tokyo, London, Paris, Sydney and New York which grew on average by 32% since 2005 and the new, or emerging, economies of Shanghai, Singapore, Hong Kong, Moscow and Mumbai which grew, on average, by 123% over the same period. It appears that the debt-induced crisis of 2008 was suffered most by the Old World cities. The biggest Old World value rebounds have been experienced in those cities that are most open to New World Investments notably London, Sydney and Paris. Hong Kong is the most expensive city in which to buy all the properties to house the Shoot Em Up (SEU). It is followed by London with Tokyo, Singapore and Paris close behind. After five years of very high price growth, Hong Kong is now significantly more expensive than the other 10 cities. It has limited land supply for expansion and price growth has been fuelled by overseas cash particularly from mainland China.

While Asia is clearly not immune to the global economic slowdown and financial market turmoil, the consensus view indicated that the current slowdown might be short-live and the region will recover towards the end of the year.

In Asia Pacific, domestic demand conditions are still robust, evident in the ongoing strength in imports and narrowing trade surpluses. This reflects a number of factors including massive government investments in infrastructure, strong business expenditures, supportive financial institutions and solid employment gains that bolster consumer spending.

ASEAN was the market of which the middle class was expanding with the rising purchasing power and 'everybody knows that the Europeans are knocking the door'. This was because 85% of trade and energy sources came from ASEAN countries, which were also an important market to the global community. At present, China, Japan, S. Korea, Australia and India were among those working with ASEAN countries. ASEAN's Secretary General, Dr. Surin Pitsuwan has said at the International Conference on Global Movement of Moderates at Kuala Lumpur on 18 January 2012 that any growth or development in the region would be done with respect to the sustainability of the environment.

The gap between rich and poor is at its highest level in most OECD countries in 30 years.[8] Today, the richest 10% of the population in the OECD area earn 9.5 times more than the poorest 10%. By contrast, in the 1980s the ratio stood at 7:1.

The average incomes at the top of the distribution have seen particular gains. However, there have also been significant changes at the other end of the scale. In many countries, incomes of the bottom 10% of earners grew much more slowly during the prosperous years and fell during downturns, putting relative (and in some countries, absolute) income poverty on the radar of policy concerns.

The increase in income inequality is evident not just in a widening gap between the top and bottom income deciles, but also in the Gini coefficient, a broader measure of inequality (which ranges from zero, where everybody has identical incomes, to 1, where all income goes to only one person). In OECD countries in the mid-1980s, the Gini measure stood at 0.29; by 2011–12, it had increased by 3 points to 0.32.

The Gini coefficient increased in 16 out of the 21 OECD countries for which long time series are available, rising by more than 5 points in Finland, Israel, New Zealand, Sweden and the United States and falling slightly only in Greece and Turkey (FOCUS on Inequality and Growth, December 2014).

The evidence is strongly in favour of one particular theory for how inequality affects growth: by hindering human capital accumulation income inequality undermines education opportunities for disadvantaged individuals, lowering social mobility and hampering skills development.

The trend increases in income inequality have dragged down growth in many OECD countries has significant policy consequences. In particular, it challenges the view that policymakers necessarily have to address the trade-off between promoting

8. Source: OECD (2014), "Focus on inequality and growth — December 2014." This document as well as figures and underlying data can be downloaded via www.oecd.org/social/inequality-and-poverty.htm

growth and addressing inequality. While previous work by the OECD has clearly shown that the benefits of growth do not automatically trickle down across society, the new evidence closes the circle by suggesting that inequality also matters for growth. Policies that help to limit or reverse inequality may not only make societies less unfair, but also wealthier.

It is not just poverty or the incomes of the lowest 10% of the population that inhibits growth. Instead, policymakers need to be concerned about how the bottom 40% fare more generally. This includes the vulnerable lower-middle classes who are at risk of failing to benefit from and contribute to the recovery and future growth. Anti-poverty programmes will not be enough. Not only cash transfers but also increasing access to public services, such as high-quality education, training and healthcare, constitute long-term social investment to create greater equality of opportunities in the long run.

Policy also needs to confront the historical legacy of underinvestment by low income groups in formal education. Strategies to foster skills development must include improved job-related training and education for the low-skilled, over the whole working live.

Key Findings

- The gap between rich and poor is now at its highest level in 30 years in most OECD countries.
- This long-term trend increase in income inequality has curbed economic growth significantly.
- While the overall increase in income inequality is also driven by the very rich 1% pulling away, what matters most for growth are families with lower incomes slipping behind.
- This negative effect of inequality on growth is determined not only by the poorest income decile but actually also by the bottom 40% of income earners.

- This is because *inter alia* people from disadvantaged social backgrounds underinvest in their education.
- Tackling inequality through tax and transfer policies does not harm growth, provided these policies are well designed and implemented.
- In particular, redistribution efforts should focus on families with children and youth, as this is where key decisions on human capital investment are made and should promote skills development and learning across people's lives.

9

BRICS: A New World Economic Order

The balance of economic power from the west (which has been dominated from the last four to five centuries) dramatically shifted to the east since 2007 when major capitalist developed countries including the U.S. face economic recession. As an emerging regional block the BRICS play a significant role through acquiring the technological capacity and internalise capability to exploit resources, develop infrastructure and finally reduce the gap between demand and supply through improving production capacity and the distribution networks with the principles of collective self-reliance at the South–South level.

BRICS have increased their trade, financial as well as technical cooperation and established distinct ways and means of economic cooperation, especially through south–south cooperation with three continents, namely, Africa, Latin America and Asia. BRICS are striving for more economic and political influence, thereby challenging western domination 'global economic order' maintaining currency supremacy like dollar and euro through international financial agencies like World Bank and IMF since the Second World War.

Global economic recession and instability has given an opportunity to forge new mutually beneficial partnerships in the fields of economic, trade, energy security and technology which will ultimately act as an engine of economic growth and socio-economic development among the developing countries. The quest for the exploration of the newer paradigm led to the birth of an idea called BRICS — it is about the tremendous force of solidarity, which can help overcome even the biggest challenges confronting the world. It has potential to bridge the technological gap to improve capability, and ensure equal distribution of resources, opportunities and freedom, to abolish foreign currency domination (like dollar and euro) and imperialist military domination, which would ultimately achieve the goal of self-reliance. With the influential and remarkable progress through promoting local currency (for de-dollarisation), regional FDI and regional trade, BRICS economies have emerged, and took a new space in the twenty-first century.

Russia hosted the seventh BRICS summit 9–10 July 2015, in Ufa, the capital of the Republic of Bashkortostan, gathering the heads of state of the five countries. Expanding investment cooperation and exploring a strategy for multilateral economic cooperation was the centrepiece of Russia's 2015 agenda in the framework of the BRICS. The crossroads of Asia and Europe, BRICS have decided to launch various projects of the Silk World Order of trade and integration. It is no coincidence, however, that the Seventh BRICS and Fifteenth SCO summits have been combined as one large international summit, to use the opportunity to bring the integration process of the Silk World Order. One informal session at Ufa was including not only all the members of the BRICS and the SCO, but also all the members of the Eurasian Economic Union (EEU).

Armenia has also attended the joint BRICS and SCO summit in Bashkortostan, since all the other members of the Eurasian Economic Space are either full SCO members or, in the case of Belarus, an SCO dialogue partner. The BRICS-SCO-EEU talks were 'a sign that Russia is aiming for political block-building', Azerbaijan and Turkmenistan were also participated in informal meeting of the BRICS, SCO and EEU. The Eurasian and global convergences in Ufa used the links that already exist between the two, China's New Silk Road and the Russian-led EEU begins a roadmap to fuse together in Bashkortostan as the pivotal axis of rotation in the Eurasian space.

While the New Silk Road and the EEU come together in Ufa, the BRICS initiates together a development map while the SCO also outlined its expansion plans for new full members. The applications of India, Iran and Pakistan for full membership have been discussed. Moreover, Egypt and several other countries have applied to join the SCO in come context. Ufa is being used to stamp out a roadmap for the 'Eurasian Century' and a Silk World Order that goes beyond Eurasia, which includes everything from a transcontinental mega railroad network connecting the Iberian Peninsula to the South China Sea and to what has been dubbed as the 'modern city of the Eurasian continent' in Belarus.

The Chinese are busy building trade infrastructure and transport networks. In Belarus, the Chinese are building the first 'modern city of the Eurasian continent' in the forests next to the Minsk National Airport as part of what *Bloomberg* calls 'a manufacturing springboard between the European Union and Russia'. Upon completion, the new export-oriented city in Belarus, which is being built on the route of the European highway that links Berlin, Warsaw, Minsk and Moscow, will be the largest manufacturing and industrial park in Europe.

The Silk World Order that is being shaped in Ufa is determined to replace the existing Bretton Woods financial architecture of the world unravelled. It is to be replaced by the BRICS that is no longer dominated by the trilateral grouping of the United States, Western Europe and Japan. The monopoly of the World Bank and the IMF, which has benefited Washington, is at its end. The U.S. dollar as a currency in bilateral and multilateral trade is being scraped by the BRICS, SCO and EEU — Washington's flooding of oil markets was partially aimed at derailing this by forcing renewed dependence on the U.S. dollar for energy trade.

Background of BRICS

BRIC (Brazil, Russia, India and China) concept launched by Jim O'Neill occurred amid a need of developing countries to get out of the shadow of industrialised nations (G-7). Dominated by scepticism at first, the five emerging economies had become, for a decade, a symbol of change of power in the global economy and an important representative of the developing world in the development and cooperation relations at bilateral, regional and even multilateral level. BRIC was formed in 2001, and subsequent accession of South Africa in 2011 formed the new BRICS.

BRICS encompass over 26% of the world's land coverage with 44% of the world's population. Over the past 10 years, BRICS countries increased their share of global gross domestic product from 18% to 28%. Approximately, 24.4% sharing in gas production in the world, 36.3% share in gold reserve, 40.2% share in traditional energy production, 20.7% share in oil production, 32% agricultural land areas, 50% contribution to the world GDP and 10.8% share in defence sector. Currently, BRICS hold a combined GDP (PPP) of 18.486 trillion dollars, and almost 20% to global trade, inspire of the economic challenges that are experienced throughout the world today. In 2015 over 30% of the world's biggest corporations in the Fortune 500 list were Southern corporations. BRICS may account for 41% of the world's market capitalization by 2030 (Prabhakar, 2015).

BRICS encompass:

- over 26% of the world's land coverage
- 44% of the world's population
- 28% share to global gross domestic product.
- 24.4% sharing in gas production in the world
- 36.3% share in gold reserve
- 40.2% share in traditional energy production
- 20.7% share in oil production
- 32% agricultural land areas
- 50% contribution to the world economy

- 10.8% share in defence sector
- BRICS hold a combined GDP (PPP) of 18.486 trillion dollars, and
- 20% share to global trade
- BRICS may account for 41% of the world's market capitalization by 2030.

In 2014 the combined economic output of Brazil, Russia, India, China and South Africa almost matched the U.S.'s GDP. Back in 2007, the U.S. economy was double that of the BRICS.

India and Russia signed up as the next two biggest contributors to the China-led Asian Infrastructure Investment Bank among the 57 member-nations. The United States and Japan are absent from the ranks in what's seen as a rival to the IMF and World Bank.

China has been the clear breakout economy, with its GDP jumping from about equal to its four peers combined to more than 50% larger.

Russia and Brazil, stars in the early BRIC days, have lost their lustre more recently as sliding commodity prices and political stresses cloud their outlooks. Indian economy is in high gear, having eclipsed Russia's and closing in on Brazil's.

The BRICS' sixth summit was hosted in Fortaleza, Brazil, on 14–16 July 2014, and the fifth summit hosted in Durban in March 2013, the five countries' leaders announced that a 'New Development Bank' will focus on infrastructure investment in developing countries, which, they said, was constrained by 'insufficient long-term financing and foreign direct investment'. They pledged to make an initial capital contribution to the bank that would be 'substantial and sufficient for the bank to be effective in financing infrastructure'. A second initiative announced in Durban was the creation of a $100 billion contingent reserve facility to deal with 'short-term liquidity pressures'. New Development Bank (NDB) of BRICS has been set up with 100 billion dollars (six lakh crore India Rupees) assets with 100 billion dollars contingency reserve arrangement, where 41% China's share, Brazil, Russia and

India sharing 18% and South Africa's share is only 5%. In the world economy, BRICS have one-fifth share (1/5) but only 10.3% voting share in the IMF, where the United States has 19.2% share (in term of purchasing power) in world GDP but enjoys with 16.8% voting rights in the IMF but China has only 3.8% voting rights when its share is 16.1% in the world GDP.

India contributes 6.0% in world GDP but voting rights of India is only 2.3% in the IMF. India and China contribute 22.1% combined to the world GDP but combined share of voting rights is 6.1% only. At least, 1 trillion dollar is needed for investment in infrastructure development in developing countries. Unfortunately, multilateral development bank provides just 40% of their requirements but for the basic infrastructures like electricity, transportation, telecommunication, water, health, education, developing countries need more investment; then the IMF and the World Bank provide loan.

The key issue on the agenda is the establishment of a joint development bank with capital stock of US$100 billion (€72 billion). The development bank is a sign of the economic power of the BRICS countries and their willingness to advance financial cooperation with each other.

Counterweight to U.S. Dominance

In Brazil, the veto by the U.S. Congress caused an outcry, further deteriorating the already strained relations between the two countries. Following the surveillance scandal revealed by former NSA contractor Edward Snowden, Brazilian president Dilma Rousseff distanced herself from Washington, promptly cancelling her planned meeting with U.S. president Barack Obama in September 2013.

Rousseff's predecessor Luiz Inacio Lula da Silva, in office from 2003 to 2011, had established a counterweight to the political dominance of the United States in Latin America by expanding the south–south cooperation. Growing trade among emerging markets resulted in China replacing the United States as the primary buyer of Brazilian products in 2009. Since 2012, the Chinese have also been Brazil's most important import partner.

For Rousseff, the political and strategic cooperation with China is even more important than the growing trade between the two countries. Brazil views the participation of Chinese president Xi Jinping at the BRICS summit in Fortaleza as an absolute priority. His official visit is the first of a Chinese head of state in Brazil and in the region. After the BRICS summit, a meeting is planned with the heads of state of the Community of Latin American and Caribbean States (Celac).

The Ukraine crisis is accelerating the strategic orientation of Brazil towards Asia and Africa. It appears that the greater the Moscow's isolation, the better the coordination among the BRICS members. Neither Brazil nor China, India or South Africa has commented on the events in Kyiv or Crimea. The principle of non-intervention has clearly welded the otherwise heterogeneous countries together.

'For Brazil, the BRICS countries are a platform to benefit as a mediator and reformer on the international stage', said Cristina Pecequilo, a political scientist at the University of Sao Paulo, adding that she doesn't view Russia's G8 exclusion as so tragic. 'The emerging countries are better represented by BRICS than by the G8' (Tables 9.1–9.3).

Table 9.1: Intra-BRICS Balance (Outflow–Inflow) of FDI in US$ Million.

	Brazil	China	India	Russia	South Africa
FDI in other BRICS	2628	41,133	22,082	12,365	10,013
FDI received from other BRICS	17,806	25,891	20,286	15,637	8601
Net result	−15,178	15,242	1796	−3272	1412

Source: Greenfield Investment Data from the Financial Times Database.

Table 9.2: Bilateral FDI among the Five Countries (January 2003–July 2013 in US$ Million).

Source Country	Brazil	China	India	Russia	South Africa	Total
Brazil		1.613	462	528	25	2.628
China	12.769		14.273	12.272	1.818	41.133
India	3.568	10.622		2.511	5.381	22.082
Russia	117	5.895	4.976		1.377	12.365
South Africa	1.352	7.761	574	326		10.013
Total	17.806	25.891	20.286	15.637	8.601	88.220

Source: Greenfield Investment Data from the Financial Times Database.

Table 9.3: Chinese FDI into Other BRICS.

South Africa (2004–2013)	%	Brazil (2003–2013)	%	Russia (2003–2013)	%	India (2003–2013)	%
Metals	37.0	Metals	27.4	Minerals	1.4	Minerals	16.0
Automotive OEM	23.4	Automotive OEM	23.6	Automotive OEM	24.9	Metals	46.5
Chemicals	13.7	Food and tobacco	22.4	Real estate	22.1	Engines and turbines	21.0
Building and construction materials	12.2	Communications	13.7	Metals	9.8	Communications	11.4
Foods and tobacco	3.6	Financial services	3.5	Coal, oil and natural gas	7.7	Consumer electronics	6.6
Communications	3.5	Industrial machinery, equipment and tools	2.4	Building and construction materials	5.9	Industrial machinery, equipment and tools	3.5
Consumer electronics	3.0	Transportation	1.9	Chemicals	5.1	Real estate	3.1

Table 9.3: (*Continued*)

South Africa (2004–2013)	%	Brazil (2003–2013)	%	Russia (2003–2013)	%	India (2003–2013)	%
Financial services	1.0	Coal, oil and natural gas	1.7	Paper, printing and packaging	4.9	Automotive OEM	2.7
Transportation	1.0	Alternative/ Renewable energy	1.2	Industrial machinery, equipment and tools	3.9	Ceramics and glass	1.0
Industrial machinery, equipment and tools	0.5	Engines and turbines	0.5	Wood product	3.5	Textiles	0.9
Engines and turbines	0.5	Paper, printing and packaging	0.4	Ceramics and glass	2.4	Non-automotive transport OEM	0.7
Software and IT services	0.4	Plastics	0.2	Financial services	2.2	Software and IT services	0.5
Medical devices	0.1	Business machines and equipment	0.2	Alternative/ Renewable energy	2.9	Business services	0.5

Automotive components	0.2	Communication	1.7	Automotive components	0.4
Non-automotive transport OEM	0.2	Consumer electronics	1.2	Business machinery and equipment	0.3
Consumer electronics	0.1	Automotive components	0.8	Financial services	0.2
Consumer products	0.1	Electronics components	0.8	Electronic components	0.2
Software and IT services	0.1	Transportation	0.6	Plastics	0.1
Business services	0.0	Beverages	0.2	Medical devices	0.0
Medical Devices	0.0	Pharmaceuticals	0.2	Consumer products	0.0
	0.0	Business services	0.2		
		Medical devices	0.0		

Source: Greenfield Investment Data from the Financial Times Database.

Table 9.4: Indian FDI into Other BRICS.

Brazil (2003–2013)	%	China (2003–2013)	%	Russia (2003–2013)	%	South Africa (2003–2013)	%
Alternative/ Renewable energy	31.8	Automotive OEM	19.7	Coal, oil and natural gas	26.1	Coal, oil and natural gas	50.4
Metals	30.9	Financial services	17.4	Automotive OEM	17.4	Alternative/ Renewable energy	15.8
Automotive OEM	14.5	Software and IT services	17.3	Pharmaceuticals	17.0	Hotels and tourisms	6.1
Software and IT services	6.0	Transportation	8.4	Financial services	6.3	Metals	1.0
Industrial machinery, equipment and tools	4.3	Coal, oil and natural gas	7.2	Chemicals	5.3	Software and IT services	5.5
Pharmaceuticals	2.9	Hotels and tourism	7.2	Metals	4.8	Automotive OEM	4.7
Engines and turbines	2.1	Metals	3.6	Communications	4.5	Rubber	2.4

Food and tobacco	1.6	Automotive	2.6	Software and IT services	3.9	Financial services	2.3
Plastics	1.5	Components	2.6	Consumer products	3.0	Industrial machinery, equipment and tools	2.2
Financial services	1.4	Business services	2.3	Food and tobacco	2.9	Biotechnology	1.3
Non-automotive transport OEM	2.3	Engines and turbines	1.3	Plastics	2.2	Plastics	1.0
Business services	1.2	Consumer products	1.7	Hotels and tourism	2.2	Business services	0.4
Automotive components	0.4	Industrial machinery	1.3	Ceramics and glass	2.0	Consumer products	0.5
Rubber	0.2	Equipment and tools	1.3	Industrial machinery, equipment and tools and glass	1.6	Automotive components	0.4
Chemicals	0.2	Plastics	1.3	Textiles	0.6	Ceramics and glass	0.3
Consumer products	0.3	Building and construction materials	1.3	Business services	0.2	Engines and turbines	0.2

Table 9.4: (*Continued*)

Brazil (2003–2013)	%	China (2003–2013)	%	Russia (2003–2013)	%	South Africa (2003–2013)	%
		Chemicals	0.7	Electronic components	0.1	Leisure and entertainments	0.1
		Communications	0.6			Communications	0.1
		Pharmaceuticals	0.5			Minerals	4.9
		Leisure and entertainment	0.4				
		Electronic component	0.3				
		Food and tobacco	0.3				
		Medical devices	0.3				
		Textiles	0.2				
		Consumer electronics	0.6				
		Semiconductors					
		Non-automotive transport OEM					

Source: Greenfield Investment Data from the Financial Times Database.

Table 9.5: Russian FDI into Other BRICS (in %).

Brazil (2009–2013)		China (2003–2013)		India (2003–2013)		South Africa	
Coal, oil and natural gas	51.1	Coal, oil and natural gas	34.6	Coal, oil and natural gas	53.1	Metals	72.8
Financial services	21.4	Transportation	22.6	Metals	10.9	Minerals	19
Transportation	15.1	Financial services	13.1	Financial services	6.1	Aerospace	3.1
Software and IT services	5.1	Chemicals	8.0	Real estate	5.7	Coal, oil and natural gas	2.2
Textiles	4.9	Automotive OEM	7.0	Transportation	5.7	Financial services	1.4
Industrial machinery, equipment and tools	2.4	Minerals	4.0	Industrial machinery, equipment and tools	5.4	Software and IT Services	0.8
		Aerospace	3.8	Aerospace	3.9	Communications	0.6
		Metals	1.4	Automotive OEM	3.0	Transportation	0.3
		Communications	1.2	Building and construction materials	2.3		
		Consumer products	1.1	Chemicals	1.6		
		Real estate	1.1	Software and IT services	1.1		

Table 9.5: (*Continued*)

Brazil (2009–2013)		China (2003–2013)		India (2003–2013)		South Africa	
		Business services	0.8	Communication	1.0		
		Plastics	0.3	Pharmaceuticals	0.4		
		Food and tobacco	0.2	Minerals	0.3		
		Wood products	0.2				
		Software and IT services	0.3				
		Space and defence	0.1				
		Hotels and tourism	0.0				

Source: Greenfield Investment Data from the Financial Times Database.

Table 9.6: South African FDI into Other BRICS.

Brazil (2005–2013)	%	Russia (2003–2007)	%	India (2003–2012)	%	China (2003–2012)	%
Minerals	92.7	Minerals	50.3	Financial services	34.1	Coal, oil and natural gas	87.2
Metals	2.7	Consumer products	18.0	Minerals	17.0	Consumer product	4.7
Software and IT services	3.6	Wood products	11.9	Hotels and tourism	15.3	Semiconductors	3.7
Business services	0.6	Financial services	10.2	Food and tobacco	13.1	Chemicals	1.6
Communications	0.3	Chemicals	9.6	Business machines and equipment	8.6	Industrial machinery, equipment and tools	1.1
Financial services	0.3	Total	100	Beverages	5.8	Software and IT services	0.7
Hotel and tourism	0.1			Software and IT services	2.8	Transportation	0.4
Total	100			Business services	1.7	Minerals	0.4
				Coal, oil and natural gas	1.3	Business services	0.2
				Chemicals	0.3	Total	100
				Total	100		

Source: Greenfield Investment Data from the Financial Times Database.

Table 9.7: Brazilian FDI into Other BRICS (in %).

China (2003–2011)	%	Russia (2004–2009)	%	India (2004–2013)	%	South Africa (2006–2012)	%
Metals	23.3	Food and tobacco	42.9	Metals	65.5	Automotive components	41.7
Financial services	22.2	Automotive OEM	40.7	Automotive OEM	14.2	Automotive OEM	40.5
Food and tobacco	20.7	Ceramics and glass	15.4	Electronic components	10.8	Chemicals	10.1
Transportation	12.6	Electronic components	0.9	Textiles	2.8	Software and IT services	7.7
Aerospace	9.3			Software and IT services	2.8		
Automotive components	3.8			Business services	2.3		
Textiles	3.6			Medical devices	0.8		
Software and IT services	1.5			Transportation	0.4		

Business services	0.8	Industrial machinery, equipment and tools	0.4
Chemicals	0.7		
Automotive OEM	0.6		
Non-automotive transport OEM	0.6		
Coal, oil and natural gas	0.5		
Consumer electronics	0.1		

Source: The Financial Times Database.

Table 9.8: Brazilian Exports to Other BRICS (Primary Commodities and Middle- and Low-Technology Products).

Products	Russia		India		China		South Africa	
	US$ (million)	(%)	US$ (million)	(%)	US$ (million)	(%)	US$ (million)	(%)
Mineral fuels	0	0.0	3.432	60.7	4837	11.8	28	1.6
Non-fuel primary commodities	2.879	91.4	1.469	26.0	32.851	80.0	780	44.2
Resource-intensive manufactures	51	1.6	36	0.6	628	1.5	115	6.5
Low-skill and low-technology-intensive manufactures	10	0.3	245	4.3	732	1.8	62	3.5
Medium-skill and medium-technology-intensive manufactures	180	5.7	161	2.8	440	1.1	675	38.2
High-skill and high-technology manufactures	29	0.9	304	5.4	1.579	3.8	103	5.8
Unclassified products	2	0.1	8	0.1	5	0.0	3	0.2

Source: The Financial Times Database.

Table 9.9: Brazilian Imports to Other BRICS (Primary Commodities and Middle- and Low-Technology Products).

Products	Russia		India		China		South Africa	
	US$ (million)	(%)	US$ (million)	(%)	US$ (million)	(%)	US$ (million)	(%)
Mineral fuels	215	5.6	2219	45.3	225	0.6	28	3.9
Non-fuel primary commodities	1593	41.8	109	2.1	1093	3.1	165	23.3
Resource-intensive manufactures	19	0.5	690	13.5	6198	17.7	9	1.2
Low-skill and low-technology-intensive manufactures	123	3.2	207	4.0	3331	9.5	144	20.3
Medium-skill and medium-technology-intensive manufactures	54	1.4	714	13.9	10,909	31.1	82	11.6
High-skill and high-technology manufactures	1809	47.4	1147	22.4	12,732	36.3	278	39.2
Unclassified products	0	0.0	42	0.8	622	1.8	4	0.5

Source: The Financial Times Database.

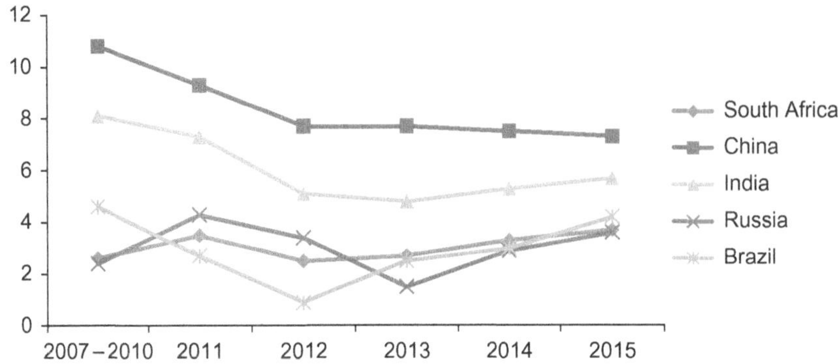

Figure 9.1: GDP Performance of the BRICS.

An Overview of the BRICS

BRICS has emerged as strongest economic and political power block — as the engine of the global economy. Based on the Forbes report released on March 2011, BRICs countries for the first time have surpassed Europe in count of billionaires by 301 billionaires or one billionaire ahead over Europe. It was the significant increase by 108 more billionaires than the previous years (Tables 9.4–9.6).

Market closeness, similarity in products and processes and business culture affinity offer investors from other developing countries greater opportunities in terms of trade and investments. The WTO Ministerial Conferences and sustained setback in the implementation of the Doha development agenda demonstrated the urgent need for a better representation of the developing country's interests in the international trading system and great solidarity amongst our countries to achieve this goal (Tables 9.7–9.9).

In this regard, intense South–South interaction and collaboration will certainly help in having commonality of approaches to major international issues like environmental problems, UN reforms, reform in the international financial system and dealing with the global financial crisis. It will also help in eradicating poverty, deprivation, malnutrition and solving problems of unemployment. In this context, the BRICS can play a significant and effective role in the ASEAN region, Asia-Pacific, Africa and Latin America. BRICS promote and facilitate their vast market access to stimulate South–South trade (Figure 9.1).

BRICS account to $230 billion of intra-trade (which was 18% out of total world trade with 43% world's population, and 53% FDI).

China–Russia Economic Corridor for De-Dollarisation

In the wake of the imposition of sanctions against Russia by the West, following Russia's opposition to Western designs on Ukraine and Western support to the Ukrainian fascists for carrying out those designs, President Putin has embarked on a course that can potentially have far-reaching consequences for the world economy. He is trying to work out trade deals with other countries which are either themselves facing Western sanctions or are willing to defy them, and the payments on these deals are not in terms of U.S. dollars or even euro, but in terms of the currencies of the countries entering into these deals.

China and Iran are the obvious partners that Putin is eyeing and Russia has just entered on May 21 into an agreement with China to the tune of US$400 billion for supplying gas to the latter over the next 30 years. The significant feature of the deal however is that the payment will not be made in U.S. dollars. For decades India had bilateral trade agreements with the Soviet Union and with other East European socialist countries, where the traded commodities exchanged against one another at agreed prices and a given exchange rate, and the trade balance was settled over a period of time without involving any movement of a so-called reserve currency from one country to another. Putin has simply taken over an idea that had been put into practice in the days of the Soviet Union.

The advantages of such an arrangement can be understood through a simple example. Imagine country A and country B trading with one another. Every transaction between the two countries would normally have to be settled in terms of a 'reserve currency', say the U.S. dollar. If country A exports US$100 worth of goods to country B over a certain period and has US$30 worth of foreign exchange reserves (in terms of the reserve currency) at the beginning of the period which it can run down, then ignoring each country's trade with other countries for simplicity, country A can buy at the most US$130 worth of goods from country B. But if there is a bilateral agreement (supplementing such trade, let us assume) and each accepts the other's currency as if it is a reserve currency, then country A can buy a lot more goods from country B. The magnitude of trade would be much larger. When both countries A and B are hard put to get the reserve currency because of sanctions, clearly bilateral trade agreements can enlarge their trade substantially.

Bilateral trade agreements in effect therefore entail that the two countries entering into agreement treat each other's currencies as if they are reserve currencies. This means a substantial increase in their foreign exchange reserves and hence trade. The increase is even more substantial when each of the partners has a shortage of the standard reserve currency, either because of sanctions by the advanced capitalist economies or because of low demand for the goods of each in the advanced capitalist economies, from whom the reserve currency could be earned (which incidentally was the rationale for India's bilateral agreements with the Soviet Union in the old days).

This substitution of other currencies for the reserve currency which in today's world consists essentially of the U.S. dollar is what the Russians are calling 'de-dollarisation'. To encourage the process Russia has enacted a law whereby companies are required to have a certain minimum percentage of their trade in roubles.

The implications of 'de-dollarisation' can be quite far-reaching. The dollar which is the reserve currency in the world economy also happens to be a currency that the U.S. central bank, the Federal Reserve Board, can print. It follows then that as long as the dollar remains a reserve currency, the United States can run any amount of current account deficit on its balance of payments, and simply print notes to pay for it. True, the other countries may not be willing to hold only the U.S. currency notes but may wish to hold some interest earning dollar asset, such as American

Treasury Bills or American government bonds. But when the U.S. central bank prints money, it puts that money into circulation in the economy by buying such assets anyway, in which case if foreigners wish to move from holding dollars to holding these assets, the central bank can simply sell these assets and take back the dollars it had printed. The basic point that the United States can run any amount of current account deficit remains valid.

If 'de-dollarisation' gets going strongly, so that other currencies are held, not just in addition to the extra dollars that would be held on account of the U.S. current account of deficit, such as was assumed in the above example, but actually as substitutes for the U.S. dollars in their role as reserves, then this ability of the United States to run whatever current deficit it wishes to gets undermined. If the United States still runs a current account deficit that is larger than what other countries are willing to hold as extra reserves, then the printing of more dollars than anybody is willing to hold would cause a collapse in the value of the dollar. Wealth-holders in such a case will move to other forms of holding wealth, including even commodities, which would cause high inflation, as had happened at the beginning of the 1970s.

On the other hand, if the United States reduces its current account deficit to match what other countries are willing to hold as extra reserves, then its absorption of goods will have to decrease, causing a socially explosive drop in living standards of its population and a loss of its military might. Since it is the leading imperialist power of the world, such a loss of military might has serious consequences.

Either way therefore 'de-dollarisation' can become a prelude to a new conjuncture entailing severe crisis and destabilisation in the capitalist world, and leading to a loss of U.S. hegemony. It is not surprising that the United States has always reacted very strongly to any effort by any country to move away from holding dollar reserves to holding reserves in other currencies of the advanced capitalist world. There was even a suspicion that one important reason for the U.S. invasion of Iraq was Saddam Hussain's reported decision to shift away from the U.S. dollar as the form in which Iraq held its considerable oil wealth.

The trend towards 'de-dollarisation' is not just confined to Russia and Iran which have both been hit by American sanctions and have good reasons therefore for 'de-dollarising'. It covers China as well. China already holds an immense amount of claims on the United States, built over the years through a persistent current account surplus vis-à-vis that country, in the form of dollars or dollar-denominated assets. It is interested therefore in diversifying away from U.S. dollar assets to other forms of wealth-holding such as gold or the euro, as a means of reducing risks (which arise for instance when all eggs are put in one basket).

China reportedly is already diversifying away from the dollar; and some attribute the recent strengthening of the euro to such diversification by China. It is also buying gold on a large scale, imitating India in this respect, though in the case of India it is not the government agencies (such as the central bank) but private individuals who are the main importers of gold.

Diversifying away from U.S. dollars however is a tricky operation for China. Since it already holds immense amounts of dollars, such diversification, if it reduces the price of the dollar, can cause large-scale capital losses for China. In such a case, diversification by China would have become a Kalidasa-type exercise of lopping off the branch of a tree on which one is standing. To prevent this, diversification for China has to be stealthy, surreptitious and gradual, so that it does not attract much notice and hence does not cause a fall in the value of the U.S. dollar (which would hurt China itself). China reportedly has been engaged in such a gradual and quiet shift away from the U.S. dollar; and its signing the bilateral agreement with Russia can be seen as one episode in this quiet shift.

The Indian government's attitude, not surprisingly, is totally different from that of Russia, China or Iran, and is much more subservient to the United States. One of the problems that the country would face, if it ever decided to break the U.S.-imposed sanctions against Iran (whatever deviation it currently has from the sanction-regime is with the 'permission' of the United States, and is based on India's promise that it would only be a temporary phenomenon), is that of obtaining insurance cover for such sanction-busting trade. Apparently even the large public sector insurance companies that could insure such trade are not large enough to manage such insurance on their own. They go even at present to Western insurance companies to obtain re-insurance for many of the transactions they cover; and the latter would certainly not provide re-insurance if trade was of the sanction-busting kind.

The obvious solution to this problem, and indeed a precondition for the country's having a degree of autonomy in its policy towards western-imposed economic sanctions on third countries, is to make the public sector insurance companies even larger, so that they do not have to run to western companies for re-insurance. But this requires infusion of government funds into these companies; and the government has steadfastly refused to make such funds available. It does not obviously contemplate getting out of its economic subservience to the United States.

A Critical Review of BRICS

It is not just an economic power that has shifted from West to East in this crisis. The global balance of respect has shifted as well. But none of the BRICS countries can afford to leave it at that, because the crisis has raised questions about their approach to economic development as well, especially China's.

Russia is now considered the odd one out of the BRICS and you can see why. Its workforce is shrinking: incredibly, the working age population is likely to fall by around a third between now and 2050. It is outside the top 10 economies by GDP and expected to remain so. Oil wealth will keep Russia at the top table of countries for some time to come, but it is unlikely to face the challenges faced by China, India or Brazil, of managing their economic success.

Endemic Inflation

Brazil also depends on commodities for too much of its growth. Like India, its infrastructure is weak and its government institutions inefficient. Inflation in both countries is more or less endemic. Brazil and India do have the great advantage of having a large home market and a lot of home consumers. Incidentally, you can say the same of Indonesia, which many think should now be an informal BRIC. None of these countries has contributed in a significant way to global current account imbalances. Indeed, in the case of the Brazilians, the problem has been that they save too little, not too much. It has also been a victim of the global imbalances, struggling to deal with big inflows of global capital. The same cannot be said of China, which has almost certainly saved and exported more in the past 30 years than any country in the history of the world, not just in absolute terms but as a share of its economy.

A handful of numbers, highlighted recently by Larry Summers, help make the point most vividly. American households now consume just over 70% of U.S. national output. The UK households spend nearly as much. As we know, that is probably too much. When Japan was an emerging market, the consumption ratio was lower: somewhere in the low fifties as a percentage of GDP. But last year, consumption by Chinese households came to barely 35% of the nation's output. That distortion, supported by Chinese policies over the past two decades, has enormous consequences for its economy and society and for the shape of world demand. Many economists, including the heads of the United States and British central banks, say China's high savings and its semi-fixed exchange rates helped cause the financial crisis by producing a glut of global liquidity. Others say there is more than enough blame to go around. But whether or not China helped cause the crisis, there is not much debate that it needs to be part of the solution, because without higher Chinese consumption in China, the only way the global economy will become more balanced in future, with less debt on countries like Britain and America, is by those countries also having little or no economic growth. This is what the G20 Summit in Cannes would have been about had it not been so distracted by Greece and the euro. But when it comes to it, China might find it easier to contribute to the European rescue fund than to contribute to a more balanced global economy.

10

China: A New Business and Economic Leader

Nowadays it is a fact that all basic goods are produced in China. According to the data of China's Ministry of Commerce, in 2014 the share of the country's global commodity turnover reached 40%, amounting to nearly half of global export. Imagine how China's Alibaba.com did business of 3.9 billion dollar just in one hour in global markets.

Rural communities in China have experienced the most remarkable complex changes in recent years. With an entrepreneurial spirit 'social entrepreneurship' led by village communities has been transformed from 'commune to company' level. This transformation has occurred in three stages:

- During the 1980s, a reform took place based on replacing the 'Commune system' by 'Company' with a 'household responsibility system', which allocated land to individual households for agri-production and agri-business.
- The second stage that began in the early 2000s was a reform based and 'voluntary cooperatives' with the emphasis on new business cooperation among villagers through village enterprises and their connection with markets.

- The third stage is a more recent reform with the slogan 'new countryside development'.

This concept is based on a comprehensive approach to develop rural community not only for economic growth, but also for the well-being of rural societies in the area of education, health care, infrastructure, other services and ecological sustainability (Hong Lan, 2014).

A Long Journey from 'COMMUNE TO COMPANY'

When the socialist reconstruction programme was launched by the Chinese Communist Party (CPC) from 1953 to 1956, there was in practice almost no private and individual business. However, some individual household business practices were established, but not more than 150,000 small units existed in the whole economy until the end of 1978. After economic reform programme to boost economy was launched by the Chinese government in 1978–2000, 3,950,000 entrepreneurs' private units registered publically. Approximately 42 million SMEs play a vital role in China today. These 42 million SMEs contributed to 58.5% of GDP, 50% of tax revenues, 68% of exports and 75% of new employment in 2009 (Zhou, 2012).

Due to openness of Chinese economy, the United States and United Kingdom transferred their manufacturing operations to China to gain the advantages of cost and scale of production when products are 'Made in China'. However, when the current global financial crisis began in 2008, the situation in China also began to change. As world stock markets fell, large financial institutions collapsed (or were bailed out) and a European debt crisis developed. Global manufacturing demand fell, causing a predictable decline in China's export growth. Therefore, China focuses mainly on internal capability and skills. China is expected to lead the world in innovation by the year 2020.

China has made significant strides in its capacity for research and innovation. In 2005, China submitted 2452 international patent applications; this represented a 44% increase over the previous year and brought China into the international top 10 for patent applications. Further, the total number of degrees granted per year in China nearly doubled from 2004 to 2007, according to the Ministry of Education of China. These substantial strides indicate that China has already begun to increase its capacity for innovation and that this precondition for a shift in entrepreneurial types — necessary for China to go global — is already being established.

Outward–Inward Rural-Urban Migration

Human capital plays an influential role across sectors in both urban and rural areas directly through both outward and inward rural-urban migration, as well as the occupational composition in the countryside, involved in construction and in the production of pressed salted duck (the so-called *Wuwei banya*) since 1985. From 1990s, it's covering a broader range of sectors, such as textile, driving, repairs, food processing, construction and other service industries, and in a broader range of destinations, including Shanghai, Beijing, Jiangsu and Zhejiang provinces.

According to official statistics, at the end of 2006, about 43% of the entire rural labour force of the county was working outside the county (Démurger, 2011). As Liu emphasised that 'the return migrants invest their savings in the rural non-farm business, which raises local labour demand and rural wages; nevertheless, income inequality is not eliminated and the rural-urban migration continues' (Liu, 2011).

However, Global Entrepreneurship Monitor says, China is not yet an innovative economy, but it is an 'efficiency-driven' and 'factor-driven' economy. There are two issues.

One is that most of the analysts — outside of China and even inside the country — do not associate China's economic success with entrepreneurship. Most commentators credit the government,

FDI and massive infrastructural construction as the reasons why the Chinese economy has surged forward. Private sector development, if it is mentioned at all, is often viewed as an afterthought — something that happened as a result of Chinese economic success rather than the cause of it.

The other is why Chinese entrepreneurship should be so vibrant in the first place. Is it not the case that this is still, at least nominally, a communist country? Is it not also true that the rule of law, market competition and its business environment are not viewed as 'friendly' to private entrepreneurs and businesses? If, as the thinking goes, communism can go hand-in-hand with vibrant entrepreneurship, why do we need capitalistic institutions — with all of their historical baggage, operational arcanery and legal complications — at all?

Trying to resolve these two puzzles is not just an academic exercise; it has real policy implications. In the past few years, as the leading Western economies are mired in financial distress, slow growth and high unemployment, developing economies are looking longingly for guidance at the Chinese model of development — with its emphasis on state-driven investments, political controls and the state-owned financial system. They are deeply sceptical of the 'Washington Consensus', a set of ideas that champions market economics, financial liberalisation and political reforms. Beijing Consensus, its polar opposite and intellectual rival, is on the rise. *Washington Post* columnist David Ignatius, invoking Richard Nixon's famous backhand tribute to John Maynard Keynes, declared 'We are all Chinese now'.

One of the least understood aspects of Chinese growth is how vital the role of entrepreneurship is. There is a reason for this lack of understanding — almost all the most dynamic and vibrant entrepreneurship in China is rural, in terms of its geography and in terms of its composition. When Americans think of entrepreneurship, they think of people like Bill Gates, Steve Jobs, Larry Page and Sergey Brin, technical geniuses who created huge business empires based on science and technology. But in a context of a poor country, technical entrepreneurship is almost by definition less relevant. We define a country as poor because it has lots of poor people. The reigning issue for entrepreneurship in developing countries is not technology but how to grow income and to create jobs for those who need income.

The modern history of entrepreneurship in China has been written by its rural people. They single-handedly created the miracle growth of the 1980s and early 1990s at a time when ideological risks of venturing into a commerce and market economy were still substantial. As recently as the mid-1990s, rural entrepreneurs represented between 30% and 50% of China's private sector. One little-noted fact about the Chinese economy is that some of its most competitive manufacturing operations are not located in the highly urbanised regions of the country; rather they are found in some of the historically more rural provinces, such as Zhejiang, Hunan, Sichuan and Anhui. Some of the best manufacturing firms in China, such as Wanxiang, an automobile supplier, and Geely, the firm that just acquired Volvo, were all started by rural entrepreneurs.

The significance of rural entrepreneurship has not diminished. In fact, it is more important than ever. As Western economies continue to struggle, with low growth rates and high unemployment, one of the key policy challenges in China is how to generate domestic consumption to replace its unhealthy dependency on exports. Rural China holds the key. Even, approximately 55–65% of the Chinese population is still rural today. Unless their income growth accelerates, China does not stand a good chance of turning around its investment-driven economic structure. As the experience from other developing countries shows, the key to get the growth of rural income going is not to artificially jack up agricultural prices but to facilitate a transition from the low value-added agriculture to higher value-added non-farm activities. Rural entrepreneurship is the key to this transition.

Some Historical Facts

During the pre-1963 period, transforming rural life through land reform, where control was taken from traditional wealthy peasants, and land lords to the state, and started collective farming system. China mechanised agriculture sector, the spread of electricity, running water and modern technology to rural areas. China attempted to accelerate collectivisation and dramatically increase the pace of industrial production throughout the country, particularly in rural areas. This mostly involved small-scale production, such as the smelting of 'backyard' steel. Through collectivisation and mass labour, China's steel production surpassed the United Kingdom within only 15 years from the start of the 'leap'. Tens of millions were mobilised to produce a single commodity that was symbolic of industrialisation — steel. Approximately 25,000 communes were set up, each with around 5000 households pre-1963. The hope was to industrialise by making use of the massive supply of cheap labour and avoid having to import heavy machinery. Small backyard steel furnaces were built in every commune where peasants produced small nuggets of cast iron made from scrap metal. Simultaneously, rural communities were collectivised.

Since 1978 China's economy shifted the approach from collective farming to household-based production quotas, in many ways reversing decades of collectivisation efforts. In many areas of China, especially southern and coastal China, the standard of living improved dramatically after Deng's reforms. Township and Village Enterprises brought industrial production to rural areas — predominantly along the southern coasts — helping open these rural communities to greater economic prosperity. (The idea of industrial production in rural areas had been attempted under Mao but with much more limited success; for instance, industrial plants in highly remote areas found their ultimate production efforts hampered.)

It is to be noted that there are two types of entrepreneurships:

1. catch-up entrepreneurship and
2. frontier entrepreneurship.

Catch-up entrepreneurship engaged in replicative activities. Those activities that have been invented by others and they are now being copied and created at competitive costs. The vast majority of Chinese entrepreneurs are of the catch-up kind. Their main economic contribution is job creation, rather than making breakthroughs in science and technology. Catch-up entrepreneurship makes relatively simple demands for stability through avoiding competition. The Chinese government facilitates basic infrastructures such as roads, electricity, water supply, transportation, public health and education, and kept the operating costs low, for example, moderating wage rate and welfare programmes. Finance is not too complicated. Supplier credits and bank loans of a modest size provide the capital and liquidity needs of catch-up entrepreneurs. Compared with the vast majority of developing countries, the Chinese political system meets these demands adequately.

However, frontier entrepreneurs ask a lot ... for strong intellectual property rights protection; and legal court system that is impartial and fair; they need a multi-tiered financing structure ...

In 2013, China announced a new plan to reduce poverty and develop impoverished rural regions by raising rural farmers' income growth and reducing obstacles in agricultural development. The plan includes the promotion of new types of agricultural businesses, such as family farms and organised cooperatives, and encouraging industrial and commercial enterprises to invest in agriculture.

'GO GLOBAL' Development Strategy

China recorded enormous growth rates based on the growth of exports. India witnessed a significant increase in service sector exports and also came up with impressive growth rates, compared to which the much lower growth rates of the pre-liberalisation dirigiste era paled into insignificance. The rise in primary commodity prices caused *inter alia* by the increasing demand of a rapidly growing Chinese economy, helped Africa and Latin America too to record impressive growth rates. With globalisation it appeared that the south had 'arrived'. And international finance capital played up this theme of diffusion of 'development', since it 'legitimised' globalisation, painting it in an extraordinarily favourable light as breaking down all past dichotomies.

'Go Global' strategy can be described as the way of adjustment of the development path carried out by the government. Thus, the government becomes the supplier of information and assistance services, as well as promoter of incentives and reduction in investment risks. There were also published guidelines, covering outward FDI to some countries and sectors, and there were conducted many infrastructural projects, connected with acquiring relatively small, but technologically advanced enterprises in developed countries and allocating production there. Chinese firms are taking to expand into international markets. Building on last year's ranking of the top 13 companies going global, this year's list demonstrates how Chinese overseas investment continues to diversify across industries and increase dramatically in magnitude. According to China's Ministry of Commerce, Chinese overseas investment totalled US$61.6 billion by the end of September 2013 — a 17.4% year-on-year increase. Chinese overseas investment is set to continue to grow at double-digit rates in 2014.

The Most Competent Chinese Business Agency

Alibaba operates a series of online marketplaces in China and elsewhere, handling more transactions than Amazon and eBay combined. Online retailer Alibaba says it sold US$3.9 billion in 2015 which is double than US$2 billion (£1.2 billion) of goods sold in the first hour of China's annual 'Singles' Day' in 2014. That compares to $3.1 billion in sales seen in the first half of 2013 event — considered the world's biggest online retail sales day. Last year, Alibaba shipped more than 150 million packages or about $5.75 billion in gross merchandise volume. Since then, it has gone on to become a massive day of sales for China's fast growing e-commerce market. The market is expected to grow at an annual rate of 25% over the next few years, from $390 billion in 2014 to $718 billion in 2017.

Global Investments: Where to Invest?

China has US$3.2 trillion currency reserves. China's Export-Import Bank says, US$3 trillion sat waiting to be spent. The China Investment Corporation (CIC) was established with the intent of utilising these reserves for the benefit of the state, modelled according to Temasek Holdings of Singapore. The state-owned Central Huijin Investment Corporation was merged into the new company as a wholly owned subsidiary company. The Corporation aims to invest in around 50 large-sized enterprises across the world. Special treasury bonds were issued to create the capital that the CIC needed. In this bond sale 1550.35 billion yuan (US$207.91 billion) was issued. The bond process was completed in December 2007. According to Lou Jiwei, the CIC needs to make a profit of 300 million yuan every day just to pay the interest on the bonds and operation costs. The low cost of capital of CIC leads to contentions that its investments are effectively subsidised by the Chinese government therefore creating an unfair advantage for CIC versus others seeking to compete for the same acquisition targets. The CIC paid its first interest on the bonds in February 2008 where it paid 12.9 billion yuan.

In 2010, CIC established a new subsidiary, CIC International (Hong Kong) Co., in Hong Kong and appointed Lawrence Lay as its Chairman. In 2011, CIC established its first foreign office in Toronto, choosing it over financial centres such as New York or London as its first office. Felix Chee will be the chief representative officer.

Over the past few years, delegations from China's big banks have been crisscrossing the globe signing a plethora of billion dollar deals with some of the world's poorest nations. China provides more loans to the developing world than the World Bank and the IMF. As the lender to go to for credit-poor governments, China's yuan is replacing World Bank dollars as the cash behind new roads, power stations, hospitals and other infrastructure. In 2010, the World Bank issued US$11.4 billion worth of loans to some 36 African countries. China also issued a host of loans to African governments. One of them, a loan facility to Ghana, reportedly is worth almost US$13 billion alone.

World Bank versus China's Export-Import Bank:

I. Cameroon: WB US$30 million; China US$743 million
II. Rep. Congo: WB US$25.5 million; China US$75.8 million
III. Ghana: WB US$313 million; China US$9.87 billion
IV. Nigeria: WB US$890 million; China US$900 million
V. Zambia: WB US$95 million; China US$315 million.

(*Source*: Data for Exim Bank are for specific reported loans; total amount of Chinese lending likely to be significantly higher.)

China Helps Finance a Hydro-Electric Project at Ecuador's Coca River

Without international organisations, without foreign investment and without international markets, you have to look for another source. That happens to be China, which has a lot of reserves and extra money. The multi-billion dollar loan from China that's helped turn the hydro dam project into a reality is to be charged at an interest rate of 6.9%. 'The risk and the appetite for risk of Chinese companies is different to other companies.'[1] Traditional partners of the continent such as those with colonial links or development partners have moved out of infrastructure financing and it's a gap that's been left and needs to be filled a swift and large push into Africa by Chinese banks. China has found the gap to its liking. In countries like Zambia and Angola, the activities of Chinese construction firms are hard to avoid. Billboards, road signs and even cash machines are now displaying Chinese symbols.

1. Hannah Erdinger from the Johannesburg-based financial consultancy firm Frontier Advisory.

In Angola, China has been offering loans since 2003 when the nation emerged from civil war. To date, it has extended credit lines to Angola worth US$15 billion as Chinese companies come over and build new infrastructure in the country. In return, Angola sends China its oil.

With the high rates of unemployment and destitution in the country, Zambians have looked to this high influx of Chinese into the country as an explanation to why they have some of the problems they have but this particular arrangement has flaws from China in Africa Project.

Cambodia was considering a $600 million loan from the World Bank that had conditions about transparency and anti-corruption and accountability. The Cambodians basically told the World Bank to go to hell and the next day they received a US$601 million loan from the Chinese with no conditions.

China Looks to Expand Currency's Global Reach

The shop assistant thumbs the red, 100-yuan bills that bear Mao Zedong's distinctive face, checks the amount is correct and places it in the till next to Hong Kong dollar notes and coins, without a sideways glance. It is a typical day in Bonjour, a cosmetics store popular with the vast numbers of shoppers from mainland China who are spending their newfound wealth in the former British colony. From vending machines selling soy milk near the Chinese border to the luxury boutiques and High Street chains in Hong Kong's financial district, payment in China's currency — known as the renminbi or the yuan — is an increasingly common sight. And it is the most visible of the steps that China, which still exerts strong control over the flow of money in and out of the country, is taking to expand its currency's global reach.

Some analysts predict that the yuan will become a dominant force in international financial markets in five years and rival the dollar, euro and yen. But no one expects the yuan to take its place alongside the world's most traded currencies quite yet, as China is still reluctant to enact many of the reforms that would make the yuan freely convertible. It's more rapid than many people had been anticipating but it is a gradual process, says Mitul Kotecha, foreign exchange strategist at Credit Agricole in Hong Kong.

Small Steps

China has been allowing the yuan to be used more widely in a number of different ways. Banks in Hong Kong, which has a freely traded currency and a separate legal system, have been permitted to hold renminbi deposits since 2004. They now total 407 billion yuan (US$62 billion; £38 billion). Chinese bank branches in Singapore and New York now allow customers to open yuan bank accounts.

In 2009, China began allowing its currency to be used to settle cross-border trade between companies in five Chinese cities and Hong Kong, Macau and Southeast Asian countries. That scheme was expanded worldwide in 2010 and includes some 67,000 Chinese firms in 20 provinces. It means that trading partners do not have to convert in and out of dollars. Multinational companies like McDonald's and Caterpillar have issued yuan-denominated bonds in Hong Kong and these bonds can be bought and sold by investors who want to bet on an expected appreciation in the Chinese currency. And soon investors will be able to buy yuan-denominated shares, following the world's first yuan initial public offering outside China.

Dollar Dominance

China has expressed concern at the dollar's status as the world's reserve currency and says it wants the global monetary system to be reformed to reduce reliance on the U.S. currency. It is feared that lowering the U.S. interest rates and soaring budget deficit could undermine the dollar and thus the value of its huge dollar reserves. China has the world's biggest holdings of dollars, largely because it still tightly manages its exchange rate in relation to the dollar.

Great Power, Great Currency?

Alistair Thornton, a China analyst at IHS Global Insight in Beijing says that China's push to make the yuan more global is also an issue of pride. There's huge privilege in being the dominant reserve currency in trade and in finance and China looks at that with envy. China's is the world's second largest economy and sees itself as a great power but the yuan is not anywhere near the yen or even the pound. Figures from the Bank for International Settlements make clear that the yuan is still a long way from mounting a challenge to the dollar. The yuan made up 0.9% of daily market turnover on the foreign exchanges in 2010, up from zero percent in 2001. The dollar makes up 85%.

China still maintains strict controls over its currency and banking system and the flow of money in and out of the country. If these controls were removed quickly, it would be difficult for China to prevent its currency from appreciating rapidly — something its leaders have long resisted. They have preferred to keep its currency relatively undervalued to boost the competitiveness of its exports on international markets. It is a policy heavily criticised by the United States and other trading partners and will again come under scrutiny as the IMF meets in Washington.

China's banks and financial markets are still relatively unsophisticated and China wants to guard against speculative inflows and outflows of money, such as those it believes were responsible for the Asian financial crisis in the 1990s.

China: A Workshop of the World

China becomes second largest economy in the world after the United States in terms of industrial output, overall GDP and purchasing power parity. Industry and construction account for 49.2% of China's GDP. Around 8% of the total manufacturing output in the world comes from China itself. Major industries include mining and ore processing; iron and steel; aluminium; coal; machinery; armaments; textiles and apparel; petroleum; cement; chemical; fertilisers; food processing; automobiles and other transportation equipment including rail cars and locomotives, ships and aircraft; consumer products including footwear, toys and electronics; telecommunications and information technology. China has become a preferred destination for the relocation of global manufacturing facilities. Its strength as an export platform has contributed to incomes and employment in China. The state-owned sector still accounts for about 30% of GDP. In recent years, authorities have been giving greater attention to the management of state assets — both in the financial market as well as among state-owned enterprises — and progress has been noteworthy.

Since the founding of the People's Republic, industrial development has been given considerable attention. Among the various industrial branches the machines-building and metallurgical industries have received the highest priority. These two areas alone now account for about 20–30% of the total gross value of industrial output. In these, as in most other areas of industry, however, innovation has generally suffered at the hands of a system that has rewarded increases in gross output rather than improvements in variety, sophistication and quality. China, therefore, still imports significant quantities of specialised steels. Overall industrial output has grown at an average rate of more than 10% per year, having surpassed all other sectors in economic growth and degree of modernisation. Some heavy industries and products deemed to be of national strategic importance remain state-owned, but an increasing proportion of lighter and consumer-oriented manufacturing firms is privately held or are private-state joint ventures.

The predominant focus of development in the chemical industry is to expand the output of chemical fertilisers, plastics and synthetic fibres. The growth of this industry has placed China among the world's leading producers of nitrogenous fertilisers. In the consumer goods sector the main emphasis is on textiles and clothing, which also form an important part of China's exports. Textile manufacturing, a rapidly growing proportion of which consists of synthetics, account for about 10% of the gross industrial output and continues to be important, but less so than before. The industry tends to be scattered throughout the country, but there are a number of important textile centres, including Shanghai, Guangzhou and Harbin.

Major state industries are iron, steel, coal, machine-building, light industrial products, armaments and textiles. These industries completed a decade of reform (1979–1989) with little substantial management change. Prior to 1978, most output was produced by state-owned enterprises. As a result of the economic reforms that followed, there was a significant increase in production by enterprises sponsored by local government, especially townships and villages, and, increasingly, by private entrepreneurs and foreign investors. The 1996 industrial census revealed that there were 7,342,000 industrial enterprises at the end of 1995; total employment in industrial enterprises was approximately 147 million. The 1999 industrial census revealed that there were 7,930,000 industrial enterprises at the end of 1999 (including small-scale town and village enterprises); total employment in state-owned industrial enterprises was about 24 million. The automobiles industry has grown rapidly since 2000, as has the petrochemical industry. Machinery and electronic products became China's main exports. China is the world's leading manufacturer of chemical fertilisers, cement and steel. By 2002 the share in gross industrial output by state-owned and state-holding industries had decreased to 41%, and the state-owned companies themselves contributed only 16% of China's industrial output.

China's construction sector has grown substantially since the early 1980s. Over half of the Chinese economy is now construction related. This sector, besides employing millions of workers, brings in tons of money to local governments; a third of local government's revenue is the sale of land lease. In the twenty-first century, investment in capital construction has experienced major annual increases. In 2001 investments increased 8.5% over the previous year. In 2002 there was a 16.4% increase, followed by a 30%

increase in 2003. The manufacturing sector produced 44.1% of GDP in 2004 and accounted for 11.3% of total employment in 2002. Industry and construction produced 53.1% of China's GDP in 2005. Industry (including mining, manufacturing, construction and power) contributed 52.9% of GDP in 2004 and occupied 22.5% of the workforce.

Energy production has increased rapidly, but it still falls considerably short of demand. This is partly due to artificial energy prices that have been held so low that industries have had few incentives to conserve. Coal provides about 75–80% of China's energy consumption. Petroleum production, which began growing rapidly from an extremely low base in the early 1960s, has basically remained at the same level since the late 1970s. There are large petroleum reserves in the inaccessible northwest and potentially significant offshore petroleum deposits, but about half of the country's oil production still comes from the major Daging oilfields in the northeast. China has much, and partially undeveloped, hydro-electric power potential and natural gas reserves. The government has made plans to develop nuclear power plants in the coastal and western regions.

Overall, the distribution of industry remains very uneven, despite serious efforts from the mid-1950s to the late 1970s to build up industry in the interior at the cost of the major cities on the east coast. While percentage growth of industry in the interior provinces generally greatly exceeded that of the coastal areas, the far larger initial industrial base of the latter has meant that a few coastal regions have continued to dominate China's industrial economy. The establishment of special economic zones in coastal areas only heightened this disparity. Shanghai by itself accounts for about 8–10% of China's gross value of industrial output, and the east coast accounts for about 60% of the national industrial output. The rate of industrialisation increased and diversified after the early 1990s. Notable were the development of aerospace, aircrafts and automobile manufacturing. In addition, China expanded rapidly into the production of pharmaceuticals, software, semiconductors, electronics and precision equipment.

Steel Industry

China is the largest producer of steel in the world and the steel industry has been rapidly increasing its steel production. Iron ore production kept pace with steel production in the early 1990s but was soon outpaced by imported iron ore and other metals in the early 2000s. Steel production, an estimated 140 million tons in 2000, was increased to 419 million tons in 2006. Much of the country's steel output comes from a large number of small-scale producing centres, one of the largest being Anshan in Liaoning. China's annual excess capacity in steel, glass, cement, aluminium and ceramics is such that it would more than meet sub-Saharan's current demand for the next three years.[2]

China is the top exporter of steel in the world. Export volumes in 2008 were 59.23 million tons, a 5.5% fall over the previous year. The decline ends China's decade-old steel export growth.

Automotive Industry

By 2006 China had become the world's third largest automotive vehicle manufacturer (after United States and Japan) and the second largest consumer (only after United States). Automobiles manufacturing has soared during the reform period. In 1975 only 139,800 automobiles were produced annually, but by 1985 production had reached 443,377, then jumped to nearly 1.1 million by 1992 and increased fairly evenly each year up until 2001, when it reached 2.3 million. In 2002 production rose to nearly 3.25 million and then jumped to 4.44 million in 2003, 5.07 million in 2004, 5.71 million in 2005 and 7.28 million in 2006. In 2007, 9 million automobiles were expected to be produced so that the country could become the world's biggest automobile manufacturer by 2020. Domestic sales have kept pace with production. After respectable annual increases in the mid- and late 1990s, passenger car sales soared in the early 2000s. In 2006, a total of 7.22 million

2. *Source*: '*Capital*' Ethiopia's Business Weekly, Vol. 12, 610, 22 August 2010.

automobiles have been sold, including 5.18 million units of passenger cars and 2.04 million units of commercial vehicles.

So successful has China's automotive industry been that it began exporting car parts in 1999. China began to plan major moves into the automobile and components export business starting in 2005. A new Honda factory in Guangzhou was built in 2004 solely for the export market and was expected to ship 30,000 passenger vehicles to Europe in 2005. By 2004, 12 major foreign automotive manufacturers had joint-ventures plants in China. They produced a wide range of automobiles, minivans, sport utility vehicles, buses and trucks. In 2003 China exported US$4.7 billion worth of vehicles and components. The vehicle export was 78,000 units in 2004, 173,000 units in 2005 and 340,000 units in 2006. The vehicle and component export is targeted to reach US$70 billion by 2010.

The market for domestically produced cars, under a local name, is likely to continue to grow both inside China and outside. Companies such as Geely and Chery are constantly evaluating new international locations, both in developing and developed countries.

Services

China's services output ranks seventh worldwide and high power and telecom density has ensured that it has remained on a high-growth trajectory in the long term. In 2005 the services sector produced 40.3% of China's annual GDP, second only to manufacturing. However, its proportion of GDP is still low compared with the ratio in more developed countries, and the agricultural sector still employs a larger workforce. Prior to the onset of economic reforms in 1978, China's services sector was characterised by state-operated shops, rationing and regulated prices. With reform came private markets and individual entrepreneurs and a commercial sector. The wholesale and retail trade has expanded quickly, with urban areas now having many shopping malls, retail shops, restaurant chains and hotels. Public administration has still remained a main component of the service sector, while tourism has become a significant factor in employment and as a source of foreign exchange. The potential for growing services in China through franchising is huge.

Tourism

China's tourism industry is one of the fastest-growing industries in the national economy and is also one of the industries with a very distinct global competitive edge. The total revenue of China's tourism industry reached US$67.3 billion in 2002, accounting for 5.44% of the GDP. It dropped, largely due to SARS, to US$59 billion in 2003. Nevertheless, for areas rich in tourism resources, tourism has become the main source of tax revenue and the key industry for economic development. The total number of inbound tourists was 91.66 million in 2003, and that of tourists staying overnight was 32.7 million, about 10 times the number in 1980. International tourism receipts were US$17.4 billion in 2003. China's ranking for both the overnight tourist arrivals and tourism receipts was among the world's top five in 2003. However, there is unlikely to be a big increase in the inbound tourism market.

China's domestic tourism market makes up more than 90% of the country's tourism traffic, and contributes more than 70% of total tourism revenue. In 2002, domestic tourists reached 878 million and tourism revenue was US$46.9 billion. The five-days-per-week and long vacation schemes have increased leisure time for the Chinese people and spurred market demand in domestic tourism and led to its prosperity.

A large middle-class population with strong consumption power is emerging in China, especially in major cities. China's outbound tourists reached 20.22 million in 2003, overtaking Japan for the first time. Currently there are 65 countries/areas open to Chinese tour groups. Putting aside the threat of SARS and other unexpected events, based on the current economic growth situation and the social development of China, China's outbound tourism is poised to achieve a new growth peak. Driven by the flourishing tourism industry, China's tourist hotel sector is expanding rapidly. At the end of 2003, China had a total of 10,093 tourist hotels and more than 820,000 rooms; 773 of these tourist hotels were foreign-funded. The number of foreign-funded (inclusive of Hong Kong, Macau and Taiwan investments) four- and five-star tourist hotels made up to 26% and 30.02% of the national total, respectively.

In 2003, there were a total of 11,522 travel agencies in China, among which, 1349 were international ones and 10,203 were domestic ones. While overall tourism market concentration rose, there was a drop in the market position of the traditional three key travel agencies. As competition heightened, China's tourism industry on the whole had begun to start earning low profits, even while it was expanding its scale of operations.

Currently, there are approximately 15,000 natural, cultural and man-made places of attraction which are above county level. Presently, Hong Kong investors are the main participants in the establishment of tourist attractions in China. In 2001, Sichuan became the first province to propose renting out the operation rights of 10 scenic areas to foreign investors.

According to the plan by China National Tourism Administration, the number of inbound tourists, foreign exchange earnings from tourism and the domestic market size are targeted to have an annual growth of 4%, 8% and 8%, respectively, in the next five to ten years. It is also forecast by the WTO that China's tourism industry will take up to 8.6% of world market share to become the world's top tourism industry by 2020.

Labour and Welfare

One of the hallmarks of China's socialist economy was its promise of employment to all able and willing to work and job-security with virtually lifelong tenure. Reformers targeted the labour market as unproductive because industries were frequently overstaffed to fulfil socialist goals and job-security reduced workers' incentive to work. This socialist policy was pejoratively called the iron rice bowl.

In 1979–1980, the state reformed factories by giving wage increases to workers, which was immediately offset by sharply rising inflation rates of 6–7%. In other words, although they were given more pay, their money was worth less and they could buy less, which meant they were poorer. The state remedied this problem, in part, by distributing wage subsidies.

The reforms also dismantled the iron rice bowl, which meant it witnessed a rise in unemployment in the economy. In 1979, immediately after the iron rice bowl was dismantled, there were 20 million unemployed people. Official Chinese statistics reveal that 4.2% of the total urban workforce was unemployed in 2004, although other estimates have reached 10%. As part of its newly developing social security legislation, China has an unemployment insurance system. At the end of 2003, more than 103.7 million people were participating in the plan, and 7.4 million laid-off employees had received benefits.

A 10% sample tabulation of census questionnaires from the 1982 census provided needed statistical data on China's working population and allowed the first reliable estimates of the labour force's size and characteristics. The quality of the data was considered to be quite high, although a 40-million-person discrepancy existed between the 10% sample and the regular employment statistics. This discrepancy can be explained by the combination of inaccurate employment statistics and varying methods of calculation and scope of coverage. The estimated mid-1982 labour force was 546 million, or approximately 54% of the total population. Males accounted for slightly more than half of the estimated labour force, and the labour force participation rates for person's aged 15 years and older were among the highest in the world. The 10% sample showed that approximately three-fourths of the labour force worked in the agricultural sector. According to the National Bureau of Statistics, in the mid-1980s more than 120 million people worked in the non-agricultural sector.

The sample revealed that men occupied the great majority of leadership positions. The average worker was about 30 years old, and three out of every four workers were under 45 years of age. The working population had a low education level. Less than 40% of the labour force had more than a primary school education, and 30% were illiterate or semi-literate. In mid-1982 the overall unemployment rate was estimated to be about 5%. Of the approximately 25 million unemployed, 12 million were men and 13 million were women. The unemployment rate was highest in the northeast and lowest in the south. The unemployment rates were higher than those of East Asian, Southeast Asian and Pacific island countries for which data were available but were lower than the rates found in North America and Europe. Virtually all of the unemployed persons in cities and towns were under 20 years of age.

I. By the 1990s and 2000s, agriculture has remained the largest employer, though its proportion of the workforce has steadily declined; between 1991 and 2001 it dropped from about 60% to 40% of the total. The manufacturing labour force has also become smaller at a slower rate, partially because of reforms implemented at many of the state-run enterprises. Such reforms and other factors have increased unemployment and underemployment in both urban and rural areas. Women have been a major labour presence in China since the People's Republic was established. Some 40–45% of all women over age 15 are employed.

II. China's estimated employed labour force in 2005 totalled 791.4 million persons, about 60% of the total population. During 2003, 49% of the labour force worked in agriculture, forestry and fishing; 22% in mining, manufacturing, energy and construction industries; and 29% in the services sector and other categories. In 2004 some 25 million persons were employed by 743,000 private enterprises. Urban wages rose rapidly from 2004 to 2007, at a rate of 13–19% per year with average wages near US$200/month in 2007.

The All-China Federation of Trade Union (ACFTU) was established in 1925 to represent the interests of national and local trade unions and trade union councils. The ACFTU reported a membership of 130 million, out of an estimated 248 million urban workers, at the end of 2002. Chinese trade unions are organised on a broad industrial basis. Membership is open to those who rely on wages for the whole or a large part of their income, a qualification that excludes most agricultural workers. In theory, membership is not compulsory, but in view of the unions' role in the distribution of social benefits, the economic pressure to join is great. The lowest unit is the enterprise union committee. Individual trade unions also operate at the provincial level, and there are trade union councils that coordinate all union activities within a particular area and operate at county, municipal and provincial levels. At the top of the movement is the ACFTU, which discharges its functions through a number of regional federations.

In theory the appropriate trade union organisations have been consulted on the level of wages as well as on wage differentials, but in practice their role in these and similar matters have been insignificant. They have not engaged in collective bargaining, as their principal duties have included assisting the party and promoting production. In fulfilling these tasks, they have had a role in enforcing labour discipline. From the point of view of the membership, the most important activities have concerned the social and welfare services. Thus, the unions have looked after industrial safety, organised social and cultural activities, and, provided services such as clinics, rest and holiday homes, hostels, libraries and clubs. They also administer old-age pensions, workers' insurance, disability benefits and other welfare schemes. More recently, however, reforms of the social security system have involved moving the responsibility for pensions and other welfare to the provinces.

In China there exist labour laws which, if fully enforced, would greatly alleviate common abuses such as not paying workers. In 2006, a new labour law was proposed and submitted for public comment. The new law, as currently drafted, would permit collective bargaining in a form analogous to that standard in Western economies, although the only legal unions would continue to be those affiliated with the ACFTUs, the Communist Party's official union organisation. The new law has support from labour activists, but has been opposed by some foreign corporations, including the American Chamber of Commerce and the European Chamber of Commerce. There is some expectation that the new law, if enacted, would be enforced. An ongoing effort to organise Chinese operations of foreign companies succeeded in 2006 at Wal-Mart. The campaign is projected to include Eastman Kodak, Dell and other companies. It was reported in 2008 that problems with sweatshops persist. By fall 2008, it was apparent that union organising efforts were widespread with emphasis on foreign corporations.

External Trade

International trade makes up a sizeable portion of China's overall economy. The course of China's foreign trade has experienced considerable transformations since the early 1950s. In 1950 more than 70% of the total trade was with non-Communist countries, but by 1954, a year after the end of the Korean War, the situation was completely reversed, and trade with Communist countries stood at about 75%. During the next few years, trade with the Communist world lost some of its standing, but it was only after the Sino-Soviet split of 1960, which resulted in the cancellation of Soviet credits and the withdrawal of Soviet technicians, that the non-Communist world began to see a speedy recovery in its position. In 1965 China's trade with other socialist countries made up only about a third of the total.

Being a Second World country at the time, a meaningful segment of China's trade with the Third World was financed through grants, credits and other forms of assistance. At first, from 1953 to 1955, aid went mainly to North Korea and North Vietnam and some other Communist states; but from the mid-1950s large amounts, mainly grants and long-term, interest-free loans, were promised to politically uncommitted developing countries. The principal efforts were made in Asia, especially to Indonesia, Burma, Pakistan and Ceylon, but large loans were also granted in Africa (Ghana, Algeria, Tanzania) and in the Middle East (Egypt). However, after Mao Zedong's death in 1976, these efforts were scaled back. After which, trade with developing countries became negligible, though during that time, Hong Kong and Taiwan both began to emerge as major trading partners.

Since economic reforms began in the late 1970s, China sought to decentralise its foreign trade system to integrate itself into the international trading system. On November 1991, China joined the Asia-Pacific Economic Cooperation (APEC) group, which promotes free trade and cooperation in economic, trade, investment and technology spheres. China served as APEC chair in 2001, and Shanghai hosted the annual APEC leaders meeting in October of that year.

China's global trade totalled US$324 billion in 1997 and US$151 billion in the first half of 1998; the trade surplus stood at US$40.0 billion. China's primary trading partners were Japan, Taiwan, the United States, South Korea, Hong Kong, Germany, Singapore, Russia and the Netherlands. China had a trade surplus with the United States of US$49.7 billion in 1997 and US$54.6 billion in 1998. Major imports were power generating equipment, aircraft and parts, computers and industrial machinery, raw materials, and chemical and agricultural products.

In 1998, China was in its 12th year of negotiations for accession to the WTO formerly the General Agreement on Trade & Tariffs (GATT), and had significantly reduced import tariffs. Previously in 1996, China had already introduced cuts to more than 4000 tariff lines, reducing average tariffs from 35% to 23%; further tariff cuts that took effect 1 October 1997 decreased average tariffs to 17%. To gain WTO entry, all prospective WTO members were required to comply with certain fundamental trading disciplines and offer substantially expanded market access to other members of the organisation. Many major trading entities — among them the United States, the EU and Japan — shared concerns with respect to China's accession. These concerns included obtaining satisfactory market access offers for both goods and services, full trading rights for all potential Chinese consumers and end-users, non-discrimination between foreign and local commercial operations in China, the reduction of monopolistic state trading practices and the elimination of arbitrary or non-scientific technical standards. China and other WTO members worked to achieve a commercially viable accession protocol.

In 1999, Premier Zhu Rongji signed a bilateral U.S.–China Agricultural Cooperation Agreement, which lifted longstanding Chinese prohibitions on imports of citrus, grain, beef and poultry. In November 1999, the United States and China reached a historic bilateral market-access agreement to pave the way for China's accession to the WTO. As part of the far-reaching trade liberalisation agreement, China agreed to lower tariffs and abolishes market impediments after it joins the world trading body. Chinese and foreign businessmen, for example, would gain the right to import and export on their own — and to sell their products without going through a government middleman. After reaching a bilateral WTO agreement with the EU and other trading partners in summer 2000, China worked on a multilateral WTO accession package. China concluded multilateral negotiations on its accession to the WTO in September 2001. The completion of its accession protocol and Working Party Report paved the way for its entry into the WTO on 11 December 2001, after 16 years of negotiations, the longest in the history of the GATT.

China's FDI Policy

Since the adoption of the open-door policy at the end of the 1970s China has been extremely successful in attracting FDI. Particularly, according to UNCTAD's *World Investment Report 1997: Transnational Corporations, Market Structure and Competition Policy*, China has become the second largest recipient of FDI in the world since 1993, after the United States. On the other hand, however, it seems less noticed that China has also become a growingly important FDI exporting country. According to UNCTAD's same report, China now ranks as one of the largest outward investors among developing economies in the 1990s. By the end of 1996, the cumulative stock of Chinese outward FDI had reached over $18 billion, next only to Hong Kong (US$112 billion), Singapore (US $37 billion) and Taiwan (US$27 billion). Consequently, China increased its share in worldwide FDI outflows from less than 0.5% until 1991 to an average of 1.3% in 1991–1995. As China is rapidly rising as a new economic power, its deepening participation in the regional and global economy, through both inward and outward FDI as well as trade, will inevitably bring about significant implications in the international political economy.[3]

China also authorised some foreign banks to open branches in Shanghai and allowed foreign investors to purchase special 'B' shares of stock in selected companies listed on the Shanghai and Shenzhen Securities Exchanges. These 'B' shares sold to foreigners carried no ownership rights in a company. In 1997, China approved 21,046 foreign investment projects and received over US $45 billion in FDI. China revised significantly its laws on Wholly Foreign-Owned Enterprises and China Foreign Equity Joint Ventures in 2000 and 2001, easing export performance and domestic content requirements.

Foreign investment remains a strong element in China's rapid expansion in world trade and has been an important factor in the growth of urban jobs. In 1998, foreign-invested enterprises produced about 40% of China's exports, and foreign exchange reserves totalled about US$145 billion. Foreign-invested enterprises today produce about half of China's exports (note that the majority of China's foreign investment come from Hong Kong, Macau and Taiwan), and China continues to attract large investment inflows. However, the Chinese government's emphasis on guiding FDI into manufacturing has led to market saturation in some industries, while leaving China's services sectors underdeveloped. From 1993 to 2001, China was the world's second-largest recipient of FDI after the United States. China received US$39 billion FDI in 1999 and US$41 billion FDI in 2000. China is now one of the leading FDI recipients in the world, receiving almost $80 billion in 2005 according to World Bank statistics. In 2006, China received US$69.47 billion in FDI.

Foreign Exchange Reserves totalled US$155 billion in 1999 and US$165 billion in 2000. Foreign Exchange Reserves exceeded US$800 billion in 2005, more than doubling from 2003. Foreign

3. Cai (2009).

exchange reserves were US$819 billion at the end of 2005, US$1.066 trillion at the end of 2006 and US$1.9 trillion by June 2008. In addition, by the end of September 2008 China replaced Japan for the first time as the largest foreign holder of U.S. Treasury securities with a total of US$585 billion, versus Japan US $573 billion. China has now surpassed those of Japan, making China's foreign exchange reserves the largest in the world.

As part of its WTO accession, China undertook to eliminate certain trade-related investment measures and to open up specified sectors that had previously been closed to foreign investment. New laws, regulations and administrative measures to implement these commitments are being issued. Major remaining barriers to foreign investment include opaque and inconsistently enforced laws and regulations and the lack of a rules-based legal infrastructure. Warner Bros., for instance, withdrew its cinema business in China as a result of a regulation that requires Chinese investors to own at least a 51% stake or play a leading role in a foreign joint venture. Outward FDI is a new feature of Chinese globalisation, where local Chinese firms seek to make investments in both developing and developed countries.

China Investment Corporation

CIC is a sovereign wealth fund responsible for managing part of the People's Republic of China's foreign exchange reserves. CIC was established in 2007 with approximately US$200 billion of assets under management, making it one of the largest sovereign wealth funds. Since then, CIC's assets have grown to US$410 billion at the end of 2010.

Governance

The management and board of the CIC ultimately reports to the State Council of China. The CIC is seen as being 'firmly entrenched' in the political establishment as the composition of its Board of Directors implies 'considerable influence on the part of China's Ministry of Finance'.

Board of Directors

I. Chairman and CEO — Lou Jiwei
II. Vice Chairman, President and CIO — Gao Xiqing
III. Executive Director, Executive Vice President and COO – Zhang Hongli
IV. Non-Executive Director — Zhang Xiaoqiang
V. Non-Executive Director — Li Yong
VI. Non-Executive Director — Fu Ziying
VII. Non-Executive Director — Liu Shiyu
VIII. Non-Executive Director — Hu Xiaolian
IX. Independent Director — Liu Zhongli
X. Independent Director — Wang Chunzheng
XI. Employee Director — Li Xin

Board of Supervisors

I. Chairman of Board of Supervisors — Jin Liqum
II. Supervisor — Linghu An
III. Supervisor — Wang Huaqing
IV. Supervisor — Fan Fuchun
V. Employee Supervisor — Cui Guangqing

Executive Committee

I. Chairman and CEO — Lou Jiwei
II. Vice Chairman, President and CIO — Gao Xiqing
III. Chairman of Board of Supervisors — Jin Liqun
IV. Executive Director, Executive Vice President and COO — Zhang Hongli
V. Executive Vice President — Peng Chun
VI. Executive Vice President and Deputy COO — Fan Yifei

VII. Executive Vice President and Deputy CIO — Xie Ping

VIII. Executive Vice President and CRO — Wang Jianxi

IX. Member of the Executive Committee — Liang Xiang

International Advisory Council

Asia

I. Zeng Peiyan (China)

II. Frederick Ma (Hong Kong, China)

III. Taizo Nishimuro (Japan)

IV. Yingyi Qian (China)

V. Andrew Sheng (Malaysia)

VI. Joseph Yam (Hong Kong, China)

Americas

I. David L. Emerson (Canada)

II. Merit E. Janow (United States of America)

III. John J. Mack (United States of America)

IV. John L. Thomton (United States of America)

V. James D. Wolfensohn (United States of America)

Europe

I. Knut N. Kjaer (Norway)

II. Jean Lemierre (France)

III. Lord Nicholas H. Stern (United Kingdom)

(*Source*: China's Ministry of Finance)

Profile. Gao Xiqing is now vice chairman of the National Council for the Social Security Fund. Zhang Hongli and Li Yong are vice ministers of finance. Zhang Xiaoqiang and Wang Chunzheng are vice ministers of the National Department and Reform Commission (NDRC), the nation's top economic planner.

Fu Ziying is assistant to the Minister of Commerce. Liu Shiyu is a central bank vice governor, Hu Xiaolian head of the State Administration of Foreign Exchange and Liu Zhongli was former finance minister.
Yang Qingwei is currently department head of fixed assets investment with the NDRC. Xie Ping is now the general manager of the Central Huijin Investment Corporation and Wang Jianxi a vice board chairman of the Central Huijin.

Hu Huaibang, Commissioner of Discipline Inspection with the China Banking Regulatory Commission, took the post as chief supervisor.

Lou Jiwei worked his way up, starting in the People's Liberation Army/Navy and becoming the deputy minister of finance.

Xie Ping, 'The Iron Fist' reorganised much of the Chinese banking system, and now firmly controls it.

Wang Jianxi holds a doctorate in accounting and lived in the United Kingdom and the United States and adopted the American first name 'Jesse'.

Previously, the Lou, Xie and Wang used $60 billion in currency reserves to clear all the bad loans from the books of the three largest state banks, allowing for stock market flotation in Hong Kong. These banks have rejoined the ranks of the world's leading financial institutions.

Investment Strategies

China has invested two-thirds of its reserves in U.S. dollars, mostly U.S. Treasury bonds and agency bonds. The devaluation of the US$ on world currency markets has provided poor returns, prompting the Chinese to create the CIC to manage China's investment in equities.

Credit Suisse predicted CIC would only take a 5–10% stake in each company, remaining a passive investor to avoid political hassles in overseas markets. CIC bought a US$3 billion stake in Blackstone, one of the largest U.S. private equity firms. CIC has refrained from influencing Blackstone's investment strategy.

The company will mainly pursue combined investments in overseas financial markets.

CIC is thought to engage in building influence for the government by buying up significant stakes in companies that have influence in western governments including airline companies as also target firms that have heavily invested in China. The investments would help the government to influence the policies of multinational companies and to protect China's interests in international spheres.

Market watchdogs want to know what would happen if China, Russia and Arab countries were to systematically acquire significant holdings in sensitive industries such as telecommunications, energy and defence.

Lou has been assigned the rank of a minister. During daily operations, he will answer to a host of other agencies, including the powerful National Development and Reform Commission, a successor to the former influential State Planning Commission. Lou said CIC will operate on the principle of 'commercial operation', and will abide by local laws of countries where it invests.

The state media had earlier speculated that the company will invest $67 billion to buy the assets of Central Huijin, the investment arm of the central bank which holds shares in most state-run banks. It was later reported that Huijin was acquired by CIC from the State Administration of Foreign Exchange for US$200 billion.

China's leadership has debated the right strategy for the government investment fund. Vice Premier Zeng Peiyan has suggested that China should invest in natural resources to increase its strategic reserves. Other high-ranking party officials would rather see the country acquire shares in high-tech companies to help China more rapidly close the gap with leading industrialised nations. Three years ago, dealers working for China Aviation Oil in Singapore, China's sole supplier of aviation fuel, suffered losses of US$500 million from miscalculations and rising oil prices.

CIC bought a US$3 billion stake of Blackstone Group in June and a 9.9% stake of Morgan Stanley worth US$5 billion on 19 December 2007. The Chinese Internet community regularly vents its anger over government losses of the people's money, and there is widespread scepticism among Chinese party leaders and the public over the extent to which the country should get involved in global equities investments. Western investment banks Goldman Sachs and Morgan Stanley will provide expert knowledge to China's state-sponsored venture capitalists.

On 2 March 2009, Chinese media reported that the CIC was shifting its investment strategy to focus more on real estate, resources and other areas more tied to the 'real economy'.

Holdings

I. Teck Resources, 3 July 2009, US$3.5 Billion, 17.2% stake.

II. Blackstone Group, 22 May 2007, US$3 billion, 9.4% stake.

III. Morgan Stanley, 19 December 2007, US$5 billion, 9.9% stake.

IV. VISA, 19 March 2008, US$100 million, > 0.1% stake.

V. China Railway Engineering Corporation, 20 November 2007, US$100 million.

VI. Noble Group, 21 September 2009, US$850 million, 12.9% stake.

VII. Nobel Oil Group, 15 October 2009, US$300 million, 45% stake.

VIII. Penn West Energy Trust, 13 May 2010, US$1.2 billion, 5% stake.

IX. GDF Suez, 10 August 2011, US$3.5 billion, x% stake.

X. Thames Water, 20 January 2012, US$900 million, 8.68% stake.

China's Investment in Nepal

The two sides reviewed the time-tested Nepal-China friendly relations and noted with satisfaction that since the establishment of diplomatic relations in 1955, China-Nepal relations have been growing in a consistent, steady and healthy manner. The relationship is characterised by equality, harmonious coexistence, ever-lasting friendship and comprehensive cooperation.

I. The two sides maintained that China-Nepal relationship is of vital significance to both the countries. Deepening bilateral friendship and cooperation serves the fundamental interests of the two countries and the two peoples, and are conducive to peace, stability and development in the region and the world at large. The two sides decided to further promote Nepal-China friendly relations of Comprehensive Partnership of Cooperation Featuring Ever-Lasting Friendship on the basis of the Five Principles of Peaceful Coexistence.

II. The two sides reiterated their commitment to respect each other's independence, sovereignty, territorial integrity, choice of social system and development path chosen in light of their respective national conditions, and respect and understand each other's major concerns and core interests. The two sides further reiterated that they adhere to the principles of the United Nations as enshrined in the Charter, five Principles of Peaceful Coexistence, non-alignment and non-intervention in each other's internal affairs, and develop friendly exchanges and cooperation on the basis of equality and mutual benefit. Both sides agreed to share development experiences and technological advancement, and enhance all round cooperation so as to achieve mutual development and prosperity.

III. Both sides believed that high-level contacts are of special importance to the development of bilateral relations. The two sides agreed to maintain the momentum of high-level mutual visits, and have meetings between the leaders on the multilateral occasions. The two sides agreed to make full use of the existing mechanisms, including the diplomatic consultations and the Nepal-China Joint Economic and Trade Committee Meeting. The two sides also agreed to form a Consultation Mechanism at the level of Minister for Foreign Affairs.

IV. The Nepali side reiterated that there is only one China in the world, and the Government of the People's Republic of China is the sole legal government representing the whole of China. Both Taiwan and Tibet are integral parts of the Chinese territory.

V. The Chinese side reiterated its commitment to the policy of non-interference in the internal affairs, and expressed firm support to the efforts made by the Nepali side in upholding its independence, sovereignty, territorial integrity, national unity and stability. As a close neighbour of Nepal, the Chinese side is pleased to see the progress achieved in the peace process in Nepal and sincerely hopes that Nepal will realise peace, stability and prosperity including the drafting of a new constitution in the near future. The Nepali side highly appreciated the goodwill shown by friendly neighbour China at this historic transition.

VI. The two sides agreed to further intensify cooperation in socio-economic development, promotion of trade and tourism, hydropower, transportation infrastructure development and other fields on the basis of equality and mutual benefit.

VII. The Chinese side agreed to expedite the implementation of various development projects, including the upgrading and expansion of existing Ring Road of Kathmandu and Tatopani Dry Port.

VIII. An Agreement on Economic and Technical Cooperation was signed between the Government of Nepal and the Government of the People's Republic of China.

IX. The two sides agreed to enhance cooperation to ensure the construction of the Upper Trisuli 3A hydropower project with concessional loan of the Chinese government. The Nepali side welcomed Chinese participation in the construction of Pokhara International Airport, and the Chinese side took a positive attitude to this.

X. The two sides congratulated the official opening of the second Nepal-China land route of Syaphrubesi-Rasuwa Gadhi Road. Both sides agreed to give full attention to the geographic proximity, and improve connectivity, particularly, the land transportation infrastructure between the two countries, to facilitate bilateral exchanges, cooperation and business ties. The two sides maintained that the Tibet Autonomous Region of China and Nepal should make full potentials and take their respective advantages to strengthen people to people exchanges in the border areas, and to promote trade, tourism and the flow of goods and services to expand mutually beneficial cooperation.

XI. The Chinese side stated that China encourages and supports competent and well-established Chinese companies and enterprises to promote investment and joint ventures in Nepal, and will provide financing assistance including loans of concessional nature, to mutually agreed projects. The Nepali side stated that Nepal appreciated and welcomed the offer made by the Chinese side. During the visit, a Memorandum of Understanding on Operationalisation of Loan Mechanism was also signed between the Ministry of Finance of the Government of Nepal and the Export-Import Bank of China. The two sides agreed to continue discussions regarding the bilateral Agreement on the Business Investment Promotion and Protection of Investment.

XII. The two sides believed that strengthening border areas management and development serves the common interests of both the countries. Both sides agreed to make joint efforts to build a boundary of peace, tranquillity, friendship and cooperation. The two sides signed the Agreement on the Management of Ports in Nepal-China Border Areas and the Agreement on Trans-frontier Pasturing by Border Inhabitants.

XIII. The two sides applauded the cooperation between the Ministry of Public Security of China and the Ministry of Home Affairs of Nepal, and agreed to improve the meeting mechanism between law-enforcement authorities of the two countries, and to deepen cooperation on border management and law-enforcement capacity-building, so as to uphold peace and stability of China-Nepal border areas.

XIV. The two sides were pleased with the momentum of bilateral people to people and cultural exchanges and announced the year 2012 as 'Nepal-China Year of Friendly Exchanges'. The two sides agreed to promote exchanges and cooperation in the areas of culture and education and between youths, media, think tanks, scholars and friendship groups of the two countries.

XV. The two sides signed the Agreement on Cultural Cooperation, and agreed to enhance cultural exchanges and cooperation. Both sides believed that China Festival held regularly in Nepal by the Chinese side has promoted cultural exchanges between the two countries, and agreed to continue the Festival. Both sides also agreed on the mutual visits between their cultural and arts group. Both sides noted with appreciation that since the establishment of the youth exchange mechanism in 2009, the youth delegations of the two countries have realised mutual visits. The two sides also agreed to expand tourism cooperation and support each other's promotional activities in their respective countries.

XVI. The two sides positively view and support each other's participation in regional cooperation, and agreed to strengthen coordination and cooperation in various regional cooperation mechanisms.

XVII. The two sides believed that the official visit of Premier Wen Jiabao to Nepal took Nepal-China relations to a new height. It also served as a milestone in the annals of Nepal-China bilateral friendly relations and cooperation. The Chinese side expressed its appreciation to the government and people of Nepal for their gracious hospitality.[4]

China-West Asia and Africa Economic Tie-up

The scale and pace of investment by Chinese companies across the African continent is picking up, with South African financial services group Standard Bank alone responsible for advising Chinese companies on recent deals worth more than R10-billion. Two large deals were concluded in 2011, namely the US$1.3-billion sale of mining company Metorex to Jinchuan and the sale of a 25% stake in black economic empowerment investment holding company Shanduka to CIC for R2-billion. Closer to home, Standard Bank was also recently worked with the Industrial and Commercial Bank of China (ICBC) to provide funding to the value of US$835 million for the Morupule B Power Project in Botswana.

Standard Bank's close relationship with ICBC stems from the Chinese bank having purchased a 20% stake in Standard Bank in 2007 for about US$5.5 billion. Other China-Africa transactions where Standard Bank was involved include a US$400-million debt refinance with Equinox, an Australian-listed mining company with African operations; a US$470-million export finance facility to the Ethiopian HydroPower plant; and a US$5.5-billion financial advisory mandate to the Ghanaian Railway. 'The scale and pace of Chinese transactions on the continent is clearly picking up pace,

4. *Source*: *The Kathmandu Post*, Posted on 15 January 2012.

especially in the area of mining and minerals,' Standard Bank Group's Brad Webber said in a statement this week. 'Standard Bank forecasts that merger and acquisition (M&A) activity between Africa and China will continue to grow and expand.'

Largest China-Africa Deal in 2011

The Meteorex sale was the largest China-Africa deal in 2011, and involved Chinese mining group Jinchuan acquiring 100% in the issued share capital of JSE-listed Metorex for US$1.3 billion. The transaction was finalised this week following several months of negotiation between the parties and efforts to obtain clearances from regulators in China, South Africa, the Democratic Republic of the Congo (DRC) and Zambia. Metorex mines copper and cobalt assets in Zambia and the DRC. 'As part of the transaction, Metorex will be delisted from the JSE but will continue to operate as an entity within the Jinchaun Group', said Webber. 'Jinchaun is a serious player in the copper space with significant resources to grow Metorex.' He said the deals highlighted Standard Bank's unique position and exposure to African and Chinese markets. 'Standard Bank Group's customers benefit from our knowledge and expertise in emerging markets, particularly Africa and in the resources sector.'[5]

China has begun a new round of engagement with West Asia and Africa. Chinese prime minister Wen Jiabao embarking on a visit to Egypt where he has participated in a key meeting of the China-Africa cooperation forum. In his address at the Arab League headquarters on Saturday, 14 November 2009, Mr. Wen stressed intensifying a dialogue among civilisations based on mutual respect and vigorous interaction. There exist diverse civilisations in the world, just like the existence of diverse species in the nature. During talks with his Egyptian counterpart, Ahmed Nazef, Mr. Wen spoke about enhancing Chinese investments in what is called the China-Egypt Suez economic and trade cooperation zone

5. *Source*: Southafroca.info on 18 January 2012 (http://www.southafrica.info/africa/africa-china-180112.htm#ixzz1l9GlLQBe).

project. Energy tie ups and infrastructure development were also identified as priority areas. Mr. Wen will travel to the Egyptian resort of Sharm El-Sheikh for a meeting on Sunday of the Forum on China-Africa Co-operation, which has linked China with 48 African countries. China reinforced its credentials as a pro-Third World economic powerhouse by offering billions of dollars of concessional loans to Africa and pledging to contribute significantly to the continent's skilled human resources base.

Addressing delegates from 50 countries, participating in the two-day Forum on China-Africa Cooperation at the Egyptian Red Sea resort of Sharm el-Sheikh, Chinese prime minister Wen Jiabao promised $10 billion of preferential loans to Africa over the next three years. China, he said, would also launch a partnership with Africa on science and technology, which would allow 100 African postdoctoral fellows to carry out scientific research in China. By 2012, Chinese government scholarships to Africa would rise to 5500, and around 20,000 African professionals would be trained over the next three years. China's ambitious plans also include building 50 schools and training 1500 school principals and teachers for Africa. Agriculture would be another focal area of the evolving China-Africa relationship. China would increase the number of its agricultural technology demonstration centres in Africa to 20.

It would send 50 agricultural technology teams to Africa and train 2000 agricultural technology personnel, to help boost the continent's food security. In the field of health care, China would provide medical equipment and anti-malaria materials worth US $73.2 million to 30 hospitals and 30 malaria prevention and treatment centres built by China. Around 3000 doctors and nurses would also be trained under this initiative. Mr. Wen said China would further open up its market to African products, with provisions of duty free access to 95% of the products produced by the least developed African countries.[6]

6. Prabhakar (2010, p. 342).

China-ASEAN Trade Treaties

China-ASEAN Free Trade Treaty is effective from 1 January 2010. China's initiative to forge closer ties with ASEAN with the aim of establishing a free trade zone between itself and the 10 member nation group is a strategic move that benefits all the countries involved. For China, the closer political and economic ties with its southern neighbours would spell greater opportunities amidst uncertainties in the global economy. Likewise, ASEAN would enjoy greater access and tariff-free goods when they participate in the free trade area. China is ASEAN's largest trading partner while ASEAN is China's third largest trading partner.

Since 2011, a year after the free trade area was established; there is an estimated total population of 1.9 billion with a combined GDP of nearly US$8 trillion and total trade volume of US$4.5 trillion within this zone. In terms of property investment, the potential is enormous, said property consultant Gavin Tee, adding that the increased business opportunities will attract many investors to this region. ASEAN will become more attractive to Chinese investors, who presently are not so familiar yet with their southern neighbours. The boom in trade will spill over to a boom in property. It will open up a whole new area for cross-border investors. Sharing his view on the growing trend in cross-border property investing is Steve Melhuish, Group CEO of Property Guru Group, the leading Asian property portal. There continues to be a growing middle class in India, Indonesia and China that is keen on investing cross-border property market. The Chinese are buying up everywhere; Indians are looking at Singapore and Malaysia while the Indonesians are looking at several new markets. At the rate the trend is growing, it will be a matter of time before this new breed of cross-border investors starts looking at the China-ASEAN Free Trade Area (CAFTA). At the centre of this area is Nanning, the capital of Guangxi Zhuang Autonomous Region in southwest China. It is a large, modern city and a transport gateway for travellers to and from Vietnam.

Gateway to ASEAN

Cooperation and communication between Nanning and ASEAN have increasingly strengthened since Nanning won the permanent host contract for the China-ASEAN Expo in 2004. An annual event, the expo has raised the profile of Nanning and catapulted it to the top 10 China's exhibition city brands. Its exhibition business has become a money maker and is increasingly attracting investors from everywhere.

Since Nanning is China's gateway to Southeast Asian countries, there is a lot of emphasis on connecting Nanning to the capitals of every Southeast Asian country. In fact, 60 acres have been allocated to each ASEAN member to build building using their own designs. Currently, Nanning's biggest project is China South City Nanning an integrated large trade and logistics centre that is expected to increase cooperation between Guangxi and ASEAN. There is a huge business potential at here, said Cheng Chung Hing, co-chairman of China South City Holdings Ltd, the developer of CSC Nanning. The trade centre will be developed in two phases with a total estimated investment of US$ 1.9 billion. The total site area is 24.4 million square feet while the gross floor area is 52.5 million square feet.

Within this is the seven stories China-ASEAN Plaza which is estimated to house 10,000 shops. The fourth floor is the ASEAN Specialties Trade Area, a 540,000 sq. ft. trade and exhibition centre which is dedicated wholly for displaying and marketing ASEAN products and services. Next to the CSE Nanning is the impressive China-ASEAN Expo Centre which is the permanent venue of the China-ASEAN Expo and China-ASEAN Business and Investment Summit.

Location wise, Nanning and its neighbouring region border Vietnam and are within easy reach of Myanmar, Laos, Cambodia, Thailand and other Southeast Asian countries. It has modern airports, railways, port facilities and highways while its urban rail transit is expected to be operational in 2014. China South City Holdings has estimated that upon completion, the trade volume of business based there can reach up to US$49.5 billion while providing jobs for up to 250,000 people.

ASEAN members based in CSC Nanning will be entitled to a series of preferential policies, such as a five year rent abatement period, to assist ASEAN economies and promote economic development and regional integration.

ASEAN Set to Be Main Driver for Export Growth

ASEAN is the third largest trade area after NAFTA and EU. The Chinese construction sectors will be benefited from ASEAN imported raw materials. Vietnam, Thailand, Cambodia's textiles, footwear and steel industries mainly will have to face Chinese competition. However, Thailand will get biggest Chinese market for their cheapest jewellery and other cosmetics commodities. Indonesia, Brunei, Malaysia, Philippines, Singapore, Thailand have agreed to reduce 90% their taxes; it would be effective from 2010. But Laos, Vietnam, Cambodia and Varma will reduce especially on textiles and electronics (at least 10% items) in 2015.

The ASEAN markets will help Malaysia's exports grow by as much as 6.0% next year. Matrade chief executive officer Dr. Wong Lai Sum said the target can be achieved provided 'all things being equal' and if the country continues to target the markets where demand continues to grow. Growth in exports for 2012 will come from ASEAN, South Asia, including China, East Asia ... basically from Asia. Many of Malaysian companies have invested in the ASEAN region. For 2011, Malaysian exports could exceed Matrade's projected 7–8% growth, based on the current performance.

The intra-ASEAN trade will continue to serve as a very significant contributor of export revenue for Malaysian goods as ASEAN's economies continue to liberalise and widen market access. The government's bilateral and regional FTAs (free trade agreements) with countries within Asia, in particular with China and India, will serve to provide Malaysian exporters with significant new market access and revenue streams in 2012 and beyond. Malaysian exports continued to expand in September 2011, increasing 16.6% compared with RM58.68 billion registered a year ago. ASEAN continued to provide a strong regional market for Malaysia with exports increasing 10.6% in September 2011. Exports to ASEAN amounted to RM13.71 billion, accounting for 23.4% of Malaysia's total exports in September 2011.

However, exports to ASEAN in the fourth quarter are expected to be impacted by the floods in Thailand. Malaysia's exports to Thailand comprise mainly industrial products, including intermediate goods. Exports to Thailand that may be affected in the fourth quarter are automotive parts and accessories, chemical and chemical products, machinery and transport equipment, and electrical and electronic products. There is single-digit growth between 4.0% and 5.0%.

For imports, it is expected a growth rate of 7.0% for 2012 and between 7.0% and 8.0% for this year. In September 2011, imports amounted to RM 49.05 billion, up 12.9%, while total trade rose 14.9% to RM107.73 billion with trade surplus in September recording RM9.63 billion. Between January and September, exports increased 8.3% to RM513.59 billion, while imports rose 8.9% to RM424.37 billion, resulting in a trade surplus of RM89.22 billion. Top destinations were mainly countries in Asia. A key component of Matrade's 2012 Work Programme will be the execution and delivery of more than 120 trade promotion activities.

China–Malaysia Tie-up

The Chinese community in Malaysia acts as a bridge for business opportunities in China. Chinese money is becoming more visible in Penang. A bridge that is currently under construction is being partly financed by a cheap loan from the Chinese government. The 4.5 billion Malaysian Ringgit (US$1.4 billion) project is set to be the longest bridge in Southeast Asia, stretching 24 km (15 miles).

In 2010, Malaysia was one of China's biggest trading partners from Southeast Asia. Two-way trade hit 147 billion Malaysian ringgit (US$46.3 billion) last year, with a push to more than double that amount by 2015. Much of the trade has been established by the Chinese Malaysian community, says Oh Ei Sun, the former political secretary on Chinese affairs to Prime Minister Najib

Razak. Malaysia was the first Southeast Asian country to form diplomatic ties with China in 1974.

China's Diaspora

I. First major emigration in fourteenth to sixteenth century by traders and seafarers.

II. Colonial powers used Chinese as labourers in SE Asia and the Americas.

III. But also have reputation for business success.

IV. There are about 30 million overseas Chinese in total.

V. Indonesia and Thailand have the biggest numbers — 7–9 million each (estimates).

VI. Singapore has the highest concentration — 3 million or 75% of its population.

As a result the two countries have a special relationship, and the Chinese in Malaysia have tried to exploit this kinship by developing business ties with China. The Chinese began arriving on Malaysian shores in the early fifteenth century. Today, they make up 24% of a population of 28 million, and have always been more prosperous than other ethnic communities.

Speaking the language. As the Chinese economy opens up, Malaysian Chinese act as a bridge because many are educated in the United States or Britain but they can also understand the Chinese language and culture. This advantage is maintained because of Malaysia's multilingual education system. Ethnic Chinese and Indians can choose to study at the primary level in their mother tongue. With the rise of China, more and more people, including non-Chinese, want to learn Mandarin.[7]

---

7. Yong Yeow Khoon, CEO of the Chinese-language newspaper *Guang Ming Daily* in Penang, who is also a board member at an independent Chinese school.

The number of non-Chinese in Chinese vernacular schools is estimated to have grown to over 60,000 over the last three decades. Even the Malay prime minister has sent his son to learn Mandarin at the Beijing Foreign Studies University. Optimists point to this as a sign of increasing acceptance of Chinese culture by the Malay community. But some say this is wishful thinking.

Malaysia's Trade

Malaysia's economy, along with that of Singapore, Hong Kong and Taiwan, will be the worst hit in Asia by Europe's debt crisis and the U.S.'s financial turbulence, says Nomura International, which forecast a 3% growth rate for Malaysia next year.[8] Its economic growth forecast for Malaysia, a slowdown from an estimated 4.7% growth this year, is believed to be the lowest by research institutions and banks. The rest have a growth forecast of 4.5% on average. Malaysia, which officially expects between 5% and 6% growth next year, is deemed vulnerable to a deteriorating external outlook, being the third most open Asian economy after Singapore and Hong Kong. Its relatively weak public finances and dependence on commodities do not help.

Malaysia is one of the economies we think will weaken the most in Asia, and the reason for that is it is a very open economy — exports make up 97% of its GDP and unlike most of Asia. It is negatively affected when commodity prices come off, and we do expect commodity prices to come off next year. Another thing is Malaysia's exposure to European banks, apart from HSBC and Standard Chartered, stood at about US$50 billion as at June 2012. This is about 19% of the country's GDP, making it the most exposed market in the Asia Pacific ex-Japan region after Hong Kong (77% of GDP), Singapore (55%) and Taiwan (19%). The region's average exposure is 9.0% of GDP of US$ 20 billion. With Europe expected to go into a recession sometime in the first half next year, its banks are likely to face more stress and come

8. Crotty (2014), Démurger (2011), Gough (2015), Hong Lan (2014), Liu (2011), Michel (2010), Prabhakar (2013, 2015a, 2015b), Xafa (2012) and Zhou (2012).

under more pressure to recapitalise. Thus, Malaysia has a large current account surplus at around 13% of GDP which should help support the ringgit (Malaysian local currency) against hefty deterioration against the USD, due to its trade performance. We just expect, that Bank Negara to cut its policy rate by 100 basis points in the first half of 2012 from 3.0% now. Inflation is expected to be low at 3.0%.

China–India Trade Treaties

China has become India's largest trading partner, with their bilateral trade volume increasing from less than US$3 billion early this century to nearly US$70 billion. Both countries have had close coordination and cooperation on climate change, food security, energy security and other global issues and upheld the common interests of two countries as well as the developing world as a whole. Both China and India are now in a crucial stage of reform and development. As emerging markets, each with its own strengths, with rich experience in infrastructure building and manufacturing, China is ready to contribute to India's development in these areas. India is advanced in IT and pharmaceutical industries and Indian companies are welcome to seek business opportunities in the Chinese market. The combination of the 'world's factory' and the 'world's back office' will produce the most competitive production base and the most attractive consumer market. As the two engines of the Asian economy, the combination of China's energy plus India's wisdom will release massive potential. There is a need to jointly develop the BCIM Economic Corridor, the initiatives of the Silk Road Economic Belt and the Twenty-First Century Maritime Silk Road, and lead the sustainable growth of the Asian economy.

China–Russia Trade Treaties

Russia and China took a small step toward undercutting the domination of the U.S. dollar as the international reserve currency. Russia's second biggest financial institution, VTB, signed a deal with the Bank of China to bypass the dollar and pay each other in domestic currencies. Russia has done a huge job to reach a new historic landmark, making note of the $100 billion in annual trade that has been achieved between the two countries.

To be sure, the Russia–China bank deal is mostly a symbolic step. Liza Ermolenko, an emerging markets economist at Capital Economics in London, said that the deal was still 'a very small one, in the grand scale of things', and that it wouldn't change Russia's reliance on the dollar 'overnight'. Most of Russia's export contracts in the oil and gas markets are still priced in dollars, she noted, and on a wider scale, replacing the dollar with the rouble is much too risky to even consider. China has agreed to the gas deal, which could see over US$450 billion of Russian natural gas flow from eastern Siberia into China over the next 30 years, Russia is not in a position to abandon its ties with Europe.

Market-Driven Global Anti-American Bloc

As Russian president Vladimir Putin visits Shanghai to meet with Chinese president Xi Jinping, the battle spaces of the twenty-first century are coming into focus in Eurasia. It is the Kremlin's opinion that the balance of power at this moment is shifting away from the United States and its reluctant NATO allies, which dominated the second half of the twentieth century, eastward to Russia, China and their Shanghai Cooperation Organisation allies.

Evidence of the transformation is not only in Ukraine and Eastern Europe — where Moscow holds a strong position to win what it wants in a decentralised Ukraine as well as to lay claim to a say in the affairs of the near abroad states of the old Soviet empire — but also in East Asia, where the reawakened potency of the Kremlin can be seen in the behaviour of Russia's rising ally, China.

After a year of standoffs in the East China Sea between China and its traditional rivals Japan and South Korea, there is fresh conflict in the South China Sea. On 1 May, China suddenly moved an oil platform into contested waters 150 miles off Vietnam in the Paracel Islands. This is well within Vietnam's claimed exclusive economic zone, yet China is enforcing a 10 kilometre security perimeter around its rig.

Anticipating trouble, China surrounded the drilling platform with coast guard vessels and, all told, more than six dozen ships of all sizes. This swift, calculated swarming into contested territory closely resembles other manoeuvres by China against its neighbours, especially against the Philippines, such as the recent news of China's building a landing zone on the cross-claimed Johnson's Reef.

Vietnam erupted at the news of the Chinese aggression. Fierce anti-Chinese demonstrations in Hanoi, Ho Chi Minh City and other locations led to the deaths of Chinese nationals and a diplomatic fusillade that has not died down, despite calls from Vietnamese prime minister Nguyen Tan Dung for order. China, not trusting that the Vietnamese nationalist reactions have played out, has launched the evacuation of thousands of Chinese nationals. The well-paced Chinese provocations against important U.S. allies in East Asia are designed to show both Asia and the world that the United States cannot be trusted to honour its mutual defence treaties.

China is also not taking risks with its Chinese National Offshore Oil Corp. property in the Paracels. Vietnamese media report that the Chinese navy has dispatched two of its largest amphibious ships, Jinggangshan and Kunlunshan, each packed with hundreds of troops, hovercraft, missiles and helicopters, in order to defend the rig from attack. In addition, the missile frigate Mianyang, carrying an ASW helicopter, will join the coast guard vessels to protect what China regards as its territory.

China's plan to deploy an overwhelming force to secure a strategic asset has more than the Vietnamese government in mind. Beijing's actions are timed to Putin's state visit and a joint Russian-Chinese naval exercise in the South China Sea. Putin's embassy aims to reaffirm economic and energy arrangements between the two nations.

Moscow is constructing *de facto* alliances in Europe with Berlin and in Asia with Beijing in order to move beyond the rudimentary Shanghai Cooperation Organisation — formed in 2001 and now including Kazakhstan, Kyrgyzstan, Tajikistan and Uzbekistan — to a land-based empire of Russia and its clients.

In Putin's grand imperial vision, what Moscow desires is a partner to secure the seas surrounding the Eurasian supercontinent. Moscow's fleet can control the Northern Passage and the northern Pacific Rim. Moscow will use the Shanghai Cooperation Organisation to trade with India and the Persian Gulf. What Moscow wants from China's fleet is to secure the southern Pacific Rim as well as to control the sea routes in the Indian Ocean approaches to the Gulf and Africa.

Trade volume between China and Russia reached US$29.1 billion in 2005, an increase of 37.1% compared with 2004. A spokesman for the Ministry of Commerce, Van Jingsun, said that the volume of trade between China and Russia could exceed 40 billion dollars in 2007. China's export of machinery and electronic goods to Russia grew 70%, which is 24% of China's total export to Russia in the first 11 months of 2005. During the same time, China's export of high-tech products to Russia increased by 58%, and that is 7% of China's total exports to Russia. Also in this time period border trade between the two countries reached US$5.13 billion, growing 35% and accounting for nearly 20% of the total trade. Most of China's exports to Russia remain apparel and footwear. Russia is China's eighth largest trade partner and China is now Russia's fourth largest trade partner, and China now has over 750 investment projects in Russia, involving US$1.05 billion. China's contracted investment in Russia totalled US$368 million during January–September 2005, twice that in 2004.

Chinese imports from Russia are mainly those of energy sources, such as crude oil, which is mostly transported by rail, and electricity exports from neighbouring Siberian and Far Eastern regions. In the near future, exports of both of these commodities are set to increase, as Russia is building the Eastern Siberia-Pacific Ocean oil pipeline with a branch to Chinese border, and Russian power grid monopoly UES is building some of its hydropower stations with a view of future exports to China.

Export growth has continued to be a major component supporting China's rapid economic growth. To increase exports, China pursued policies such as fostering the rapid development of foreign-invested factories, which assembled imported components into consumer goods for export and liberalising trading rights. In its 11th Five Year Plan, adopted in 2005, China placed greater emphasis on developing a consumer demand-driven economy to sustain economic growth and address imbalances.

The China Council for the Promotion of International Trade (CCPIT) promotes China's international economic and commercial interests. This is accomplished by developing business cooperation and exchanges with foreign countries. It also produces economic data, creates diplomatic ties and is active with trade arbitration issues. Hong Kong remains prominent in domestic trade, notably in its reliance on the mainland for agricultural products.

China was the largest trading partner of:

I. North Korea (81% in 2008)
II. Sudan (69.8% in 2008)
III. Mongolia (in 2008)
IV. Angola (48.7% in 2008)
V. Taiwan (42.2% in 2008)
VI. South Korea (39.1% in 2008)
VII. Japan (34.9% in 2008)
VIII. Iran (28.3% in 2008)
IX. Vietnam (26.6% in 2008)
X. India (20.4% in 2008)
XI. Brazil (in 2009)
XII. Australia (in 2009)

China–Venezuela Economic Relations

Since 1998 China–Venezuela relations have seen an increasing partnership between the government of the Venezuelan president

Hugo Chavez and the China. Sino-Venezuelan trade was less than US$500 million per year before 1999, and reached US$7.5 billion in 2009, making China–Venezuela's second-largest trade partner, and Venezuela China's biggest investment destination in Latin America. Various bilateral deals have seen China invest billions in Venezuela, and Venezuela increases exports of oil and other resources to China.

China–United States Trade Treaties

China and the United States established diplomatic ties on 1 January 1979. The trade volume between the two countries in 1979 amounted to only 2.4 billion dollars. At that time, what happened in the U.S. economy had little impact on China, and vice versa. But last year, China–United States trade volume amounted to more than 333 billion dollars. China has also become the largest creditor of the United States. China's trade with the United States has reached 24.9% in 2008. China has come under criticism in the United States for having a large trade surplus with the United States. In reality, China enjoys only a small part of this trade surplus as only around 30% of this is retained in China. Thus, the trade surplus that China enjoys with the United States is overrated. In China, the average import content of exports is high, about 45–53% according to several recent studies, using separate input-output tables for domestically produced and processing exports.

In China processing exports refer to a special category of goods produced by assembling and/or processing intermediate inputs that are exempted from tariffs because the final products are sold only in foreign markets. Processing exports accounted for about 55–60% of total Chinese exports in the first half of this decade. Their import content is several times that of non-processing exports; in 2002 it was around 75% against 11%. Import content is particularly high — over 80% — in sectors processing high-end manufactures such as electronics compared to low skill exports. Foreign firms are active in export processing and have particularly higher import content in their exports than do domestic firms. The estimates made for the first half of the 2000s show that the average foreign value-added content of Chinese exports was between 40% and 50%. A very large proportion of foreign content of exports consisted of imported parts and components directly used in sectors producing exportable.

This proportion was particularly high in export processing sectors. Chinese exports to the United States are found to have greater import contents than its exports to the rest of the world in large part because a very high proportion of exports to the United States — about 78% in 2002 — are processing exports. In 2002 the foreign value-added content of exports to the United States was around 63% compared to less than 50% for total Chinese exports. By contrast U.S. exports to China have very high domestic value-added content (around 87% in the same year) and very low foreign value-added content (13%). As a result, while in gross value terms the bilateral trade surplus of China with the United States was estimated to be some US$172 billion in 2005, in value-added terms this figure comes down to less than US$40 billion. In other words, China's exports to the United States contain large amounts of value-added generated elsewhere, including in its Asian trading partners and even the United States itself.

Moreover, this already reduced trade surplus in value-added terms is not all retained in China. A relatively important part of the domestic value-added generated by Chinese exports accrue to foreign firms. This is particularly the case for processing exports where foreign firms are dominant. It is estimated that of the total domestic value-added generated by Chinese exports in 2002 to the United States, around two-thirds went to capital income, some 18% to labour and 14% to indirect taxes. About 60% of these exports were by foreign firms, including firms from the United States. Even if it is assumed that such firms shared only in the direct capital income, it can be estimated that an additional 7% of the value of total Chinese exports to the United States went to foreign firms. As a result, income left in China was no more than 30% of total value of exports to the United States.

11

The Global Economic Recession: South Perspective

The world economic trend is still skating, and this will have serious consequences for the developing countries. Some prominent economists have warned that this time the crisis will be more serious and more prolonged than the 2008–2009 Great Recession. Firstly, a double-dip recession is now likely because of the sovereign debt crisis in the European region and the weakening of the U.S. economy. Secondly, the tools that helped the world quickly recover from the 2008–2009 recession (fiscal stimulus and easy monetary policy) are no longer so easily available in the developed countries (or in some countries they are not available at all). Thirdly, the kind of coordination of policy actions among developed countries (and several developing countries as well) that fought the last recession no longer seems to exist, at least in the immediate future.

A conference on 'Options for developing countries in the global economic and financial turbulence' was organised by the South Centre with the Third World Network and the Consumers' Association of Penang and held at the International Labour Organization in Geneva on 25 May 2011. The Conference brought together many experts from the developing countries as well as from international organisations such as United Nations Conference on Trade and Development (UNCTAD) and the ILO.

Diplomats and policymakers from developing countries and NGOs specialising in financial and economic issues also attended.[1]

Mostly speakers warned how the unregulated flows of capital were continuing to cause boom-bust cycles that have devastating effects on developing countries. They predicted that the boom in capital flows and in economic growth could come to an end when the global situation changes. The accuracy of these analyses and predictions has been shown by the recent events.

The world face in the next 10 years will be different, with the developed countries facing massive public debts, said Y.V. Reddy, former Governor of the Reserve Bank of India. From the developing countries' viewpoint, there will be a lot of uncertainties, and they must prepare themselves to face the uncertain future. Asian countries will be able to continue with their economic growth but at a moderate rate as most of them are not so vulnerable to currency or balance of payments problems. However the situation will be less orderly in Latin America and Africa, which are vulnerable to changes in global financial conditions and commodity markets. But there may be balance of payments crises in some major developing countries that have significant current account deficits and are thus dependent on the inflow of capital flows, since these flows may reverse.

There is risk of fiscal and sovereign debt crises in some developed countries. And the sluggish growth and high unemployment in the North will increase tension in the trading system, with the higher risk of protectionism. Systemic reforms are needed in global finance. There is a lack of multilateral discipline on financial, macroeconomic and exchange rate policies of major countries. There is an absence of control of financial markets, capital flows and speculation. And the G-20 has failed so far to address these systemic issues.

As we know, globalisation had been oversold to developing countries, which were asked to fully integrate into the global financial markets. The lesson is that developing countries should

1. The theme and tone of the Conference was set by a presentation on the current global situation by the South Centre's Chief Economist, Dr. Yõlmaz Akyüz. If the lessons of the last financial crisis are not acted on through coordinated global action, there will be a bigger crisis soon, and an even bigger one after that, he warned.

rethink their integration into the world economy. They should seek strategic integration (in areas and ways that are beneficial) but not full integration.

Three Scenarios on the New Crisis

What would happen if the systemic problems are not tackled? We can then expect another crisis, and without reforms an even bigger crisis after that, and the possibility of conflicts among countries. The financial crisis was triggered by coordination failures at the global level, and there will be more crises if this is not addressed. He gave three scenarios of what could happen:

I. First, there would be greater global policy coordination, with a world economic council setting rules for finance, disciplining major countries and establishing an independent panel for resolving debt crises.

II. Second, the present situation continues without global governance, each country sets its own policies, but there is regulation of financial institutions with cross-border effects, and a fund is set up to provide financing to developing countries hit by external shocks.

III. In the third scenario, there is only talk of reforms but no global action. Each country then tries to protect itself against a future crisis, by building foreign reserves, in a race to the bottom. This may be supplemented by regional financial measures.

Need for South to be Pro-Active

In order not to be caught as helpless victims to the new crisis, they need to take three types of action:

I. They should prepare themselves with policy responses to reduce the impact of the new crisis and the external shocks that may come with it, particularly a sharp fall in exports (including in commodity prices and demand), a reversal of capital flows and a sharp decline in value of their currency.

II. They should review their previous development strategies to see if they are still valid or whether changes are needed to respond to the changed international situation. In particular, developing countries that have relied heavily on exports to lead their growth may now find a decline in demand especially from the developed countries. They need to examine how to rely more on domestic demand and on regional South–South cooperation.

III. They should also take an active part in the discussions on reform of the international financial and monetary system, as well as on the coordination of macroeconomic policies of systemically important countries. Developing countries are adversely affected by the dysfunctional global system, and therefore have an interest in its reform. Unfortunately there is an absence of an appropriate system of global economic governance that enables the developing countries to participate fully. Thus, this is also a good time to advocate for establishing such a governance system.

There had been too much of shadow banking in the past without the knowledge of whether the institutions and financial instruments are safe or toxic. The problems of financial institutions being 'too big to fail' or 'too powerful to regulate' remain. In developing countries, it is necessary to design a financial system that not only avoids instability but also promotes development. Since the markets do not ensure stability or development, governments have to take charge and they must not give up the space for public policy.

Therefore, countries must be allowed to have the policy space. It is important that there be diversity of policies. In the developed countries, the financial institutions were practicing the same model and making the same mistakes, and this led to a failure affecting the system. Those regulators that did not follow this model were able to avoid a crisis. Up to now, the developing countries had been reactive (only reacting to others' views) in the global debates on finance. There is a need to make four policy proposals for Asian countries:

I. First, Asia should not follow the Anglo-Saxon model of finance but bring back the role of the financial sector as serving the real economy.

II. Second, Asian countries should rebalance their economic growth by reducing their export dependence and also reducing income inequalities.

III. Third, Asian countries should reinvest their savings in the region. The foreign reserves should be invested in the region itself rather than being channelled to the West only to be recycled from there to Asia.

IV. Fourth, in view of the volatility of capital flows, Asian countries should be prepared to make use of capital controls to avoid the adverse effects.

V. First we look at the current economic conditions and problems in the major economies, the United States, Europe and China; then discuss the vulnerability of developing and emerging economies to financial risks posed by advanced economies, notably the United States and Europe; and finally, GEP with respect to stability and growth.

Life after Crisis

Developing countries are facing renewed risks of instability and slowdown before fully recovering from the so-called Great Recession and the chances of averting such an outcome are becoming quite slim. This is largely because the imbalances and fragilities built-up over several years in the past as a result of misguided policies in the United States and Europe cannot be easily undone, regardless of the policy pursued today. These have resulted in distortions and imbalances in economic structures and private balance sheets and they cannot be corrected overnight. This is a main reason why recovery in advanced economies is sluggish, erratic and jobless.

The strong growth in developing and emerging economies we have been witnessing since mid-2009 is not sustainable because of the following reasons. First, it is the outcome of a strong policy response to the crisis whose effects are wearing out in several developing economies particularly in China which has been a major locomotive to commodity-rich developing countries as the number one global commodity importer. Secondly, the response to the crisis in advanced economies through excessive liquidity generation and sharp cuts in interest rates is actually creating bubbles, not in Europe and United States, but in commodity markets and the developing world. This cheap money in search for yield is a major factor behind the rapid growth in several emerging economies.

That we now have a two-track world economy is a fallacy — very much like the belief initially held during the sub-prime crisis that the developing economies would be decoupled. These economies are still highly susceptible to destabilising and deflationary impulses from advanced economies even though there is considerable diversity among them regarding the channels of transmission of such impulses, the degree of vulnerability and their ability to respond.

A double dip recession in the United States is now believed to have been averted, but there is little doubt that it is experiencing the weakest recovery in its post-war history — jobless and without much investment. This is often the case in recoveries from financial crises because incomes need to be used to address excessive debt and balance sheet distortions before being spent on investment and hiring new people.

Growth forecasts in the United States have been cut down by the Fed and growth is not seen as self-sustaining through expansion of private spending and/or exports. The policy of easy money pursued to sustain recovery has led to the weakest dollar in effective terms since 1973, and is creating bubbles in the developing world and commodity markets. With weak and erratic recovery, the United States is facing a growing public deficit, presently at some 10% of GDP. The IMF expects U.S. public debt to rise to 110% of GDP in 2016, up from 70% in 2008. Under the current growth path, there is no way for the United States to halve its public deficit by half by 2013, as it promised to the G-20.

The U.S. fiscal response to the crisis focused on raising private consumption though perhaps it should have emphasised investment, which is needed to accelerate export growth. Despite that, U.S. consumers have been retrenching. Any fiscal adjustment coming on top of consumer retrenchment would bring down growth considerably unless exports closed the gap. President Obama's National Export Initiative launched in 2009 targeted to double U.S. exports in five years, but this is unlikely to be attained — it would require 15% growth annually but so far exports have grown by an average 10% per annum, despite the bounce back from a depressed level. It is unlikely that the United States can shift to an export-led growth in the near future unless Europe deals quickly with its sovereign debt problems and restores strong and broad-based growth and developing countries, notably those in Asia, reduce their dependence on exports and maintain strong growth based on domestic demand.

There is a risk that U.S. interest rates may rise before full recovery is achieved. First, the bubble in the commodity market could be translated into inflation particularly if oil prices continue to go up, and the Fed may have to respond in the same way as it did in the late 1970s to the second oil hike and rising inflation. Second, growing concern over public debt and deficits could lead to a surge in long-term interest rates — that current yields are very low is no guarantee that they will remain so in the foreseeable future.

Europe has been grappling with sovereign debt in the periphery and is engaged in fiscal consolidation and monetary tightening in its search for stability. Eurozone growth is anaemic — one and a half percent in 2010 — and is highly uneven — Germany is growing much faster, relying on exports. For the rest of the eurozone Germany is not a locomotive but deadweight — it pursues a policy of competitive disinflation. Its unit labour costs are lower than many other eurozone countries not because of its exceptional productivity growth but because of wage suppression. This creates considerable difficulties in maintaining growth and external balance for countries incapable of cutting wages to the same extent. However, German exports and growth may not be sustained if the rest of the Europe does not do well.

The approach to sovereign debt problems in Europe invokes memories of the 1980s. It cost a decade of development to learn that debt overhang could not be removed by getting countries into more debt and cutting growth. Insisting that the debt should be fully paid can make it even less payable. The European periphery, unlike the Latin Americans in the 1980s, does not have the option of devaluing their currencies except through deflation by creating larger and larger unemployment — a cure worse than the disease, as Argentina knows very well. If the current strategy continues and the EC and ECB pretend that this is a liquidity crisis, the European periphery will remain susceptible to speculative attacks and messy defaults.

A growth-oriented adjustment in Europe calls for Germany to start acting as a locomotive. There is a need for a real appreciation of the euro for Germany, but not for the others, that is, through higher German wages. This could generate faster growth in domestic demand needed to maintain growth while reducing dependence on exports and allowing other Europeans to grow faster.

Growth and Adjustment in China

China introduced a massive stimulus programme in response to the crisis, reaching 15% of GDP, three times the United States. But it focused on investments pushing it to over 50% of GDP. Support to household incomes has remained moderate even though the country faces a problem of under-consumption, with private consumption hovering around 36% of GDP, half the level of the United States.

Chinese growth has also been pushed up because of large amounts of private foreign capital inflows. Before the crisis, private capital went almost everywhere in the developing world in search for yield. Subsequently, it was withdrawn from most countries in Central and Eastern Europe, and China has become the largest recipient. According to Chinese official estimations, one-third of net capital inflows from non-residents are now in 'hot money', meaning not linked to investment and productions. A quarter of FDI inflows are in commercial real estate, adding to the property bubble fuelled by rapid credit expansion as part of the crisis response. The economy has been overheating, and the government is now applying monetary breaks to slow it down.

China needs to reduce its dependence on exports and rely on domestic markets for growth. Its current account surplus fell from a peak of 11% of GDP in 2006 to around 5% in 2010, now lower than the German surplus. Chinese adjustment needs to be based on significantly faster growing household income — that is, rapid expansion of wages without a pass-through to prices, and employment. This would appreciate the currency while simultaneously creating domestic demand to offset the slowdown in exports. By contrast, a nominal appreciation of the RMB would not necessarily translate into faster domestic demand. In fact, it could result in a slowdown in domestic demand if the burden is passed on to wages.

China now recognises the needs to shift to consumption-led growth. It has recently taken several measures in terms of minimum wages, higher wage growth, faster job creation, emphasising the services sector, better social safety nets, etc. The 12th five-year plan envisages several measures on these fronts, but a shift from export-led to consumption-led growth is a slow process particularly since it requires a significant redistribution of income from corporations to households, increased government transfers and faster job creation.

Before the crisis Chinese exports were growing at 25% per annum in real terms. According to my calculations, around 50% of Chinese growth was due to exports, including spillovers to domestic consumption and investment. But this figure was around 90% for Germany and between the two for Japan even though all the attention has been on China. Now China's five-year plan projects a 7% growth, in recognition that China cannot keep on raising its real exports 25% per annum as it did for seven or eight years before the crisis. If Chinese export growth fell to some 10%, its GDP growth rate could indeed come down to 7 or 7.05% without a massive shift to consumption. Attempts to fill the gap with a new surge in investment could simply amount to postponing the under-consumption crisis, to come back even with a greater force.

Impact of Chinese Slowdown on Other Developing Countries

What will happen if China slows down? Its strong growth has been a major factor in the recent commodity surge. Commodity stockpiling was a reason for the emergence of a trade deficit in the first quarter of this year for the first time for many years. A slowdown from double-digit rates to 7% could have a serious adverse impact on commodity exporters. On the other hand, over the longer term, a successful shift to consumption-led growth could also shift the Chinese demand from hard to soft commodities, particularly grains and meat, aggravating the global food shortage. It has indeed already turned from a grain exporter to an importer.

A slowdown in Chinese exports to the United States would hurt other countries linked to the Sino-centric production network even if this is fully compensated by increased Chinese domestic consumption. This is because Chinese consumption has little foreign content, directly or indirectly. Some countries in the region are already facing the so-called middle-income trap with low investment and sluggish consumption but large current account surpluses, like Malaysia at 16% of GDP. An interregional redistribution of investment from China to the other countries in the region is needed. Countries in Southeast Asia also need to expand domestic consumption, and again the problem here is worsened income distribution. But a shift of China from exports to domestic demand would be good for some newcomers in labour-intensive industries such as Vietnam, which could actually make more headway into U.S. markets.

Capital Flows and Bubbles

Following a short-lived interruption after the Lehman collapse in September 2009, private capital flows to developing countries recovered rapidly, particularly to those with higher interest rates and better growth prospects. While almost all emerging economies have seen their currencies appreciate, appreciations have been faster in deficit countries such as Brazil, India, Turkey and South Africa than Asian surplus countries. Like China, most deficit countries are also facing credit and asset bubbles, with, credit growth in the range of 25–35% per annum, risking a hard landing.

There is a remarkable correlation between recent movements in capital flows to developing countries, commodity prices and the dollar. After the outbreak of the sub-prime crisis until the Lehman collapse, capital flows to developing countries held up. Similarly, commodity prices which had started rising in 2003 and accelerated in 2006 reached the peak in the middle of the crisis in summer 2008 when oil hit US$150 pb. Why? The factors which kept up capital flows to developing countries also kept the flows into commodity markets. The downturn was seen as a hiccup and the growth was expected to pick up quickly — in fact, the IMF was upgrading its global growth projections in the middle of 2008. But when Lehman collapsed, commodity prices and capital flows plummeted and the dollar shot up as a result of flight to safety. But, from the first quarter of 2009 onwards, all these were reversed; dollar started weakening, capital flows began picking up and commodity prices started rising again. Strong Chinese growth was an important factor in the commodity surge. But commodity speculation has also played an important role.

FDI into Indonesia

Indonesia's FDI hit a record US$20 billion last year, with Singapore, Japan and the United States among the Southeast Asian nation's top investors, the trade minister said on 19 January 2012. Gita Wirjawan said the figure was 'a new historic level' and an 18.4% hike over 2010 as foreign money flowed into the country's fast growing economy. The record figure comes a day after Moody's Investors Service restored Indonesia's investment grade sovereign credit rating, weeks after a similar move by rival ratings agency Fitch. Indonesia, Moody's said, had earned the bump following steps to bring down its debt-to-GDP ratio as well as having a 'well managed financial system'. Indonesia's total investment in 2011, from both domestic and foreign sources, was 251.3 trillion rupiah, surpassing the government's 240 trillion rupiah target. Foreign investment accounted for about 70% of the total, adding that offshore money flows also accounted for about 67% of 400,000 jobs created last year in Indonesia. Foreign capital flows dipped 0.4% in the fourth quarter.

FDI in the transport, storage and communications sectors totalled US$3.8 billion, followed by US$3.6 billion in mining and US$1.9 billion in electricity, gas and water supply. Singapore led the list of foreign investors with US$5.1 billion, following by Japan and the United States with about US$1.5 billion each. The Netherlands and South Korea invested US$1.4 billion and US$1.2 billion, respectively.

Moody's upgrade of Indonesia's credit status to investment grade is set to spur capital inflows into the country, with fund managers tipping that to mainly benefit government bonds and stocks with exposure to domestic consumption, such as PT Unilever Indonesia Tbk. Moody's Investors Service on 18 January 2012 became the second credit-ratings agency in just over a month to give Southeast Asia's biggest economy an investment grade rating, paving the way for more fund managers to allocate money to Indonesia. Most bond funds can only invest in a country if it has investment grade ratings from at least two of the three major agencies — Moody's, Standard and Poor's and Fitch Ratings.

How the Capital and Commodity Bubbles Might Be Ended?

How will all these end up? There are four possible scenarios. First, these bubbles could end with an abrupt monetary tightening in the United States.

Second, a significant slowdown of growth in China, possibly aggravated by the bursting of the credit and property bubble, could bring an end to the boom in commodity markets and capital flows. It could not only depress Chinese demand for commodities but also trigger a massive exit of speculative capital flow from commodity markets.

Third, a balance-of-payments crisis in a major developing economy can bring an end to the boom in capital flows by leading to a contagion across emerging markets. For example, Turkey now has a current account deficit close to 10% of GDP, and deficits are also high and growing in some other emerging economies. A sudden change of moods in markets, as in East Asia during 1997, could trigger a currency and payments crisis in such countries.

Finally turmoil in the eurozone resulting from sovereign debt difficulties in the periphery could cause a flight to safety in much the same way as the Lehman collapse resulted in the reversal of capital flows even in emerging economies with sound fiscal and payments positions and banking sectors.

In any of the four of these scenarios, it is highly likely that the downturn in capital flows will be associated with a reversal of commodity prices. As a result, the most vulnerable countries are those which have been enjoying the twin benefits of global liquidity expansion, that is, the surge in capital inflows and the commodity boom. This is more or less what happened in the 1980s. Mexico which had enjoyed the twin booms in the 1970s in international lending and oil prices was the first country to get into trouble in Latin America in the early 1980s. Commodity importers such as Turkey and India may benefit from a downturn in commodity prices even though they may get hurt by capital reversal.

In this regard, Asia is less vulnerable to balance of payments and currency crises, because of sound balance of payments positions and strong reserves. However, outflows could explode bubbles, notably in the property markets, as happened during the Lehman collapse. Still, Asia can be expected to achieve an orderly moderation of growth. But adjustment in commodity-dependent and deficit economies may not be so orderly. Unlike Asia where reserves are earned from current account surpluses in deficit countries they are borrowed, coming from capital inflows. Hence, with a reversal of capital flows they can disappear as fast as they were accumulated.

Major Lessons from the Crisis

1. The crisis illustrated how far-reaching contagion can be in globally integrated financially markets. By and large, with exceptions like Australia and Canada, the direct effects of the financial contagion in the form of threats to financial systems involved major financial markets in advanced countries. However, the effects of this contagion on interest rates and prices have been felt globally — by emerging-market and other developing countries — as have the challenges to policies in areas like the control of capital movements.
2. Regulation with a primarily micro-prudential focus does not adequately monitor and control systemic or macro-prudential risks.
3. Regulation must keep up with transactional and institutional innovation and other changes. Failures to exercise control or even to actually outright prohibit certain activities and products can exacerbate micro prudential and macro-prudential risks.
4. Regulatory models relying heavily on market signals provide inadequate incentives for effective risk management.
5. Questions need to be faced concerning both the reality and the desirability of the policy objective of increased global financial integration based on concepts like an international level playing field and progressive removal of obstacles to the expansion

of international banking and to cross-border financial transactions. The crisis has highlighted the huge divergence between the capacity of advanced and developing countries to subsidise financial activities (which in some cases in advanced countries was required to ensure the survival of large financial institutions and thus their continuation as participants — and thus competitors of institutions from developing countries — in international financial markets). Furthermore the case for 'speed bumps' in financial markets is now stronger.

Concluding Remarks

1. Work on the agenda of financial reform is still in flux. The bank lobbies continue to exert formidable pressures in both the United States and the EU regarding many features of proposed reforms. A threat to the timely and full implementation of the Dodd-Frank Act in the former has emerged in the form the reluctance of Congress to provide the funding required for finalising sections of the Act and then implementing it.
2. The reforms enunciated under the international agenda have been very much a response to problems revealed by the crisis in the regulatory regimes of advanced countries rather than emerging-market and other developing ones. Statistical data concerning the latter suggest that at the aggregate level their banks should be able to introduce the capital standards of Basel 3 without major problems, though some of its rules for capital requirements for particular sectors or activities may require modification in the light of local circumstances. A source of greater difficulties may prove to be the rules on liquidity management whose designers appear to have had fairly highly developed financial markets in mind.
3. Beyond the debate on policy towards financial institutions that are 'too big to fail', the international reform agenda has not addressed issues posed by concentration in major

countries' banking sectors (often greater since the current crisis) or by the extreme difficulty of establishing effective supervision, management and internal controls for large complex financial institutions.

4. There are reasons to doubt whether measures taken or envisaged so far have properly aligned incentives and risks in the financial sector. Remuneration in the form of shares was widely and ineffectively used in several financial firms before the crisis. Eventual success of the new rules on remuneration of the reform agenda is likely to depend on the effectiveness of provisions on claw back in response to positions taken by employees eventually shown to entail excessive risk. I dream of reintroduction of unlimited liability partnerships for investment banks/broker dealers (still common until relatively recently and requiring bankers to write cheques to their institutions in some years) or, if this too radical, of arrangements which mimic the functioning of such partnerships.
5. Adam Smith, regarded as the father of free-market economics by many (who often have probably never read him), recommended the joint-stock-company form (as opposed to that of the 'private copartners') as appropriate only to banking whose operations were of a routine character and reducible to strict rules. It is reasonable to assume that in making this argument he had in mind speculative bubbles in his not too recent past.[2]

2. *Source*: 'International Conference on Global Financial Turbulence: Options for Developing Countries.' The prominent participants and speakers were former Central Bank Governor of India Dr. Y.V. Reddy; former Nigerian Central Bank Governor Dr. Charles Soludo; Chairman of the G77 and China (Geneva Chapter), Ambassador Mothae Maruping of Lesotho; President of the UNCTAD Trade and Development Board, Ambassador Homero Hernandez Sanchez of Dominican Republic; Arturo O'Connel (Advisor to Central Bank Governor, Argentina) and Raymond Torres, Director of the Institute for International Labour Studies of the ILO.

12 Conclusion

The global economic recession, the onset of which was in December 2007 from the west to the east, the north to the south or the most advanced developed nations to developing countries, has been facing the challenges of recovering a level of economic growth. While the uneven performance of the U.S. economy and the eurozone has led economists such as Paul Krugman and Larry Summers to ask whether the U.S. has succumbed to 'secular stagnation': Is the economy now burdened with structural impediments which will make strong and sustained growth difficult to achieve? International finance capital and military-based marketisation and globalisation process of the world capitalist regime has crashed, not only fallen in demand both public and private at a global level (e.g., from Russia to European countries, Malaysia to European countries, India, China, Japan and S. Korea to the United States and European countries), but the world's GDP (the growth rate) plunged, with balance of payment problems impending enormous fall in value of local currency everywhere. The core capitalist economies of the world including Japan entered into a double-dip recession. Unemployment has been rising at mass scale. Inflation has increased in upward direction at a global level. State-led welfare programmes have adjourned, resulting in the destitution of billions of people. The eurozone (especially Greece) has continued to experience nearby stagnation. The U.S. economy recovered slightly and creates larger job opportunities in the last few months, which has been accredited to military-based industry.

In short, there are gathering clouds of recession over the world economy as a whole.

The Financial Institutional Crash of 2007–2008 was an acute crisis of market disequilibrium which has imposed itself upon an economics discipline still giving pride of place to models where market forces nudge economies in the very opposite direction — towards equilibrium. Crises of disequilibrium have occurred with increasing frequency over the past 30 years: with the Latin American debt crises of the 1980s, the American Savings and Loans collapse of the late 1980s, the Scandinavian banking crisis of the early 1990s, the Asian and Russian financial crises of the late 1990s, the American 'dotcom' bust of 2000 and the Crash of 2007–2008 itself which has been global in impact.

Since classical, neo-classical and modern economics emphasised to achieve general equilibrium point as theories suggested that market-led economy automatically leads when producers focus on economic specialisation, profits, prices of commodities, quantity and quality improvements of goods/commodities will be determined by the demand and the supply forces on the basis of comparative advantage. Keynesian economists recommended reduction in aggregate expenditure to fight inflation. Thus Keynesian economics emphasised management of aggregate demand through the adoption of proper fiscal and monetary policies. These policies could prove successful when there was either high inflation or high unemployment, that is, when high inflation and high unemployment did not exist simultaneously.

Under capitalist system in the era of hegemony of international finance capital cannot, for reasons already mentioned (namely the need of the system to act always in a manner that makes finance capital appear to be socially necessary), rely on Keynesian 'demand management' to stimulate its level of activity; the only stimulus available to it therefore is the formation of 'bubbles' in asset prices that can give some boost to the level of aggregate demand. These 'bubbles' however get formed only if there are 'exuberant expectations'; but in a situation of crisis such as now the prospects of such exuberant expectations getting formed are remote. Hence the world capitalist economy has no alternative but to remain mired in stagnation and to keep 'bumping along the floor', with occasional minor upturns being followed by recessions.

The financial system of the largest economic bloc in the world is threatened by a fiscal and financial crisis that has so far eluded policymakers' efforts to contain it. The formation of that bubble and its collapse are episodes which are themselves embedded within a deeper structural crisis that afflicts contemporary capitalism, one related to the phenomenon of 'globalisation'. The present globalisation is no different from, indeed as a continuation of, the previous episode of globalisation that had been interrupted by the two world wars, the Great Depression and the post-war adoption of State interventionism within broadly national economic regimes. This view however is erroneous. The present globalisation is a *sui generis* phenomenon that makes contemporary capitalism differ in important respects from all that has preceded it.

Capitalism prior to the current globalisation had been characterised by three basic features. First, labour did not have free mobility from the 'south' to the 'north'; indeed it still does not have. The 'long nineteenth century', lasting until the First World War, had seen two large waves of migration across the globe. There was a migration from Europe to the temperate regions of white settlement like Canada, the United States, Australia, South Africa, Kenya and New Zealand where the migrants occupied land by dispossessing the original inhabitants. They kept up their own standard of living and therefore also the actual wage back home. This was a 'high wage, temperate-to-temperate region migration'.

There was a second wave of migration at the behest of capital that was from tropical or subtropical countries like India and China to other tropical regions, where the migrants were employed as coolies or indentured labourers on mines, plantations and construction projects, such as countries like Malaysia, Indonesia, Kenya and South Africa. The countries from which the migrants came had witnessed substantial 'deindustrialisation', in the sense of the destruction of traditional craft production by the import of manufactures from the capitalist metropolis which had thrown large numbers of people out of work and intensified the pressure on the limited land mass. This had led to extraordinarily depressed real wages. This second wave of migration therefore was a 'low wage tropical to tropical region migration'.

Each of these waves involved approximately 50 million people, but they were kept strictly separate. Tropical labour was not allowed to move freely to Europe; it was also restrained from moving to the temperate regions of white settlement. Even in the post-Second World War years, migration occurred on a larger scale than before from the 'south' to the 'north'; it still remained as controlled migration, regulated in accordance with the needs of capital. There was no free labour mobility.

The second feature of pre-globalisation capitalism was that capital did not move freely from the 'north' to the 'south'. Here, there were no juridical restrictions upon its moving; nonetheless it moved only to plantations, mining, export activities and the infrastructure required for such activities, such as railways (where typically the rates of return were guaranteed by the colonial State). There was no migration in any significant sense to manufacturing, despite the lower real wages prevailing in the 'south'. Why there was so little migration of capital from the 'north' to set up manufacturing units in the 'south' has been much discussed. We need not enter that discussion here; we merely note the fact that capital from the 'north' did not move freely to the 'south' despite there being no juridical restraints upon its doing so.

The third feature was that the import of manufactured goods produced in the 'south' was taxed heavily in the north. Because of this, the emerging local capitalists, even if they did manage to set up manufacturing units within the 'south' (despite the numerous hurdles placed in their way by the colonial regimes) were precluded from entering the 'northern' markets. They were confined at best to their own local markets; and even there they had to face competition from 'northern' manufactured goods without any protection given to them.

The net result of these three features was that the world economy became 'segmented' into two parts, and the real wages in one part, the 'north', were not restrained by the massive labour reserves of the other, the 'south'. To be sure, there was a reserve army of labour located within the 'north' too (capitalism can never function without such a reserve army), which restrained 'northern' wages; but its size being relatively small, its restraining influence on 'northern' wages was not so absolute as to tie these wages down to some 'subsistence' level.

Put differently, world capitalism had two reserve armies of labour: there was a relatively small one in the 'north' which, though it restrained wages, did not prevent their rise, through trade union action, with increases in labour productivity. Then there was a huge reserve army in the 'south' which prevented wages there from rising above a bare subsistence level (and thereby helped to achieve price-stability in the metropolis by preventing any autonomous cost-push for raw materials), but did not restrain 'northern' wages owing to this fact of segmentation. What this segmentation meant therefore was that while real wages in the 'north' rose with labour productivity, real wages in the 'south' continued to stagnate at a bare subsistence level under the pressure of its massive labour reserves.

In addition however it also contributed to bolstering the internal demand within the global 'north'. The rise in real wages along with labour productivity helped to prevent the emergence of the problem of demand deficiency. A rise in real wages along with labour productivity to be sure is neither a necessary nor a sufficient condition for thwarting a possible deficiency of demand: after all even with a constant share of wages and even with all wages being consumed, demand deficiency can still arise because of a waning of the drive to invest; and likewise euphoric expectations about prospective profits among capitalists can push up investment to a point where even a declining wage share does not cause a deficiency of aggregate demand. But a rise in real wages does help in boosting aggregate demand: it keeps the level of demand higher than it would have been for any given level of investment.

The current globalisation has broken down this segmentation of the world capitalist economy. Even though labour from the 'south' is still not free to move 'north', capital from the 'north' is now moving 'south' to locate plants there for exports to the world market as a whole including to 'northern' markets which are now open to such exports from the 'south'. This also means, however, that the workers in the 'north' are now exposed to the baneful consequences of the massive labour reserves of the 'south'.

One obvious implication of this has been the decline in the strength of trade unions in the advanced countries. The essence of workers' 'combinations' in the form of trade unions, as Marx had noted in *The Poverty of Philosophy*, is to restrict competition among workers. Globalisation, by exposing the workers in the advanced countries to competition from the workers from the 'south', undermines the trade unions in the former. Quite apart from the effects of the actual relocation of plants from the 'north' to the 'south', the very threat of such relocation hangs like a Damocles sword over the workers of the 'north' limiting the strength of their trade unions.

The second related implication is that the real wages of the workers in the advanced countries can no longer rise with labour productivity; under the pressure of the massive labour reserves of the 'south', they tend to remain stagnant. They do not, of course, tend towards equality with the real wages of the 'south' (since there is a certain temporal irreversibility about real wage levels for political reasons if nothing else); but the vector of world real wages, consisting of wages both in the 'north' and in the 'south', tends to remain unchanged, even as labour productivity increases in the world economy. It is not surprising that in the United States, in the last three decades or more, the real wage rates have remained stagnant even in absolute terms.

The stagnation in the vector of real wages even as labour productivity increases in the world economy implies an increase in the share of surplus. This amounts to an increase in the income inequalities in the world. World income inequalities in fact would continue to rise in the era of globalisation unless the world labour reserves get progressively exhausted. This however is not happening and is not even likely.

The other implication of this rising share of surplus is an *ex ante* tendency towards overproduction owing to inadequate demand, which follows from the fact that workers devote a larger proportion of their incomes to consumption compared to capitalists. Such an *ex ante* tendency does not necessarily mean an actual *ex post* occurrence of crisis and stagnation on account of it. State intervention in demand management can always ward off such a tendency. (Indeed Baran and Sweezy had argued in the context of post-war America that military expenditure played a major role in keeping up the level of aggregate demand in that economy despite an *ex ante* tendency towards overproduction stemming from a rising share of surplus.) But here we come to another important aspect of the current globalisation. The globalisation of capital, above all of finance capital, entails that, in a world of nation-States, every such State must willy-nilly pursue only those policies which are demanded by finance capital, or otherwise it faces the prospect of finance capital leaving its shores *en masse* and unleashing a financial crisis upon its economy. And finance capital is invariably opposed to State intervention in demand management for keeping up the level of activity in the economy, an opposition that gets expressed through its insistence upon 'sound finance' (which holds that governments should balance their budgets, or at the most have a fiscal deficit not exceeding a certain fixed percentage of GDP).

Since governments are restrained from increasing taxes in a world of globalised finance (since this would drive finance capital away), and also from increasing their borrowings (because of the pressure to adopt 'sound finance', or what is now called 'fiscal responsibility'), they cannot intervene directly to raise aggregate demand, and hence cannot offset the *ex ante* tendency towards overproduction that the de-segmentation of the world economy brings in its wake.

The only antidote to stagnation under these circumstances, when there are no colonial markets 'on tap', and when State intervention in demand management is undermined by the opposition of globalised finance capital, is provided by the formation of 'bubbles'. Indeed in the period since the decline of Keynesian demand management, while the average growth rate of the advanced capitalist world has slowed down, such growth as has occurred has owed its occurrence to a set of 'bubbles' in the United States in particular: the 'dotcom bubble' followed by the 'housing bubble'.

Hence the view which attributes the current global economic crisis to the formation of bubbles and argues that regulatory measures to prevent such bubbles would produce a crisis-free capitalism is completely off the mark. In the absence of such bubbles, contemporary capitalism would be permanently mired in stagnation and mass unemployment. Bubbles today provide the only basis for booms, just as their collapse causes recessions and slumps. The predicament of contemporary capitalism therefore arises not from the fact that it has experienced 'bubbles' together with their inevitable collapse, both of which were avoidable; it arises from the fact that it needs precisely such 'bubbles' to provide whatever relief it can from stagnation and mass unemployment.

The global economic crisis thus consists not in the collapse of the bubble but in the fact that capitalism is caught in this structural predicament, where it will continue henceforth to experience protracted stagnation and mass unemployment, relieved occasionally by the temporary palliative offered by a bubble.

The cause of the problem was located in the fundamental defect of the free market system regarding its capacity to distinguish between 'enterprise' and 'speculation' and hence, in its tendency to become dominated by speculators, interested not in the long-term yield assets but only in the short-term appreciation in asset values. The crisis was not the result of some 'mistakes' or 'aberrations'. It was just a failure of the system.

The current capitalist crisis has ended talk of the triumph of capitalism. The struggles and movements of the people in Europe can bring about a substantial change only when a strong political alternative in the form of the Left forces is built up. In Latin America, the Left has maintained its advance. A number of countries with Left governments have rejected the neo-liberal model and are implementing policies which are an alternative to neo-liberalism. Increasingly it is becoming clear that the only alternative to the exploitative neo-liberal capitalism is socialism.

In the countries of the South, the strategy of the world oligopolies is to transfer the weight of the crisis on these peoples (devaluation of money reserves, fall of the export raw resource prices and rise of import ones). In counterpoint the crisis presents the opportunity for the renewal of national, popular, democratic alliance of working classes, and on that basis the move from a pattern of capitalist-dependent development with growing exclusion of majorities towards an alternative pattern of inclusive development, in other words 'delinking'. This involves:

I. The national control of monetary and financial market (moving away from the integrated global monetary and financial 'market').

II. The control of modern technologies, accessible now (defeating the exclusive monopoly of the North, overprotected by WTO rules on industrial property).

III. The recuperation of the use of natural resources.

IV. The defeating of global management, dominated by the oligopolies (WTO) and the military control of the planet by the United States and their allies.

V. The liberation from the illusions of an autonomous national capitalism system as well as of passeist myths (para-religious or para-ethnic).

The agrarian question lies in the heart of decisive choices in Third world countries. An inclusive pattern of development needs an agrarian radical reform that is a political strategy based on the access to the soil for all peasants (half of humankind). On the opposite, the solutions proposed by the dominant powers — to accelerate the privatisation of arable soil, and its transformation into merchandise — lead to massive rural disintegration. The industrial development of the concerned countries being not able to absorb this overabundant manpower, this one crowds together in shantytowns or risks its life trying to escape in dugouts via the Atlantic Ocean. There is a direct link between the suppression of access to the soil and the migratory pressures.

Keynesian Intervention

As John Maynard Keynes had advocated during the post-1930s Great Depression, 'Active State Intervention' is the only manner in which capitalism could achieve full employment through public investments. This, according to him, was the only way to save capitalism and, thus, protect it from the imminent takeover of socialism. Capitalism has a tendency to even ignore the boldest of writings on the wall, as Marx had once said that capitalism 'has conjured up such gigantic means of production and of exchange, it is like the sorcerer who is no longer able to control the powers of the nether world whom he has called up by his spells'. Thoroughly examining the data from all corners and surveying of literature, we have reached the conclusion that the current 'decade-long crisis' is not just a simple mistake by the policymakers nor de-regulation, but it is a systemic crisis of capitalism that the internal 'motion' produces and creates again and again in cyclical order by its own capitalist's internal physical forces. It is not because of the greed or avarice of individuals. The only true liberation for humanity can come with the overthrow of this system.

The top largest level private and public transnational corporate sectors are highly subsidised and tax-privileged for long periods. The current international financial regime has failed to meet the obvious requirements: of preventing instability and crises, to provide full employment and reduce inflation and of transferring resources from richer to poorer economies. Not only have we experienced much greater volatility and propensity to financial meltdown across emerging markets and now even industrial countries, but even the periods of economic expansion have been based on the global poor subsidising the rich.

These global failures are so immense that they constitute enough reason to abandon this system. But there are other associated failures in terms of what the regime has implied within national economies: it has encouraged pro-cyclicality; it has rendered national financial systems opaque and impossible to regulate; it has encouraged bubbles and speculative fervour rather than real productive investment for future growth; it has allowed for the proliferation of parallel transactions through tax havens and looser domestic controls; it has reduced the crucial developmental role of directed credit.

So we clearly need a new system, even if the goals remain the same as that of the original Bretton Woods: to ensure currency stabilisation through international monetary cooperation; to encourage the expansion of international trade in a stable way; and to promote development by facilitating productive investment.

To achieve this in the current context, four elements are crucial. First, the belief that self-regulation supported with external risk assessment by rating agencies is an adequate way to run a financial system has been blown sky-high. There is no alternative, therefore, to systematic state regulation of finance.

Second, since private players will inevitably attempt to circumvent regulation, the core of the financial system — banking — must be protected, and this is only possible through social ownership.

Therefore, some degree of the socialisation of banking (and not just socialisation of the risks inherent in finance) is also inevitable. In developing countries it is also important because it enables public control over the direction of credit, without which no country has industrialised.

Third, to cope with the adverse real economy effects of the current crisis, fiscal stimulation is essential in both developed and developing countries. Enhanced public expenditure is required to prevent economic activity and employment from falling, to manage the effects of climate change and promote greener technologies and to advance the development project in the south.

Fourth, we need an international economic framework that supports this, which in turn means that capital flows must be controlled and regulated so that they do not destabilise any of these strategies.

It may be argued that such an international system based on state regulation will reduce the possibility of developing countries to access much-needed capital for their own economic expansion. But this perception is wrong, because in fact the current liberalised system did not provide for a net transfer of resources to the developing world. In the past six years, there has been a net flow of financial resources from every developing region to the north, primarily the United States, even as global income disparities have increased. And within countries, the idea that deregulated finance could put more resources in the hands of the poor (as in sub-prime lending) has proved to be unsustainable.

The Shadow Banking System Creates Financial Bubbles

Paul Krugman described the run on the shadow banking system as the 'core of what happened' to cause the crisis. 'As the shadow banking system expanded to rival or even surpass conventional banking in importance, politicians and government officials should have realised that they were re-creating the kind of financial vulnerability that made the Great Depression possible — and they should have responded by extending regulations and the financial safety net to cover these new institutions. Influential figures should have proclaimed a simple rule: anything that does what a bank does, anything that has to be rescued in crises the way banks are, should be regulated like a bank.' He referred to this lack of control as 'malign neglect' (Michel, 2010).

The shadow banking system became critical to the credit markets underpinning the financial system, but was not subject to the same regulatory controls. Further, these entities were vulnerable because they borrowed short term in liquid markets to purchase long-term, illiquid and risky assets. This meant that disruptions in credit markets would make them subject to rapid deleveraging, selling their long-term assets at depressed prices. In early 2007, asset-backed commercial paper conduits, in structured investment vehicles, in auction-rate preferred securities, tender option bonds and variable rate demand notes, had a combined asset size of roughly US$2.2 trillion. Assets financed overnight in tri-party repo grew to US$2.5 trillion. Assets held in hedge funds grew to roughly US$1.8 trillion. The combined balance sheets of the then five major investment banks totalled US$4 trillion. In comparison, the total assets of the top five bank holding companies in the United States at that point were just over US$6 trillion, and total assets of the entire banking system were about US$10 trillion (Michel, 2010). The combined effect of these factors was a financial system vulnerable to self-reinforcing asset price and credit cycles.

Commodity Bubble

A commodity price bubble was created following the collapse in the housing bubble. The price of oil nearly tripled from US$50 to US$140 from early 2007 to 2008, before plunging as the financial crisis began to take hold in late 2008. Experts debate the causes, which include the flow of money from housing and other investments into commodities to speculation and monetary policy or the increasing feeling of raw materials scarcity in a fast-growing world economy and thus positions taken on those markets, such as Chinese increasing presence in Africa. An increase in oil prices tends to divert a larger share of consumer spending into gasoline, which creates downward pressure on economic growth in oil-importing countries, as wealth flows to oil-producing states.

System Failure

The current crisis of the capitalist world is commonly explained as resulting from 'a lack of government regulation of the financial sector', 'insufficient supervision allowing reckless lending by financial institutions', 'the unbridled greed of the financiers', in short a series of mistakes and aberrations. These have contributed to a 'systems failure' in the words of Joseph Stiglitz, the distinguished economist and Nobel Laureate. This entire line of reasoning, however, misses the point. The crisis is not a 'failure' of the system; it is central to the mode of functioning of the system itself. It is not the result of some 'mistakes' or 'aberrations'; it is inherent to the logic of the system. If indeed government regulation in the United States had prevented 'reckless lending' by the financial institutions, if indeed there had been no 'sub-prime lending', then the housing boom would have been truncated much earlier.

Mass unemployment would have reared its ugly head much earlier, and even the entire world economy would have got into a state of recession much earlier. The fact that these things did not happen, the fact that the boom was kept going by sustaining the bubble in the housing market through enlarging the disbursement of credit, is precisely because the policy of the U.S. Federal Reserve was to make the financial system accommodative. And this is now being called 'irresponsible' and 'reckless'. It is precisely this so-called irresponsibility and recklessness that underlies booms in capitalism. Or, putting it differently, growth in conditions of modern capitalism is caused by financial, or more generally asset price, bubbles. And crises, such as what the capitalist world is experiencing today, are the necessary sequel of the bursting of such bubbles. What Stiglitz calls a 'system failure' is actually the 'system' itself (Prabhakar, 2013).

Centralisation of Capital

Capitalism has reached a certain level of centralisation of capital that cannot be compared to the situation, even 50 years ago. At this stage, where a mere 5000 odd oligopolies control every production and organisation of exchange in the world. This is a terrific level of centralisation of capital, very different from the scenario prevalent in the early twentieth century, dominated by monopolies. That these oligopolies have the capacity to control not merely the economic but the political sphere is striking. This centralisation is the basis on which unequal distribution of incomes has become possible. But it has led a shift in gravity from the productive sector to the redistribution of profit among the oligopolies through the means of financial investment. This is the secret behind the financialisation of the global capitalism. The emergence of new forms of global integration of production processes via direct investment, combined with the re-emergence of older forms via financial flows, has consolidated rather than undermined the fundamental difference in the material conditions of class formation that separates the North from the South (Prabhakar, 2013).

Fairness and Equity

Fairness and equity, as basic ingredients of sustainability, are increasingly violated by the predominance of finance and finance-driven globalisation which have been a major factor in growing inequality in wealth and income distribution. Almost everywhere income earned on financial assets and property has been rising relative to labour income. There has been a major shift in the global balance between labour and capital. Wages often lag productivity growth because of increased competition among the global labour force and financial incomes are lightly taxed because of the threat of footloose capital.

Income and wealth distribution is further distorted by financial boom-bust cycles. The benefits of credit and asset bubbles are generally reaped by private individuals but the costs of crises impinge on all segments of the society — very much like costs and benefits of exploitation of natural capital. The distributional consequences of crises are aggravated by financial bailout operations. In the United States, crisis interventions have increased financial concentration; systemically dangerous, 'too big to fail institutions' are now even bigger, and executive bonuses have been restored while labour incomes remain depressed.

Financial markets, rating agencies and international financial institutions ignore inter- and intra-generational equity and environmental sustainability and focus almost entirely on debt and balance-of-payments sustainability in their ratings and lending decisions. The emphasis on financial sustainability is a source of increased inequality. It also tends to undermine environmental sustainability by leading to acceleration of exploitation of natural resources to fill income and foreign exchange gaps.

These finance-related disruptions imply that any programme of action designed to promote sustainable development should contain, as its integral part, regulation of financial markets and institutions and fundamental changes in the international monetary and financial system to secure greater stability and reduce the likelihood of crises.

Greater Income Inequality

The wealth of the world's billionaires now stands at $7.3 trillion, an increase of 12% from last year (The Wealth of the Billionaires, 2014). There are a record 2,325 billionaires in the world, up from 2,170 in 2013 and 1,360 in 2009, the first year following the financial collapse. Billionaires make up .000033% of the world's population, or to put in another way, there are about 3 million people for every 1 billionaire. Yet this exceedingly small social layer possesses about 4.5 times the total wealth of the bottom half of the population, or 3.5 billion people. All the money of bankers, shareholders, land owners and manufacturers is nothing else than accumulated unpaid for labour of the working class.

The stock market and finance capital are the driving forces behind the wealth of the world's billionaires. The top industry for billionaires, according to Wealth-X, is 'finance, banking and investment', which accounts for close to 20% of the total billionaire population, followed by industrial conglomerates at 12% and real estate at 7%. More than one in six billionaires resides in the financial capitals of New York, Hong Kong, London, Mumbai, Singapore and Moscow.

Behind these figures lies a social relationship essential to the functioning of the capitalist system. The corporate and financial aristocracy has benefited from a massive redistribution of wealth, aided and abetted by the major capitalist states and central banks. It is not just that enormous wealth stands side by side with enormous poverty, but the one is the direct product of the other.

Six years later, stock markets continue to post record highs. Both benchmark U.S. indices — the Standard & Poor's 500 and the DJIA — closed above previous highs. The latest surge came after the Federal Chairman Janet Yellen said the central bank would keep interest rates at nearly zero (i.e., provide banks with essentially free cash) for a 'considerable time'. As a result, American billionaires have seen their number grow by 57 over the past year. The country is home to the largest number of billionaires in the world (571), nearly 25% of the total global billionaire population and three times more than any other country. Wall Street investors are buying up stocks; even corporations themselves are funnelling record cash hoards back into the market, rather than increasing production. In the first half of this year, U.S. companies bought back $338 billion in their own shares, more than any six-month period since 2007. This is the real state of world capitalism: sustained by an unending stream of cash, run by a financial aristocracy addicted to speculation and a sustained assault on the working class, and headed towards another and even greater collapse.

World investment trends now shifted from the United States, the EU and Japan to the newly emerging regions like Mexico, Indonesia, New Zealand and Turkey (so-called MINT), Brazil, Russia, India, China and South Africa (BRICS), Asia-Pacific region (21 nations group) and ASEAN since 2008 financial crisis, where private corporations or MNCs found the most attractive prospects to maximise their profits. However, some analysts assume that Chinese demand for raw material wanes, and as higher wages and strong currencies make many emerging economies less competitive. The bigger issue is that the explanation here appears to be addressing the symptoms of the crisis (global capital flows) rather than the disease (excess credit and an unstable global economic system).

India's new central bank chief suggests that there were four main causes for the 2008 financial crisis:

- Rising inequality and the push for housing credit in the U.S.A. Growing income inequality in America, exacerbated by technology replacing low-wage jobs and an inadequate education system which failed to re-skill people, led to politicians allowing easier credit conditions to boost asset prices and make people feel wealthier. That resulted in the sub-prime and housing crisis.

- Export-led growth and dependency of several countries including China, Japan and Germany. The debt-fuelled consumption in the U.S. would have been inflationary were it not for these countries not meeting the consumption needs of Americans. In other words, they aided and abetted the consumption binge in the U.S.
- A clash of cultures between developed and developing countries. This relates back to 1997 when the Asian crisis force countries in the region to go from being net importers to substantial net exporters, thereby creating the conditions for a global glut in goods.
- U.S central bank policy pandering to political considerations by focusing on jobs and inflation at any cost. The bank acted in accordance with the wishes of politicians by keeping interest rates too low for too long. They did this to maintain high employment, one of the bank's two central mandates.

It is important to note that none of these issues has been resolved. In fact, many of them have worsened. And any hint of adjustments to one or more of these problems results in further crises. If these adjustments were to happen in full, it would result in plunging global asset prices as excessive debt loads are unwound. This deflationary action is anathema to the world's central bankers as deflation is enemy number one. Hence, they shall do 'whatever it takes' to produce inflation. And if that means flushing currencies down the urinal, so be it. The battle between inflation and deflation is ongoing (James, 2014).

The weapons of choice for central bankers to fight off deflation are QE and zero interest rates. Central bankers tell us that these policies are necessary for economies to heal. I'd suggest this is baloney and they're exacerbating the aforementioned problems. It is important to understand that interest rates are the central price to signal off which all assets are priced. If central banks keep rates artificially low, it distorts these asset prices. And if you keep rates low for long enough, it distorts prices to such an extent that it's impossible to know what the real value of certain assets are. Another issue is that by keeping rates low, businesses which should go bankrupt stay alive. That's why government bail-outs of almost any private company are a bad idea. Keeping zombies businesses alive means economies become less competitive over time. Witness Japan since 1990.

There are three possible endgames to the current situation:

- There's a global deflationary shock where all asset prices fall and fall hard. A la 2008. In this instance, central banks would go in all guns blazing with more money printing on an even grander scale. This would risk inflation if not hyperinflation as faith in currencies is diminished, if not lost.
- You have a gradual global recovery and inflation stays tame enough for a smooth exit from current policies.
- There's a recovery but central banks are slow to raise rates and inflation gallops, which forces tightening and a subsequent economic slowdown.

In this regard, Asia is less vulnerable to balance of payments and currency crises, because of sound balance of payments positions and strong reserves. However, outflows could explode bubbles, notably in the property markets, as happened during the Lehman collapse. Still, Asia can be expected to achieve an orderly moderation of growth. But adjustment in commodity-dependent and deficit economies may not be so orderly. Unlike Asia where reserves are earned from current account surpluses in deficit countries they are borrowed, coming from capital inflows. Hence, with a reversal of capital flows they can disappear as fast as they were accumulated.

Policy Recommendations

The developing countries could thus face serious economic problems. In order not to be caught as helpless victims to the new crisis, they need to take two types of actions:

- They should prepare themselves with policy responses to reduce the impact of the new crisis and the external shocks that may come with it, particularly a sharp fall in exports (including in commodity prices and demand), a reversal of capital flows and a sharp decline in value of their currency.
- They should review their previous development strategies to see if they are still valid or whether changes are needed to respond to the changed international situation. In particular, developing countries that have relied heavily on exports to lead their growth may now find a decline in demand especially from the developed countries. They need to examine how to rely more on domestic demand and on regional south–south cooperation.

They should also take an active part in the discussions on reform of the international financial and monetary system, as well as on the coordination of macroeconomic policies of systemically important countries. Developing countries are adversely affected by the dysfunctional global system, and therefore have an interest in its reform. Unfortunately there is an absence of an appropriate system of global economic governance that enables the developing countries to participate fully. Thus, this is also a good time to advocate for establishing such a governance system.

This study also examined the export dependence of Asian countries and called for a review of development strategies about how the unregulated flows of capital were continuing to cause boom-bust cycles that have devastating effects on developing countries. The boom in capital flows and in economic growth could come to an end when the global situation changes.

However, Asian countries will be able to continue with their economic growth but at a moderate rate as most of them are not so vulnerable to currency or balance of payments problems. However, the situation will be less orderly in Latin America and Africa, which are vulnerable to changes in global financial conditions and commodity markets.

There may be balance of payments crises in some major developing countries that have significant current account deficits and are thus dependent on the inflow of capital flows, since these flows may reverse. There is risk of fiscal and sovereign debt crises in some developed countries. And the sluggish growth and high unemployment in the North will increase tension in the trading system, with the higher risk of protectionism.

Systemic reforms are needed in global finance. There is a lack of multilateral discipline on financial, macroeconomic and exchange rate policies of major countries. There is an absence of control of financial markets, capital flows and speculation. And the G20 has failed so far to address these systemic issues.

Globalisation had been oversold to developing countries, which were asked to fully integrate into the global financial markets. The lesson is that developing countries should rethink their integration into the world economy. They should seek strategic integration (in areas and ways that are beneficial) but not full integration.

Three Scenarios on the New Crisis

The financial crisis was triggered by coordination failures at the global level, and there will be more crises if this is not addressed. Three scenarios of what could happen:

- First, there would be greater global policy coordination, with a world economic council setting rules for finance, disciplining major countries and establishing an independent panel for resolving debt crises.

- Second, the present situation continues without global governance, each country sets its own policies, but there is regulation of financial institutions with cross-border effects, and a fund is set up to provide financing to developing countries hit by external shocks.
- In the third scenario, there is only talk of reforms but no global action. Each country then tries to protect itself against a future crisis, by building foreign reserves, in a race to the bottom. This may be supplemented by regional financial measures.

Need for 'SOUTH' to Be Pro-ACTIVE

There had been too much of shadow banking in the past without the knowledge of whether the institutions and financial instruments are safe or toxic. The problems of financial institutions being 'too big to fail' or 'too powerful to regulate' remain. In developing countries, it is necessary to design a financial system that not only avoids instability but also promotes development. Since the markets do not ensure stability or development, governments have to take charge and they must not give up the space for public policy.

Therefore countries must be allowed to have the policy space. It is important that there be diversity of policies. In the developed countries, the financial institutions were practicing the same model and making the same mistakes, and this led to a failure affecting the system. Those regulators that did not follow this model were able to avoid a crisis. There is a need to re-examine the realities in developing countries and to be pro-active in making some policy proposals for Asian countries.

- First, Asia should not follow the Anglo-Saxon model of finance but bring back the role of the financial sector as serving the real economy.

- Second, Asian countries should rebalance their economic growth by reducing their export dependence and also reducing income inequalities.
- Third, Asian countries should reinvest their savings in the region. The foreign reserves should be invested in the region itself rather than being channelled to the West only to be recycled from there to Asia.
- Fourth, in view of the volatility of capital flows, Asian countries should be prepared to make use of capital controls to avoid the adverse effects.

Finally, the strategy of the world oligopolies is to transfer the weight of the crisis on the developing countries (devaluation of money reserves, fall of the export raw resources prices and rise of import ones). In counterpoint the crisis presents the opportunity for the renewal of national, popular, democratic alliance of working classes, and on that basis the move from a pattern of capitalist-dependent development with growing exclusion of majorities towards an alternative pattern of inclusive development, in other words 'delinking'. This involves:

- The national control of monetary and financial market (moving away from the integrated global monetary and financial 'market').
- The control of modern technologies, accessible now (defeating the exclusive monopoly of the North, overprotected by WTO rules on industrial property).
- The recuperation of the use of natural resources.
- The defeating of global management, dominated by the oligopolies (WTO) and the military control of the planet by the United States and their allies.
- The liberation from the illusions of an autonomous national capitalism system.

Bibliography

Alford, P. (2009, February 16). Japan headed for longest, deepest post-war recession. *The Australian*. Accessed on April 10, 2009.

Allen, P. (2009, January 29). Global recession – Where did all the money go? *The Guardian (London)*. Accessed on April 10, 2009.

Barro, R. J. (1979, May). Second thoughts on Keynesian economics. *American Economic Review*, *69*, 58.

Barro, R. J. (1984, May). Rational expectations and macroeconomics in 1984. *American Economic Review*, *74*, 180.

Bernanke, B. S. (2004). *Money, gold, and the great depression*. Washington, DC: Board of Governors of the Federal Reserve System. March 2, 2004.

Bernstein, M. (1987). *The great depression: Delayed recovery and economic change in America, 1929–1939*. New York, NY: Cambridge University Press.

Bezemer, D. J. 'No one saw this coming'. Understanding financial crisis through accounting models. Available via: MPRA, esp. p. 9 and appendix.

Cai, F. (2009). *Why rapid economic growth in China: The success story*. Retrieved from www.academia.edu

Chua, A. (2003). *World on fire: How exporting free market democracy breeds ethnic hatred and global instability*. New York, NY: Doubleday.

Cingano, F. (2014). *Trends in income inequality and its impact on economic growth*. OECD SEM Working Paper No. 163. Retrieved from www.oecd.org/els/workingpapers

Cole, H. L., & Ohanian, L. E. (2004, August). New deal policies and the persistence of the great depression: A general equilibrium analysis. *Journal of Political Economy*, *112*, 779–816.

Crotty, J. (2009). Structural causes of the global financial crisis: A critical assessment of the new financial architecture. *Cambridge Journal of Economics*, *33*(4), 531–538.

Crotty, J. (2014). Structural causes of the global financial crisis: A critical assessment of the new financial architecture. *Oxford Journals, Cambridge Journal of Economics, 33*(4), 563–580.
Darity, W. (2014). Crony capitalism. In *International encyclopedia of the social sciences* (2nd ed., Vol. 2). Detroit, MI: Macmillan Reference USA. 2008. 180. *Global Issues in Context.*
Démurger, S. X. (2011, April 27). Return migrants: The rise of new entrepreneurs in rural China. *World Development, 39*, 1847–1861.
Dunkley, J. (2008, October 10). Singapore slides into recession. *The Telegraph (London).* Accessed on January 4, 2009.
Eichengreen, B. (1992). *Golden fetters: The gold standard and the great depression, 1919–1939.* New York, NY: Oxford University Press.
Engels, F. (1969). *Anti-Duhring.* Moscow: Foreign Language Publishers, p. 341.
Engels, F. (1969). The under consumption of the masses. *Anti Duhring* (pp. 340–341), Moscow.
Eric Rauchway on the Great Depression and the New Deal. (2008, December 1). Econtalk podcast.
Evans, A. (2009, April 16). IMF warns over parallels to great depression. *The Telegraph (London).* Retrieved from Telegraph.co.uk. Accessed on January 21, 2010.
Evans-Pritchard, A. (2008, September 25). Ireland leads eurozone into recession. *The Telegraph (London).* Accessed on January 4, 2009.
Evans-Schaefer, S. (2010, September 20). Street rallies around official recession end. *Forbes.* Archived from the original on September 20, 2012.
Field, A. J. (1992, June). Uncontrolled land development and the duration of the depression in the United States. *Journal of Economic History, 52*, 785–805.
Finch, J. (2009, January 26). Twenty-five people at the heart of the meltdown. *The Guardian (London).* Accessed on April 10, 2009.
Fisher, G. (2001, June 29). *Housing in the new millennium: A home without equity is just a rental with debt.* Retrieved from Ssrn.com. Accessed on November 20, 2012.
Fitzgibbons, P. (2008, November 14). *Topwrap 10-Germany, China, US feel pain of global downturn.* New York, NY: Reuters. Accessed on January 4, 2009.
Fried, J. (2012). *Who really drove the economy into the ditch?* (p. 148). New York, NY: Algora Publishing.
Friedman, M., & Schwartz, A. J. (1963). *A monetary history of the United States, 1867–1960.* Princeton, NJ: Princeton University Press.
Funnell, W. N. (2009). *In government we trust: Market failure and the delusions of privatisation/Warwick Funnell, Robert Jupe and Jane Andrew.*

Sydney: University of New South Wales Press. ISBN 9780868409665 (pbk.).

Furuhashi, Y. (2011, April 26). Dean Baker. Further house price declines in the United States. Retrieved from Mrzine.monthlyreview.org. Accessed on August 17, 2013.

Glasner, D. (1989). *Free banking and monetary reform*. New York, NY: Cambridge University Press.

Global Economic Prospects. (2012). Public Documents – World Bank. Retrieved from pubdocs.worldbank.org/.../Global-Economic-Prospects-January-2012

Gough, N. (2015, September 8). China's export data points to a deepening industrial downturn. *The New York Times*.

Greenwald, D. (Ed.), *Chief. The McGraw-Hill encyclopedia of economics* (2nd ed., pp. 96–104). New York, NY: McGraw-Hill, Inc. See Business Cycles, by Geoffrey H. Moore.

Gullapalli, D., & Anand, S. (2008, September 20). Bailout of money funds seems to stanch outflow. *Wall Street Journal*. Retrieved from http://www.wsj.com/articles/SB122186683086958875

Hall, T., & Ferguson, J. D. (1998). *The great depression: An international disaster of perverse economic policies*. Ann Arbor, MI: University of Michigan Press.

Hansen, A. (1938). *Full recovery or stagnation?* New York, NY: Norton.

Harman, C. (2009). *Zombie capitalism: Global crisis and the relevance of Marx*. London: Bookmarks Publications. ISBN 9781905192533.

Heng, M. S. (2010). *The great recession: History, ideology, hubris and nemesis*. Singapore: World Scientific.

Hetzel, R. L. (2010). *The Great Recession (Studies in Macroeconomic History)*. Kindle Edition.

Hetzel, R. L. (2012). *The great recession: Market failure or policy failure*. Cambridge: Cambridge University Press.

Higgs, R. (1997). Regime uncertainty: Why the great depression lasted so long and why prosperity returned after the war. *Independent Review*, *1*(Spring), 561–590.

Hong Lan, Y. Z. (2014, June). The role and characteristics of social entrepreneurs in contemporary rural cooperative development in China: Case studies of rural social entrepreneurship. *Asia Pacific Business Review*, *20*(3), 379–400.

Hulbert, M. (2010, July 15). It's dippy to fret about a double-dip recession.

Ian Traynor, E. (Ed.). (2009, January 31). Governments across Europe tremble as effects of global recession prompt angry people to take to the streets. *The Guardian (London)*. Accessed on May 15, 2012.

James, C. (2014). Global Status of Commercialized Biotech/GM Crops: 2014. ISAAA Brief No. 49. ISAAA: Ithaca, NY. ISBN: 978-1-892456-59.

Karlsson, S. (2004, November 08). *America's unsustainable boom.* Mises Institute. Retrieved from https://mises.org/library/americas-unsustainable-boom. Accessed on January 4, 2009.

Keilis-Borok, V. I. et al. (2008). Pattern of macroeconomic indicators preceding the end of an American economic recession. *Journal of Pattern Recognition Research, JPRR, 3*(1). doi: 10.13176/11.106

Kevin, G. C. (2009, February 12). Outward foreign direct investment: A novel dimension of China's integration into the regional and global economy. Published online in *The China Quarterly.*

Keynes, A. (1934). *Critique of crisis theory.* Retrieved from https://critiqueofcrisistheory.wordpress.com

King, S. S., & Cushman, D. P. (1997). *Lessons from the recession: A management and communication perspective.* Albany, NY: State University of New York Press.

Klamer, A. (1983). *The new classical macroeconomics; conversations with the new classical economists and their opponents* (p. 41). Totowa, NJ: Rowman and Allanheld.

Krugman, P. (2009a). *The return of depression economics and the crisis of 2008.* New York, NY: Norton. ISBN 978-0-393-07101-6.

Krugman, P. (2009b, January 4). Fighting off depression. *The New York Times.*

Krugman, P. (2010, January 3). That 1937 feeling (Op-ed). *The New York Times.* Accessed on June 6, 2012.

Labaton, S. (2008, October 03). Agency's '04 rule let banks pile up new debt, and risk. *The New York Times.* Accessed on May 24, 2010.

Lall, S. (2008, April 9). *IMF predicts slower world growth amid serious market crisis.* Washington, DC: International Monetary Fund.

Lawrence & Wishart. (1977). *Capital* (Vol. 1, p. 224). New York, NY: Penguin.

Liu, J. (2011). Human capital, migration and rural entrepreneurship in China. *Indian Growth and Development Review, 4*(2), 100–122.

Mankiw, N. G. (2003). *Macroeconomics* (5th ed., Chapter 1, p. 4). New York, NY: Worth Publishers.

Marx, K. (1992). *Capital: A critique of political economy* (Vol. 1). New York, NY: Penguin.

McCarthy, R. (2010, October 22). *How American income inequality hit levels not seen since the depression.* Retrieved from huffingtonpost.com. Accessed on October 24, 2010.

McKay, T. (2011). *Explaining the 2008 financial crisis: A comparative analysis of Stiglitz and Harvey.* Discussion paper CSGP D2/11, Canada.

McLean, B., & Nocera, J. (2010). *All the devils are here: The hidden history of the financial crisis portfolio* (pp. 104–107). New York, NY: Penguin.

Merline, J. (2012, April 20). *A record 5.4 million workers and their dependents have signed up to collect federal disability checks since President Obama took office, according to the latest official government data, as discouraged workers increasingly give up looking for jobs and take advantage of the federal program*. Retrieved from News.investors.com. Accessed on April 22, 2013.

Mian, A., & Sufi, A. (2014). *House of debt*. Chicago, IL: University of Chicago. ISBN 978-0-226-08194-6.

Michel, C. (2010). The global economic crisis, the great depression of the XXI century. *Global Research on Globalisation*.

Mishkin, F. S. (2009). *The economics of money, banking and financial markets* (9th ed., p. 8). New York, NY: Pearson.

Mishra, S. (2007). *Agrarian scenario in post-reform India: A story of distress, despair and death*. Working Paper, Indira Gandhi Institute of Development Research, Mumbai.

Nagle, J. (2009). *How a recession works*. New York, NY: Rosen Publishing Group.

OECD (2011), Divided we stand: why inequality keeps rising.

OECD. (2014, December). Focus on Inequality and Growth.

OECD (2014a), Rising inequality: youth and poor fall further behind — Income Inequality Update — June 2014.

OECD (2014b), Focus on top incomes and taxation in OECD countries: was the crisis a game changer?

Nakamura, E., Sergeyev, D., & Steinsson, J. (2012). *Growth-rate and uncertainty shocks in consumption: Cross-country evidence*. NBER Working Paper No. 18128. SSRN 2079921. Accessed on August 17, 2013.

O'Brien, A. P. (1989, November). A behavioral explanation for nominal wage rigidity during the great depression. *Quarterly Journal of Economics, 104*, 719–735.

Patnaik, P. (2009, January). *Speculation and growth under contemporary capitalism*. Kale Memorial Lecture, Gokhale Institute of Politics and Economics.

Paul, K. (2014, July 1). Learned economic helplessness.

Paulson, H. (2010). On the brink. London, Headline. ISBN 9780755360543.

Peppers, L. (1973). Full-employment surplus analysis and structural change: The 1930s. *Explorations in Economic History, 10*(Winter), 197–210.

Pettifor, A. (2008, September 16). America's financial meltdown: Lessons and prospects. openDemocracy. Accessed on January 4, 2009.

Plumer, B. (2012, August 31). *Low wage jobs are dominating the U.S. recovery*. Retrieved from Washingtonpost.com. Accessed on August 23, 2014.
Polleit, T. (2007, December 13). *Manipulating the interest rate: A recipe for disaster*. Mises Institute. Accessed on January 4, 2009.
Popa, D., & Carp, L. (2013). *The influence of foreign trade and foreign direct investment on BRICS economic growth*. Romania: Economy and Business Economics.
Popper, N. (2013, May 23). Fed fears shake global markets but fade on Wall St. *The New York Times*. Accessed on May 24, 2013.
Prabhakar, A. A. (2015, October). Foreign direct investment, trade and economic growth: A new paradigm of the BRICS. *Modern Applied Science*, *9*(12), 32.
Prabhakar, A. A. (2015a, October). A critical appraisal of comparative advantage theory under free market crony capitalism. *Investment Management and Financial Innovations*, *12*(3), 93.
Prabhakar, A. A. (2015b, September). Evaluation of technology, trade, and inclusive development: Chinese experiences. *Investment Management and Financial Innovations*, *12*(2), 180.
Prabhakar, A. C. (2010). *Globalisation and development strategy: The new dynamics of south-south cooperation* (p. 342). Saarbrücken: Lambert Academic Publishing.
Prabhakar, A. C. (2013). World economic trends: An enquiry. *International Journal of Management Studies (IJMS)*, *20*, 109–163.
Prabhakar, A. C., Abidin, A. S. Z., & Saha, A. (2015). A critical appraisal of comparative advantage theory under free market crony capitalism. *Investment Management and Financial Innovations*, *12*(3), 93.
Prabhakar, A. C., Ahmad, A. R., & Khan, S. J. M. (2015). Evaluation of technology, trade, and inclusive development: Chinese experiences. *Investment Management and Financial Innovations*, *12*(2).
Renaghan, T. (1988). A new look at fiscal policy in the 1930s. *Research in Economic History*, *11*, 171–183.
Rhodes, D., & Stelter, D. (2010). *Accelerating out of the great recession: How to win in a slow-growth economy*. New York, NY: McGraw-Hill.
Robert, A. R. (2005, July 14). *The crisis intervention (Handbook)* (3rd ed.). New York, NY: Oxford University Press.
Robert Higgs on the Great Depression. (2008, December 15). EconTalk Podcast.
Roberts, M. (2009). *The great recession*. London: Lulu Enterprises.
Roubini, N. (2009, January 15). A global breakdown of the recession in 2009. *Forbes*.
Rutenberg, J., & Thee-Brenan, M. (2011, April 21). Nation's mood at lowest level in two years, poll shows. *The New York Times*.

Saint-Etienne, C. (1984). *The great depression, 1929–1938: Lessons for the 1980s*. Stanford, CA: Hoover Institution Press.

Sharma, A. N. (2005). Agrarian relations and socio-economic change in Bihar. *Economic and Political Weekly, March*(5), 960–972.

Smiley, G. (2002). *Rethinking the great depression: A new view of its causes and consequences*. Chicago, IL: Ivan R. Dee.

Smith, A. (2012, October 31). *Eurozone unemployment hits record high*. Retrieved from Money.cnn.com. Accessed on August 17, 2013.

Sowell, T. (2009). *The housing boom and bust* (pp. 57–58). New York, NY: Basic Books. ISBN 978-0-465-01880-2.

Stack, M. K. (2009, January 17). Protests spread in Europe amid economic crisis. *Los Angeles Times*. Accessed on May 15, 2012.

Steffens, L. (1902). The shame of the cities: Steffens on urban blight – History matters. *McClure's Magazine*, October.

Stiglitz, J. (2008). The fruit of hypocrisy. *The Guardian*, September 16, 2008.

Stiglitz, J. (2010, January). Nobel Prize winning economist, said at the African Development Bank meeting.

Strupczewski, J. (2008, November 14). *Euro zone in recession, December rate cut expected*. Brussels. Retrieved from Reuters.com. Accessed on January 4, 2009.

Sun, Y. (2005). Corruption, growth, and reform: The Chinese enigma. *Current History*, *104*(683), 257–263.

Temin, P. (1976). *Did monetary forces cause the great depression?* New York, NY: Norton.

Temin, P. (1989). *Lessons from the great depression*. Cambridge, MA: MIT Press.

Temin, P. (1990, June). Socialism and wages in the recovery from the great depression in the United States and Germany. *Journal of Economic History*, *50*, 297–308.

Temin, P., & Wigmore, B. (1990, October). The end of one big deflation. *Explorations in Economic History*, *27*, 483–502.

The Economics of Global Turbulence. (1998). New Left Review. p. 93.

The Economist. (2012, March).

The Economist. (2013). Buttonwood. Companies and the economy: The mismatch. *The Economist*, June 25.

The World's Billionaires List. (2014). *Forbes*. Retrieved from www.forbes.com/billionaires/list

Tropeano, D. (2010). The current financial crisis, monetary policy, and Minsky's structural instability hypothesis. *International Journal of Political Economy*, *39*(60-2010).

United Nations Human Development Report. (2011). Retrieved from www.hdr.undp.org. [Source: Prabhakar, A.C., Ahmad, A. R., Khan, S., & J. M. (2015). Evaluation of technology, trade, and inclusive development: Chinese experiences. *Investment Management and Financial Innovations*, 12(2)].

Wallison, P. (2013). *Bad history, worse policy*. Washington, DC: AEI Press. ISBN 978-0-8447-7238-7.

Wallison, P. J. (2008, November). *Cause and effect: Government policies and the financial crisis*. Washington, DC: American Enterprise Institute.

Wallison, P. J. (2011, January). *Dissent from the majority report of the financial crisis inquiry commission*. Washington, DC: American Enterprise Institute. Accessed on November 20, 2012.

Walton, G. M. (Ed.). (1979). *Regulatory change in an atmosphere of crisis: Current implications of the Roosevelt years*. New York, NY: Academic Press.

Waterfield, B. (2009, March 25). EU resists deficits. *The Telegraph (London)*. Retrieved from Telegraph.co.uk. Accessed on January 21, 2010.

Wearden, G. (2008, June 03). Oil prices: George Soros warns that speculators could trigger stock market crash. *The Guardian (London)*. Accessed on April 10, 2009.

Weinstein, M. (1980). *Recovery and redistribution under the NIRA*. Amsterdam: North-Holland.

Wilson, K. (1999). Patterns of accumulation and struggles of rural labour: Some aspects of agrarian change in central Bihar. In T. J. Byres et al. (Eds.), *Rural labour relations in India* (pp. 316–354). New York, NY: Routledge.

Wingfield, B. (2010, September 20). The end of the great recession? hardly. *Forbes*.

Wolf, M. (2012, April 27). *The impact of fiscal austerity in the Eurozone*. Retrieved from Blogs.ft.com. Accessed on August 17, 2013.

Woods, T. E. (2009). *Meltdown: A free-market look at why the stock market collapsed, the economy tanked, and government bailouts will make things worse*. Washington, DC: Regnery Publishing. ISBN 1596985879.

World Economic Outlook. (2012, April). IMF 'Global financial stability reports'. New York, USA. Retrieved from www.imf.org/external/pubs/ft/weo/2012/01

Wright, G. (1974, February). The political economy of new deal spending: An econometric analysis. *Review of Economics and Statistics, 56*, 30–38.

Xafa, M. (2012, June 12). Sovereign debt crisis management: Lessons from the 2012 Greek debt restructuring. *CIGI Papers Series*.

Yadav, S. N., & Khatri, P. V. (2009). *Global financial crisis*. New Delhi: Jhanda Prakashan.

Zhou, D. (2012, February). Chinese entrepreneurs go global. *Technology Innovation Management Review*.

Zuckerman, M. B. (2011, April 26). *The national debt crisis is an existential threat*. Retrieved from Usnews.com. Accessed on August 17, 2013.

Index